A Northern Chronicle of the Civil War

*Commemorative military roster of Company E of the Thirty-seventh Massachusetts Regiment;
almost half this regiment was recruited from Berkshire County.*

A Northern Chronicle of the Civil War

Stuart Murray

Berkshire House Publishers
Lee, Massachusetts

A Time of War: A Northern Chronicle of the Civil War
Copyright © 2001 by Stuart Murray

Library of Congress Cataloging-in-Publication Data

Murray, Stuart, 1948-
A time of war : a northern chronicle of the Civil War / by Stuart Murray.
    p.   cm.
Includes bibliographical references and index.
ISBN 1-58157-011-2
1. Berkshire County (Mass.)—History, Military—19th century. 2. Berkshire County (Mass.)—History, Military—19th century—Sources. 3. Berkshire County (Mass.)—Social conditions—19th century. 4. United States—History—Civil War, 1861-1865—Social aspects. 5. Massachusetts—History—Civil War, 1861-1865—Social aspects. 6. United States—History—Civil War, 1861-1865—Personal narratives. 7. Massachusetts—History—Civil War, 1861-1865—Personal narratives. I. Title.

F72.B5 M86 2001
974.4'103—dc21
                00-058580

ISBN: 1-58157-011-2

Editor: Glenn Novak. Cover, book design, and typsetting: Jane McWhorter, Blue Sky Productions. Index: Diane Brenner, Map of Berkshire County: Ron Toelke.

Berkshire House books are available at substantial discounts for bulk purchases by corporations and other organizations for promotions and premiums. Special personalized editions can also be produced in large quantities. For more information, contact:

Berkshire House Publishers
480 Pleasant St., Suite 5, Lee, MA 01238
800-321-8526
E-mail: info@berkshirehouse.com
Web site: www.berkshirehouse.com

Printed in the United States of America
10 9 8 7 6 5 4 3 2 1

To every thing there is a season,
and a time to every purpose under the heaven: . . .
A time to love, and a time to hate;
a time of war, and a time of peace. . . .

— Ecclesiastes 3: 1-8

For Ron Toelke and Barbara Kempler-Toelke

This, at least, in future say, with honest pride,
"Berkshire boys right nobly fought, and bled, and died";
Ever let their actions be rehearsed in story,
And their names encircled with a wreath of glory.

From "The Charge of the Forty-ninth"
by Samuel B. Sumner of Great Barrington, Massachusetts
Lieutenant Colonel, 49th Massachusetts Volunteers
May 27, 1863, before Port Hudson, Louisiana

Such a war and such a peace deserve a memorial that shall last as long as yonder mountains shall look upon this valley. . . . Here let it remain . . . standing like a sentinel at the dawn of morning, at noon, at eventide, in the soft moonlight and beneath the stars.

David Dudley Field, Williams College '25
Oration at the July 28, 1868, dedication
of a monument commemorating the thirty
Williams men who died in the Civil War

ACKNOWLEDGMENTS

Thanks to all who gave so unstintingly to the research, writing, production, and publishing of this book. To them belongs the credit for what is right, and the author takes responsibility for the rest.

Thanks to Berkshire House editor Glenn Novak, editorial director Philip Rich, and publisher Jean Rousseau and his associates Carol Bosco Baumann and Mary Osak; thanks also to book designer Jane McWhorter.

Special thanks to expert readers James Parrish, former regional historical preservation commissioner for Berkshire County; William Bell, a former longtime editor at the *Berkshire Eagle;* Dr. Edwin Redkey, emeritus professor of history at Purchase College of the State University of New York, and Civil War re-enactors Ron Toelke and Edward Stanard (who manages a web site for the Tenth Massachusetts).

Thanks also to: the local history staff at the Berkshire Athenaeum, including Katharine Westwood, Kathleen Reilly, Maureen Marrone, Rick Leab, and Ann-Marie Harris; Kathryn Beebe, Berkshire Museum registrar; Sylvia Kennik Brown, archivist of Williams College special collections at Sawyer Library; Thomas Hayes, collector of Massachusetts Civil War letters, which he puts online at blue&gray@worldnet.att.net; Mark Spies and his mother, Mary-Joy Spies, who published the war letters of their ancestor, Thomas Reed; Sue Greenhagen of the SUNY Morrisville library; the staff of the Crane Museum of Papermaking, Dalton, Massachusetts; the librarians at the Chatham, New York, Public Library, and at the New York State Library in Albany.

Thanks to all those who so generously opened doors, gave direction, and offered advice: Lila Parrish of Great Barrington; Bernard A. Drew, Great Barrington historian; *Berkshire Eagle* Editor David Scribner; Bette Roan, descendant of Windsor's Edward Stearns of the Forty-ninth Massachusetts; Lani Sternerup, archivist at Herman Melville's Arrowhead, and Arrowhead's director, Susan Eisley, and curator Ned Allen; Dennis Lesieur, director of the Lenox Library; Barbara Allen, Stockbridge Library local history director; Charles Flint, former president of the Lenox Historical Society; G. Bartlett Hendricks of Lanesboro, former director of the Berkshire Museum; John D. Sisson, president of the New Marlborough Historical Society; Jane Phinney of the Savoy Historical Commission; Sarah Poland of the Washington Historical Commission; Lisa Sartori of the West Stockbridge Historical Commission; Eugene Michalenko of Adams; Paul Marino of North Adams; Wanda Styka, archivist at Chesterwood, the museum of sculptor Daniel Chester French in Stockbridge, Massachusetts; Steve Cotham, manager of the Calvin M. McClung Historical Collection at the Knox County Public Library, Knoxville, Tennessee; Boyd Murphy, reference archivist, Florida State Archives; David Hartmann of Florida State University; Howard P. Beckmann of California for information on Claudius W. Sears and the Seventeenth Mississippi Regiment; Cheryl McCraw, librarian, State Library of Florida. Thanks also to Tom Reardon and Mark Swirsky for their work scanning the book's images.

Thanks, in memoriam, to the late Donald Little, the Hoosac Valley High School teacher who in 1996 encouraged his pupils to study and put online the letters of William Riley Norcutt of Savoy, ancestor of then-student Jason Wandrei; and thanks to the Wandrei family of Adams, who preserved the letters.

And thanks to all those who have labored, over the years, to compile written records of the Civil War generation, many of which records are now available online. Thanks for online assistance to Garry Earles, on the Thirty-fourth Massachusetts; Grace-Marie Moore Hackwell, researcher on the history of the First Massachusetts Cavalry Regiment; Ralph Osgood, researcher on the Eighth Regiment Massachusetts Volunteer Militia; Dr. Richard Sommers, assistant director for archives, and associate Randy Hackenburg, at the United States Military History Institute, Carlisle, Pennsylvania; and Lynne Kennedy, manager of the Second Massachusetts Regiment web site. And thanks to the managers of and contributors to various web sites dedicated to the Civil War, including the regimental sites for the Twentieth, Twenty-first, Thirty-fourth, and Fifty-fourth Massachusetts regiments, and the Seventy-first Pennsylvania (First California) and the Seventeenth Mississippi.

Thanks and apologies to those whose names ought to be included here but are not.

And, as ever, thanks to my wife, Els.

CONTENTS

PREFACE

"Berkshire County is a state of mind," said Great Barrington's Lila Parrish, a longtime local historian. Mrs. Parrish's ancestors came to Berkshire with the first white settlers, so she ought to know.

Berkshire County is a state of mind.

When she said this to me just after I had finished writing *A Time of War,* I understood what Mrs. Parrish meant, though I am not a Berkshirite (I have been a New York State close neighbor for many years). I understood because I had delved into the story of Berkshire in the Civil War, discovering a depth of Berkshire character that put me in awe.

So many Americans of the Civil War era who stood up for human liberty, and for the Union, knew well that Berkshire County, Massachusetts, symbolized their highest ideals of sacrifice, courage, patriotism, and honor.

Already in 1861, Berkshire was a state of mind.

Stuart Murray
East Chatham, New York

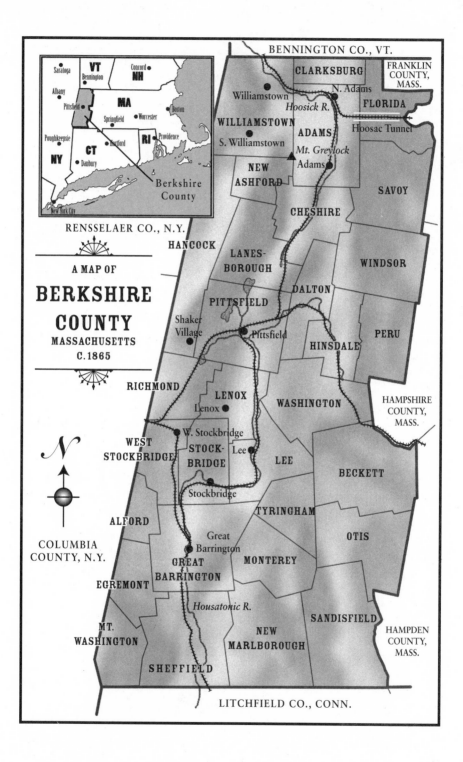

BENNINGTON CO., VT.

FRANKLIN COUNTY, MASS.

CLARKSBURG

N. Adams

Williamstown

Hoosick R.

FLORIDA

WILLIAMSTOWN

S. Williamstown

ADAMS

Hoosac Tunnel

Mt. Greylock

Adams

NEW ASHFORD

SAVOY

CHESHIRE

RENSSELAER CO., N.Y.

HANCOCK

LANES-BOROUGH

WINDSOR

DALTON

PITTSFIELD

Shaker Village

Pittsfield

PERU

HINSDALE

RICHMOND

LENOX

Lenox

WASHINGTON

HAMPSHIRE COUNTY, MASS.

WEST STOCKBRIDGE

W. Stockbridge

STOCK-BRIDGE

Lee

LEE

BECKETT

Stockbridge

ALFORD

TYRINGHAM

Great Barrington

OTIS

COLUMBIA COUNTY, N.Y.

GREAT BARRINGTON

MONTEREY

EGREMONT

Housatonic R.

MT. WASHINGTON

SANDISFIELD

HAMPDEN COUNTY, MASS.

NEW MARLBOROUGH

SHEFFIELD

LITCHFIELD CO., CONN.

Saratoga

VT

Bennington

Concord

NH

Albany

Pittsfield

MA

Boston

Springfield

Worcester

Poughkeepsie

Hartford

RI

Providence

CT

NY

Danbury

Berkshire County

New York City

Prologue

THE BERKSHIRE JUBILEE

There probably was never a nobler family-reunion," wrote Pittsfield, Massachusetts, historian Joseph E. A. Smith, describing the 1844 Berkshire Jubilee celebrating the centennial of the state's most western county.

Smith's history of Pittsfield, published in 1876, was not so long removed from that 1844 celebration, a reunion of residents of Berkshire with more than a thousand of her "emigrant sons." At eleven in the morning of August 22, a warm and muggy Thursday, many of the returnees gathered in the town hall for the Jubilee welcome, resident and emigrant sons alike dressed fashionably in high hats and coats with tails, the ladies with bonnets, wide gowns, and parasols. On behalf of the emigrants, the Reverend Russell S. Cook of New York, an organizer of the Jubilee and a New Marlboro native, accepted the welcome:

> From the four quarters of the land, we have come to our Berkshire
> home, to revive the friendships and associations of our boyish years,
> and live over again in memory and imagination the days of our youth.

There was much to be jubilant about on this day, which had been originally planned as a way to introduce prominent men who had left Berkshire County to those who had remained. The year 1844 was a heady time of progress, growth, and peace in America and in Berkshire, a pastoral region bounded by a hilly plateau to the east and the Taconic mountain ridge to the west. The southeast corner of the county was more than a hundred miles from the metropolises of Boston and New York, which bought her agricultural products and manufactures and took in many of these emigrant sons and daughters, too.

The 1844 Berkshire Jubilee at Maplewood in Pittsfield.

COURTESY BERKSHIRE ATHENAEUM

The first purpose of the Jubilee was to stimulate business contacts, at the same time alerting Berkshire natives in far-flung places about others like them, who were living in their neighborhoods or positioned to cooperate with them for mutual benefit. This intent alone was a worthy one, for so many of those who had left their native county had risen to influence and wealth, and in some cases to national fame.

The unusually high standard of living in Berkshire, and its population's respect for education, independence, and hardworking diligence, had produced men and women who were highly regarded from Boston to San Francisco. The Berkshire Jubilee, with the county's centennial as its centerpiece, was a perfect way to draw them back, and their very coming was proof of the strong attachment they held for the forested hills and deep, narrow valleys of their homeland.

With the nation embroiled in bitter debate between pro- and antislavery camps, the Reverend Cook, the emigrants' spokesman, made it a point to stress the harmonious spirit of the Jubilee:

> We have left all political prejudices and animosities, and all business cares and troubles, behind us; and have devoted these few days to social and patriotic feeling.

Political prejudices and animosities certainly needed to be left behind on this day, for although the returnees were either from Berkshire or descendants of Berkshire folk—"Berkshire-borners," natives termed themselves—they were loyal first of all to their adopted new homes. One of the most successful emigrant sons was the wealthy Thomas Allen, now a leader in Missouri politics, cultural life, and business. Allen had made a special trip back from St. Louis to attend the Jubilee, and for much of the remainder of his life he would summer at his mansion in Pittsfield. There was dark irony in the fact that he had been brought up to oppose slavery, as did most people of Berkshire, but his adopted home, where he was prospering in railroads and finance, was a slave state.

America was prosperous and expanding westward, with a new-coined philosophy of "Manifest Destiny," which justified taking control of the land from coast to coast, but sectional and political conflicts were threatening to make the nation ungovernable. One of the most successful Berkshire-born practitioners of Manifest Destiny was not at the Jubilee: Great Barrington's Anson Jones was the last president of the Republic of Texas, which would be annexed to the United States in 1845. Jones's ranch, "Barrington," grew cotton and tobacco, and he owned slaves. Though personal animosities and political differences were temporarily buried for the Jubilee, Jones would have found few kindred spirits had he attended, for most of Berkshire County's upper class—the ones who organized and led the Jubilee—were strongly against slavery.

Another departed son living in the Southwest was military engineer John G. Barnard of Sheffield, a career army officer and an 1833 graduate of West Point, the United States Military Academy. Stationed on the Gulf Coast, Barnard was soon to be a hero of the approaching conflict with Mexico. His older brother, Francis A. P. Barnard, was a professor at the University of Alabama. Also teaching in the South was Claudius W. Sears, a native of the town of Peru and an 1841 graduate of West Point. Sears now was teaching mathematics at a private military school in Mississippi.

One of many successful Berkshire-born entrepreneurs was industrialist and inventor Hiram Sibley of North Adams, who was involved in enterprises ranging from textiles to the telegraph, and was increasingly influential in both western New York and Washington, D.C.

A remarkable number of those who had stayed at home in Massachusetts or who had adopted Berkshire as their own were as successful as the best of those who had gone. Among them was the Jubilee's most eminent guest and its nominal president, Governor George N. Briggs, a native of South Adams. If any Berkshire son was a stellar example of success, it was the witty and much-admired Governor Briggs, who had just taken office after years of serving as a state senator and a congressman. Briggs was respected at home for personal achievements that went hand in hand with genuine modesty. As historian Smith one day would say about the soldier depicted on Pittsfield's Civil War monument, Briggs was the kind of "bold, frank man" who was "capable of either commanding or obeying," and who would do either with dignity and with regard for others.

Another Berkshire man of comparable stature was Pittsfield attorney Julius Rockwell, born in Connecticut, but married to a Lenox woman. Rockwell, who gave an entertaining after-dinner talk at the Jubilee, had a bright future as a jurist and as a representative at the state and national levels. He would go to Congress this year, appointed to replace Governor Briggs. One other notable rising star from the county was the Reverend Mark Hopkins of Stockbridge, president of Williams College in northern Berkshire; the Reverend Hopkins also had been invited to speak at the festivities.

Author Catharine M. Sedgwick of Stockbridge and Lenox, who came to believe the Civil War was a holy crusade to destroy slavery.

Perhaps the most famous Berkshire native of all was a woman—Lenox author Catharine Marie Sedgwick. Born and raised in Stockbridge, Miss Sedgwick reigned as the most popular and admired American novelist of the day. She attended the Jubilee, and though not a speaker, her words would be heard before it was finished.

While many residents, returning emigrants, and seasonal visitors attending the Berkshire Jubilee were notable in American society, the general population of the county had itself achieved a remarkable level of prosperity. Churches were numerous, public schools were increasingly well-attended, and private schools educated the youth of Berkshire's wealthier class. The roads and bridges were well-maintained, and there was employment to be had in factories such as woolen mills, ironworks, paper mills, and flouring mills, as well as on the farm. A railroad had been built through Pittsfield, and rails linked Berkshire with New York state to the west, Boston to the east, and Connecticut and New York City to the south. Plans were underway to build short-line railroads that in a decade would unite most of the county, which was roughly fifty miles long north to south, and a little more than twenty-five miles at its widest point.

With the debate over slavery becoming ever more heated, and a Mexican war threatening, everything was not well in the United States. Governor Briggs and many in Berkshire opposed going to war with Mexico on grounds that it would be "an unjust invasion of a sister republic," as historian Smith put it. In these years of growth and prosperity, new political coalitions were breaking up the old alliances that had been in place since the War of 1812. With the coming of the telegraph and railroad and the advent of steam power in commerce and industry, nothing would be the same in America after the 1840s. For these two summer days, however, the thousands who attended the Berkshire Jubilee intended to enjoy themselves thoroughly, and the only forbidding clouds of the moment were those westward-rising thunderheads looming over the Taconic Mountains.

At two on that humid afternoon, a procession was organized at the park in the middle of Pittsfield, which once had been the village commons.

There stood an enormous, ancient elm tree, towering above the buildings, and higher even than the church spires. The first pioneers, who established Pittsfield in the mid-1700s, purposely left the elm standing, diverting their roads around it, for the tree was so majestic. Homes and a meetinghouse were built around the tree, horses and teams hitched to it, and as the community grew into a village, the common with its landmark elm was the scene of important public meetings and militia musters. The Marquis de Lafayette had been formally welcomed beneath this tree, the symbol of Pittsfield, when he passed through Berkshire in 1825. The age of the elm was unknown, but it was one hundred and twenty-six feet tall, with no branches for ninety feet up the trunk. Berkshire folk revered the tree, artists sketched it, and visitors were astonished by it.

While visiting Pittsfield a few years before the Jubilee, young New England novelist Nathaniel Hawthorne had been so impressed by the "Old Elm," as it was called even in those days, that he described it in his journal:

> [I]n the centre of the town . . . rises an elm, of the loftiest and straightest stem that I ever beheld—without a branch or leaf upon it, till it has soared seventy or perhaps a hundred feet into the air.

In 1841, lightning had struck the top of the tree, splitting off limbs and slashing a white scar straight down the bark all the way to the ground. The elm seemed doomed. Then a young man of the village—a former sailor used to climbing a ship's rigging—got up the tree to paint the scar with a preservative, and now three years later the beloved elm still stood, a noble remembrance of Berkshire's heritage.

The Jubilee parade wound its way past the park with the elm and through the tree-lined streets to high ground west of the village, a place thereafter to be called Jubilee Hill. With its commanding view of Pittsfield and the surrounding Berkshire countryside of farmland and wooded ridges, this was a fitting spot from which to see the county being celebrated this day. A speaker's stand faced seating for the five or six thousand in attendance, "a large portion of them ladies," Smith wrote. To open the festivities, an anthem, "Wake the Song of Jubilee," was sung, and a prayer offered.

Then it began to rain hard.

Pouring down in sheets, the deluge drove everyone to shelter, but the audience soon reassembled in the First Congregational Church to hear an hour-and-a-quarter sermon by the Reverend Hopkins, who said, "We have come to revive old and cherished associations and to renew former friendships" in a spirit of "local thanksgiving in one sense, but extended in another sense. This day our family affection is thrown around a whole country."

As Smith described it, Hopkins gave thanks that "God had dealt bountifully" with the folk of Berkshire "in granting them those aspects of nature and influences of society by which they were surrounded." Hopkins offered "a graphic description of our loved Berkshire; bestowed high compliments upon the industry and benevolence of its citizens, and upon those who had achieved a distinguished and enviable fame in the walks of literature."

In Hopkins's own words: "It is remarkable, secluded as this county has been, that the three American writers most widely and justly celebrated in their several departments, have lived and written here."

Those three writers were Jonathan Edwards, William Cullen Bryant, and

Miss Sedgwick. Edwards, the eighteenth-century missionary and theologian who had lived in Stockbridge, was described by Hopkins as "our great metaphysical writer." Bryant, a native of nearby Cummington in Hampshire County, had lived until 1825 in Great Barrington, where he had written poetry that the speaker said "has not been excelled since the world stood." Miss Sedgwick's writing and "universal sympathy with all that is human" had given her a place of "eminence" in the "public estimation."

Following Hopkins, several gentlemen read poems about Berkshire County written by other gentlemen and by several ladies. Although the revered William Cullen Bryant had been asked months earlier for a contribution, his muse had failed to inspire him, and he had apologized in a letter to the Jubilee organizing committee:

> [A]fter attempting again and again, I produced nothing that would not disgrace me by its flat and commonplace character. I have torn up the verses, and acknowledge that I cannot fulfill the engagement. It is mortifying, but I find no alternative.

In 1820, however, when still an unknown young Barrington attorney, Bryant had been inspired to write an ode for the annual Agricultural Society cattle show, praising the bounty of Berkshire as "Our triumphs o'er reluctant earth." In 1844, if the famous Bryant could not conjure up poetry for the Jubilee, others could, and with gusto. A poem composed and read by the Reverend William Allen of Northampton was one hundred and eight stanzas long, "alluding to many historical events and personages of Berkshire," according to Smith. And as was fitting for a people who mingled passionate love of home and country with staunch religious devotion, the "public exercises of the day closed with the doxology and a benediction."

Most of the poetic tributes to Berkshire were delivered at the continuation of the Jubilee the following day, Friday, after a stormy night that did not permit the visitors from afar to socialize house to house, as had been planned. The morning was pleasant as the thousands gathered once again on Jubilee Hill for more prayers, songs, poems, and orations. Early that afternoon, wrote Smith, "the assembly proceeded to the grounds of the Young Ladies' Institute, where, under a large pavilion, tables were arranged, calculated to accommodate over three thousand persons." After the dinner, Governor Briggs spoke, again welcoming the emigrants and concluding with:

> The County of Berkshire—she loves her institutions and her beautiful scenery; but feeling the sentiment and borrowing the language of the Roman mother, she points to her children and exclaims, "These are my jewels."

The many distinguished speakers of this day took up subjects that included the history of the long-gone Mohegan tribe known as the Stockbridge Indians, praise for the vitality of Berkshire literature, and a remembrance of the many missionaries sent out into the world. There were historical sketches of Berkshire's past as a seventeenth-century trade route shared by the native peoples and the fledgling white settlements of New England and New Netherland, and descriptions of colonial developments and wars of the last century. The county's most recent history included the burgeoning of industrial centers such as Pittsfield, North Adams, Lee, and Great Barrington. Most significant of late were the railroads, built at great cost to local communities and private investors. Rails soon would supersede the traditional water routes along the region's south-flowing rivers and would open commerce with the great markets and granaries of the far west, further linking Berkshire to the outside world.

Also important to Berkshire County in 1844 were the wealthy Eastern families who visited in the summertime, enjoying the serenity of its beautiful countryside and sometimes joining intellectual circles such as those of Hopkins in Williamstown and Miss Sedgwick and her family in Lenox. Among these visitors was Charles Sumner, a promising Boston attorney who soon would be a mighty force in antislavery politics. Another was Sumner's good friend, the famous English actress Frances Anne "Fanny" Kemble, who was a part-time resident in Lenox, that well-known hive of antislavery adherents. Miss Kemble was legally Mrs. Pierce Butler, the wife of a prosperous Georgia slaveholder, a social position that gave her heartache, for she despised slavery. She and her husband would separate this year. On the occasion of the Jubilee, Miss Kemble wrote "Ode to Berkshire," which was read by a gentleman, as was proper, since ladies were expected to be modest and demure, although neither term described the vivacious Fanny Kemble.

Among the most famous speakers at the Jubilee was the philosopher, educator, and poet Dr. Oliver Wendell Holmes of Cambridge, Massachusetts. Holmes's middle name was well known in Pittsfield, belonging to his maternal grandfather, who in 1735 had invested in the 24,000-acre "Pontoosuc Plantation" tract that eventually became the village and surroundings. Four years after the Jubilee, Holmes would build a country home on the southern edge of Pittsfield and become a seasonal Berkshire resident for seven of the happiest summers he and his family ever would know.

Holmes told the admiring audience at the Jubilee: "If I am not a son or grandson, or even a nephew of this fair county, I am at least allied to it by hereditary relation." He closed with his own verses, which commenced with "Come back to your mother, ye children."

The Reverend Joshua N. Danforth of Alexandria, Virginia, had done just that. Danforth had been born in Pittsfield in 1798, the son of a leading

Berkshire settler, and was related to the twenty-five direct descendants of a prominent Williamstown founder who were in the Jubilee audience. He had attended Lenox Academy as a boy and graduated from Williams, but had lived mostly in the South since the late 1820s, except for a four-year term as pastor of the Congregational Church in Lee. Danforth cherished his hereditary ties to Berkshire, saying with feeling and simplicity, "The scenes we witness today are indeed impressive." It was just as well that he did not repeat what he once had said about those who wanted to forcibly abolish slavery: that they had "more blood than brains."

There followed a pointed and telling tribute, read by Governor Briggs and written by Catharine Sedgwick. It honored the abolitionist Dr. William Ellery Channing, a well-known antislavery minister whose last public address had been given in Lenox two years previously; he had died soon afterwards. Lenox, with its many prominent abolitionists, such as Miss Sedgwick and her brother, Charles, and his wife, Elizabeth Dwight Sedgwick, was a haven and inspiration for members of the growing antislavery movement, and Miss Sedgwick's tribute to Channing called upon both her Berkshire neighbors and those who were visiting to join that movement.

> Men of Berkshire, whose nerves and souls the mountain-air has braced, you surely will respond to him who speaks of the blessings of freedom, and the misery of bondage. I feel as if the feeble voice which now addresses you, must find an echo in these forest-crowned heights. Do they not impart something of their own power and loftiness to men's souls? Should our commonwealth ever be invaded by victorious armies, Freedom's last asylum will be here. Here may a free spirit, may reverence for all human rights, may sympathy for all the oppressed, may a stern, solemn purpose to give no sanction to oppression, take stronger and stronger possession of men's minds, and from these mountains may generous impulses spread far and wide.

Catharine Sedgwick wrote that no one should "be satisfied with the distinction of being natives of Berkshire, but strive in whatever clime, under whatever circumstances they may be placed, to wear always the Berkshire badge—Industry, Uprightness, Humanity." Her antislavery message was clear to these Berkshire-connected Northerners, Southerners, and Westerners alike: the institution must be opposed, rooted out, and destroyed. Many listening at the Jubilee did not agree, however—not if open hostility to slavery would endanger the existence of the United States.

In 1844, few in Berkshire County or anywhere else in America were prepared to unsheathe the sword in the name of abolition. Although opposed in principle to slavery, the majority of folk in Berkshire were not "Radical

Republicans," as the most vehement faction of a new national party soon would come to be known. Most Berkshire voters favored preserving the Union, free and slave states compromising, letting the emancipation of slaves take a natural, inevitable, and peaceful course.

The Union, on the other hand, was a sacred covenant to the people of Berkshire. The Union must be defended at all costs, and to the death, if need be.

Chapter One

THE METEOR OF WAR

The shadow of civil conflict lengthened over the United States in the decade of the 1850s, but the country prospered, and so did Berkshire. Work began on an east-west railroad tunnel, four and a half miles long, through Hoosac Mountain in northern Berkshire. The tunnel was an awesome feat of engineering that put the nearby towns into debt as they optimistically invested in the project. Telegraph lines and railroads continued to extend in the county, and the iron, paper, and textile industries steadily grew.

Proof of the community's prosperity was the founding of the Berkshire Life Insurance Company, with former governor George Briggs as its first president. Having served as governor from 1843-50, re-elected six years in a row, Briggs had been voted out after he took a controversial stand in opposition to the Mexican War. Further, the general change in political alliances among Free-Soilers, Unionists, compromisers, and antislavery factions also left him on the outside. After leaving office, Briggs returned to Pittsfield, where he made his home on West Street and was active in public affairs. He also served as head of several major associations, such as the American Baptist Missionary Union, the American Temperance Union, the American Tract Society, and the State Sabbath School union.

Self-educated, and a prodigious reader, Briggs was recognized by Williams College, which gave him an honorary master of arts degree; and Williams, Amherst, and Harvard awarded him honorary doctorates in divinity. Briggs could also be proud of the accomplishments of his offspring, especially his youngest son, Henry S. Briggs, who was following his father into the field of law. The younger Briggs was also reorganizing Pittsfield's militia company, which had disbanded in 1833.

Since the Jubilee of 1844, many more of Berkshire's most ambitious young folk had migrated across America, whether for fortune or to make a new home, on business or seeking an education. Lee's Augustus V. Shannon, for example, well known in central Berkshire as a musical instructor, took his talents to Texas and taught music in a seminary there. In 1858, promising young attorney Hamilton N. Eldridge of South Williamstown went to Chicago after graduating from Williams and from law school in Albany. Also in Chicago was Sheffield native George F. Root, composer of popular music, gospel hymns, and ballads, who opened a music shop in that city in 1859.

Berkshire continued to produce outstanding individuals, one of the most famous being the entrepreneur Cyrus W. Field of Stockbridge. Field acquired a fortune in manufacturing by the middle of the 1850s, and in the fall of 1858 his home town and all the United States celebrated the news that he had completed the task of laying the trans-Atlantic cable that would carry telegraph messages between Europe and America. All over the country, bells were rung and cannon fired to honor Field's achievement, which fit perfectly into the nation's belief in its right to assume a place as one of the world's leaders.

Other individuals had journeyed extensively before coming to Berkshire to settle down, as did Bostonian Charles M. Whelden, who had joined the California gold rush of 1849, traveled through Central America, and then moved to Pittsfield to practice his profession as a pharmacist. Another was Vermonter Elisha Smart, who had moved to the county in the late 1840s after years of traveling and five years' military service that included fighting in Florida's Seminole War. In North Adams, where he was a skilled gardener known for practical jokes and for drinking too much, Smart served in the militia company as fourth lieutenant. Englishman Thomas Trend, who worked at the Crane Paper Mills in Dalton, was perhaps the only man in Berkshire with more military experience than Smart. The much-decorated Trend, a former cavalryman in the renowned Light Brigade, had survived his regiment's doomed but famous charge against Russian defenses during the Crimean War in the mid-1850s.

One notable family that moved into Berkshire was headed by the Reverend Miles Sanford, who came to North Adams from Michigan in 1853 to take charge of the First Baptist Church. The Sanfords were highly regarded, and their son, Charles, graduated Williams College, served as librarian for the local library association, and would finish law school at Albany in 1861. The elder Sanford was an outspoken abolitionist who, with several other area ministers, scathingly denounced anyone from North or South who profited from slavery.

Some radical Berkshire people journeyed away from home in order to populate western territories, such as Kansas, and keep them "Free-Soil" regions by voting to forbid slavery there. Other folk fled to Berkshire from the slave states. These last were former slaves, some of them fugitives, some having been liberated legally, and for decades they had been coming to the county to live in freedom. Their pastor was Pittsfield's Reverend Samuel Harrison, himself born in Philadelphia and eventually given his freedom. While employed as a shoemaker, Harrison had studied for the Congregational ministry, then came north in 1850 to serve the black community of Berkshire, which in Pittsfield alone counted at least eight hundred male taxpayers.

Many of the new arrivals to Berkshire were well-to-do seasonal visitors from Boston and New York. One of these families was that of the Reverend Henry Ward Beecher, a Congregationalist minister famous for delivering fire-breathing antislavery sermons at his church in Brooklyn. In 1853, the Reverend Beecher bought a farm in Lenox and liked it so much that his city congregation worried he might move permanently to Berkshire County. In this same year, Beecher's sister, Harriet Beecher Stowe, who lived in Maine, published her melodramatic novel about slave life on the plantation. The best-selling *Uncle Tom's Cabin*, which infuriated slaveholders and rent the hearts of abolitionists, was an international sensation, translated into more than twenty languages. The emotions it stirred up deepened the schism between North and South.

Berkshire was gaining a reputation for its private schools, and leading Eastern and Southern families sent their children to the prestigious finishing academies that had become well established in the county. Among the best were Elizabeth Sedgwick's academy for girls in Lenox, Pittsfield's institute for young ladies, called Maplewood, and the Lenox Academy for boys; others were the Southern Berkshire Institute, in New Marlboro, the Rose Cottage Seminary, and the Maple Grove Academy (Miss Allen's), both of Great Barrington. As a result, Berkshire came to be known by upper-class Americans from Boston to New Orleans.

By the mid-1850s, William Cullen Bryant had been replaced as a Berkshire literary light by the arrival of Herman Melville, an author almost as celebrated. Melville bought a home on the edge of Pittsfield, a community where he had longstanding family connections, his late uncle having lived in the county early in the century. The farm was on the southern edge of Pittsfield, near land that once had belonged to this uncle; Melville named it Arrowhead because of the many Indian artifacts found there.

Pittsfield's Park Square in the 1830s, with the Old Elm rising prominently in the center.

In the late 1830s, when Melville had been just in his mid-twenties, he had won international fame with stories of seafaring adventure, such as *Omoo* and *Typee*, but soon after he bought the Pittsfield farmhouse, his writing career began to collapse. He became embittered by harsh criticism hurled at his epic novel *Moby Dick*, written for the most part at Arrowhead during his first year there. (The Pittsfield elm is hinted at in *Moby Dick*, as a character's scar is likened to "that perpendicular seam sometimes made in the straight, lofty trunk of a great tree, when the upper lightning tearingly darts down it, . . . leaving the tree still greenly alive, but branded.") Furthermore, *Moby Dick* was a financial failure, and publishers were unwilling to take a chance on Melville's latest writing, so steeped in allegory, and considered to be too morose, even incomprehensible. By the late 1850s, although he was famous, Herman Melville no longer wished to write fiction at all. Instead, he was writing poetry, but he told no one about it other than his immediate family.

In the first years at Arrowhead, Melville had the summertime company of Oliver Wendell Holmes and family, who were close neighbors. These two giants of American literature, living on the same country road, attracted the attention of locals and tourists, and in August 1854, the *Springfield Daily Republican* remarked upon them in an article, "Lenox and Its Attractions," by "Beta," who took the reader on a drive southeast of Pittsfield and across a bridge:

> Now do you see yonder pink, faded looking house, as square as it is ugly? . . . Would you ever imagine that to be the residence of a poet, and the poet, Holmes? . . . And here on the other side of the road . . . dwells Melville, the author of Typee, Omoo, etc. . . . There he sits now in the front "stoop" with a party of friends around him. He presents outwardly no very salient point which you can seize to describe him by.

One very salient point describing Herman Melville just then was despondency, for he was disillusioned both with the decline of his career and with the course America was following. Forty years old in 1859, and at what should have been the height of his powers, Melville was in despair, suffering from artistic uncertainty and financial difficulty as well as from painful attacks of rheumatism. Moreover, the Melvilles had put Arrowhead up for sale, meaning to move back to New York City, where they would not feel so isolated. No one wanted to buy the place, however, and Melville became increasingly reclusive and withdrawn, even from his wife, Elizabeth, and their four young children. He worried his friends and family, who at times feared for his sanity. Though Melville was personally liked around Berkshire, some considered him too moody, too often given to spouting archaic philosophy that harked back to Homer.

In the late 1850s, Williams College student Titus Munson Coan, Hawaiian-American by birth, made a literary pilgrimage to Arrowhead. After a "weary walk through the dust" from Pittsfield village, Coan was cordially welcomed by Melville, but was disappointed to find that his host had little interest in answering questions about the fascinating characters of those South Seas adventure tales. Instead, Melville swept into "a full tide of talk—or rather of monologue," steeped in classical philosophy and praising ancient times as having been far better than the present.

> But he would not repeat the experiences of which I had been reading with rapture in his books. In vain I sought to hear of Typee and those Paradise islands, but he preferred to pour forth his philosophy and his theories of life. The shade of Aristotle rose like a cold mist between myself and Fayaway. We have quite enough Greek philosophy at Williams College, and I confess I was disappointed in this trend of the talk.

Disappointed, too, was the once-adoring audience that had snapped up those thrilling early works by Melville. Coan's attitude matched that of the general public, which wanted more of Melville's cannibals and adventurers, not the agonized ravings of *Moby Dick*'s Captain Ahab. Coan succinctly described Melville's outward persona: "He seems to have put away the objective side of life and to shut himself up in the cold North as a cloistered thinker."

That cloistered thinker was in financial distress as a result of losing his audience. Readers and publishers found his metaphysical digressions boring and gloomy, as did former admirer and sometime Berkshire resident Nathaniel Hawthorne, whose own career was in full flower. Still, Melville was determined not to write in his former style and was even unwilling to take to the profitable lecture circuit, for he could not stomach playing the role of enter-taining public speaker. He longed to cast off the mantle of adventurer-author, and become instead the profound poet-philosopher of America.

Oliver Wendell Holmes had taken much pleasure in long, thoughtful talks with Melville, and when the Holmes family left to return to Boston one autumn day in 1855, no one realized they would never come back to their summer home. The Berkshire estate was simply too costly to keep up, and Holmes sold it that winter, although the family maintained its many close connec-tions to the county. (Holmes, too, once wrote about the ancient elm tree in Pittsfield's park, saying so few branches were left that it was "sadly needing a new wig.") The Holmes family still visited Berkshire from time to time, and Oliver Wendell Holmes, Jr., who had entered Harvard, was particularly attracted to some local girls he wanted to see again.

Near the Melvilles at Arrowhead lived the Morewoods, wealthy New Yorkers who summered in an eighteenth-century farmhouse that once had belonged to Herman's uncle. Sarah Morewood and her husband, John Rowland Morewood, both in their mid-thirties, were socially active in Berkshire society, always ready for lighthearted fun, and they admired Melville's writ-ing. The friendship of the Morewoods, who were dear to Herman and "Lizzie," as Elizabeth was called, soothed the irritation of being unable to sell Arrow-head and move back to the city.

The actress Fanny Kemble, too, was delightful company when she came up to her summer home in Lenox, six miles from Pittsfield. She had been divorced by her planter husband, who had wearied of her assailing him for owning slaves. Whenever Miss Kemble returned to England to visit, she spoke out publicly in favor of supporting the American Union and against the proslavery interests. It was clear that if civil conflict ever developed in the United States, the British government was inclined to support the slave states, because so much profitable commerce passed between Britain and the South.

Everywhere in the United States, pro- and antislavery sentiments deep-ened, and national politics became ever more divisive, until at last the Union that most Northerners considered a heaven-forged compact threatened to crack and shatter.

Boston abolitionist Charles Sumner, now a Republican senator from Massachusetts, fiercely opposed the extension of slave territory. For years, Sumner led the fight in Washington against the "peculiar institution" that for more than a century had propped up the Southern economy. He made bitter enemies in the South, especially when he railed against civil strife in Kansas Territory, one of the hotbeds of open conflict over the slavery issue.

At one point, Sumner insulted a South Carolina senator and two days later was assaulted in the Senate by a South Carolina representative, who beat him senseless with a cane. Though left debilitated for years, Sumner held his Senate seat, relentlessly calling for emancipation of the slaves. He—and with him Massachusetts—came to symbolize everything the people of the South so despised in the "meddling" North, which they accused of hypocrisy, because so many Northern workers were held in thrall as "wage slaves" in factories and mills.

During the 1850s, Eastern folk who had migrated to Kansas Territory to settle as Free-Soilers had to fight the proslavery forces with gun in hand. One of them, Great Barrington native Samuel Phillips, was murdered by a proslavery mob in 1855, and his brother, Jared, was wounded in the same struggle. A North Egremont native, Grosvenor P. Lowrey, had gone to Kansas as the secretary to the federally appointed territorial governor, but in 1856 an insurgent proslavery faction forced the Free-Soil governor and his staff out of the territory under threat of arrest for treason. Also influential among the Free-Soilers in Kansas was David R. Anthony of Adams, brother of women's suffrage leader Susan B. Anthony, who lived in western New York. As the outspoken editor and founder of the *Leavenworth (Kansas) Times*, David Anthony was ever in peril during those years of factional fighting in what came to be known as "Bleeding Kansas."

The most violent antislavery man in Kansas was John Brown, a Connecticut native who, before going west in the early 1850s to carry on his crusade, had lived for a time in Springfield, just east of Berkshire. Messianic, and in his later years characterized by a long, flowing beard, Brown called for armed assaults on the slaveholders, and for a full-scale uprising of the slaves. He was financed in large part by Massachusetts abolitionists, some with links to, and even living in, Berkshire. It is said that Brown, a marked man, had secretly passed through the county while meeting with abolitionist sympathizers, raising money, and in one case had been given a gun. William M. Walker of Pittsfield was a "pioneer abolitionist" who owned a watch and jewelry store in town. One day in the late 1850s, Walker was visited by a "tall, dark-featured" stranger—as later described by one who observed the meeting. After a whispered discussion, Walker took a field glass and revolver from behind a showcase and passed it over to the stranger, saying, "God bless you, John Brown." With that, they clasped hands, and the man "hastily left the store and the town."

In 1859, using arms paid for by New Englanders, Brown took his crusade to northern Virginia and lit the tinder that set America ablaze. Attempting to spark a slave rebellion in Harpers Ferry, Brown was captured by Federal troops and put on trial for treason. Found guilty, he was promptly hanged from a tree close to the courthouse in nearby Charlestown.

Herman Melville considered John Brown's raid and execution as "The

Portent" of civil war, and in a poem with this title he described the executed man, "Hanging from the beam," face hidden by the hood of execution placed over his head:

> But the streaming beard is shown
> (Weird John Brown),
> The meteor of the war.

In the wake of Brown's failed insurrection, abolitionists and proslavery advocates alike became ever more furious with each other. William Lowndes Yancey, a leading Alabama congressman and one of the "fire-eater" secessionists, was the most passionate opponent of what he considered to be an intensifying Northern threat to Southern stability. Yancey once had been a student at Lenox Academy, and in the early 1830s had been dismissed from Williams College as an incorrigible disciplinary problem.

Born in Georgia, Yancey had been brought north to Troy, New York, at the age of eight, when his mother married Nathan S. S. Beman, a leading Presbyterian minister and a vehement abolitionist. (Beman later served for twenty years as president of Rensselaer Polytechnic Institute in Troy.) Beman's stepson came to despise abolitionists, especially because Williams was a seed bed of antislavery sentiment. In 1823, students had formed the Anti-Slavery Society of Williams College, the first such organization in Massachusetts and the second in all New England. Although the society went out of existence with the appearance of other abolitionist groups, as late as July 1831 its members participated in annual Fourth of July festivities by sponsoring a poem or oration on the subject of slavery. That was the same year sixteen-year-old William Yancey first entered the college.

Yancey's disciplinary record from February 1831 to February 1833 shows he was punished thirteen times for infractions ranging from "absence from prayers"—eight of the thirteen—to playing cards, public intoxication, disturbing a religious meeting, and disorderly conduct in the town of Adams. He was suspended twice, let back in twice, and violated probation one last time by again being absent from prayers.

There is a tradition at Williams that the strict discipline of the college developed Yancey's "pugnacious and irascible" temperament while at the same time the professors taught him masterful rhetoric and imparted a commanding style on the public speaking platform—a talent for which the college's men were very well known. Yancey made the most of his Williams education, becoming a brilliant orator and lawyer, building his political career by obsessively battling for secession. He was the figure who, in the fall of 1860, led the embittered Southern Democrats out of their party's convention. Splitting the party in this way left the path open for Lincoln and the Republicans to win the presidential election. Yancey well knew that victory by the antislavery Republicans could spark the wholesale secession of the South.

Yancey was so influential among Southerners that one historian wrote, "It would seem presumptuous to say that without him there would have been no Confederate States of America, but it is probably so."

Herman Melville's financial support came in part from his father-in-law, Lemuel Shaw, Jr., chief justice of Massachusetts. Respected as one of the finest jurists in the state's history, Shaw had enraged abolitionists in the 1850s by ordering a fugitive slave to be forcibly returned to his Southern owners. Judge Shaw's standing with liberals and Republicans had been ruined by this difficult decision, but Democrats, such as Melville and his core family in the area of Albany, New York, backed the decision as respecting the rule of law. That law led back to the Constitution of the United States, which bound the states together, and therefore that law must be heeded or the Union would be threatened.

The wealthy Shaw, who was almost eighty and ready to retire, gave the Melvilles loans, at one point purchasing Arrowhead from Herman to clear debt and then turning the farm over to Lizzie. This step was taken in 1860, just before Melville set off on a sea voyage around Cape Horn, at the southern tip of South America. Shaw was glad his son-in-law was taking that journey, reckoning it essential for Melville's mental and physical health. At the same time, Shaw was anxious that the family ultimately sell Arrowhead and move either to Boston or New York, where his daughter would not be so lonely, and her depressed husband could avoid being cooped up on the farm. The Melvilles were increasingly anxious to sell Arrowhead, but there were still no takers.

While her husband was on the voyage, Lizzie and influential contacts in New York's literary world attempted to find a publisher for his new collected verse. The volume was to be called simply "Poems" by Herman Melville. So decided was he about breaking with the adventure stories that had won him fame, that Melville told Lizzie and his friends, "For God's sake don't have By the author of 'Typee' 'Piddlededee' etc., on the title-page."

As it was with his other work these days, however, publishers were not interested in Melville's poems.

If John Brown was a "meteor of the war," a portent of disaster, he was not the only one, for in 1860 a comet appeared in the southern hemisphere, a phenomenon said to predict the coming of war. On Melville's voyage through the South Atlantic, he first saw this comet, which soon would appear in the night sky above the United States.

During the presidential campaign this year, William Cullen Bryant introduced Republican candidate Abraham Lincoln of Illinois to a skeptical audience at a lecture hall in New York's Cooper Union. Lincoln gave an electrifying speech that day and won the hearts of New Yorkers and New Englanders alike, hurrying his languishing candidacy on to triumph in the election that fall. Shocked by Brown's crusade to inspire a slave rebellion, the Southern states—led by William Yancey—had moved ever closer to seceding from the Union, and Lincoln's election in November drove them over the brink. The first to go was South Carolina, officially seceding in December and laying siege to Fort Sumter, the Federal bastion in Charleston harbor. Other states followed, and the government of the Confederate States of America was formed, with Mississippi's Jefferson Davis as president and Georgia's Alexander H. Stephens as vice president.

Like Yancey, Stephens had been a student at Lenox Academy—as was the last Republic of Texas president, Anson Jones, who had died in 1858. (The ambitious Jones had taken his own life in an abyss of mental anguish at failing to be elected to national office.) By late 1860, the many Berkshire folk who had gone south or west found themselves compelled to make choices for or against the Union. Some would go north, others would choose for the Confederacy.

Throughout that presidential campaign of 1860, Herman Melville was aboard ship, sailing around South America and up to San Francisco. On his return, Melville took a train across Central America and sailed from there to New York, reaching the city just after Lincoln's victory. He found the nation in a tumult of emotions, but at the same time he knew that the advent of the new administration in Washington would mean government positions to be handed out to Lincoln supporters. Melville had not voted in the election, but he hoped to use family and social connections to win a post as customs house inspector in New York harbor. Friends suggested he might even become consul to a foreign country. Such a position would give him the regular income he so desperately needed, and he could then write whatever he wished.

Before Melville returned to Berkshire, he joined Lizzie in Boston, where her father had taken seriously ill. While there, Melville experienced a brutal windstorm that swept over New England, destroying buildings and even toppling the spires of churches—a symbolic event not lost on the metaphorically inclined author. Back at Pittsfield that December, he found the folk of western Massachusetts worked up about the threat of the Union's being dissolved. Most swore to fight it.

Chapter Two

THE LAST DAYS OF PEACE

The reorganized Pittsfield militia company, now known as the Allen Guards, was training regularly under its elected captain, thirty-six-year-old Henry S. Briggs. Over the past half year, the company had been funded in large part by Thomas Allen, who had contributed $1,500 toward the $2,000 raised to finance it. Though his home was in St. Louis, Allen retained close ties to Berkshire and maintained a handsome mansion in Pittsfield, which he visited in the summer.

For all that Berkshire opposed secession and was proud of the Guards, its new "Minute Men," Abraham Lincoln had won only a narrow majority in the county, for there were many Berkshire Democrats who feared his election would result in a sudden spiral down to disunion and armed conflict. Throughout the county, the subject of much discussion and worry was the threat of disunion and how to prevent it—or perhaps whether just to let it happen, as some believed was better than going to war over it. Farmers near Great Barrington met every weekday evening at the distillery and grist mill of Orrin Curtis on the Seekonk River while their cattle and swine were fattening up on still slops, and the men inevitably talked politics, or about the "Impending Conflict," as they termed it.

One participant recalled those "warm discussions" years later:

> On such occasions some good reader was selected to read the stirring news which appeared from day to day in the Journal of Commerce. [This news was] hotly discussed by old line Whigs, newly fledged Republicans, and Jackson Democrats. It was in the evening of Nov. 9, 1860, that we heard of the election of Lincoln, and that the Mahaiwe Bank at Great Barrington village, in common with others, had suspended specie payments. This, exclaimed all those present, means war, for there will be an uprising in the Southern States.
>
> And so it proved, for that same evening we heard that South Carolina had seceded. News of the secession of other states followed in a few weeks, and thus the winter glided swiftly away, like a "night of fateful dreams."

Brigadier General Henry S. Briggs, original commander of the Allen Guards and first colonel of the Tenth Massachusetts.

COURTESY BERKSHIRE ATHENAEUM

December was hard and cold in Berkshire, with the temperature at twenty below zero on the thirteenth. Pittsfield began to consider how to celebrate its own centennial jubilee that coming spring of 1861. With an eye on the Southern secessionists, the village paraded its militia company, by now admirably drilled and equipped. Ably led by Captain Briggs, the Allen Guards were joined by the musicians of Hodge's Band from North Adams, and the military performance inspired an admiring audience of thousands. Thomas Allen's contributions had been well spent, for the seventy-eight members of the Guards were turned out smartly in cadet-gray uniforms with white crossbelts and gold trim. The militiamen had become quite proficient in the manual of arms and in executing marching maneuvers, and to display their style, the Guards fired volleys in salute to outgoing president James Buchanan.

This salute was followed by a commemoration of the continuing siege of Fort Sumter, and the Guards fired volleys in honor of the fort's embattled commander, Major Robert Anderson.

The cold, snow, and heavy rains of winter isolated farms like Arrowhead, and the damp- ness continued to cause Melville debilitating pain from his rheu- matism. Immersing himself in writing and reading poetry, he acquired volume after volume of works by the likes of Alfred Lord Tennyson and Andrew Marvell. He read hungrily—studying, it might be said—the poetry of Emerson, Shelley, Robert Herrick, volumes of British bal- lads, and translations of Schiller and Homer. Perhaps his closest friend in this time was Joseph A. E. Smith, later to become Pittsfield's historian, and in 1861 the strongly abolitionist editor of the *Berkshire County*

Herman Melville in 1861, from a photograph taken by the Rodney Dewey studios in Pittsfield.

COURTESY BERKSHIRE ATHENAEUM

Eagle. Smith's inflammatory editorials against slavery agitated the reading public so much that his more conservative publisher, Henry Chickering, ordered him to tone down the rhetoric.

Nor would Melville have supported Smith's radical antislavery position, for as ever with him, preserving the Union was more important than civil war—"man's foulest crime," as it might have been described in "Misgivings," a poem he was writing. All around Melville, among his friends, in the news, and in his very own home, was the specter of fatal conflict between abolition and slavery. Not only were editor Smith, the Sedgwicks, the Morewoods, and most society folk of Boston adamantly resolved to fight slavery to the bitter end, but Arrowhead itself was believed to have been a "station" on the secret network known as the "Underground Railroad," which had illegally spirited fugitive slaves north to Canada. Dr. John Brewster, the former owner of the farm, had kept a "slave room" to conceal fugitive slaves waiting for the next stage of their flight. It was said that in Brewster's next home, on East Street in Pittsfield, he had built a similar room to continue his efforts.

Yet there were many who opposed the approach of civil war and called for compromise. At first they spoke out boldly, often in frank public discussions that were the heritage of New England democracy, but as feelings grew more impassioned, some accused the antiwar faction of being Southern sympathiz-ers, which the vast majority certainly were not.

From Arrowhead's north piazza, Melville could see the top of "yon black" Mount Greylock, at almost 3,500 feet the highest peak in the state. In the shelter of his piazza, he could contemplate the moods of nature, remembering last year's vicious windstorm that had come at the same time as the tumultu-ous presidential election and the move toward secession—a storm that had knocked down New England church steeples. Melville compared the "dark side" of natural phenomena to national politics, and contemplating storms and Greylock, he wrote about his "Misgivings" as he anticipated what was coming upon the United States.

> When ocean clouds over inland hills
> Sweep storming in late autumn brown,
> And horror the sodden valley fills,
> And the spire falls crashing in the town,
> I muse upon my country's ills—
> The tempest bursting from the waste of Time
> On the world's fairest hope linked with man's foulest crime.
>
> Nature's dark side is heeded now—
> (Ah! optimist-cheer disheartened flown)—
> A child may read the moody brow
> Of yon black mountain lone.
> With shouts and torrents down the gorges go,
> And storms are formed behind the storm we feel:
> And hemlock shakes in the rafter, the oak in the driving keel.

Was the hemlock rafter a symbol for the home? The oaken driving keel the ship of state? It is thought "the world's fairest hope" meant the United States, but did "man's foulest crime" signify slavery or fratricide? Or both?

Not all social commentary of the day had to do with doom and war, how-ever, for some of it was about ordinary life in western Massachusetts.

Oliver Wendell Holmes published his novel *Elsie Venner,* a mildly anti-Calvinist tease, which annoyed many Berkshire residents who recognized their community—"Rockland" was a thinly disguised Pittsfield—or perhaps saw themselves or family depicted and did not always like what they read. Holmes's Rockland, like Pittsfield, had a mountain nearby that "gave it its character, and redeemed it from wearing the commonplace expression which belongs to ordinary country villages." And "Elm Street was the pride of Rockland, but not only on account of its Gothic-arched vista," as he described the overarching elms, but "in this street were most of the great houses, or 'mansion-houses.'"

Sarah Morewood replied to a New York literary friend who had written her to ask what she thought of *Elsie Venner*, which had appeared in installments in the prestigious *Atlantic Monthly*:

> *Much,* and that not of the best natured say either— You knew of course many of the localities he meant and Characters too—did you not? It is certain he has not cared about a strife of the winds—for he has created a Storm in many quarters.

When it came to more serious matters, Holmes poured out his liberal heart in a poetic appeal to South Carolina, which had blockaded Fort Sumter and was threatening a bombardment if it were not surrendered. Newspapers told of efforts being made by steamship to resupply and reinforce Sumter, but these vessels were turned back by cannon fire from Charleston's harbor forts. "Brother Jonathan's Lament for Sister Caroline" was published on March 25, the title playing on the well-known nickname for Yankees—"Brother Jonathan"—while referring tenderly to the seceding state as "sister." Like Melville, Holmes refers to America as "the hope of the world."

SHE has gone,—she has left us in passion and pride,—
Our stormy-browed sister, so long at our side!
She has torn her own star from our firmament's glow,
And turned on her brother the face of a foe!

Oh, Caroline, Caroline, child of the sun,
We can never forget that our hearts have been one,—
Our foreheads both sprinkled in Liberty's name,
From the fountain of blood with the finger of flame!

You were always too ready to fire at a touch;
But we said, "She is hasty,—she does not mean much."
We have scowled, when you uttered some turbulent threat;
But Friendship still whispered, "Forgive and forget!"

Has our love all died out? Have its altars grown cold?
Has the curse come at last which the fathers foretold?
Then Nature must teach us the strength of the chain
That her petulant children would sever in vain.

They may fight till the buzzards are gorged with their spoil,
Till the harvest grows black as it rots in the soil,
Till the wolves and the catamounts troop from their caves,
And the shark tracks the pirate, the lord of the waves:

In vain is the strife! When its fury is past,
Their fortunes must flow in one channel at last,
As the torrents that rush from the mountains of snow
Roll mingled in peace through the valleys below.

Our Union is river, lake, ocean, and sky:
Man breaks not the medal, when God cuts the die!
Though darkened with sulphur, though cloven with steel,
The blue arch will brighten, the waters will heal!

Oh, Caroline, Caroline, child of the sun,
There are battles with Fate that can never be won!
The star-flowering banner must never be furled,
For its blossoms of light are the hope of the world!

Go, then, our rash sister! afar and aloof,
Run wild in the sunshine away from our roof;
But when your heart aches and your feet have grown sore,
Remember the pathway that leads to our door!

Back in Lenox, abolitionist Catharine Sedgwick was not feeling so
conciliatory. She wrote about her feelings to her niece Katherine Minot, the
daughter of her brother, Charles, who had died several years earlier.

> As for that bullying state of South Carolina, one would not much
> care. As C. (Cousin C.) says, "Let the damned little thing go!" or as
> C. B. (two of the most humane men I know) says, "Plow them under,
> plow them under! It has been a little wasp from the beginning!"

Presumably her cousin "C. B." was referring to South Carolina's fractious-
ness at the very establishment of the nation just after the Revolution. Though
a free-thinking Unitarian, Miss Sedgwick was somewhat fatalistic about it
all, with mixed feelings that caused her to dread civil war, but at the same
time she was praying that the leaders of Massachusetts would concede nothing to the secessionists. Earlier that year, Miss Sedgwick had written a friend
about her confusion over how the impending struggle should best resolve
itself, whether in full-scale war or in reconciliation and compromise:

I am hopeful as to the issue. I cling to the Union as an unweaned child does to its mother's breast. But it seems to me we should stand in awe and only pray that God's will may be done in this great matter. It may be that he will permit the Southern suicidal madness to rage and *prevail* to the great end of blotting slavery from the land it poisons. Massachusetts is condemned as a hot-bed of abolition fanaticism—I hear nothing but ultra concession and conservatism.

That spring, Melville journeyed to New York and Washington, D.C., to press his case for an appointment as a consul, probably to Florence. He had the endorsement of well-connected friends and family and an introduction to the influential Massachusetts senator Charles Sumner. Melville also had been warmly recommended in a letter signed by some of the leading men of Berkshire, including Judge Julius Rockwell, who asked Sumner to oblige him with the personal favor of recommending Melville to President Lincoln for a post. Rockwell also sent his best regards to Lincoln, whom he knew.

In March, Washington was a madhouse of office-seekers and solicitors, with long receiving lines winding into the White House. Melville got in one of those White House lines, though it was against his grain to personally solicit a government post. He shook hands with Lincoln, seeing for the first time the much-maligned president who, in newspaper articles and cartoons, had been portrayed as homely, even ugly.

Melville wrote home to Elizabeth:

Old Abe is much better looking [than] I expected and younger looking. He shook hands like a good fellow—working hard at it like a man sawing wood at so much per cord. . . . The scene was very fine altogether. Superb furniture—flood of light—magnificent flowers— full band of music, etc.

Melville's quest for a consulship had little chance, however, for Sumner represented the most radical of Republicans, and at this time the Lincoln government was striving to set a middle course, hoping to appeal to moderates and prevent the outbreak of war. Then, on March 29, Elizabeth's father again fell ill in Boston, and Herman was compelled to meet her there. They arrived too late. Lemuel Shaw, Jr., died at home on March 30. Shaw's death marked the passing of the generation that had held the Union together despite quarrel after quarrel, a generation that had steadily built the country by adding states and territories, striking compromises, always cherishing peace more than the victory of one section over another. It was not so with Melville's generation and the next one, just maturing, for they were ready to fight.

Melville's poem about that spring of 1861, entitled "Apathy and Enthusi-asm," expresses how those elders "Mourned the days forever o'er."

> And recalled the forest proverb,
>   The Iroquois' old saw:
> *Grief to every greybeard*
>   *When young Indians lead the war.*

The weather became warmer in Berkshire, as April rains turned meadows green and brought the first trees into leaf. Life went on, but tension was in the air because of South Carolina's ongoing siege of Fort Sumter.

Henry Briggs, son of the former governor, was in Boston, prosecuting a ten-year-old claim by a circus company against the town of Adams. In 1850, the circus had lost an elephant, which had fallen through the Park Street bridge over the Hoosic River and been injured mortally. "Columbus" had been much loved by the children of Berkshire and the region, who had eagerly awaited the appearance of the circus each year. A dozen or more youngsters used to ride in a huge sedan chair strapped to the gentle Columbus's back, and they fed him sweets whenever he reached backwards with his trunk. The lawsuit accused the town of negligence, and several unresolved trials had been held, with juries failing to agree on the amount due the circus, which wanted $15,000 in damages. Columbus had been buried in Lenox, where he had died a week after the accident, and his hide had for a time been hung in Briggs's law office. Eventually, the skeleton was exhumed and taken to the Natural History Society of Williams College to be mounted.

During those weeks presenting his elephant case before the state supreme court in Boston, Briggs had also been lobbying Governor John A. Andrew on behalf of the Allen Guards, which Briggs wanted to be among the first called out if militia were needed to defend Washington. The politically well-connected Briggs, who was a graduate of Williams and had studied law at Harvard, got Andrew's attention.

Briggs did not have long to wait for the moment to come. On Friday, April 12, Fort Sumter was fired upon by South Carolina artillery. It was the sixty-first birthday of his father, former governor George Briggs.

News of the bombardment of Fort Sumter reached Berkshire on the stormy, rain-soaked evening of April 13. Most people did not hear about it until the next day. Other than in the weekly newspapers—such as the *Sun* or the *Eagle* of Pittsfield, the *Courier* in Great Barrington, and the *Hoosac Valley News and Transcript* in northern Berkshire—the quickest way to get the latest news reports was to look at the bulletin boards generally outside a newspaper or telegraph office, where important public messages were usually posted. Sometimes messages or clipped articles were put up there by employees in the offices, and in other cases citizens took the initiative to tack up newspaper clippings, whether from local or big-city publications.

In Great Barrington, someone suspended a bulletin board between two buildings in Railroad Street, and there many read the startling news of the attack on a national fort—of treasonous South Carolina actually firing on the American flag. Shock swept Berkshire County, and most folk were enraged when that Sunday, April 14, Fort Sumter surrendered to the forces of South Carolina. The move was on to mobilize militia companies across the country as President Lincoln called for the states to send 75,000 men to the defense of Washington, D.C., which he believed was threatened by attack from armed secessionists. Militia companies in the Northern states were summoned to muster, but very few were ready to answer Lincoln's call immediately. The Eighth Massachusetts Militia regiment was ready to go, except that it needed two more companies to fill its complement. The Allen Guards were chosen as one of those companies, and would be the only militia unit from western Massachusetts to participate in the first defense of Washington.

On the evening of April 17, Henry Briggs telegraphed to Pittsfield for Henry H. Richardson, his first lieutenant, calling for the militia company to assemble and board a train within twenty-four hours. Briggs let the court case languish and headed back to Springfield to meet his company and the rest of the Eighth. When the court was next called to order to continue the case, the judge was told that the elephant-suit attorney had "gone to Washington at the head of his company." The case eventually would be settled by compromise.

Henry Richardson was a contractor and master builder who had erected many of the finest residences in Berkshire County. In his mid-thirties, Richardson was drilling the Allen Guards in West's Hall armory when the telegraph came in about 8:30 p.m. at the House Printing Telegraph Line office in the passenger station at the foot of Depot Street. This historic message was dated April 18, 1861, and was printed on a long strip of paper, which Richardson read aloud to the company: He was to get the Allen Guards to Springfield the next day, and there meet Briggs and the Eighth regiment for the journey southward by rail.

After instructing the company, Richardson hurried over to the Berkshire House inn and read the message to the men who happened to be there, some of whom—such as George Campbell and George H. Laflin—would be instrumental throughout the war in organizing and supporting Berkshire regiments. All agreed they would have to organize a second militia company, and they immediately planned to raise the funds. Their efforts would be firmly supported by leading Pittsfield businessmen, such as Robert Pomeroy and William Pollock.

Historian Joseph Smith described the scene in Pittsfield after the telegram arrived from Briggs:

> The night of the 17th, and the following day, was an interval of excitement, animation, and preparation, such as had not been known in Pittsfield since the revolution. The members of the guard and their families were of course busy in making their personal arrangements. And as soon as the order calling for the company became public, a large number of the wealthier citizens met and guaranteed the sum of five thousand dollars, to provide for the comfort of its members and the aid of such of their families as might need assistance during their absence.

Since some of the older militia men were not fit enough to take part in what might well become a strenuous military campaign, several resigned, their places taken by younger recruits. Among the newcomers was new-made private Daniel Hughes, a tall and lanky nineteen-year-old Pittsfield boy, and soon another would be William W. Rockwell, twenty-one-year-old son of Julius Rockwell. Young Rockwell was in New York City just then, where he would join the company as soon as it arrived. The Allen Guards were partly in the keeping of Third Sergeant Israel C. Weller, who was twenty-one and employed by his family firm, Isham & Weller, flour dealers. The company's second sergeant was Daniel J. Dodge, one of the first to appeal to the community for financial support of the Allen Guards; it was Dodge who, ten years earlier, had climbed the Old Elm to paint its scar with preservative and prolong its life.

At noon on April 18, war bells rang all over Pittsfield, calling people to the town hall, where patriotic addresses were given and the Allen Guards publicly thanked for their "alacrity in responding to the call of the government." There was not an hour to lose, for at any moment armed secessionists might march by the thousands on Washington, which had virtually no defensive force at hand. At this time, the United States Army numbered only 16,000 men in widely scattered posts.

By 6:30 that evening, the Allen Guards shouldered muskets and marched through Pittsfield's crowded streets toward the railroad depot. Smith wrote:

> Railroad square was thronged with men, women, and children, surging with excitement and enthusiasm; and evidently brought by the scene before them to a clearer realization of the grandeur and sadness of the conflict, which the thick coming telegrams of the day foreshadowed; while, on the platform, closer around the position of the guard, were witnessed the varied partings of kindred, lovers, and

friends, with those never so well loved as then; partings in which pride and joy struggled strangely with grief and sad forebodings.

Amid cheers from friends and family, and only twenty-three hours after the telegram reached Richardson, the train pulled slowly out of the Pittsfield depot, carrying the troops of the Allen Guards, who waved from doors and windows to friends and loved ones watching them go. No one knew how this all would end, or whether their men would come home safely.

Chapter Three

ON TO WASHINGTON, ALMOST

The Allen Guards arrived at Springfield, a few hours by train southeast of Pittsfield, and were greeted with resounding ovations from a crowd of five thousand well-wishers, including paraded militia and fire companies.

Reunited with its captain, Henry Briggs, the Guards that evening met the rest of the Eighth Massachusetts Militia Regiment, which had come out from Boston. The other companies of the Eighth were all from the eastern part of the state, the regimental commander Brigadier General Benjamin F. Butler, Boston attorney and politician. One of the Eighth's volunteers, calling himself "Leatherstocking," wrote to a Massachusetts paper about the enthusiastic reception in Springfield:

> Indeed, it seemed as though we were war-worn veterans returning from victorious battlefields, covered with glory, rather than untried recruits and volunteer militia, on the way to duty for the protection of our common flag. We were ushered into the city amid the ringing of bells, the blazing of bonfires, firing of cannon, and inspiring music of military bands. It made our hearts bound with joy, and thrill with emotions of pleasure, to find so many warm and patriotic hearts in Western Massachusetts. All honor to the men and women of Springfield and its surroundings.

It was the same at every station along the way to New York City, a hundred and thirty-five miles to the south, with excited crowds rushing up to the tracks to wave and cheer the soldiers on. For this regiment, and for General Butler's personal ambition, it was not only crucial to garrison Washington before secessionists took possession, but it was important to be among the first to answer Lincoln's call. The Sixth Massachusetts Militia Regiment was already en route, and, in fact, the honor of being the very first to arrive had already been dubiously snatched by a ragtag gang of unarmed young men from Pennsylvania, who had hurried to the capital but were in no position to mount a defense.

The Seventh New York Militia Regiment marches down Broadway in the city on its way to Washington, received by cheering crowds, as was the Eighth Massachusetts Militia, which passed this way a few hours

Earlier in the day, the Sixth Massachusetts had marched down Broadway in Manhattan, past cheering crowds, then took trains across New Jersey to Pennsylvania and Maryland. It soon would enter Baltimore, a hotbed of secessionist sympathizers, among them local officials who had publicly warned that Northern troops would not be allowed to pass through the city.

Another militia regiment aspiring to be among the first to defend Washington was the Seventh New York, made up of wealthy young men from leading families of the city and state. These were distinguished fellows in white gloves and immaculate uniforms, virtually all with college educations and socially well-connected. They were well drilled and disciplined, having often paraded before New York's high society. The Eighth Massachusetts, in turn, was also made up of men from leading families of its state, and the Allen Guards uniform was styled after that of the Seventh New York.

The Eighth arrived in New York City the next morning, April 19, at 6 a.m., some hours before the Seventh New York was ready to depart. With the Allen Guards officially designated as Company K, the Eighth followed a line of march through a happy, admiring Manhattan throng. It was very thrilling, but by now the hungry, tired troops just wanted a good meal. Half the men dined at the plush La Farge House, and the rest at the Astor House, where "we were met by a perfect shower of applause," wrote Leatherstocking.

> After a hearty breakfast we once more resumed our onward march towards the South. In marching down Courtland [sic] street the crowd was so immense that it [required] guides to keep their post. Thousands [of] streamers floated from the stores and public buildings. The demonstrations were such as to assure us that the city of New York was true to the Union. We proceeded to the Jersey City Depot, followed by thousands of citizens of New York. From Jersey City to Philadelphia we received the same warm expressions of favor and congratulations, such as bands of music, bonfires, ringing of bells, &c.

At six o'clock that Friday evening, the Eighth detrained at Philadelphia, where the streets were so mobbed with supporters that the regiment could barely get to its quarters in two hotels, the Continental House and the Girard. The Berkshire men stayed at the latter, unrolling their bedding on the floor as vague but troubling reports arrived, telling of rebel forces occupying railroad crossings, ferry slips, and strategic towns in Maryland and northern Virginia. At two in the morning, they were awakened with the grim news that the Sixth Massachusetts had been attacked by a large mob while passing through Baltimore. Four volunteers had been killed and thirty-six wounded. The mob had paid a much higher price, and the Sixth had pressed on to Washington, but it was certain the next Northern regiment to arrive in Baltimore would be met just as savagely.

As the Eighth took its uneasy rest on the floors of the Philadelphia hotels, the New York Seventh Regiment entered the city and quartered for the night at the railroad depot, intending to go through Baltimore the next day.

Leatherstocking wrote:

> But on hearing of the disgraceful attack on the Massachusetts Sixth Regiment . . . by the Baltimore mob, and also meeting . . . Pennsylvania troops returning, and they saying it was impossible for any northern troops to pass through Baltimore, they concluded to remain at Phila-

delphia. But the "old Eighth," of Massachusetts, under the command of Brig. Gen. Butler, determined to cut their way through all opposes and mobs. Their destination was Washington, and thither they were bound to go.

The order was given for the train to start, and on we went. . . . We steamed on through Delaware, where we had the pleasure of still beholding on the public buildings, and also on houses and barns, our country's flag—the glorious stars and stripes, the "flag of the free." . . .

When we arrived at a small station about thirty miles from Havre de Grace, the report came that 1,600 Baltimoreans were in position at the latter place, to dispute our passage to the Capitol; and it was also reported that they had taken possession of the ferry boat, and had her anchored in the stream. The regiment was supplied with ball cartridges, ten rounds to a man, and, as almost every man was supplied with a "six shooter," we could give the mob sixteen rounds of lead, and the balance in steel!

As the train continued on its way towards the ferry, the men commenced to load their muskets and revolvers. The report came so direct, and being confirmed, as we thought, by a subsequent messenger, we made up our minds that a fight must come off in half an hour's time. And let me tell you, sir, that there would have been no child's play in this matter. As we neared Havre de Grace we took each comrade's hand, and some of us concluded for the last time on earth. The cars here moved on very slowly.

Lookouts thought they saw the gleam of enemy bayonets in the sunshine, and the train stopped. The regiment got out and formed up in battle order, the Allen Guards positioned as a flank company on the left of the main force, which advanced in column, "steadily and firmly; not a man flinched; all seemed cool and collected." Fortunately, there was no enemy in sight, and the regiment boarded the ferry, a railroad car transport named *Maryland*. Soon, the Eighth was steaming down the Chesapeake as night came on.

The landlubbers of Berkshire County suffered from seasickness on the *Maryland*, which was packed with nearly a thousand soldiers, their gear, stacked muskets, sheathed bayonets, and haversacks mostly jammed into corners, out of the way so the men could sleep and smoke, play cards, or more likely try not to be seasick. Someone knocked over a stack of loaded muskets, and one went off, but no one was hurt.

The steamer anchored that night off Annapolis, the capital of Maryland and home of the United States Naval Academy. Forty miles overland to the west was Washington, and every man knew that thousands of armed, hostile adversaries were swarming through that region, waiting for them. Most of the Massachusetts troops remained aboard, cramped and fatigued, while Butler went ashore to consult with uneasy naval officers and the city's mayor on how to get to the capital and to ask how much opposition awaited them. Many rebels were, indeed, in arms, said the mayor, the railway line torn up, and the roads to Washington would be impassable to so few soldiers.

The next morning, the troops on the *Maryland* awoke to see that the famous War of 1812 warship, *Constitution,* was tied up at a nearby wharf. Fondly nicknamed "Old Ironsides," she was still in use as a training vessel for the naval academy, and her reputation stirred the men, as Leatherstocking said:

> It was indeed a beautiful sight, that noble old frigate in all her pride, with the figure of Jackson on her bow. "The Union, it must be preserved," came to every mind, and it was repeated by every tongue. One of my friends stood by my side, and, with tears in his eyes, exclaimed: "I love that old noble ship! We mean to take her from her present position, and send her into free waters. The keeping of the Constitution from the secessionists is of more glory to us than the fighting and winning of a battle!" "Amen!" I exclaimed, and every heart responded, "Amen!"

None other than Oliver Wendell Holmes had immortalized the *Constitution* in his 1830 poem "Old Ironsides," which had brought him national acclaim and prevented the frigate from being routinely scrapped by the navy. The Eighth intended to keep "Old Ironsides" from being taken by the rebels, who were likening themselves to the revolutionaries of 1776. Two Massachusetts companies were detached to board and protect the venerated ship, one of them the Allen Guards, and it was towed by the *Maryland* away from the lightly defended naval academy, eventually to be sent to New York.

The rank and file of the Eighth remained confined to these two vessels for days, the men uncomplaining, but resigned, as they ate only hard biscuit and salt pork, quickly growing weary of the tedious monotony so well known to every soldier on campaign. They had been wondering whether they were the only volunteer troops available to cross the peninsula and attempt to reach Washington; then a ship full of soldiers came into sight. Alert for any sign of surprise attack, the Union men readied themselves for a fight, as Leatherstocking described the moment:

> It was a relief to us when the steamer Boston, with the Seventh Regiment on board, came steaming up the bay. They were first supposed to be secessionist, and every man stood with his musket, ready to give them a warm reception.

The gentlemen of the Seventh New York joined forces with the Eighth Massachusetts as the regiments finally landed at Annapolis. Companies of the Seventh were positioned in advance and on the flanks to prevent an attack, while the Massachusetts troops worked hard to repair railroad tracks that had been ripped up by rebels and rebuild bridges the insurgents had torn down in an effort to blockade Washington. Men of the Eighth even repaired sabotaged locomotives and got a train going to transport rails and timbers for their track-laying labors in the hot spring sun of Maryland.

In one remarkable effort, the Eighth Massachusetts took the lead in laying twenty miles of railroad track, working through the night, without rest. Members of the Seventh regiment occasionally took part in the track-laying and reconstruction, and some skilled civilians were hired to work, but the brunt of the physical labor fell on the Massachusetts men. Still, a friendship sprang up between the two regiments, for the Yankees were running out of supplies, and the Yorkers generously shared their food with them. Generations of state hostility melted away during this slow, determined advance on Washington, through uncertain country held by dangerous bands of armed rebels.

The Allen Guards were not involved in the track-laying effort, however, for the company had been detached from the regiment and shipped aboard a small steam tug to support the Federal garrison of Fort McHenry, the citadel in Baltimore harbor. McHenry had been the scene of the War of 1812 siege and British bombardment that had ended with the "Star-Spangled Banner" still waving the following morning, inspiring the famous verses by patriot Francis Scott Key. Though the Berkshire men were not in the railroad-repairing advance, Fort McHenry held danger enough, for it was constantly under threat of attack, facing Baltimore and its bloodthirsty rebel mob.

On April 20, secessionists moved on the Federal navy yard at Norfolk, Virginia, but before they got there Union troops destroyed many of the ships, setting them ablaze or scuttling them to prevent capture. One of the naval vessels tied up at Norfolk was the obsolete *United States*, the frigate on which Herman Melville had sailed during a journey from Hawaii to Boston in 1843-44. The Union men who destroyed the ships to keep them out of rebel hands did not bother to sink the decrepit *United States*, thinking her worthless. As it turned out, Confederate commander Robert E. Lee placed her in commission as the very first vessel of the Confederate States of America's new navy. Armed with guns to help defend harbors, and also intended to serve as a training ship, *United States* kept her original name, although some rebels wanted to rename her *Confederate States*.

It did not take long for Allen Guards men to venture from Fort McHenry into Baltimore, which had not yet been occupied by Union troops, although most of its insurrectionists had apparently left the city and joined the forces blocking the way to Washington. The following was reported in a Pittsfield newspaper:

FIRST IN BALTIMORE—The first Massachusetts uniforms seen in Baltimore after the fatal affair of the 19th of April were worn by a party of the Allen Guards consisting of Goodrich, Wardwell, Van Loan, and A. H. Whipple, who went over last Saturday afternoon. They strolled through the city, visited the best stores and other places of resort and were everywhere treated with the utmost courtesy. (It must be remembered that this was *before* the arrival of Gen. Butler's command at [the encampment on] Federal Hill.) The only approach to ill will shown to them being an exclamation as they passed a liquor saloon, "There goes some of those d—d Northerners!" Deducting the D—D rather a compliment than otherwise.

Entering Barnum's Hotel, they were greeted by a gentleman whose appearance at once gained their good will, which further acquaintance increased. He proved to be Mr. McLaughlin, the proprietor of the hotel, and father of Wm. B. McLaughlin, who, for good reason, is excused from the present service. Mr. McLaughlin enquired to what corps they belonged, and being informed, said he had a son who belonged to that company, and at once cordially invited them to the hospitalities of his house, which ranks with St. Nicholas of New York, and it is not a little to the credit of both parties that they appreciated the kindly feelings of their host even more than the richness of his fare. One of them exclaims emphatically, "he does know how to keep a hotel."

Since the above was written, we learn that Willie Rockwell and C. R. Strong visited the city, in uniform, and strolled about at their pleasure. Both parties were warned that they would not come back alive, and both experienced only kindness and courtesy, even from those who acknowledged sympathy with the south. We trust that this feeling will increase as the troops and citizens know each other better.

Additional regiments from New York and New England arrived at Annapolis, guaranteeing that the relief of Washington would succeed once the rail line was rebuilt and secured.

With troops of the Seventh loaded onto open flatcars slowly drawn by a locomotive, the advance went forward, although it was required to stop frequently to check for loose rails, replace missing ones, or make repairs. Often, rails had to be laboriously searched for in the nearby countryside, where rebels had thrown them after tearing them up. The advance sometimes was no more than one mile an hour, and rebels often returned in the night to destroy work that had been done so arduously the day before. Then, on April 24, word came to the Seventh New York that a train had been sent out from Washington on repaired lines in hope of meeting the troops. The Seventh was assembled and ready when that train arrived. The regiment jumped aboard and got to the capital the next day, sprucing itself up before parading through the streets to the cheers of the deliriously happy thousands who crowded the parade route. The Eighth Massachusetts, minus the Allen Guards at Fort McHenry, did not reach the city for another day, when they trudged in without ceremony or much in the way of cheers. Even the city's newspapers did not take special note of their arrival. They were dirty and tired from their long days laboring on the railroad, and were glad for a chance to rest at their temporary quarters in the Rotunda of the unfinished Capitol building. The Seventh New York was already settled in the chambers of the House of Representatives, the Sixth Massachusetts housed in the Senate building.

As the weary men of the Eighth assembled in formation around the inside of the Rotunda, they were surprised and delighted to see, in the middle of the huge chamber, fifteen kegs of lager beer, two thousand boiled eggs, heaps of cheese, crates of lemons and oranges, smoked beef, bread, pies, and tobacco—all the gift of the New York Seventh. The men of these two regiments would become fast friends during their three months of service together defending Washington (the Eighth Massachusetts would stay in service almost four months, one month more than their enlistment required). In time, many of these men—such as the Seventh's Robert Gould Shaw of New York and Boston,

Union troops drill near the Rotunda of the Capitol Building, which was under construction in 1861.

Herman Melville's cousin Henry Gansevoort, and the Eighth Massachusetts's Henry Briggs and Henry Richardson—would become able commanders of Union regiments.

After a week at the Capitol building, the Eighth was sent to a position known as the Relay House, on a rail line seven miles south of Baltimore, which by now had been occupied by Union troops. The Allen Guards rejoined the regiment on May 16, after their detached duty in McHenry for more than three weeks. From the Eighth's "Camp Essex" in Howard County, Maryland, a soldier correspondent calling himself "W. A. F." sent a letter that day to the newspaper known as *The Bay State*.

> Yesterday, the 15th, we received our camp tents from Massachusetts, and at once set about putting up our "duck houses." Our camp is

situated in one of the most beautiful and picturesque spots in the state, or the world. It is on a highland, overlooking a large range of country, fine in the extreme. On our right is the small village of Elk Ridge. In front is a beautiful stream, which empties into the river, and finds its way into the beautiful, and ever to be remembered by us, Chesapeake.

This is indeed a rich country; but alas! the "institution" of slavery darkens and despoils this fair portion of "our common heritage." It only wants our New England farmers here to make it "the garden of Eden."

As I am writing, the spirit-stirring drum is heard; the glorious "old Sixth" Regiment, of Massachusetts is filing past our camp, into their quarters on the opposite hill, and with them come again our friends and former comrades, the Allen Guards, of Pittsfield, commanded by Capt. Briggs, a son of Ex. Gov. Briggs, of our state. It causes the warm blood to thrill, as we behold our friends and brothers of Pittsfield filing into our camp. Cheer upon cheer greets them, and a general "shake all round" is going on. They are a noble set of fellows. We parted from them at Annapolis, as they were ordered aboard the Constitution. . . .

War excitement swept through Berkshire that spring, and three more companies were raised—a second in Pittsfield, and one each centered in North Adams and Great Barrington. The incessant beating of drums and the cadence of marching and musket drills were heard in many places in Berkshire, outdoing the springtime sounds of bird song.

This martial rumble of a nation arming for civil war was the forewarning of an earthquake that would shudder open a chasm between America's past and its future. That chasm was the war, which would become ever wider, dividing the country that had been from what it was to be. The United States and Berkshire County would never be the same after that spring of 1861. Even the beloved Old Elm in Pittsfield's park would be lashed by another bolt of lightning this year, losing more of its few remaining branches, and seeming doomed at last.

Chapter Four

INTO THE ABYSS

April 21 was the centennial anniversary of the founding of Pittsfield, but with all the commotion over the firing on Fort Sumter, the occasion was hardly noticed.

The *Pittsfield Sun* displayed its patriotism by printing the words to the "Star-Spangled Banner," and the community got into the patriotic spirit as people wore cockades of red, white, and blue. Businesses bought large flags, which appeared flying on buildings all around the county, one of the largest suspended over Pittsfield's North Street with the emblazoned motto, "Constitution and Union." The Pittsfield Woollen Company, owned by leading citizens and with Robert Pomeroy as president, erected a flagstaff on its mill near the fairgrounds north of the village and proudly flew a new Stars and Stripes.

During the send-off for the Allen Guards, a touring minstrel company had caught the spirit and had sung the "Star-Spangled Banner" in front of a cheering crowd on North Street. Afterwards, there had been prayer meetings and speeches to comfort the families of those who had gone to a fate that no one could foretell. Immediately, women and girls gathered to organize informal groups to support the men, and to make sure the troops received clothing, delicacies, and remembrances from home. With Parthenia Fenn of Pittsfield

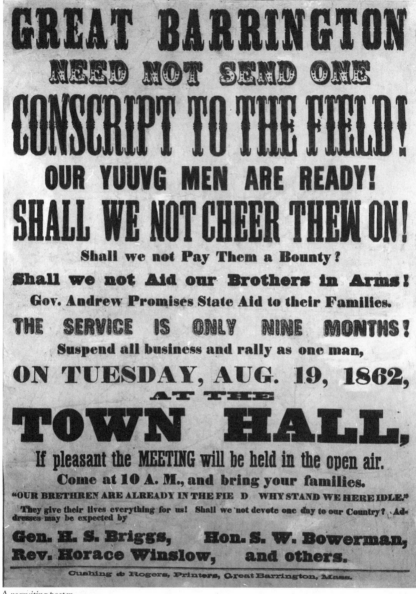

A recruiting poster.

as their guiding light—there was never to be a formal, elected organization—they began to knit socks and scarves, and to prepare packages to send the soldiers. In time, women and girls would be kept busy with a more foreboding task, scraping hundreds of yards of linen strips to soften them for "lint," which was needed as bandages.

Soon, another company of Berkshire militia was organized, as Scottish-born industrialist William Pollock, a resident of Pittsfield, donated a thousand dollars to equip the unit, which took the name "Pollock Guard." Pollock was one of the most successful men in Berkshire, having built a large textile factory in South Adams. The militia company he sponsored was quickly filled and, in preparation for joining a new Massachusetts regiment, began to drill with muskets that had been turned out by the musket works once owned by the Pomeroy family, a business that had prospered in Pittsfield decades earlier.

That spring a Pittsfield newspaper reported on the new company:

> The Pollock Guard—The drill of this company goes on at the Agricultural Grounds, where they are having comfortable quarters and a pleasant time generally. The proficiency in drill in the company is remarkable, although as yet they have only a few of the old Pomeroy muskets for arms. When properly uniformed and armed, as one hopes they will be, we have good reason to believe that our citizens will be surprised at the appearance of a corps so recently raw recruits.
>
> At an election of officers, on Saturday, Thomas W. Clapp was chosen Captain; Charles Wheeler, 1st lieutenant; Dwight Hubbard, 2nd lieutenant, and George E. Hagar, 3rd lieutenant.
>
> Capt. Clapp is a son of Col. Thaddeus Clapp of this town and a brother of the new marshal of Florida. Messrs. Wheeler and Hubbard are Dalton men and exactly qualified for the post. They attracted the attention of observers from the first moment of their enrollment. Lieut. Hagar is a Pittsfield man but has been for some time employed in Dalton. The whole roll of officers is an excellent one and we congratulate the company on its choice.

Not long after the Allen Guards left, Berkshire was visited by former president Franklin Pierce and the recently defeated vice presidential candidate of the compromise party, Edward Everett, a former Massachusetts representative to Congress. Both men were opposed to the coming war, and they had many sympathetic allies in Berkshire, though the fervor for military glory and the crusader's zeal to punish Southern "traitors" dominated the mood of the day.

Pierce spoke to the crowd from the balcony of the Eagle Hotel in Pittsfield, his speech optimistically anticipating the peaceful reunification of the country before it was too late. Bands played, flags were raised, schoolchildren sang, and Everett gave an oration of his own—a very long one, as was expected from a man recognized as one of the finest public speakers of the day. Speeches of an hour and a half in those times were not considered especially long.

Melville might well have attended the festivities, and his mind could have been on the welfare of his cousin from Albany, Henry Gansevoort, with the Seventh New York. In the news were reports of preparations underway at the

Brooklyn Navy Yard, where another New York cousin, Guert Gansevoort, a career naval officer, was rising in importance as the government called for experienced officers. Guert Gansevoort had heavy responsibilities readying warships and transports for sea and handling the myriad tasks of vessel maintenance, construction, and supply.

The tense drama of this moment in America's history served to ignite Melville's interest, stirring him out of the gloomy moods and rheumatism-wracked routine of his past few years at Arrowhead. He was following the war news whenever he came to town and could be found outside the newspaper office, reading the latest bulletins along with the rest of the citizenry. Although Melville was against the war, he was caught up by the momentum of the times. At home, he labored away on his verses with the intent of making some significant statement about the United States on the brink of disaster. He did not expect to be able to divert his country's course, for his verse was kept secret, but he did want to capture something of its essence, its power, in his poetry.

Like many of his countrymen, Melville was undergoing the "Conflict of Convictions" that made one pray for the armies to be called back, while being sensible to the mocking cynicism of those who said war was unavoidable. Melville's verses of this title spoke of the eternal battle between cosmic forces— Satan, the mighty fallen angel, against Raphael, the archangel over the spirits of men, the healing angel, who might this time be overwhelmed.

> On starry heights
>   A bugle wails the long recall;
> Derision stirs the deep abyss,
>   Heaven's ominous silence over all.
> Events, they make the dreamers quail;
> Satan's old age is strong and hale,
> A disciplined captain, gray in skill,
> And Raphael a white enthusiast still;

Of all Berkshire families, perhaps none was more patriotic or cultured than the Sedgwicks of Lenox. This close-knit household had suffered from the loss of Charles in 1856, but since then had welcomed in the German-born wife and two children of his son, William. Elizabeth Sedgwick had been sickly since the death of her husband, but her grandchildren were her joy, and she grew close to daughter-in-law Louisa.

The imposing Will Sedgwick, twenty-nine years old, had studied in a private Stockbridge school and then at home before going to Europe, mainly to Germany, to continue his education. There, he met and married the daughter of a university professor, and after seventeen months abroad, Sedgwick had returned with his wife and children to Massachusetts, and for a year had attended Harvard's law school. Then he moved with his family to St. Louis to open up a law practice, which by 1861 was thriving. When Fort Sumter was bombarded, Sedgwick—who had been active in a local pro-Union militia company in this sharply divided border state—prepared to enlist.

Before coming back east with his wife and children, Sedgwick wrote home to Lenox:

> St. Louis, Missouri, April 18, 1861.
> The excitement increases here daily. I do not expect any outbreak to occur here for the present, but at the same time a breaking out of hostilities here at almost any moment would scarcely surprise me. Men like Mr. G— and Mr. C—, who still profess to be thorough Union men, say that . . . to try and whip in the Cotton States is madly hopeless; and that when war breaks out . . . the Border States must infallibly defend their "Southern brethren." Mr. G— thinks, moreover, that one Southerner is equal to two Northerners, and that the recognition of the Southern Confederacy by the European powers is so palpably certain as to leave no possible room for a contrary expectation.

This peace-loving young man, brought up in an idealistic, Unitarian household, was surprised by his own willingness to go to war. But then, this was a hot-blooded time, when an abolitionist minister like Henry Ward Beecher could consecrate a musket on the altar of his Brooklyn church and call his flock to arms in a holy war against slavery.

Sedgwick wrote to Lenox:

> We are drilling here, under a pledge to obey any call made on us by the United States authorities, to resist attack or rebellion here. I am longing, as I never should have thought to do, to join the Massachusetts Volunteers. Perhaps I may not be able to "hold myself in," if matters come to the point of actual war. I'm very sure that I would rather die in battle 20 times, than have Washington captured, or than that the North should now yield her principles to accommodate those of the South. At the same time I cannot avoid feeling grief and distress in the knowledge that so many people I esteem, and could agree with on every question of morality, except in these pro- and anti-slavery issues, are quite as capable of being aroused to enthusiasm on the side of this monstrous wrong as any of us at the North on the other side. God send us a good issue!

Sedgwick soon was nominated to serve as a lieutenant in the new-formed Second Massachusetts, which, with the Twentieth Massachusetts, was one of the so-called "Harvard Regiments," because so many of its officers had attended that college. One of the Second regiment's captains was Robert Shaw of the Seventh New York Militia.

That spring Sedgwick returned to Lenox to recruit for the regiment and was successful at inspiring men to join the Second Massachusetts. The Sedgwick name was highly regarded by Berkshire workmen and farmers—the group that made up the core of a regiment's enlisted men—since, for generations, lawyers and judges in the Sedgwick family had vigorously defended the rights of the common man as well as those of blacks.

Sedgwick wrote to his German father-in-law, who dreaded the young man's taking part in the war and risking his life.

> Your views are perfectly normal; but the same reasons which should induce me to withdraw from the service of government would, if adopted by all those to whom they apply . . . break up our armies and leave us at the mercy of Southern dictators. In one prediction I have seen already that I was quite right,—in saying to my friends . . . that every one would be needed; even now we have barely enough to stand on the defensive. After having once taken the step, and feeling as I do, I know you could only despise me, should I forsake my country's cause because you regard it as almost hopeless. Were these views, which I believe are general, not only in Germany but in all of Europe, to prevail throughout the North . . . we should be lost indeed. . . . [I]f my country is to perish, my hope is to perish with her. I could not wish to survive the downfall of what I regard as the world's hope. Should America cease to be a first-class power, and be broken up in contemptible little fragments, what would you think would become of England? How long would it be before she would lie before the feet of France? What would become of the surplus population of Europe? What chance would be left to Germany and Italy in the struggle for eventual freedom after the failure of the grandest experiment of a free government that the world has known? Utter discouragement and dejection would fall upon the friends of freedom everywhere, should the North now yield to the entreaties of those who say, "Do not persist in this war, for you will be only shedding blood to no purpose."

In accordance with his principles, William Sedgwick was commissioned on May 25, 1861, as first lieutenant in the Second Massachusetts Volunteers, which joined the corps commanded by Major General Nathaniel P. Banks, a former Massachusetts governor. Sedgwick soon was brought onto the head-quarters staff as ordnance officer, and it was not long before he was transferred to the staff of Major General John Sedgwick, a distant cousin from Connecticut, who eventually had him promoted to the rank of major.

O n May 25, the same day as Will Sedgwick was commissioned, Edward Aylesworth Perry, a native of Richmond, Massachusetts, enlisted in the Pensacola Rifle Rangers, destined to become Company A in the Second Florida Infantry Regiment of the Army of the Confederate States of America.

A Pensacola attorney, the thirty-year-old Perry was a graduate of Richmond Academy and had attended Yale for a year. Quitting college, he had moved South in the early 1850s and had practiced law in Pensacola for the past few years. Perry soon would be elected captain of his company, which would depart for Richmond, Virginia, after basic training was completed. Richmond was a key city for the Confederacy, lying close to Washington and vulnerable to an expected Northern invasion that loyal Southerners were determined to repulse.

Confederate brigadier general Edward A. Perry, who eventually became governor of Florida, left his home in Richmond, Berkshire County, to practice law in the South before the war.

Although Lincoln had called out the militia in the spring of 1861, the Confederate States of America had made no overtly hostile move against the capital in that time. Instead, the secessionists were claiming the North was the aggressor, gathering an army to invade the South.

Claudius W. Sears of Peru, Massachusetts, was somewhat farther down the road to war than Perry and the Pensacola Rifle Rangers. Elected captain in the Confederate Guards company that on April 22 was mustered into the service of the State of Mississippi at Holly Springs, Sears was preparing to lead his men north as Company G in the Seventeenth Mississippi Regiment. He had been elected to replace the original captain of his company, former congressman Winfield Scott Featherstone, who had been elected colonel of the regiment. Mississippi regiments were being hurried to the front line developing near Manassas Junction in northern Virginia; the Florida troops soon would follow. In a few days, the Seventeenth would leave Corinth, Mississippi, and after a long train journey arrive at Manassas to join the main Confederate army that had been assembling there.

Music teacher Augustus Shannon of Lee, on the other hand, would re-main in Texas no longer now that it had seceded, and he booked passage aboard one of the last northbound ships before the Union placed a coastal blockade on the Southern states. Shannon returned home to Berkshire, and before long was ready to go to war himself. Sheffield's Frederick A. P. Barnard also refused to remain in the South, resigning, with profound regret, as chan-cellor of the University of Mississippi, a position he had held since 1856. Dr. Barnard made his way to Washington, D.C., where his younger brother, General John G. Barnard, was in charge of building up the fragile defenses of the capital.

General Barnard had served as superintendent of the Military Academy at West Point in 1855-56, and until 1861 had spent several years in charge of the harbor fortifications of New York. Soon, he would be the key staff officer who would select the site in northern Virginia for meeting the rebel army in the first major battle of the Civil War. It seemed almost everyone, soldier and civilian alike, was looking forward to that.

The movements of the Eighth Massachusetts militia regiment with its Allen Guards company were keenly followed in Berkshire by folk reading the regu-lar reports of Corporal Fred Smith, whose journal was published in the *Eagle*. Smith detailed the uncertain but mundane life of the soldier, the rainy sum-mer weather, his nights on guard duty or fitfully trying to sleep in a cramped, leaky tent. He told of rumors of fighting and of imminent armistice, of the arrival—or not—of longed-for mail and packages from home, and of regi-ment after regiment from many states coming to defend the capital.

After daily duties and letters from home, uppermost in the men's minds were food and comfort. Their fancy militia grays had become worn and were set aside in favor of the blue fatigues of the regular soldier. Corporal Smith wrote the *Eagle* to thank Pittsfield's Charles Whelden for bringing overcoats all the way to "the seat of war," as the Washington region was being termed.

> The Allen Guards feel under great obligation to Adjut. Whelden, for his untiring efforts in procuring overcoats. What we would have done without them through this severe rain storm which now prevails is more than I can say.

Whelden had been a Pittsfield militia captain and adjutant (a position similar to the role of secretary), but had graciously resigned to permit Henry Briggs to take his place and become commander of the new-formed Allen Guards.

All over Berkshire County, young men were looking for militia units to join, and Pittsfield, North Adams, and Great Barrington were the main hubs of enlistment as new companies were authorized by the state and funds were donated to equip and feed them.

In Barrington, some patriot climbed a giant pine tree near the main road opposite the house of Sylvester Hulbert in the west part of town and raised a Stars and Stripes on a flagstaff he attached to the top of the tree. This flag would remain there all summer, until windstorms tore it to pieces. Other worked-up young men around town were looking for alleged Southern sympathizers to chastise and threaten, but by now open opposition to the government's policy was less evident.

In every community, newspapers immediately sold out whenever important war news broke, and what papers could be had were read and reread by several people, often at the same time. The reports of the Baltimore mob attacking the Sixth Massachusetts on April 19 and killing several soldiers caused intense agitation in Great Barrington. At Sunday service in the Congregational Church a few days later, the Reverend Horace Winslow had trouble giving a sermon, as a witness later recalled, for the minister "was so overcome with emotion that he paused and declared he could go no farther with his subject." Winslow "therefore began an earnest exhortation on the situation, and in conclusion urged his hearers to make immediate preparation for war."

That Tuesday, handbills were posted around Barrington, with the heading, "Patriots Attention," and calling for a public meeting at the town hall in order to adopt measures to support the national government. On the afternoon of April 24, the people of Great Barrington and surrounding communities assembled at "The Convention," as the meeting was called, to pass resolutions that included raising and financing a militia company. Schools were dismissed early that day in order to give the entire community a chance to participate in the momentous events. Students at the Academy on upper Main Street eagerly scanned the latest postings on the Railroad Street bulletin board, and several of the boys, including Frederick N. Deland of Sheffield, were determined to join up in a year or so, as soon as they were seventeen. They hoped the war would last that long.

This "great war meeting," as it was known, was the first of its kind since the days of the Revolution. The convention's leaders included prominent local businessmen, such as Joseph Tucker, David Leavitt, Increase Sumner, and James Sedgwick, as well as representative clergy, who instilled their crusader's zeal into the excitement of the moment. The Reverend Winslow "offered a fervent prayer to the God of battles," and speeches and resolutions at the packed and overflowing Barrington town hall were accompanied by blasts from a cannon placed in front of the nearby blacksmith shop and "fired at frequent intervals," as a participant later recalled. There was also appropriately inspiring music by the brass band from South Egremont.

Committees were formed to authorize a local militia company, and resolutions "were unanimously adopted amid great applause." A roll was prepared for the signatures of volunteers, and several men in the audience signed up at once, the first being Barrington attorney Ralph O. Ives, a native of New York City. The volunteers were put in his charge, to be quartered in the Agricultural Hall at the fairgrounds, where they would begin to drill. The Great Barrington "Convention" adjourned until May 1, when the community gathered once more to learn that fifty volunteers had signed up, and almost five thousand dollars had been contributed to the cause.

That day a flagpole one hundred and fifteen feet in height was raised near the Berkshire House on Main Street, and the next day a Ladies' Soldiers' Aid society was formed, with Mrs. Clara Sumner, wife of Increase Sumner, elected president. More men signed up, and by May 13, the seventy or so recruits had elected their officers, with Ives chosen captain. (This election would not be recognized by Massachusetts as being official and had to be repeated in a couple of weeks, after the company was formally accepted as a state organization.)

The enlistees came from communities all around southern Berkshire, and in one case a traveling soap salesmen who had served in the Mexican War sold out his wares and joined the company. They included Barrington tailor John Donovan, a talented artist, who was a deaf mute. The volunteers numbered seventy-nine soon after May 15, when Governor Andrew received permission from Secretary of State William H. Seward to raise six regiments in response to President Lincoln's call for soldiers to serve a term of three years.

The longstanding Massachusetts Tenth Militia Regiment, headquartered in Springfield, was reorganized into the Tenth Massachusetts Volunteer Infantry. Three of the new regiment's eleven companies were to be raised in Berkshire: A, B, and D came respectively from Great Barrington, North Adams, and Pittsfield. The rest of the Tenth's companies were mainly made up of men from the western Massachusetts counties of Northampton, Hampden, Franklin, and Hampshire. Some Berkshire men enlisted in other Tenth Regiment companies, as was the case with nineteen-year-old George Gaylord Strickland, a bookkeeper from Stockbridge but living in Springfield, who joined Company F, called the Springfield City Guards.

With the eagerness of so many young men to join up—including Southern students, who were going home—some of the Berkshire schools had to close for the duration of the conflict. The venerable Lenox Academy, founded in 1803, was compelled to shut down without knowing when, or if, it would open again. The Maple Grove Academy in Great Barrington, which had been failing in the 1850s but by the spring of 1861 was showing signs of a revival, was also forced to close its doors for lack of pupils this year. It would never reopen.

Chapter Five

VOLUNTEERS

As in south county, rising martial enthusiasm also gripped central and northern Berkshire that spring, with the Pollock Guard being drilled at Pittsfield, and the new North Adams company replacing a recently disbanded state militia company. Before the coming of war, there had been a state militia unit in North Adams known as the Greylock Light Infantry, which in mid-April 1861 was reorganized into the Johnson Greys. The company was named in honor of prominent Adams businessman Sylvander Johnson, chairman of the town committee and a key promoter and supporter of the organization.

Enlistment notices appeared in the *Hoosac Valley News and Transcript*, the North Adams village newspaper, and a recruiting office was opened there. More than $5,600 was contributed to a committee formed to create the company and to guarantee that the volunteers' families would be supported. One of the lieutenants in the original Greylock company had been Elisha Smart, the ne'er-do-well former soldier who had come to Massachusetts from Vermont. Smart, who was in his mid-thirties, was well liked in northern Berkshire, for all that he was thought to have fled for some reason from his native state, and there was even some question about his true name. High-spirited and friendly, he was always forgiven for his practical jokes, which allegedly once included forging doctors' prescriptions to help his pals get liquor when its sale had been proscribed by a state law.

Upon the establishment of the Johnson Greys, Smart was one of the first to enlist, prepared to serve as a private or a noncommissioned officer, since for the most part only educated gentlemen were expected to fill the higher ranks, to which they were invariably elected by the men. In those first weeks, as the Johnson Greys drilled and became steadily more serious, Smart's training and war experience shone through, and the others began to depend on him for advice and instruction. The dignified leading citizens who backed the company had always looked down on the penniless Smart as an irresponsible, hard-drinking rogue who never attended church, and certainly could not imagine him as an officer. Yet he became ever more dedicated and worked hard with the men right from the start.

COURTESY BERKSHIRE ATHENAEUM

Dashing and fun-loving Captain Elisha Smart of the Johnson Greys company from Adams.

Then a distinguished friend, whom Smart respected, had a long talk with him about the responsibilities of an officer. Someone later said Smart was so moved that he pledged from that moment on to "abandon his bad habits, arise to the emergency in which he was so unexpectedly placed, and with the help of God be a true man." Elisha Smart performed soberly, indeed, and with unswerving dedication, drilling the men three times a day in the Phoenix fire department engine house. The raw recruits came to love and respect him as their natural leader and, when the time came, unanimously elected him captain of the company.

On April 30, Smart took formal command of his eighty-two men. One of his key assistants was twenty-seven-year-old Sergeant Napoleon "Boney" P. A. Blaise of North Adams; another good man, also from North Adams, was Private John Atwood, twenty-two. On May 4, the Greys moved into newly established Camp Johnson, at the site of the old Arnold and Ray brick factory, later the Arnold Iron Works. To celebrate the event, cannon were fired, and patriotic speeches and prayers given. A Ladies' Soldiers' Aid society was formed, with Mrs. Miles Sanford, wife of the venerable minister, elected president. Their son, Charles, was already terminating his plans to open a law practice and would instead enlist as soon as an officer's position in a new regiment became available. The ladies of northern Berkshire immediately went to work in Burlingame & Ray's hall, where they made flannel shirts for the company, while the firm of Chapin & Briggs made up handsome new uniforms of cadet gray.

More than once, volunteers had to be disciplined for secreting liquor in the camp, and Smart did not hesitate with punishment and keeping them to the regulations. The Johnson Greys had no weapons at first, but under his direction they drilled with dummy muskets, and by the time the company received its muskets and bayonets, the men showed themselves to be superior soldiers to the previous state militia company—thanks to the unswerving diligence of Captain Elisha Smart.

Late in May, Herman Melville took his four young children to watch Pittsfield's Pollock Guard parading at the county fairgrounds, which had been named "Camp Seward" in honor of Lincoln's secretary of state. The grounds were on the north side of town, just across Onota Brook.

In the middle of the drill, a fire alarm went up, for the Pittsfield Woollen Mills were ablaze. The militiamen, most of them volunteer firefighters, dashed off to help extinguish the fire, but soon there was little left to save. More than one hundred and fifty jobs were lost with the destruction of the mill, but vastly more manufacturing work was to appear in the near future, as war requisitions for textiles, iron, clothing, and flour began to pour into Berkshire.

One poignant loss in the burning of the woolen mill was the new Stars and Stripes that had first been proudly raised over the building when the Allen Guards set off for Washington. Now the flag was half-charred, but what was left of it was saved as a memento, and early in June when the Pollock Guard marched away to join the Tenth Massachusetts, the color bearer carried that damaged flag before them.

The volunteers with the Eighth Militia Regiment near Washington were troubled by bad food, not enemy bullets, as they began to count the days until their return home. While the men of the Eighth carried out their mundane duties, signs of war were all around, and there was unsettling news of the repulse of a Union force that had been commanded by Major General Benjamin Butler, their own leader, who had been promoted in rank. Butler had landed a body of troops on the Virginia coast and unsuccessfully engaged the enemy at a hamlet known as Big Bethel.

The *Roxbury City Gazette* published an Eighth Regiment letter signed by "G. H. W.," who observed how Maryland and northern Virginia seemed empty of civilian men of fighting age. He also met one of the wounded soldiers from Butler's defeat—a member of Duryea's Zouaves, as the Fifth New York Infantry was known. It was an outfit that counted volunteers from Berkshire in its ranks.

The greater part of young men in Alexandria have joined the Southern Army, and all would if they could escape our guards. The ladies remain, and in every way they can, display their hospitality to our soldiers. The day's ride and scenes were full of interest. To-day I met a wounded soldier of Duryea's Zouaves on his way home. He was a bright, intelligent, handsome fellow, formerly clerk in a drug store, in New York. He was struck with a Minnie ball in his thigh, at the battle of Great Bethel, and was just now only able to travel home. He was a hero though he knew it not. The ball is terribly destructive. In this instance it carried with it and left in the wound it made, the piece of pants it cut through, while itself whirled and passed through the leg. That piece of cloth remained irritating the wound, he told me, until yesterday, when he saw it and drew it out.

Looking at him and others I have seen, I thought truly it is the flower of our young men who have gone to the war.

The Great Barrington Company, as it was generally called, drilled daily at the Housatonic Agricultural Society fairgrounds in the village, where the men were quartered in the agricultural building. With Captain Ives at their head, they paraded several times a week up and down Main Street to show off their progress.

Although there was no subversive threat anywhere in sight in south county, strict military custom was maintained at the fairground, with sentries posted before the gates, challenging anyone they did not know. The soldiers even became presumptuous about who could pass on Main Street without being challenged. This became more pronounced after a rumor arose that a Vermont gunpowder firm was shipping wagonloads of black powder to the Confederacy via Berkshire County roads. One morning, before dawn, a dutiful sentry at the fairgrounds gate saw two covered wagons coming rapidly down Main Street, and in his most soldierly voice challenged the drivers with, "Who goes there?"

There was no answer, and the wagons kept on coming. The guard stepped out and repeated his demand several more times, but the wagons passed in front of the gate to the fairgrounds, with no acknowledgment of the sentry's challenge. So he raised his musket and fired through one of the wagons. The terrified drivers hauled their teams to a stop, wondering what had happened. Upon looking closer, the guard discovered that these were no surreptitious ammunition wagons bound for the rebels, but only a local butcher's meat carts trundling to the slaughterhouse to pick up their daily supply.

On May 19, the Great Barrington Company recruits donned their new gray uniforms, trimmed with black, to attend services at the Congregational

Church. They made an impressive sight in their handsome uniforms, ranged solemnly in the pews.

On the twenty-eighth, a large number of people from southern Berkshire gathered on Main Street as the troops officially and unanimously elected their officers. Captain Ives took command, and the Reverend C. A. L. Richards, rector of St. James Church, presented each man with a New Testament. Then Ives gave the order to fall in, and the company marched along Main Street, escorted by twenty-four leading citizens on horseback. The procession stopped before the residence of Mrs. Judith Bigelow, who formally presented the colors, which she had made. The presentation speech was by Barrington's Samuel B. Sumner, son of Increase and Clara Sumner, and a highly respected young attorney in the community. One who was there at the ceremony later described Company A's flag:

> It was a beautiful piece of work, six feet long by three wide, of silk of the finest texture. On this were gilt stars bordered with yellow fringe. The staff had a silver plate with appropriate inscription, surmounted with golden ball and eagle, with two frillon tassels hanging therefrom.

Captain Ives was moved to make a speech and, with tears running down his cheeks, knelt before Mrs. Bigelow to say, "Madame, I swear to carry this banner through the South and protect its honor on the battlefield." To his men, he said, "My boys, if ever I lead you astray, if ever I hesitate to stand in the front rank and take the . . . brunt of battle, may my right arm be paralyzed, and my tongue cleave to the roof of my mouth."

The next couple of days were busy with other such emotional ceremonies, dinners at a local inn, and marches down Main Street. There was a dance on May 27, to the music of the Curtis Band, and the next day the citizens of the towns presented a stand of colors while the local Bible Society gave each man a small New Testament. After dinner at the Collins House, the company marched to Mount Peter, where a liberty pole had been erected in 1775, and each man swore his fealty, kneeling to kiss the national flag. Another meal and more patriotic speeches followed.

The next afternoon, the company prepared to leave the fairgrounds and march a few miles eastward to the railroad line, where it would "take the cars"—go by train—to Springfield. The troops formed up at the corner of Main and Railroad streets and set off, escorted by brass bands and riders. As they marched up what was known as Three Mile Hill, they noticed South Carolina's "Palmetto flag," flying above a shack. Company member Mark Nickerson of Cornwall, Connecticut, later wrote:

The men took it as an insult, and the way they went to work to tear down that house was a caution. When they got through with it, it looked as though a cyclone had hit it. The boards and timbers were scattered in every direction.

Apparently, the shed's owner had wanted it torn down, and in fun put the palmetto flag on its roof as encouragement for the recruits to destroy it. One man, however, was seriously hurt by flying boards and beams.

A southern Berkshire farm boy who longed for the glory of donning a fighting man's uniform was sixteen-year-old Charles Gates of Lee, who begged his parents to let him join the Great Barrington Company. His elders refused, much to Charlie's disappointment, as the war news intensified and the drumbeat of enlistment was to be heard everywhere. The Gates family needed the boy on the farm, and more than that, they thought he was too young to go to war.

Charlie heard that the Barrington volunteers were preparing to leave for Springfield, and he again pleaded with his family, to no avail. There was work to do. One morning in the last week in May he was given a dinner basket and an ax and sent off to work in a woodlot, driving a few cows to a pasture along the way. A good-natured and cheerful lad with a sense of responsibility, Charlie got the cows into the pasture and closed the gate securely behind them. Then he hid the ax and emptied the basket of food and hid that, too, and hurried over the hills for Becket, nine miles away, where he knew the company would be that very day.

Charlie Gates caught up, enlisted, and became a soldier of the Tenth Massachusetts.

On June 2, an ailing Catharine Sedgwick, who had been sickly for a year and suffered from bouts of epilepsy, wrote from Stockbridge to her niece Kate Minot, the married sister of William Sedgwick. Miss Sedgwick hinted at her illness and expectation of death in the near future. Then she spoke of the Berkshire men who had gone to join the new-formed Second Massachusetts, along with her nephew Will.

The Second was in training at Brook Farm, near Boston, which for years had been a well-known resort and meeting place for Transcendentalists, freethinkers, and abolitionists of the Northeast. Miss Sedgwick ended the letter to her niece with:

> Perhaps you know that our warriors of the Valley went Friday to the Brook-farm camp. There were thirty-nine. Your Aunt Susan and half the village were at the station at 6 o'clock to take leave of them. Her blessing was the best munition of war they took with them.

Perhaps the leading patron of Brook Farm as a retreat was the fabulously wealthy Francis Shaw of New York and Boston. Shaw's son, Robert, a captain in the Second, was a frequent visitor to Berkshire County, for his sweetheart was Annie Kneeland Haggerty, daughter of one of the leading families of Lenox and New York. As the regiment was forming, Shaw wrote to his mother about the Berkshire recruits, describing them as "a company of fine-looking men from Lenox & vicinity. . . . Sedgwick, got most of them." Among those new recruits was Private Adam Miller, son of John Miller of Stockbridge, but born in Bavaria and considered by Lee as one of its own. The twenty-one-year-old Miller would become a sergeant in Company D by mid-June and a second lieutenant within a year. Another recruit was former seaman Orrin G. Smith of Great Barrington, a corporal in Company H, commanded by Captain Shaw.

When the Barrington Company entered Springfield, it was met by the local "Horse Guard" and the city's own two companies of the Tenth Massachusetts. On the way to to their quarters at Hampden Park, the Berkshire men paraded like heroes through the crowded streets. On June 4, they were photographed individually and given a picture of Confederate president Jefferson Davis, "that he might be recognized and shot on sight."

Spirits were high, and in some cases too high, as a man was drummed out of the company for drunkenness. Before the company was mustered in with the rest of the regiment, two others were accused of desertion, stripped of their uniforms, "heads shaved, arms pinioned, and they were escorted off the grounds of Hampden Park to the 'Rogue's March.'"

If some men were not up to the discipline of military life, John Donovan was, though he could not speak or hear. Private Donovan was faithfully with the regiment as it drilled and trained, preparing to move toward Boston and then to join the Union army assembling before Washington. He was also making detailed sketches of the regiment's encampment, and he proved to be a fine illustrator.

Early in June, Captain Henry Briggs of the Allen Guards accepted command of the new Tenth Massachusetts Regiment. Promoted to colonel, Briggs turned over command of the Allen Guards to Lieutenant Henry Richardson and returned to Massachusetts to assume his new tasks.

Captain Ralph Ives's sincerity apparently was convincing to fellow attorney Briggs, who personally endorsed Ives to Governor Andrew as a worthy captain of Company A. After the Tenth had been some time in camp at Springfield, however, others in the regiment were not so sure about either Ives or Company A. Sergeant Charles Brewster of Company C at first considered the Barrington troops the "worst Company in the Regiment."

Around this time, the Berkshire newspapers reported that two North Adams ministers had volunteered to serve as chaplains to Massachusetts troops: the Reverend B. F. DeCosta and the Reverend F. Russell Jones, both former rectors of St. John's Episcopal Church.

A sense of determination united the people of Berkshire County, as formal resolutions to support the national government were passed by the various communities. Committees were formed and funds appropriated to equip volunteers, as well as to sustain their families after the men were gone. At a meeting of the Sheffield townsfolk, the community heard the reading of a patriotic resolution passed by the town on June 18, 1776, early in the Revolutionary War. In Lee, a resolution calling for loyalty to the national government was worded in a way that would have been familiar to Northern towns anywhere. Without such resolutions, the militia companies might not have been legally raised and financed, and the state volunteer regiments composed of these companies would never have come to be:

> Resolved: That the inhabitants of Lee deem it important that the Government of the United States should have the hearty and earnest encouragement and active assistance of every loyal citizen in suppressing the treasonable Rebellion which aims at the overthrow of our laws and the Constitution of the land, and that as citizens of Lee, actuated by a love of our country and of universal liberty, we are ready to share in the common effort of sustaining the Government; and as a town, we assure those of our citizens who shall enter into the service of the Government as volunteer soldiers, that their families dependent upon them shall be well and honorably provided for, and sustained during their entire absence. . . .

The people of Lee were far-sighted enough not to presume their volunteers would serve only a short time. There is no mention of the controversial issue of fighting to liberate the slaves, but the subject is hinted at with the assertion that the community is "actuated by a love . . . of universal liberty." The resolution included borrowing $3,000 and establishing a committee to use the funds for raising a militia company called the Valley Guards. Governor Andrew did not have a place for the unit in his military establishment, however, so most of the volunteers joined Company A in Great Barrington.

As it was with the young men of most Berkshire towns, Lee volunteers were scattered throughout several regiments, some in units from other states. Later in 1861, twenty-six Lee men joined the Twenty-seventh Massachusetts; in 1862, fourteen went to the Thirty-first Massachusetts, and a sizable number joined the Thirty-seventh Massachusetts, making up most of Company B. Others enlisted in the Forty-ninth Massachusetts that same year, most of them included in two companies, F and H. Several went to the Second Massachusetts, which had Lee's William T. Fish as its sutler—the civilian merchant permitted to follow a regiment and sell the men wares that were not normal army issue. Men from Lee went to New York and became troopers with New York cavalry, while others joined Duryea's Zouaves.

Eventually, Lee men would serve in more than a dozen Union regiments.

From the outset of the war, some Berkshire folk were alert to preventing any situation that might benefit the Confederacy. Some Southern businesses still bought and sold goods in the North, including in western Massachusetts. This spring two men who were skilled paper manufacturers for a well-known company in Lee received an order for special watermarked paper from a New York City firm. That paper was to have the mark "C.S.A.," and when a Lee "patriot" learned about it and guessed it was for printing Confederate bank notes, he reported what he knew to the United States Treasury Department. Soon, government detectives appeared in Berkshire and confiscated the paper, stopping all further production.

Sylvanus Grant, a strapping twenty-four-year-old from Lenox, offered to enlist in the regiments then being formed, but he was turned down, told that the army was not using "colored" soldiers.

Many in the North, especially among the abolitionists, wanted to enlist blacks, but the national government was against it. Every effort was taken to keep the army in the field, and that required avoiding the controversial issue of fighting to liberate the slaves, for declaring this as a reason for war-making would have caused many would-be volunteers to turn away, perhaps even cause a mutiny among the soldiers. Many would have felt betrayed by their government if abolition had been declared a war aim after they had signed up.

The light-skinned Grant went back to his profession as a woodsman, skilled with an ax and expert at felling even the largest trees.

Chapter Six

THE LAST HAPPY FOURTH

With the outcome of Butler's campaign around Big Bethel on the Virginia coast still undecided, Catharine Sedgwick wrote to her niece Kate Minot, describing the beauty of the Berkshire countryside in "this most lovely month of June"; and yet,

> one can not long keep up to the symphonies of nature in war-time, and with all my earnest feeling and love for this divine month, I was even to-day crying out of the window and breaking the Sunday still-ness by an appeal for a newspaper H. had in his hand, we . . . having missed that daily food yesterday and being at the starvation point.

Mr. "H" assured them that reliable reports indicated "there would be no battle this campaign," Miss Sedgwick wrote, saying that "took the edge off our hunger." Many friends shared her insatiable appetite for war news—so much so that when an acquaintance was thrown by her mount and

> saw her horse's heels in the air, and coming down, as she thought, on her head, what one throb of anguish at parting life think you she had? "Oh, I shall never hear about the battle at Bethel!" It takes a Berkshire to generate such enthusiasm as that!

It turned out that the fight at Big Bethel earlier in June was no more than a skirmish and never developed into a major campaign. Both sides fought bravely, as General Butler's forces—including Massachusetts men—failed to capture the rebel position, although it cost eighteen Northern lives, including that of a former member of the Seventh New York: Major Theodore Winthrop, a thirty-two-year-old native of New Haven, and a direct descendant of John Winthrop, the first governor of Massachusetts.

Miss Sedgwick's friend, Mr. "H," had unreliable sources, however, for there would indeed be a battle this campaign, a disastrous one for the Union cause.

In the Twentieth Massachusetts Regiment was Harvard's Oliver Wendell Holmes, Jr., son of the famous poet and himself a well-known personality in Berkshire. Commissioned a second lieutenant, young Holmes had a crush on Mary Agnes Pomeroy, called Agnes, the daughter of a leading Pittsfield citizen, Robert Pomeroy.

During the regiment's recruitment, Holmes and fellow Harvard man Captain William Francis Bartlett of Haverhill came to Pittsfield to sign up enlistees. While in town, the dashing young officers attracted the attention of a group of girls who played at soldier, terming themselves the "Campbell Guards," after the gentleman who had given them a drum. There were half a dozen of them, mostly from a well-to-do neighborhood on East Street, not far from the Pomeroy mansion. The girls wore homemade uniforms of matching knee-length dresses with high necks and short sleeves, and decorated with broad stripes of red, white, and blue. They had white cambric caps with stiff visors and fitted with a cloth that draped down the back of the neck in imitation of "havelocks," headgear worn by British troops in India.

Carrie Cushing played the drum as they drilled with wooden guns and were led by her sister, Captain May Cushing, whose brother had officially presented her with a sword, presumably also wooden. At the end of the guns were wooden holes into which firecrackers could be fitted for effect.

One day, while the Campbell Guards were parading on the adjoining lots of the Plunkett and Cushing families, Lieutenant Holmes, in full uniform, made an appearance. Wendell, as he was called, cheerfully put them through some marching and musket drills that the girls would remember fondly for the rest of their lives. Holmes was a success with the Campbell Guards, but he was losing ground to Captain Bartlett, who also had been smitten with Agnes Pomeroy, and the feeling appeared to be mutual.

July 4, 1861, was unsurpassed in patriotic outpourings of sentiments and excitement in Berkshire, with bold speeches and fireworks all over the county. Pittsfield held a parade and invited marching companies, bands, firemen, and social organizations from the surrounding towns. Cannon salutes and bell-ringing went on into the evening, the celebration fueled by an inspired populace convinced it was waging a crusade against unholy Southern treason.

Those residents who were against civil war spoke up even less frequently now that so many young men were under arms. To most people, especially the eager volunteers, war was a lark, an adventure, and few thought Southerners would be courageous enough to stand and fight. Some soldiers worried that the fighting would be over before they ever got to the front.

The defenses of Washington included signal camps—such as this one overlooking the Potomac River at Georgetown Heights—which communicated with one another by flags; the Capitol dome rises in the distance, and the Washington Monument is in the middle foreground.

One of the organizations leading the Fourth of July procession was the new militia company known as the Independent Zouaves, captained by Charles Whelden, the pharmacist. Whelden's company drilled in the Pittsfield streets several evenings a week, and he had aspirations of his own to lead troops to war. For the moment, Whelden was doing much to support and supply the Allen Guards near Washington and the Pollock Guard in the Tenth Massachusetts. So-called zouave companies such as his existed all over the country, North and South, inspired by several popular marching companies that had toured the United States in the years before the war. Wearing wide pantaloons that were usually red, and with turbans or a tasseled fez, zouave companies imitated colonial troops from North Africa who had won fame fighting for France earlier in the century. The Independent Zouaves of Berkshire County usually wore uniforms "of the regular Zouave pattern, crimson cap with blue tassel, dark blue jacket over a white blouse, light blue pants, [and] russet gaiters."

At the start of the Civil War, many zouave-styled volunteer regiments took to the field in full-dress uniforms, but the hardships and realities of war soon forced most of them to don the dark blue of the Union or the gray or butternut of the Confederacy. On this July Fourth in Pittsfield, however, Berkshire zouaves marched in all their gaudy glory, joined by a company of boys called "Sarsfield Zouaves." The unit had been named in honor of M. Sarsfield, a gentleman who had presented each of them with "a neat Zouave uniform." The boys marched in parade behind their new flag, which had been presented by G. Abraham, another patriotic citizen. They followed a band playing martial music and were one of the day's highlights as the parade passed through the tree-lined streets.

Not to be outdone, the most prominent girls' company of patriots was a mounted organization calling itself the "DiVernon Phalanx," also an attractive part of the Fourth of July parade. Missing from the annual Independence Day celebration was Hodge's Cornet Band of North Adams, an outstanding group in a day when every town, fire department, and community organization fielded a brass band of its own. The North Adams band had enlisted en masse in the Tenth Massachusetts and were now in camp at Springfield. Another missing local figure was Herman Melville, who had gone to New York City, in part to visit his cousin Guert Gansevoort at the Brooklyn Navy Yard, and in part to get away from Lizzie's awful bouts of hay fever at this time of year.

For those who were in Berkshire County in this last Independence Day before the descent into the unimaginable misery and heartache of civil war, the hot and raucous celebration was everything anyone could want. It was complete with the emotion of having loved ones in uniform, willingly serving the country in its most desperate crisis.

The comet Melville had seen last year from the southern seas had just appeared in the night sky across the eastern United States. Though, superstitiously, a comet was a portent of war, few in the country could believe that some monumental catastrophe was about to break upon them. In such a confident, prosperous time, with the best of their young men looking so grand in uniform, both North and South were spoiling for a fight after so many tense years of hostility.

This intensely emotional, heady, and bittersweet moment at the Fourth of July, 1861, would not soon come again to Berkshire County. The thrill of it would not even last the month.

Among those Berkshire men living elsewhere and joining other regiments was schoolteacher George S. Massey, formerly of Richmond. Twenty-eight at the time of his enlistment, Massey joined Company C of the First California Regiment, a unit raised mainly in Philadelphia and New York and initially intended to be filled with men who had connections to California or Oregon.

Without enough volunteers in the East who met that criterion, the regiment enlisted anyone willing to sign up for three years. Like many other "Californians," as he and his comrades were termed, Massey enjoyed the first thrill of soldiering as the regiment went into action that summer after briefly crossing the Potomac River, the recognized border between the hostile armies. On July 5, Massey wrote to the *Eagle* from Martinsburg, in northern Virginia, proudly reporting that the letter was written on a captured "drum the secessionists left behind, which was marked 'Wise's Artillery.' " He described the action:

> We passed a place called Falling Waters, so called from the fact that the stream runs across the road and falls down into a ravine—it is a very pretty spot. Well, we had got about two miles from that place, moving along very briskly, as it had rained the day before and the air was very cool and bracing. The morning was beautiful, but not a cloud was to be seen, the men moved forward joking, laughing and chatting. There were very few people along the road or in the houses, for . . . they all fled over into Maryland. . . . [W]e had got about two miles from Falling Waters when [bang] went one of our artillery pieces, and . . . bang, bang went two more, then came a volley of musketry, then came the order to drop our knapsacks, food bags and canteens. They were off in a moment. I am sorry I threw my water canteen off, for water is one thing [a soldier] needs most in a fight. We pitched ahead double quick, the firing becoming more brisk [step] by step. We filed to the left into the fields, the artillery rushed ahead of us and stopped about 20 yards from the woods where the rascals were. They opened their fire at this side while about a half of a mile on the right of the road was another one of our batteries firing into them. Our regiment did not fire as musketry would not have done much good, while they were in the woods. Every now and then they pointed at us and the shot whistled over our heads in beautiful style. I felt . . . queer at first, but I soon got eager and I wanted badly to get them out where we could get a shot at them. We had not waited long before they ran and we after them. We chased them two miles but they had the advance and we could not keep up with them. . . . During the chase we had to cross a swamp which was up to our knees, and a pretty looking sight we were when we gave up the chase. It is very exciting and one scarcely thinks of, or feels fatigue. We stopped to rest in a clover field and the men went out foraging. We lived high that day and ever since—chickens, bacon, ham, honey, molasses, milk, gingerbread, flour, bread, and every kind of eatables were seized on and eaten up double quick, and if any was left we took it with us. . . . I forgot to say that as we passed into the field I saw one fellow lying dead, while another had his head wounded and another was bleeding in the breast. I had not time to let the sight worry me, though.

Massey not only saw his first casualties on this foray, but he also witnessed the "wanton destruction of property" caused by a retreating force, in this case the Confederates his regiment was skirmishing with. When relieved from guard duty, he went to a nearby railroad yard to witness a sight that disgusted him.

> [I]f you want to see some of the outrages perpetrated by the Southern chivalry, just come and look at the locomotives destroyed by them. Over fifty locomotives of nearly a million dollars value, are burnt till the iron has twisted and broken itself into a hundred shapes. They stand on the track and are not worth buying for old iron. [On] the bridge just below the town . . . a locomotive lies with the front hanging down nearly touching the pike road underneath—it may fall at any moment. At the other end of the bridge is a creek and two locomotives . . . dangling down, one in the creek and the other resting on it, both of them burnt and broken into old iron. Further down are six or seven locomotives still burning and the ashes of the cars burnt are still hot. Above the town are 2 or 300 coal, passenger and freight cars. Every locomotive and car on the road is burnt, I believe.
>
> They will get paid in their own coin, I'll venture.

Upon hearing a report that a civilian living nearby was secretly a "secessionist" and had helped destroy the locomotives, Massey, his lieutenant, and another private went to the suspect's home and arrested him. This made Massey feel as if he had done his duty, as if the suspect were a common vandal.

In mid-July, Berkshire heard the happy news that the Allen Guards had received orders to set out for home in ten days. Preparations soon were under way to give the militiamen a rousing reception after their service of more than three months. The Guards had not come under fire, but their prompt arrival in Washington, garrisoning forts and establishing encampments in the region in a time of great peril, had paved the way for the safe arrival of more than 60,000 Union men in scores of new regiments, most of them similarly enlisted for only one hundred days.

The Guards had faithfully done their duty, and usually extremely tedious duty at that, even if often under threat of danger. They had garrisoned Washington, had taken control of the famous Old Ironsides, and had defended historic Fort McHenry. These Berkshire boys had been greeted as heroes in some of the nation's greatest cities and had met hundreds of men from distant states, which before had only been names in books. They had even seen examples of marvelous new steam-powered inventions—engines and bake ovens and water pumps. One of Corporal Fred Smith's most memorable experiences was an off-duty Saturday spent visiting a Baltimore home for wayward boys, which was run by a Massachusetts man. On that beautiful summer afternoon, Smith had especially enjoyed watching the boys fly more than twenty kites from the lawns of the home. Smith's journal, published in the *Eagle*, recounted the Guards' service, and ended with,

> As a company we have endeavored to do our duty at all times. . . . If we have not been called into an engagement, it was not our fault. We went with the expectation of meeting the enemy, and if we did not it is their fault.

Among the women and girls laboring three or more times a week to do what was needed to prepare packages for the new companies taking the field was pretty Lilla Reeve, a seventeen-year-old student at Pittsfield's Maplewood Young Ladies' Institute. Miss Reeve was the daughter of Major Isaac V. D. Reeve, a regular army officer serving in Texas, who had been taken captive by the rebels. From the start, she threw herself passionately into working for the sake of the volunteers. Understandably distraught at her father's imprisonment, and worked up emotionally, she worried her teachers at Maplewood, who thought her health was suffering.

Very well liked by friends and teachers, Miss Reeve was persuaded one day to join an outing to Waconah Falls, a lovely spot for picnics about ten miles from Pittsfield. As soon as they arrived there, some of the excited youngsters wanted a look at the falls, and a few, including Miss Reeve, ventured too far out on the slippery rocks. The girl lost her footing and fell, striking her head, and tumbled into the whirlpool below. She could not be rescued in time, and she drowned.

Upon the sad news reaching him, Major Reeve was released by the Confederates to travel to Berkshire for the mourning. He was officially exchanged late in 1862, returned to active duty, and was promoted to lieutenant colonel of the Thirteenth U.S. Infantry.

On July 8, a few days after receiving its battle flag from the ladies of Boston, the Second Massachusetts, with its large contingent of Berkshire men, left for western Maryland, eventually to occupy Harpers Ferry, Virginia.

Fifty miles northwest of Washington, Harpers Ferry was a strategic railroad junction at the confluence of the Potomac and Shenandoah rivers. Since it was there that John Brown had begun his failed slave insurrection in 1859, some soldiers and officers of the Second—especially those strong for abolition—felt they would be treading on hallowed ground, and were excited at the prospect.

Militarily, the town was the doorway to the Shenandoah Valley, a rich agricultural region of Virginia and an excellent point of departure for an invasion toward Richmond.

On July 18, the Tenth regiment prepared to leave its camp at Springfield and go into training for some weeks at Camp Adams in Medford, just outside Boston.

Before departing, the regiment received its silken battle flag—one of its "colors"—as a gift from the ladies of Springfield. Attending the ceremony were fifty persons who had hurriedly arrived by excursion train from Pittsfield. Most were "of the female persuasion," reported the *Eagle*, which added that more Berkshire friends and family would have been on hand for the poignant farewell, but the notice of departure had been unexpected, allowing little time to organize a larger group for the occasion.

In the next few days, the Tenth would receive yet another unexpected, and even more urgent, call to depart, this time for the battle front, where the cause of the Union would be in great distress.

The following poem, excerpted from unsigned verses published around this time in the *Valley Gleaner*, a western Massachusetts newspaper, captures the heartache of both the departing soldier and the woman who stayed at home. It was likely written by a genteel woman, for lady contributors to publications were expected to remain anonymous.

THE SOLDIER'S TEAR
Upon the hill he turned
To take a last fond look,
Of the valley and village church
And the cottage by the brook;
He listens to the sounds,
So familiar to his ear,
And the soldier leant upon his sword
And brushed away a tear.
Beside that cottage porch
A girl was on her knees,
She held aloft a snowy scarf,
Which fluttered in the breeze;
She breathed a prayer for him,
A prayer he could not hear,
But he paused to bless her, as she knelt,
And wiped away a tear. . . .

On the day the Tenth regiment left camp in Springfield, the *Eagle* reprinted comments of praise for Colonel Henry Briggs from a *Boston Post* soldier correspondent—likely one of the Eighth Massachusetts Militia Regiment. The *Eagle* introduced the comments with:

While Pittsfield has reason to be proud of all the officers and most of the men which she has sent to the service of the country in this as in former wars, there are few men in the present war who do her more honor than the Colonel of the Tenth regiment, and we are glad to see by the following extract from an eastern correspondent of the Boston *Post* that his merits are well understood in that part of the state.

The *Eagle* then quoted the *Post* writer regarding Briggs:

He deserved his promotion, and, if called to active duty in the field, will vindicate the propriety of his appointment. Few men in our State, not educated for the army, have been more thorough students in military science, and no man surpasses him in zeal for the service, in knowledge of what it demands, and in honest determination to do his whole duty. He is a prudent man, and a brave man. He will never forget the men under his command, and while he relaxes nothing in discipline, will pretermit no effort to secure their health and comfort. I wish all the officers from Massachusetts were equal to Henry S. Briggs.

Such confidence in the man who would lead them into battle was absolutely essential to the success of a fighting regiment. Unlike Colonel Briggs, as suggested by the correspondent's remarks, every officer did not evoke that confidence from his subordinates. A demanding taskmaster, Briggs was compelled to enforce strict discipline as soon as the Tenth reached Medford, for that first night a hundred men left the camp without leave and went into Boston.

"But they were brought back again by picket guards, and made to dig wells and perform double guard duty for their amusement," a Berkshire newspaper reporter wrote.

Medford was "a beautiful village . . . four miles from Boston, on the Charlestown side" of the Mystic River, said the reporter. There, instructors from the regular army would train the Tenth's commissioned and noncomissioned officers in basic drills that in turn would be taught to the enlisted men. Now the troops experienced something of campaign life, having to sleep in tents, without a mattress of straw but, instead, on thin rubberized tents spread over the hard ground. The companies were required to cook for themselves, being issued raw rations and expected to make the best of it.

Each volunteer regiment in the armies of North and South was organized along the same lines, with a colonel in command, next a lieutenant colonel, and then a major. There were various other officers, including an adjutant, who served as assistant to the colonel, and the quartermaster, responsible for the regiment's supplies and equipment.

Ideally, a regiment was made up of approximately a thousand men, divided into ten or more companies, each given a letter designation, beginning with "A" and continuing in "K," but skipping the letter "J." Each company, with men usually raised from the same town or region, was commanded by a captain, who was aided by first and second lieutenants. Along with the field officers, these "line officers" had to be officially commissioned by the governor to hold their ranks. The enlisted men of each company were in the immediate charge of noncommissioned officers, which included half a dozen sergeants aided by as many corporals.

On July 21, while the Tenth trained, expecting to remain at Medford for some weeks more, calamity struck the Union cause as the two green armies collided at Manassas Junction in northern Virginia, and the Federal troops withdrew in confusion from the field.

The Union soldiers had fought well enough, but poor organization, inexperience, and false rumors of close enemy pursuit turned the crowded roads into a panic-stricken mob scene. Battle-weary soldiers trying to get to the rear found the roads and bridges clogged by hundreds of fleeing civilians, who had gone out to watch the engagement as if it were picnic entertainment. Terror gripped the city of Washington, which suddenly filled up with wounded, dying, and shell-shocked, demoralized troops. Many in the North feared the secessionists were too strong to be defeated in battle. Others knew, however, that this was just the beginning of a long and terrible war.

The Union army, under the command of Brigadier General Irvin McDowell, had been demoralized by Southerners led by his West Point military academy classmate, Brigadier General P. G. T. Beauregard. The site of the battle had been chosen by McDowell and Lincoln with the advice of the army's chief engineer, General Barnard of Sheffield. At sixty-one years of age and although almost deaf, Barnard was the leading military engineer in the Union cause. Eleven years earlier, he had led a scientific mission to search, unsuccessfully, for a railroad or canal route across Central America. As the former superintendent of West Point in 1855-56, and an instructor in military engineering, Barnard was perhaps the most qualified of the day at his profession. Only an obscure Confederate general named Robert E. Lee of Virginia had comparable military engineering experience. After serving as superintendent of West Point in the years 1852-55, Lee had been succeeded by Barnard, and like him had been honored previously for gallantry in the Mexican War. At present a military advisor to the Confederate government, Lee had spent most of his career designing and building coastal fortifications

In the past few months, Barnard had analyzed the prospects of an advance against Richmond, and the plan he helped devise had made McDowell's first objective the strategic railroad junction at Manassas, near a stream called Bull Run. McDowell had moved against the Confederate left wing, but his advance troops had been driven back by unexpectedly fierce resistance and resolute counterattacks at Blackburn's Ford, a key crossing point. This surprise repulse of the Union advance had forced McDowell to alter his plans and delayed the development of his overall strategy, giving Southern reinforcements time to arrive, counterattack, and emerge victorious.

At the forefront of the stout Confederate resistance at Blackburn's Ford had been the Seventeenth Mississippi, with Peru, Massachusetts, native and West Point graduate Captain Claudius W. Sears courageously leading his company into action.

General John G. Barnard.

COURTESY BERKSHIRE EAGLE

Chapter Seven

HUMILIATION

All Berkshire was jarred by the defeat at Bull Run and deeply shocked to hear of almost three thousand Northern men dead, wounded, or missing. The South lost two thirds that number. Neither side had expected such slaughter. Both had thought the other would run, and in the end too many Union troops had done just that, making the North ashamed and smarting for revenge.

One man recalled that when news of the defeat reached Great Barrington, "the greatest excitement prevailed" in the village.

> Unless a person was a regular subscriber or a news dealer, it was almost impossible to buy a paper for love or money. Those who had been clamorous for war were somewhat fearful, while a few professed to believe the Federal cause was lost.

Herman Melville's poem "The March into Virginia" described the naive elation of going off to war in beautiful countryside for the three days of campaigning leading up to that bloody engagement, where volleys of muskets flashed across the field and killed young men by the hundreds: Melville wrote, "All wars are boyish, and are fought by boys" who were blithely unaware of what awaited them, thinking only of glory, not at all about "battle's unknown mysteries."

Melville alluded to the picnicking civilians who foolishly came out from Washington for the Battle of Bull Run, as gleeful and ignorant as the young soldiers, many of whom fell out of the march to pick berries.

> The banners play, the bugles call,
> The air is blue and prodigal.
>   No berrying party, pleasure wooed,
> No picnic party in the May,
> Ever went less loath than they
>   Into that leafy neighborhood.
>   * * *
> But some who this blithe mood present,
>   As on some lightsome files they fare,
> Shall die experienced ere three days are spent—
>   Perish, enlightened by the vollied glare. . . .

With the defeat at Bull Run, the Tenth Massachusetts was immediately ordered to the front, and on the morning of July 25 struck its tents and prepared to entrain for Boston and then take steamships to Washington. Before boarding the train, the men formed up in a hollow square and were addressed by former governor George Briggs, who gave them and his colonel son a warm send-off. By midafternoon, the regiment was disembarking from the train at Boston and boarding the steamers *Ben De Ford* and *Spaulding*.

After the Tenth left, Camp Adams was renamed Camp McClellan, in honor of the new commander of the Union army, General George B. McClellan.

A few regiments defending Washington, such as Massey's Californians, which had not taken part in the July defeat, stood ready for an enemy attack. Most, however, were wondering whether the meddling politicians would allow McClellan to do his best or would treat him as badly as they had General McDowell. The unfortunate McDowell shouldered far too much of the blame for the July defeat, for his strategy had been sound. His troops, however, had been too inexperienced to carry out the required maneuvers. Most had been militia, enlisted for only three months and ready to go home, which was why the Federal government had demanded McDowell go on the offensive too soon.

The Union army had not been ready, but if McDowell had waited much longer, so many troops would have been mustered out that he would have had no army at all. Still, Lincoln dismissed McDowell as commander-in-chief, blaming him for the defeat, although the general remained an important field commander in the Union army. The president retained General Barnard, who was recognized for his unmatched ability at fortification design and engineering.

Late on the afternoon of July 27, the Tenth Massachusetts landed at unhappy Washington, which was mobbed with unattached soldiers, its littered streets and alleys filled with despairing civilians and disgruntled, hungry troops. The city and the surrounding district swarmed with thousands of soldiers; wounded and dead had been brought into Washington by the wagonload, and groups of surly men from broken regiments were everywhere, some sleeping in doorways, most depending on charity and kindness for food, few knowing where to go. Much of the capital had lapsed into a turmoil of disorder, drunkenness, and bad morale.

Exemplary in this gloomy time were the harried, exhausted civilian and military doctors and nurses who staffed the unprepared hospitals and makeshift infirmaries. Working day and night, without adequate medical supplies or beds, they saved life and limb many times, but all too often lost one or the other. Hundreds of suffering soldiers found themselves at Washington's Columbia Hospital, if they were lucky enough to be brought there from the battlefield or from a sickbed in a regimental campsite. At Columbia, they might meet volunteer nurse Caroline A. Burghardt of Great Barrington, who took a position at the hospital early in the war. Until now few, if any, men from Berkshire had come through there.

The Tenth Massachusetts parades at Camp Brightwood near Washington; pictured seated near the wagon at right is the artist, John Donovan, who was deaf and dumb.

Several days after the Tenth's arrival at Washington, resplendent in their gray uniforms, they were marching past the Capitol dome on the way to an encampment at Kalorama Heights, two and a half miles northwest. Within a week, the regiment was issued Union blues and was hard at work digging trenches and building fortifications to protect the frightened capital. Soon, the Tenth was moved to a new encampment, named Camp Brightwood, but their construction labors continued.

Colonel Briggs worked with pick and shovel alongside his men, digging trenches, building earthworks and rifle pits, and cutting down trees. This was the regiment's duty for half the day in the heat of the Washington summer; the other half was taken up drilling and practicing back at camp with their new English Enfield rifles, Briggs overseeing everything. Often, when the troops were drilling, artist John Donovan was permitted to sit on his folding campaign stool and draw pictures, creating vivid illustrations of the regiment at Brightwood.

The Tenth received many compliments and was soon considered one of the best-drilled regiments in the army. Before long, the men were happy to get new government-issue caps and be rid of the "hideous mud-colored felt hats" they had brought with them from Massachusetts. One unusual situation was either not noticed by the higher-ups, or was allowed to go on in the fashion of earlier armies, and that was the arrival of the wife of Captain Ives, who moved in with him as the weather began to get colder.

The Confederacy did not have the inclination or the resources to press its advantage and move against Washington after the Battle of Bull Run. Time was on the side of the secessionists, and all they need do was stand on the defensive, show their strength, and eventually the Confederate States of America would be officially recognized by the rest of the world.

At the end of July, concerned that enough men might not enlist—and well aware of the need to defeat the Confederate army in the field—Congress passed the "Crittenden Resolution," which stated flatly that the war was being fought "to defend and maintain the supremacy of the Constitution, and to preserve the dignity, equality, and rights of the several States unimpaired." The abolitionists wished their cause had been uppermost in the hearts of Congress and Unionists, but common sense told them that while hundreds of thousands of patriotic Northerners would go to war to save the Union, far fewer would willingly lay down their lives for the sake of abolishing Negro slavery.

In this time, a strong current of disgruntlement with the war was present in the North and in Berkshire County, too, as evidenced by a comment in the *Hoosac Valley News and Transcript* that "Secessionists have quieted down since the Home Guard was formed." The mustering of militia companies, "home guards," which sometimes drilled and at other times were only a list of names on paper, made it clear that anyone speaking out against the war might one day be confronted by resentful, armed neighbors. Worries about opposition to the war were strong enough that a number of South Adams men collected funds to purchase a hundred muskets from a Springfield manufacturer and quietly distributed them among loyal citizens in case an insurrection broke out.

In Berkshire, fear that the Union cause might be doomed because of the defeat at Bull Run mingled with elation at the expected return of the Allen Guards.

Wearing their original dress uniforms, patched and cleaned, the Eighth Massachusetts Militia regiment left Baltimore at dawn on July 30 and arrived in Philadelphia that afternoon, where they "found ample refreshment provided . . . by the patriotic citizens of the city," wrote Corporal Fred Smith.

That evening, after a train journey across New Jersey, the Eighth disembarked onto a station platform, expecting to take the ferry over to New York City. For some reason, known only to the top officers, the men were left on the platform that night, and no one thought to permit them to unsling their knapsacks, so they were obliged to sleep as best they could on the floor, "strapped up in all our equipments," said Smith. "We got but little rest, but being tired, of course slept soundly."

The next morning, the Eighth crossed by ferry to New York City and marched to a park, where they were able to wash up and were given liberty to walk around for a few hours. At noon, the regiment was paraded up Broadway, hailed by the crowds, and heartily honored—especially by its former comrades-in-arms, the New York Seventh Regiment, which had returned home weeks earlier. Many of the New Yorkers already had been commissioned officers in various regiments—such as Robert Shaw in the Second Massachusetts, and Herman Melville's cousin Henry Gansevoort, now a lieutenant in a regular army artillery battery.

For all the excitement they found in New York, reported Smith, the parade through steaming New York was wearying to the Allen Guards in their heavy, stifling uniforms.

> The day was hot, and the march to the Fifth Avenue Hotel, where we halted, was very tedious, but we were amply repaid for all our toil by the grand reception which we received here from the 7th regiment.

Afterwards, the Eighth marched to the dock for the steamboat *Bay State*, which would take them on a nightlong journey to Fall River, Massachusetts, where they would board a train to Boston. Glorious receptions were given in Fall River and Boston, where the militiamen were celebrated as the heroes who had saved the nation's capital. In Boston, after a meal and a regimental drill demonstration, the Eighth listened patiently to a farewell speech by a Massachusetts official before being officially mustered out. The companies then went their separate ways, the Allen Guards taking an express train to Springfield, where they were again feasted and heard more speeches.

For all the glory of it, the men were exhausted.

At one o'clock on Friday, August 2, bells were rung and cannon fired all over Berkshire to announce that the company was aboard a train from Springfield, and that the Pittsfield escort should assemble and march to Depot Square for the parade. On this very hot summer's day, Pittsfield's streets were full of cheering people as the train chugged into the station at 3 p.m. The Guards disembarked, to be swarmed by loved ones who rushed joyfully toward them. When order was restored, the parade began.

First came a column of county dignitaries, then the sixty Independent Zouaves led by Captain Whelden, all smartly uniformed in white shirts and black pants—the weather was too hot for their jackets, although the unfortunate Allen Guards were in full dress uniform. Whelden's company was followed by a young cadet company and then the youthful zouave group; next came the engineers and assistants of the fire departments, then Housatonic Engine Company No. 1, the Greylock Hook and Ladder Company, the Taconic Hose Company, and a procession of citizens riding in carriages. The column went down South Street, turned left onto East Housatonic Street and then Pomeroy Avenue, and up East Street to the park.

It was the "most attractive [parade], although not the longest, ever seen in town," said the *Eagle* reporter.

> Of course, the main feature of the procession was the sunembrowned and way-worn soldiers, with their gray uniforms, their arms, huge knapsacks and other well-worn accouterments, marching to a step that showed more of the true soldier than has been seen in these streets since the War of 1812.

The parade units and crowd assembled at the park with the Old Elm and a speaker's platform sporting red, white, and blue bunting and a Stars and Stripes. A banner was suspended from tree to tree with the words, "WELCOME HOME, ALLEN GUARD." The Mendelssohn Glee Club sang patriotic songs, and more speeches were made, the keynote speaker being Thomas Allen himself. The ceremony was presided over by George Briggs, whose son, the Allen Guards' first commander, was conspicuously absent, serving with the Tenth Regiment near Washington. After the speeches, the three sisters of Captain Henry Richardson, who now was in command of the Guards, presented a banner emblazoned with the Latin phrase that translated as "I Triumph in Life as in Death." It was accepted on behalf of the company by Captain Richardson.

Observing these welcome-home festivities was Charles Moulton, a young reporter for the *Springfield Republican*. A Great Barrington man, Moulton wrote about the scene in a letter to the *Berkshire Courier*, based in that village.

Dear Courier: Yesterday was the occasion of an enthusiastic excitement and a hearty welcome—a day of scenes appropriated to such a
cause as was never before experienced in this citified town of Pittsfield.

With a true reporter's objectivity, the eighteen-year-old Moulton was one
step removed from the excitement of the moment and revealed sympathy for
the soldiers who were enduring the heat; he said they "stood it out bravely," but

ought not to have been put to such a tedious march as they were—
for, estimating the heavy weight of their guns and knapsacks, besides
their blankets, overcoats, and thick uniform, their conditional feelings must have been anything rather than comfortable and, as it was,
I believe there were one or two cases of either sunstroke or exhaustion among them.

Moulton showed a keen ability to look penetratingly at the scene before him.
That characteristic and his common sense would continue to show in his reports
on military matters. Moulton saw beyond the flag-waving and cheering.

At 5 p.m., after the ceremonies, the Allen Guards were invited to the
home of Captain Whelden, escorted there by the zouaves. Some men were
considering re-enlisting in the new regiments, this time for three years. Captain Richardson was already recruiting for the Twenty-first Massachusetts,
then being organized at Worcester, and the Twenty-seventh was being formed
at Springfield, mainly with men from western Massachusetts.

Sergeant Israel Weller went back to the family flour business, and others,
like Private Daniel Hughes, returned to the farm, not expecting to serve again.
Patriotism would inspire some to re-enlist immediately, while the responsibilities of daily life made strong demands on others to stay home. Within the
next year, however, many of the Allen Guards would march out once more
behind the colors of another regiment on the way to the "seat of war."

The *Berkshire County Eagle*'s description of the company's return ended
thusly:

We close our report here from the fact that just about this time there
was a general disappearance of the married men of the company, and
that there was a large number of unmarried gentlemen . . . escorted
by bonnets, shawls, balmoral skirts, and very good looking faces and
figures. The public can draw its own inferences. We don't want to.

The Allen Guards were safely home, but the war was just beginning.

On August 4, the *Berkshire Eagle* ran the next letter from George Massey,
writing from the California Regiment's camp near Washington, D.C. Massey

was in "Camp Oregon," so named because his regiment's colonel was Senator Edward D. Baker of Oregon, who alternated between attending sessions of the Senate and overseeing his regiment. Baker was a staunch friend of Lincoln's, and the California Regiment had been raised at his instigation. Since California's military organization was so far away, the regiment was placed under the authority of the Federal government. (In that distant California organization was Great Barrington's Charles A. Sumner, a San Francisco newspaper editor and brother of Samuel, the Berkshire attorney. These days, Charles was serving as a captain of volunteers in Nevada Territory.)

By now, George Massey's taste for soldiering had dulled considerably, blunted by the daily drudgery of camp life, especially in the period of disillusionment right after Bull Run. Yet, the army was reorganizing amazingly well under McClellan, whose mastery of military organization instilled renewed discipline and hope in the Union forces. New regiments were pouring in, most enlisted for a term of three years, as were the Californians. Massey wrote:

Editor Eagle: [I]t is well for the good folks at home to know something of the incidents of the soldier's everyday life. Brilliant deeds on the battlefield are always eloquently described by brilliant writers. The unflinching firmness, the undaunted courage and the irresistible charge of the men, are themes that have exhausted the descriptive powers and inventive genius of many writers, and created in the minds of many readers a picture of the soldier which might truly represent him one day in a hundred, while during the ninety-nine that he remains inactive in camp the picture would have about as much resemblance to him as the very showy gentleman who appears on the stage of the theater at night has to the same person next morning.

It is possible that I may destroy the romantic sensations of some sweet miss who has a "lover" in the army; but while I will not be cruel or give pain to any, I deal in facts,—stubborn facts,—and it is a fact, sad, perhaps, but true, that when divested of a very little romance that is attached to it, the soldier's life is very dull and common place indeed.

Fancy the stern, unyielding warrior, bending over a tub washing his shirt. Just imagine, dear young ladies, if you can, your ideal soldier seated on a knapsack in an ungraceful attitude sewing up a ghastly rip in his "government trousers." Such sights are common. Many volunteers come fresh from the counter and the counting-room. They are redolent of perfume and have fine glossy curls. A short time in camp works a wondrous change in them. Good looks become less, and comfort more desirable. The curls disappear, and stubby bristles take their place. The delicate complexion is lost, and when the blue shirt and overalls are donned, the transformation is complete. He who was handsome before is ugly now. It may be well to state that the modern warrior makes nearly as much use of the "shovel" and "pick" as he does of his gun; and while the former are less genteel, they are far more conductive to health and long life than the latter. . . .

Our Colonel, Senator Baker of Oregon, divides his time between the Senate chamber and camp. Every evening he comes out to "dress parade," usually bringing a brother senator or officer with him. . . . Great confidence is reposed in him, and from the well known energy of the man, it may be inferred that if he leads a regiment or brigade into action, the victory or defeat will be complete. There will be no half way work about it.

Massey's last statement about Colonel Baker was exactly right, unfortunately, and amazingly prescient.

In this same letter, he also reported on the Californians parading down Pennsylvania Avenue and seeing Lincoln, who was showing the strain brought on by the country's strife.

Friday afternoon the regiment marched down the "Avenue" to the grounds of the "White House," and were there reviewed by the President. Mr. Lincoln looked much thinner and more care-worn than when I saw him in February. His homely but sad, and, I think, attractive countenance, cannot be forgotten. I saw him first when he raised the flag that first flowed in the breeze over "Independence Hall." There was something in the act, and something in the man, on that occasion, that caused tears to flow from many eyes. I well remember my own feelings on that morning. As the noble flag reached its height and proudly waved in the morning breeze, it seemed as if the "Stars and Stripes" were destined ever thus to wave over this land, and Abraham Lincoln's the hand destined to protect them from the assaults of those who would pluck them down. If he does not succeed in doing so, it will not be the fault of the hundreds of thousands of volunteers who forgot their troubles and sacrifices in the proud thought that they are fighting not only for the "dear old flag," but for the permanency of republican institutions.

Around this time, Charles Moulton wrote home to his mother, Fannie Easlund Moulton, a West Stockbridge native who lived in Great Barrington. Her son was in the *Springfield Republican* office, finishing his regular shift as a sometime writer who more often worked as a typesetter. It was one in the morning. He wrote that Springfield was mobbed with off-duty soldiers, many in the ever-popular zouave uniform. The day before, Moulton had been going to and from the train station, expecting to see the new Twenty-seventh Massachusetts regiment pass through, but they had not yet come. Then,

> [t]his morning about 6 o'clock I was awakened by a great noise and got up to find it was the soldiers. I got dressed in a hurry and went up just in time to see them. There was 800 and a drunker lot I never saw—but we must give them a complimentary notice 'cause they're our "soger" boys.

Unlike so many of his young age, Charles Moulton had remarkably few illusions about soldiering.

On August 29, the *Eagle* ran a letter from Cyrus N. Chamberlain, surgeon of the Tenth Massachusetts, who expressed the regiment's gratitude for the many essentials that had been sent from home.

Stationed at Camp Brightwood, the regiment was still busy building fortifications, one of them known as Fort Massachusetts, later to be named Fort Stevens. It is likely that the flannel "bands" mentioned in the letter were for wrapping around the waist as back supports and for warmth, preventing chills of the kidneys, which men who slept on the ground were liable to suffer.

> Dear Sir: I have the honor to acknowledge the receipt of your favor of the 13th inst., and also a package of seventy-seven flannel bands. The other package which you spoke of has not been received, I regret to say. Those received are being distributed to the men that need them most.
>
> It would be very pleasant and profitable to have enough to supply the whole regiment, as I think they are a valuable means of preserving the health of the men. . . .
>
> Our regiment is pretty well supplied with the various necessaries of camp life, and I will not now make any further requisition upon your generosity. The addition of vegetables to their cuisine, is perhaps as important as anything. These they are supplied with to a limited extent, and they can also be procured of the farmers here for money.
>
> I think the generosity of our friends in Massachusetts could hardly find a more important channel, or form, than that of money, supplied to the Captains of the various companies, for the purchase of such luxuries as may from time to time be desirable. . . .

On September 4, Berkshire County was shocked to hear that George Briggs had been accidentally shot in a mishap at his mansion on West Street in Pittsfield. Briggs had been reaching into a closet to put away a coat when he knocked over a loaded shotgun, which went off, the charge striking him squarely in the body.

Briggs, who was sixty-one, lay near death for several days and died on the eleventh. His son, Colonel Henry Briggs, hurried home for the funeral from the Tenth's encampment at Washington. With the death of the much-loved Governor Briggs, another strong link to Berkshire's peacetime past was irrevocably gone.

Chapter Eight

DEFEAT, AGAIN

After the initial shock and discouragement following the Union loss at Bull Run, a new wave of war excitement swept over Berkshire, and more volunteers began to enlist.

That August, six men from Great Barrington and one from Sheffield joined Harris's Light Cavalry, part of the Second New York Cavalry. These men always rode together and were labeled the "Great Barrington delegation." Their regiment was commanded by the daring Hugh J. Kilpatrick, a New Jersey man who had been a captain in Duryea's Zouaves and surely knew a number of Berkshire volunteers. By September, a recruiting office was opened on Main Street in Barrington, managed by Dr. Samuel Camp, who had received the authority to enlist men. As was customary, a commission was paid to Dr. Camp for each man he signed up, and as a physician, he could also examine them before they were accepted.

Berkshire men were now mainly joining two new regiments: the Twenty-seventh and the Thirty-first Massachusetts. That fall, twenty enlisted at Barrington for the Thirty-first regiment alone. Most of this regiment's recruits came from western Massachusetts, for it had been authorized by the United States War Department as one of two Federal regiments to be raised in the state, one in the east and one in the west. At the outset of its career, the

Thirty-first, established at Pittsfield, was officially known only as the "Western Bay State Regiment" and had no state designation. A serious problem arose when Governor Andrew challenged the right of the Federal government to raise national regiments in his state. Although the formation of the regiment proceeded under the command of General Butler, bitter conflict would rage for months to come between State and War Department officials over ownership of the regiment. The acting lieutenant colonel was Charles Whelden of Pittsfield, chosen by Butler, who promised to name him lieutenant colonel once the regiment was officially accepted by the government.

Whelden proved an able and well-liked commander, and the Western Bay State Regiment steadily took shape, although the cloud of controversy hung over it. By accepting the position of lieutenant colonel of this War Department regiment, Whelden made an enemy of Governor Andrew. Butler, too, stirred intense hostility against himself at the Massachusetts Statehouse.

Will Sedgwick of Lenox, like the men of the California Regiment and the Twentieth and Second Massachusetts regiments, had not been at Bull Run. In September, Sedgwick, now a major, was serving on the headquarters staff of Brigadier General Sedgwick, stationed along the Potomac River. In a letter home, he wondered whether the Union defeats meant the North would lose its appetite for war, and if abolition would ever come to pass:

Camp Near Darnestown, September 12, 1861.
How do people that you meet talk about the war? Does Northern spirit and determination seem to you unabated, and do you see many signs of an increase of the desire to see slavery abolished? I pray God that it may come to that. Not that I would have total and immediate abolition declared; but I want a policy adopted and persevered in, which shall look to the speediest abolition possible.

George Massey and his First California were eager to come to grips with the enemy. In a letter to the *Eagle* published late in September, he told of miles of fortifications and armed camps being constructed to protect Washington. His regiment, under Brigadier General Edward Baker, was stationed near the famous "Chain Bridge," which crossed the Potomac from the District of Columbia into northern Virginia and symbolized the North's determination to keep this invasion route open.

Camp Advance, Va.,
Sept. 26, 1861.
Editor Eagle: During the last three weeks the 1st Regiment of Gen. Baker's Brigade, has been engaged on the extensive fortifications near

[the] chain bridge. It, in connection with several other regiments, has made a grand change in the appearance of the country within two miles of the Potomac. . . . [N]ow instead of dense forest, thousands of tents cover these hills and hill sides. [Yet] it seems our friends at the North cannot yet get rid of the idea that Washington is in danger of falling into the hands of the rebels. . . .

Massey's letters told Berkshire about his regiment's stints of picket duty at the edge of no-man's-land, where the opposing troops took potshots at each other and tried to capture prisoners. He wrote of his regiment making a reconnaissance in force the day before, testing the enemy's strength and readiness to fight. Though he was not arrogant, Massey spoke for many in the swiftly growing Union army when he said he had no fear of the Confederates and was eager to fight them. He declared that the enemy seemed to melt away whenever a strong body of troops probed the region the Confederates occupied across the Potomac River.

We of the Army, know that the capital is safe. I don't know whether the object of [our] advance [yesterday] was accomplished or not; but I do know that the enemy are not anxious to fight. If they were they would not need so much coaxing as we gave them yesterday.

The California Regiment wanted a chance to prove it could beat the Confederates in battle, especially because there were rumors the regiment soon would be disbanded, its men dispersed to other units. The Twentieth Massachusetts, also stationed between the rebels and Washington, likewise wanted to make an offensive move against the enemy.

The first northern Berkshire death of the war came home this fall, with the return of the body of Savoy's Edward Sherman, seventeen years old, of the Tenth Massachusetts. Sherman had fallen ill with typhoid fever and was taken to Columbia Hospital in Washington, where he died. A large number of county dignitaries attended his funeral at the Methodist Church in Savoy Hollow. Young Sherman would be followed by many more Berkshire youths, including others who would return home with sickness or wounds, there to die. Illness would kill two Union soldiers for every one fatality resulting from battle wounds.

At the end of September, there were beds enough in the Washington hospitals to handle sick and wounded, but that would change when George Massey and the men of the California Regiment and the Twentieth Massachusetts got their wish to cross the Potomac and go into action.

On October 21, unclear orders from the Union high command sent elements of several regiments across the Potomac River on a reconnaissance mission that was too weak to stand and fight and too numerous to be easily brought back if a powerful enemy force were encountered. Ferried over to high ground known as Ball's Bluff, the troops were under the command of General Baker of the First California. In the force were men from that regiment and others, including the Twentieth Massachusetts, with Colonel William R. Lee at their head and captains Oliver Wendell Holmes, Jr., and William Francis "Frank" Bartlett leading their companies.

The crossing was made thirty miles or so upstream from Washington, and within easy reach of thousands of Union soldiers. If needed, however, reinforcements would not be available, because there were too few boats to ferry them across. The troops on this expedition to the Virginia side were mostly brought over on two scows that went back and forth in a tedious process requiring an hour or more each trip. Once across, small groups of men would spring from the boats, run along the river's edge, and have to clamber, single file, up a steep and slippery bank to assemble on an open field. Once there, they felt like sitting ducks, for the field was bordered on three sides by a wooded ridge, and on the fourth side, behind the troops, was the brink of the cliff, one hundred and fifty feet above the swirling waters of the Potomac, swollen by recent rains. The Union men even managed to wrestle three cannon up that slope.

Their commanders expected a fight, admitting this was a poor position to start from, but they told the troops that reinforcements soon would be advancing along the Virginia side after having crossed somewhere downstream.

General Baker, garbed elegantly in his finest dress uniform, called out, "Boys, you won't be able to retreat; all we want is to keep the ground for one hour, by that time the reinforcements will come up and we will be all right, but the odds are against us."

That hour and four more passed with no reinforcements. Meanwhile, Confederates were entering the woods, gathering in strength, and preparing to attack the exposed Union soldiers formed up dutifully in battle order in the middle of the field. Some Union skirmishers pushed into the woods to take forward positions there, but most were in the open. The troops had been on the move since the previous night and had not eaten much, if anything, all day. By midafternoon, they were tired and wondering why they had been ordered to this place. Enemy snipers began to fire, dropping men here and there, especially from the California regiment.

Then heavy firing sounded from the woods, and the Union skirmishers were driven back. The main body of Union soldiers, about 1,700 men, could not see the enemy, but bullets whistled past as they prepared to meet an attack. Captain Bartlett of the Twentieth and his company came under increasingly heavy fire, and he ordered his men to lie down. He himself nonchalantly walked along the line, encouraging the men, expecting at any moment to be hit. The Californians and Massey's Company C were under even heavier attack, but they stood and volleyed courageously, some companies even going on the counterattack for a short distance, but the situation was becoming desperate.

The Union cannon were hardly fired, for their crews were soon shot down. Bartlett saw his colonel, William Lee, trying vainly to serve one of the guns himself.

Then the rebels began to make frontal attacks at parts of the line. Some assaults were driven back, others gained ground and forced the Union troops into an ever-shrinking pocket against the edge of the high bank above the Potomac. The air was thick with bullets. Suddenly, General Baker fell, hit by half a dozen slugs at once. Other officers fell, dead and wounded. Union soldiers were falling back everywhere, many doggedly firing in slow withdrawal, others trying to get to the few boats down at the river's edge, while others were dragging wounded friends to the rear. In the smoke and confusion and roaring musketry, Bartlett could not find the Twentieth's Colonel Lee, but it was clear the battle was lost.

Writing later of his own regiment, Bartlett said, "They acted . . . with great coolness and bravery . . . even after the intimation had been given that we must surrender in order to save the men that had been left. . . ."

No one was braver than Bartlett, who had no intention to surrender. Managing to collect twenty men from his own regiment and sixty from other units, he led them away from the firing and along the river bank to an old mill. There, he found a sunken rowboat, had it bailed out, and began the process of sending five or six men at a time across the water. He concealed most of his followers in the mill, and after some hours of anxious work managed to save them all, crossing himself in the last load. Bartlett's own colonel and major had been captured, Wendell Holmes badly wounded, but rescued.

In those thick Virginia woods, leading Company G of the Seventeenth Mississippi, was Berkshire's Claudius Sears, whose regiment had been guarding this stretch of the river. When the Yankees had crossed, the Seventeenth had been reinforced by more Mississippi and some Virginia troops. Late in the afternoon, when the number of Southern men in position was about the same as the Union had, the battle was joined in earnest. Soon after General Baker fell, the Union troops had begun to retreat, and the Confederates moved in line of battle across the open field toward them. The fighting was bitter and at close range, and the Virginia regiment ran out of ammunition, leaving only the two Mississippi regiments to carry on the fight. These advanced until more than a thousand Federal troops were crowded against the edge of the high bluff, unable to get away.

Then, Sears's colonel, the former congressman Winfield Scott Featherstone, bellowed, "Charge, Mississippians, charge! Drive them into the Potomac or into eternity!"

The Union troops heard this, and suddenly, there "ensued an awful spectacle!" according to a Virginia private, who wrote about the battle:

> A kind of shiver ran through the huddled mass upon the brow of the cliff; it gave way; rushed a few steps; then, in one wild, panic-stricken herd, rolled, leaped, tumbled over the precipice. The descent was nearly perpendicular, with ragged, jutting crags, and a water laved base. Screams of pain and terror filled the air. Men seemed suddenly bereft of reason; they leaped over the bluff with muskets still in their clutch, threw themselves into the river without divesting themselves of their heavy accouterments—hence went to the bottom like lead. Others sprang down upon the heads and bayonets of those below.

Many Union soldiers drowned trying to escape. Of the approximately 1,700 engaged, forty-nine were killed in action, 158 wounded, and 714 missing—most of them prisoners, but many presumed drowned. So close on the defeat at Bull Run, the Ball's Bluff debacle further shocked the North, especially because the general who had sent the troops across the Potomac had poorly managed the movement. This was West Point graduate General Charles P. Stone, a Massachusetts man and a respected veteran of the Mexican War, who until then had a sterling reputation as a regular army officer. Stone was subsequently arrested, but released, with no formal charges leveled against him. Much of the blame for inexpert handling of the troops and poor tactical decisions was eventually placed on the late General Baker.

Another body of Union troops, which had managed to cross downriver and was supposed to have joined Baker, had been unable to break out because of stiff enemy resistance, dooming the Ball's Bluff expedition from the start.

Two Twentieth Regiment men from Berkshire—Sergeant John Merchant and George F. Kelly, both of Pittsfield—were among those killed at Ball's Bluff. They were the first battle fatalities from the county. Merchant was a married man, a tailor by profession, and thirty-one years of age. Kelly, nineteen, was the son of Patrick Kelly, who owned a clothing store on North Street. Both were in Company A and had been in the service about two months.

Some weeks later, Berkshire readers of the *Eagle* found George Massey's letter describing the Ball's Bluff defeat. In a letter dated December 12, Massey was writing from a military prison in Richmond, Virginia.

Circumstances of a nature more forcible than agreeable, have contributed to bring me to Richmond, considerably in advance of the "Grand Army" and in a manner reflecting little of the "pomp and circumstance of glorious war."

The events at Ball's Bluff of the 21st of October, are well known, and it is not my intention [to give] in detail [an] account of what I saw and experienced on that fatal day; suffice it to say, that after five hours' hard fighting, with not more than ten minutes' cessation at any one time, we retreated to the river. Our situation could not well have been worse. Surrounded on three sides by the enemy, with the river on the other and no means of crossing—the leaky old scow in which we went over, being sunk—it only remained for us to swim the river, surrender or die.

A flag of truce went up the hill, but many of us did not learn with what result till long after. We got in the most sheltered places we could find, and calmly awaited our fate, whatever it might be. During the long dreary hours that we sat upon the river bank that night, I saw much of the sickening horrors of war. Just below me lay a mortally wounded man, who only ceased his groans to implore someone to kill him and relieve his misery. All around lay the wounded, and their groans were piteous to hear, while the dying shrieks of many who entered the cold and rapid current in the vain endeavor to reach the other shore, as they sank beneath the surface, or were borne down by the current were truly heartrending.

At 10 o'clock we were in the hands of the enemy, and on the road to Manassas. We marched all day Tuesday through a drenching rain and reached the Bull Run battlefield at dusk, when we bivouacked for the night. At seven next morning we were in Manassas, and at the same hour next day securely caged in a tobacco warehouse in this city.

Our life here, as may be imagined, is very monotonous, and although our ingenuity is taxed to the fullest extent, we cannot invent ways of "killing time" as effectually as not sometimes to feel all the misery of those who have "nothing to do."

A rough sketch of what I see going on around me may be interesting. Directly in front of me is a party of card players, surrounded by interested spectators; still farther along are several engaged in the disagreeable but commendable duty of shirt-washing. Quite a large number are engaged in cutting rings from bones, which is the nearest approach to a regular occupation we have. Chess, checkers, and other games are receiving a fair share of attention. A few are reading papers, which we are permitted to purchase, every morning, a privilege for which we are truly thankful. A majority of the others are doing nothing, and thus passes day after day with little variation.

We are well fed and receive no indignities, from officers or citizens, in fact we have little to complain of as prisoners of war. Letters come to us almost weekly and it may be easily imagined how they are received. But not withstanding our good treatment we are naturally anxious to enlarge the area of our freedom, and extend our privileges. Many of us have no blankets of our own, and there are not a dozen here who are in the fortunate possession of two shirts apiece, and as a shirt is a thing that must be washed occasionally, we are for a period doomed to go shirtless, and are very liable to take cold at such times—

All this and much more not enumerated is very disagreeable. If our united views could reach the ears of the authorities at Washington, we would ask in thunder tones, whether justice and humanity do not demand some action on the part of the Government to relieve those who, when they volunteered to fight to maintain it in its integrity, accepted all the evil the war necessarily entailed, but none that could be overcome or avoided. We confidently expect to hear before many weeks have passed, that some system of exchange has been adopted, and that the day of our liberty is not far distant.
George S. Massey,
Company C, 1st California Reg't.

Before long, Massey's shattered regiment would be reorganized and designated the Seventy-first Pennsylvania Volunteers, but would retain its nickname, the "Californians."

Herman Melville's poem "Ball's Bluff" was subtitled "A Reverie." It was as if, from his home in Berkshire, he were observing the soldiers departing, their hearts "fresh as clover in its prime / (It was the breezy summertime) / Life throbbed so strong."

The verses contemplate seeing the youths go and, later, hearing news of their defeat.

> One noonday, at my window in the town,
>   I saw a sight—saddest that eyes can see—
>   Young soldiers marching lustily
>   Unto the wars,
> With fifes, and flags in mottoed pageantry;
>   While all the porches, walks, and doors
> Were rich with ladies cheering royally.

Weeks passed; and at my window, leaving bed,
  By night I mused, of easeful sleep bereft,
  On those brave boys (Ah War! thy theft!);
    Some marching feet
Found pause at last by cliffs Potomac cleft;
  Wakeful I mused, while in the street
Far footfalls died away till none were left.

Chapter Nine

THE APPROACH OF
WAR'S FIRST WINTER

Headquarters of Brigadier General John Sedgwick in northern Virginia.

Late that autumn, the two armies confronting each other across the Potomac began to settle in for cold weather, building huts and barracks, and trying to stay warm. There was military activity in the West, as the Mississippi River region was known, and sporadic action along the southeast coast, but in rain-soaked, muddy northern Virginia and Maryland, no more fighting was expected until springtime.

Stationed at Brigadier General John Sedgwick's headquarters near Washington, Major Will Sedgwick struggled with the unhappiness that followed news of the losses at Ball's Bluff, which included friends in the Twentieth Regiment. Soon after the skirmish, he wrote in his journal of his heartfelt hope for the future:

> Camp Sacket, October 24, 1861. My faith does not begin to be shaken yet, though, so far as I can see or learn, every "impartial observer" abroad professes the unqualified conviction that this government cannot succeed in re-establishing its sway over the Southern States. I long for the day to come when the government shall declare the war to be one of emancipation, and be supported as now by the great mass of Northern men.

At home, in Berkshire, hundreds more families saw their sons, brothers, fathers, and husbands departing with the army, as the Twenty-first and Twenty-seventh Massachusetts regiments were filled.

The Twenty-first—the regiment seen to be drunk as its troop train passed by reporter Charles Moulton in Springfield—was organized at Worcester and went to Annapolis, where it would remain until January. More than eighty Berkshire men had enlisted in this regiment. The Twenty-seventh was raised in Springfield, and had almost four hundred Berkshire men in its ranks. It would leave the state in November, also heading for Annapolis, where with the Twenty-first it would prepare for a campaign on the Southern coast in an expeditionary force under the command of General Ambrose E. Burnside.

Through the fall, the Western Bay State Regiment, organized by the War Department and General Butler, was still in camp at Pittsfield. That December, an accord was reached between the War Department and Governor Andrew, and the regiment would be redesignated as the Thirty-first Massachusetts. By February, it would move to Lowell, and then join the operation against the Southern coastline—eventually to attack New Orleans, the South's greatest city. Virtually all this regiment's recruits came from the counties of western Massachusetts, and it included Pittsfield's William Walker and Daniel Hughes, who had marched out with the Allen Guards and now decided to go off again. This time, Walker would become a captain and Hughes a corporal.

The custom was for the officers of a regiment to be officially commissioned by the state's governor, but the continuing anger of Governor Andrew over the War Department's raising of troops in Massachusetts led him to snub this new regiment, particularly Charles Whelden, its acting lieutenant colonel, who had been appointed by Butler. Although Whelden was a popular and able commander, he would not receive his commission from Andrew, and so would be compelled to resign in favor of a regular army officer. The commission had, in fact, been grudgingly signed by Andrew and then tossed onto a pile of Statehouse papers. There, it had been found by an unscrupulous state official who was an enemy of General Butler's. The official intentionally diverted Whelden's commission from its proper channel, and it never reached him.

After all his devoted work assisting the Allen Guards and raising the new regiment, Whelden was hurt and disappointed, but eventually joined Butler's headquarters staff and served throughout the war, not learning what had actually happened to the missing commission until years later.

Another new regiment formed in the fall of 1861 was the First Massachusetts Cavalry, which had more than one hundred and fifty men from Berkshire. It, too, was destined for Annapolis at the end of the year, and later would be broken up into smaller units for picket duty between the two armies or for reconnaissance missions, riding on dangerous patrols into disputed territory.

Other Berkshire men enlisting with regiments from different states included South Williamstown attorney Hamilton Eldridge, who in 1862 would join the 127th Illinois Regiment at Chicago. Eldridge was elected lieutenant colonel of the regiment, and his many friends in Chicago presented him with a magnificent horse and all the military trappings of his rank. The 127th would operate in the western theater under up-and-coming commanders such as Ulysses S. Grant and William T. Sherman.

Lee natives Chauncey and Charles Bassett joined the Sixth Michigan Volunteers, the older Chauncey as a captain, and Charles as a member of the regimental band. Charles H. Barker of Adams joined the Eighty-third New York, which had been raised in New York City from the core of the existing Ninth New York Militia. Barker's regiment, nicknamed the "City Guard," had left New York in late May to the music of "The Girl I Left Behind Me," and arrived before Washington to take part in its defense during those first uncertain weeks. Barker soon was promoted to sergeant, and throughout his enlistment wrote home faithfully to his parents, Dr. John L. and Marie E. Barker of Adams.

There was not much more that worried parents could do for their soldier sons than write letters and help contribute to the Ladies' Soldiers' Aid Relief Association, which had circles in most of the main towns and villages of Massachusetts and other states.

In that first year of the war, the Pittsfield ladies, guided by Parthenia Fenn, encompassed the full range of social classes, with Fanny Kemble, Sarah Morewood,

Catharine Sedgwick, and Lizzie Melville at the upper end. Mrs. Fenn's husband, Curtis, was manager of an industrial plant in Pittsfield. Her devotion, relentless energy, and determination to do all she could for the troops brought her to the fore of the aid effort, though her circle never elected officers.

Catharine Sedgwick wrote a letter to a relation, expressing how delighted she was to see the "gallantry of some of our young men," and

> there is nothing that pleases me better than the zeal among our young women (young and old) in working for the hospitals. We hear no gossip, but the most rational talk about hospital-gowns, comfortable socks, and mittens. Our whole community, from Mrs. Kemble down to some of our Irish servants, are knitting. You may meet E[lizabeth Sedgwick] any hour of the day going about to distribute yarn she has purchased, to persuade some to knit for love, and to hire blind women and old women to do the work. Small things become great with such motives and such actions.

Pittsfield's railroad yards in 1861, with a soldier guarding military freight; view is looking west from North Street bridge.

COURTESY BERKSHIRE EAGLE

While Sarah Morewood was summering in Berkshire, she worked hard to prepare packages for the local soldiers, although it soon became apparent that she herself was ill and weakening. Suffering from consumption, as illnesses such as tuberculosis were called, Mrs. Morewood did not let her health hinder her selfless labors, which increased by the week as the women found themselves confronted with trainloads of wounded that began to pass through from the battle front. Pittsfield was a rail crossroads; while fresh regiments from Vermont, Maine, and New York were journeying through, headed either south, or east to Boston, and in need of home-cooking and kindness at stations along the way, growing numbers of wounded and sick also passed through on their way home or to military hospitals in Boston or Albany. Their trains often stopped for a while at Pittsfield, where ready hands—usually female—ministered to wounds, changed dressings, and provided food and comfort.

Naturally, men of the cloth also appeared and did what they could for the well-being of the suffering soldiers, but it was the women who carried most of this burden. The small hospitals in Pittsfield began to fill up with sick and injured Berkshire soldiers, who soon were far more numerous than anyone had anticipated. Once-robust men came back as invalids from service with regiments that had not yet been in battle, but which might have been encamped in unhealthful country or were lacking shelter or wholesome food. A huge Union force, inexperienced in campaigning in the field, was collecting around the Washington region, where exposure to chill autumn rains and constant dampness could break a man's health. The women at home were the last resort—often too late—to restore that health.

Sometimes, the deaths of Berkshire men living in other states were reported, as it was with Lee's Charles Bassett, band member of the Sixth Michigan, who this fall died of typhus in a Baltimore hospital, at the age of twenty-three.

The largest soldiers' relief organization was the Women's Central Association of Relief, based in New York City, which had been founded and gone into action at the very outset of the conflict. In cooperation with the newly formed United States Sanitary Commission, which took much responsibility for the state of military hospitals and the health of the troops, these volunteer organizations were efficient and effective compared to the tangled, often inept, military hierarchy that tried to care for the soldiers.

As described by leading Massachusetts participant Mary A. Livermore, the work of the Sanitary Commission and the relief organizations—"an outgrowth of patriotism in women"—was a godsend to the troops. At the beginning, government officials belittled as "quixotic" the plan to create the Sanitary Commission. Those officials shrugged and conceded that at least the effort could do no harm, according to Mrs. Livermore, who wrote a definitive report on the work of the Massachusetts soldiers' aid societies.

In a few months, however, the baseless prejudice against the commission died, and the army surgeons, first opposed to it, became enthusiastic in its praise.

The commission did more extensive work than was contemplated . . . [and] was an enterprise that sprang from the hearts of the people, and which planted itself firmly on their generosity, for it received no government aid in money or sanitary stores. It depended wholly on the voluntary contributions of loyal men and women throughout the nation. . . .

Immediately after the conflict began, wrote Mrs. Livermore, the surge of patriotic zeal in "men who forgot sectarian and political differences in their quickened love of the country, was paralleled by a similar uprising in women."

Men mustered the battlefield [at the] call of the President and women mustered in churches, school-houses and parlors asking what they could do and calling for instruction. Within fifteen days of the President's call for seventy-five thousand volunteers, scores of associations of women were formed, pledged to the service of an imperiled republic, to supplement it in its care of the sick and wounded soldiers, and to assist the care of the dependent families they left behind. These associations increased to hundreds in a few months.

Springfield, a key military transit point between New England and the front, housed the larger soldiers' aid facilities in the region. Pittsfield was another center for relief, but subordinate to the main operation in Springfield.

According to Mrs. Livermore, volunteers who contributed to the relief societies and supported the Sanitary Commission had

a resolute determination in their hearts that neither inexperience nor dogged adherence to army routine should cause such wholesale slaughter of their beloved citizen soldiers as lack of sanitary care and proper food had wrought among British soldiers in the war of the Crimea, only six years before.

Stockbridge's Catharine Sedgwick was getting on in years, her own health not the best. There were those who thought Miss Sedgwick should move back to her other home in Boston for the duration of the war. She did return there for the coming winter, as usual, but would come back to Berkshire the following spring. Her sister-in-law, Elizabeth Sedgwick, herself physically weakened after the loss of her husband, also worried for her son, Will, stationed at the front. Mrs. Sedgwick's daughter-in-law, Louisa, was expecting a third child. After the baby was born, Louisa intended to travel to Germany for a few months to be with her own family.

In this time, Elizabeth Sedgwick's Lenox school for young ladies was beginning to fail, in part because she and Catharine were losing the ability to continue managing it. Within a few years, the prestigious Sedgwick school, which had counted among its pupils such names as Marcy, Delano, Van Buren, Jerome, and Saltonstall, would have to close its doors.

Before returning to Boston for the winter, Catharine Sedgwick wrote to a friend, describing some of her feelings:

> The year is fast waning, and our lives are speeding away, and few the lights still burning in our narrowed circle. . . . We shrink from these intimations of change that must come, that is certainly near, and why do we, except from the defect of faith. . . . I must make an honest confession: I have an intense desire to live to see the conclusion of our present struggle; how order is to be brought out of the present confusion; how these adverse principles are ever to be harmonized; how peace and good neighborhood are ever to follow upon this bitter hate.

At this point, she was willing to see South Carolina "humbled in the dust," but had no ill will for the rest of the South, whose people

> are cursed and borne down by their slavery, and maddened by their ambitious leaders; made to believe, not a lie, but bushels of them, and they can only be cured of their frenzy by being made to feel their impotence. . . .

The Berkshire agricultural fair went on as usual at Pittsfield this autumn, though much of the spontaneous fun had gone out of it. Despite the uncertainty of the future, the annual fair was part of the fabric of life, and normal life did have to continue.

In the state elections that fall, Pittsfield gave a small majority to the Republicans—the party that represented war rather than compromise with the secessionists. The *Pittsfield Sun* reported that C.S.A. president Jefferson Davis had visited Colonel William Lee of the Twentieth, who was imprisoned in Richmond after having been taken at Ball's Bluff. Years ago, those two had been good friends, and Davis now promised to do what he could to exchange Lee for a Confederate officer of comparable rank among prisoners held by the Union.

Thanksgiving in Massachusetts was celebrated on November 21, and the weather was absolutely perfect in Berkshire. Quartered at the Berkshire fairgrounds, the men of the Thirty-first Massachusetts were visited by hundreds of friends and family on Thanksgiving Day and provided with the best food the community could offer. The mood was poignant, for so many young Berkshire men were away in the service and, after Bull Run and Ball's Bluff, it was clear that some would never again come back for Thanksgiving.

Two days later, Berkshire's hills lay under a heavy autumn snowfall. The dampness worked on Herman Melville's sciatica, making it difficult for him to write. Already, he could feel the long isolation of winter at Arrowhead, and he was more than ready to leave. The Melville family was preparing to live between Boston and New York that winter, but they spent the holidays at Arrowhead.

On November 14, the Reverend Joshua N. Danforth, Pittsfield native, son of an aide to George Washington, guest speaker at the Berkshire Jubilee in 1844, and former minister in Lee, died at Newcastle, Delaware, surrounded by the tumult of war between his native New England and his adopted South.

The Reverend Danforth had ended his career as pastor of the Second Presbyterian Church of Alexandria, in the heart of the region known to his friends and relations back in Berkshire as "the seat of war." At the 1844 Jubilee, Danforth had said, "The Home of our fathers, revisited today in our persons—our hearts never depart from it."

Deeper trouble with Great Britain developed late that year as a result of Union warships blockading the Confederacy's coast and interrupting Britain's once-booming trade with the South. British vessels were stopped if they tried to run the Federal blockade, and in one incident two Confederate agents to Europe were forcibly taken off a British ship.

The agents soon were released to the British government, which had angrily protested the action, but the affair was a slap in the face to Britain, long recognized as lord of the seas. At his brigade camp near the Potomac, Will Sedgwick wrote home that winter:

> War with England seems to me not unlikely, though I have been very slow to believe in it. If it comes, we must bid good by to the hope of a speedy peace, and every man who can will have to turn soldier. Were it not for my wife and children . . . I should require only the assurance that the North would continue in harmonious action to put forth its entire strength, to enable me to accept cheerfully the prospect of a war which, if [the nation remains disunited] will grind us to powder. If such is to be the result, we must accept it, believing that, though we cannot interpret God's designs or appreciate the tendency of the means he uses, his designs will yet be carried out,

and that we, his instruments, are doing his work. . . .

Leave me the faith I have now that we are engaged in a righteous war, and I shall never allow myself to despair; and as yet I am very far from that point. . . .

As it was with most of the Union army, only a handful of the officers of Sedgwick's Second Massachusetts counted slavery among their reasons for going to war. For example, Captain Robert Shaw was no radical abolitionist, although he firmly opposed slavery. Shaw expected the war would be a long one, and he wanted to see the secessionist states thoroughly defeated first, then allowed to go off on their own to avoid repeated conflict between North and South. The slave states must, however, be "hemmed in" by free states and not allowed to expand, he said. Unlike the abolitionists, Shaw did not believe blacks would ever be allowed to enlist as Federal soldiers.

Will Sedgwick, on the other hand, wanted the United States to declare once and for all that the central purpose of the war was emancipation for the slaves. As did his family in Berkshire, he considered slavery a "curable disease" and was prepared to keep fighting as long as necessary to eradicate it.

I should be glad to have the war last ten years, if it must, so that its end may leave slavery in its death-throes. And I do not propose to abandon the cause while life and strength are spared me; for I believe it to be a holy one, and devised by God, however much unholiness mingles with it, as it mingles with everything involving the joint action of masses of men in this world.

Major Wilder Dwight of the Second regiment, Sedgwick's cousin from Springfield, believed abolishing slavery should not be put forward as the main object of the war. Dwight said abolition would be the natural result of victory on the battlefield and told Sedgwick that a crusade against slavery should not be formally announced, lest thousands who were enlisted in the Union cause violently object. The demands of abolitionists, Dwight believed, would only undermine the Union forces.

Keep it back. Say nothing. Let the war continue to be for the grand purpose which first inspired it, and which has united and quickened a whole people. The inevitable consequence must be the death-wound of slavery; but that is incidental . . . not forced.

What counted most, according to Dwight, was decisively defeating the treasonous rebellion and reuniting the country. That was cause enough to fight for and, if need be, die for.

Late in the year, the Second regiment was stationed at Frederick, Maryland, many men having suffered ill health from constant service along the Potomac River during cold, rainy weather. For all the marching, countermarching, and picket duty the Second had endured since coming south, it had not yet seen action. Knowing that the resolve of the North to fight on had been shaken by unexpected defeats, Captain Shaw hoped "the war will not end without a good, fair battle, as we should never hear the end of Bull Run."

Second Florida Infantry Captain Edward A. Perry, of Richmond, Massachusetts, was now stationed in eastern Virginia, at Yorktown, building fortifications in case McClellan decided to invade from that direction. Commanded by the brilliant West Pointer, General Joseph E. Johnston, the Confederate forces in this region erected dummy fortifications, painting logs to make them look like bristling artillery. Johnston marched columns of troops back and forth, day after day, to give the false impression that many thousands of rebels were stationed there.

It was an effective deception. The cautious, methodical McClellan, slowly building up a mighty army for just such a move through Yorktown against Richmond, was hoodwinked into believing that far more rebel troops were defending Yorktown than there actually were. He could have swept aside Perry and his comrades with one bold assault, but instead kept enlarging his army to improve the odds, meanwhile losing precious time.

With a potentially hostile Britain lurking in the wings, time was on the side of the Confederacy.

Chapter Ten

THE FIRST
RESOUNDING STROKE

Newspaper reporter Charles Moulton moved back from Springfield to Great Barrington late in 1861, and then to Pittsfield to work for the *Berkshire County Eagle*. While in Springfield he had been a correspondent for the *Berkshire Courier* in Barrington, describing southbound troop movements that were increasingly frequent. One troop train included a battery of artillery and more than twelve hundred men, all loaded onto seventy-six cars and "headed by a steam calliope, which will discourse its sweetly musical patriotic tones all along the route."

Moulton himself was tempted to enlist, and rumors to that effect reached his family in Barrington. He dispelled them, but the urge was there, and he might have joined if it would "not affect mother so," as he wrote to his brother, Frank.

> I think it is the duty of every young man to enlist and especially when there is nothing more to prevent one from so doing, than there is to me. Parents may feel grieved at first, but upon meditating and thinking it over, they cannot fail to resolve that it is "all for the best."

From Springfield, Moulton had reported to the *Courier* on regiments that had Berkshire men, especially men from the Barrington area. Now that he was in Pittsfield, he reported on the organization of the Thirty-first Massachusetts, at the time still under Lieutenant Colonel Charles Whelden, and with more than seven hundred men in Camp Seward. Moulton remarked on Whelden's popularity and on his ability as a disciplinarian, "as is well shown by the quietness which reigns in the camp, and by the alacrity with which the men obey orders." This would be the third regiment—after the Tenth and the Twenty-seventh—to be formed wholly from the western counties of the state.

According to Moulton, the large number of volunteers from the region indicated "the existence among these old hills of the same spirit which animated our fathers in fighting the battles of the revolution." He described the boxes of blankets, sheets, and gloves donated to the regiment, with even the pacifist members of the communal order known as Shakers doing their part for the sake of the Union. Seventeen Shaker communities existed in the Northeast and Midwest, two of them in Berkshire, and the society was a significant manufacturer of household and agricultural tools and items that were sold all over America.

> Contributions are received about every week by the soldiers from the ladies in the several towns. . . . The Shakers of Hancock and West Pittsfield, though in principle opposed to the war, contribute largely to fill the boxes with useful articles, and are said to be a little anxious to hear of a Union victory.

In December of 1861, Herman Melville pondered the Navy's recent policy of attempting to block Southern ports by sinking old vessels in the main channels. Many of those ships were filled with stones to make them heavier and more difficult for the rebels to clear away. This wasteful, "unkindly" scuttling of so many once-proud vessels—popularly known in the press as the "Stone Fleet"—was hard for the former seaman Melville to accept; he put his feelings into verse.

The following is from "The Stone Fleet," subtitled "An Old Sailor's Lament."

> I have a feeling for those ships,
>   Each worn and ancient one,
> With great bluff bows, and broad in the beam:
>   Ay, it was unkindly done.
>   But they so serve, the Obsolete—
>   Even so, Stone Fleet.

You'll think I'm doting; but do think
  I scudded round the Horn in one—
The Tenedos, a glorious
  Good old craft as ever run—
    Sunk (how all unmeet)
    With the Old Stone Fleet.

This Union tactic did not succeed in closing ship channels for long. An effective blockade of the South required armed warships taking on and decisively defeating the Confederate navy. In the Brooklyn Navy Yard, a completely new fighting ship was being built, and Melville's cousin Guert Gansevoort was closely involved in her development: Monitor was a small "ironclad" steamer designed by a Swedish-born engineer, and if all went well, no wooden vessel could stand up to her in an engagement. High-grade iron for Monitor's plating was said to have come from Berkshire mines and furnaces.

Late in December, the Melvilles left Berkshire to spend the winter between Lizzie's family in Boston and Herman's in New York. At first, Lizzie would stay in Boston with the children while her husband went on to New York. It is likely that while visiting cousin Gansevoort at the navy yard, Melville would get a close look at the "pill box on a raft," as Monitor would come to be described. Guert Gansevoort was primarily responsible for the work of mounting Monitor's guns. It was known that the Confederates, too, were building C.S.S. Virginia, their first ironclad gunboat, converted from a vessel known as Merrimack. If it got among the Federal blockading fleet at Hampton Roads, Virginia, before Monitor was launched to meet it, Virginia might wreak great destruction.

That winter, Melville was so miserable from the pain of his terrible rheumatism that Lizzie had to hurry from Boston with the children to care for him.

The technical ingenuity of men from Berkshire was again hailed nationally, as in 1861 North Adams native Hiram Sibley oversaw the construction of the first transcontinental telegraph line, which was built by his fledgling firm, the Western Union Telegraph Company. Within a few years, Sibley would be busy building western railroads and amassing land and a fortune.

Industry in Berkshire was beginning to develop new momentum as government orders came in for everything from paper collars to shoes, from cloth for uniforms to Lee marble for the Capitol building, from wooden matches to iron for train wheels and armaments. In this time, Lee was the leading center in the nation for the manufacture of paper, with approximately twenty-five working mills—which explains why the Confederacy would have put in an order there for currency paper.

New mills were erected in Berkshire and old ones enlarged, but there was a need for more railroad capacity to enable the region to compete with industry farther east, such as that in Holyoke, a major manufacturing area. To that end, the most remarkable technological enterprise in Berkshire was being undertaken just southeast of North Adams, where for ten years hundreds of men had been drilling and digging to open a railroad tunnel four and a half miles long through the rock of Hoosac Mountain. One of the greatest engineering projects of the day, the work was directed by Herman Haupt, a brilliant West Point-educated civil engineer and contractor who had constructed a number of railroads, viaducts, and at least one tunnel during the past decade, and had authored the definitive textbook on the theory of bridge construction.

Originally from Philadelphia, Haupt had become the Hoosac Tunnel project's chief contractor in 1856, when the cost of the tunnel had been estimated at $4 million, with half of that budget coming from a promised state loan. By 1861, Haupt was completely absorbed with the demands of directing the work, while being cruelly tormented by political infighting and conspiracies at the state level, intended to ruin him and his efforts. Since the tunnel would open a northern line from Troy and the Hudson River to Greenfield and so compete with other railroad interests in Massachusetts, unscrupulous efforts were underway to stop the project. Haupt's enemies manipulated politicians and stirred up slanderous controversy full of bare-faced lies about his character, and falsely accused him of misappropriating state loans. They publicly called Haupt a swindler, hypocrite, and blackguard, though in fact he had a sterling reputation, had invested his own personal fortune in the tunnel project, and had even borrowed more cash to keep the work moving when the Massachusetts government reneged on the promised funds to complete the work.

At last, the tunnel's opponents achieved decisive influence with Governor Andrew, who had been elected in 1860. Beholden to these corrupt railroad interests, Andrew refused to approve the second half of the state loan to the Hoosac Tunnel contractor, even though a designated committee of the state legislature courageously opposed him and voted to pay the funds that had been appropriated for the project and were rightfully due. Andrew coolly promised to veto such a bill and demanded the state take over the tunnel by forcing foreclosure on the first half of the promised loan.

With the situation at an impasse, Haupt faced financial ruin; but even when he appealed to the governor for a personal interview on the matter, he was flatly ignored. Haupt had many supporters among Berkshire's most prominent citizens, but the political influence of his opponents was too powerful to overcome. In the winter of 1861-62, as he considered withdrawing from the Hoosac Tunnel project, he received a telegram from Secretary of War Stanton asking him to come to Washington and direct the reconstruction and development of railroads for the war effort. Haupt discussed the matter with a close friend, Jonathan E. Field, a state representative from Stockbridge, who encouraged him to go to Washington and promised to do his best to protect the engineer's financial interests in the tunnel.

COURTESY BERKSHIRE ATHENAEUM

An early view of the east portal of the Hoosac Tunnel construction.

The ingenious Haupt went on to become one of the most important weapons the Union would have in its arsenal, while the Hoosac Tunnel project would be taken over by the state, and he would lose most of his personal fortune as a result. This crisis, however, did not defeat Haupt, who went on to engineer the repair and new construction of railroad bridges, the laying of track, and restoration of train service, all in an amazingly short time. He labored tirelessly, and President Lincoln praised him in the highest terms:

> I have just seen the most remarkable structure human eyes have ever rested upon. That man Haupt has built a bridge in four days across the Potomac Creek, 400 feet long and 100 high, over which loaded trains are running every hour, and upon my word, gentlemen, there is nothing in it but bean poles and cornstalks.

Appointed a brigadier general, Haupt went on to make the railroads and the speed of movement they afforded one of the foremost reasons for the military superiority of the North. In one notable example, he bridged Georgia's

Chattahoochie River with a span seven hundred and eighty feet long and ninety feet high, and did it in four and a half days.

One of Haupt's key associates throughout the war was Matthew P. Wood of Adams, who served as a superintendent of motive power during the Civil War and was also a confidential agent of Secretary Stanton. A civil engineer, scientist, and author, Wood wrote technical and engineering works that remained long in use by leading engineers in America and abroad.

Not only was Berkshire's Hoosac Tunnel becoming nationally known, but county native George F. Root was winning widespread acclaim for his war song that inspired the North and perhaps was the most popular pro-Union tune of all.

Having moved from Sheffield at the age of six, Root had been raised in eastern Massachusetts and had taught music in Boston and New York and studied voice in Paris before going to Chicago. There he ran a music store and the music-publishing company Root & Cady. As a composer, Root had met with some success writing gospel and minstrel tunes, and when the war came, he had tried to catch the Union's fancy with his "Columbia's Call."

> O, come brothers all, 'tis Columbia's earnest call,
>   To make her people one again. . . .

Since the national mood was for fighting, not reuniting, this song had gone nowhere. What was wanted was a war cry, a rallying song that praised the Union, a song to lead loyal men into combat. In 1861, when the Union cause seemed to be failing, and Lincoln wanted three hundred thousand more volunteers, Root was asked offhandedly by a performer friend to write a song for a war rally in Chicago's Court House Square. The composer dashed it off and sent his friend away with it. The song electrified the crowd. Evoking great emotion and patriotism, the "Battle Cry of Freedom" was everything a Union man needed to inspire him to join with brother soldiers from all over America. The first stanza:

> Yes, we'll rally 'round the flag, boys,
> We'll rally once again,
> Shouting the battle cry of freedom;
> We will rally from the hillside,
> We'll gather from the plain,
> Shouting the battle cry of freedom.

Before the final stanza had been sung by the performers, the thousands in Court House Square were singing along with the chorus:

The Union forever, hurrah! boys, hurrah!
Down with the traitor, up with the stars;
While we rally 'round the flag, boys,
Rally once again,
Shouting the battle cry of freedom.

Root had caught the fighting spirit of the North. He would go on to compose thirty-six of the one hundred and fourteen songs recognized as the most popular of the Civil War era, including, "Tramp, Tramp, Tramp, the Boys Are Marching." He wrote two of the most moving songs of the war, "The Vacant Chair" and "Just Before the Battle, Mother." For Northerners, no song was more loved than "Battle Cry of Freedom," and Union soldiers often went into an engagement singing it. One commander actually ordered his troops to sing it before a battle, and at least one color bearer rallied his broken regiment by standing fast and singing "Battle Cry of Freedom."

Many a soldier—in blue and gray—would remember campfire singing and long marches to Root's tunes, which were sung and sung again, sometimes with Confederate words instead of Root's. There were times when Union and Confederate encampments faced each other across a river, with hundreds of campfires glittering in the darkness on the hillsides. Often, one group of singers would inspire men on the other side to join in, and then more men on both sides would take up the song, until ten or twenty or thirty thousand lonely, heartsick soldiers would all be singing the same song, their combined voices rising, united, into the night.

In the winter of 1861, a seventeen-year-old private who had gone west and joined the Thirty-fourth Illinois regiment began to write letters home to his mother, Sarah Sanders, in Savoy. William Riley Norcott, known as Riley, was delighted to be adventuring in the army and serving in the warmer climate of Tennessee, and he teased those at home about it:

> This is the place for me. The rest of the folks may stay there on the mountain and wallow through the snow if they want to. They will never have me to help them anymore. Don't worry about me, for I am big enough to take care of myself.

Mrs. Sanders faithfully saved her son's letters, which came at least once a week, sometimes more often. In the depth of the Northeast winter, he wrote home that "It is as warm here now as it is in Savoy in the month of May." As was to be expected, the boyish adventure soon went out of soldiering, but Riley still liked the South's milder weather—as long as it was not raining, which unfortunately for him it often did during the cold months in the Tennessee hills.

Many folk in Berkshire found the winter of 1861-62 a time of heartache, with so many young men gone to war and the prospects looking dim for Union arms ever being triumphant. As long as there was no resounding Federal victory, the secessionists could afford to wait, grow stronger, and make their separation from the United States more irreversible with every passing week. In the North there was even doubt as to whether the rebels could be beaten in the field, at least in Virginia, where a powerful force under Johnston was ready to meet any move McClellan might make against Richmond.

Life had been transformed by the war, which at first had charged the Berkshire community with such patriotism and confidence. Sarah Morewood remarked on how the once-tranquil village of Pittsfield had been so changed, with spirits sagging after defeats and loss of life, and the prospect of many more months of war. Fanny Kemble wrote a letter about what she saw in Berkshire, and what was to come if the war dragged on. As an Englishwoman, Kemble could look upon the conflict with a different perspective; and as someone who had lived in the South, she knew the reckless gallantry of Southern courage. Yet, she also knew what would come upon that region if the North threw its full might into an all-out assault.

> Our daily talk is of fights and flights, weapons and wounds. The stars and stripes flaunt their gay colors from every roof among these peaceful hills, and give a sort of gala effect to the quiet New England villages, embowered in maple and elm trees, that would be pretty and pleasing but for the grievous suggestions they awake of bitter civil war, of the cruel interruption of an unparalleled national prosperity, of impending danger and insecurity, of heavy immediate taxation, of probable loss of property, and all the evil, public and personal, which springs from the general disorganization of the government, and disruption of the national ties.

One piece of good news early in 1862 was that the Union prisoners captured at Ball's Bluff were for the most part being exchanged. By the end of January, George Massey and others who were healthy enough were returning to their regiments.

In February, news came of General Burnside invading coastal North Carolina and capturing Roanoke Island. This stirred Berkshire and all western Massachusetts, because so many soldiers from the region were in the invasion force, which included the Twenty-first and Twenty-seventh regiments. Then the attention of Berkshire newspaper readers suddenly turned westward, to the river valleys of the Tennessee and the Cumberland, where the Confederates had fortified strong positions to prevent Union invasions down the Mississippi River. One of the strongest fortifications was Fort Donelson on the Cumberland, garrisoned by 15,000 troops, and in mid-February news broke that General Ulysses S. Grant had surrounded it.

Herman Melville's poem "Donelson" expresses what it was like in those anxious, wintry days of February 1862, when small crowds would gather in front of a bulletin board to read the latest news about the battle. A Union victory was so desperately needed that a defeat would shake Northern resolve at its very foundations. Although Melville was in New York City at the time, the crowd in his poem might be in any Berkshire town—in West Stockbridge, North Adams, or Williamstown, or standing on Railroad Street in Great Barrington before the community bulletin board someone had placed there.

When, pelted by sleet in the icy street,
   About the bulletin-board a band
Of eager, anxious people met,
And every wakeful heart was set
On latest news from West or South.
"No seeing here," cries one—"don't crowd"—
"You tall man, pray you, read aloud."

The "tall man" reads that Grant with thirty thousand men has Donelson under siege. The fort is described as a stronghold on a river bluff, surrounded by rifle pits and "fixed entrenchments in their hush," and the weather "Is clear and mild, much like May. . . . / A dreamy contrast to the North."

The Union troops, mostly men of the prairies, are in good spirits and prepared for a long siege.

Washed by the storm till the paper grew
Every shade of a streaky blue,
That bulletin stood. The next day brought
A second.

The crowd gathers once more to read that Grant's army has fought for "Each wood, each hill, each glen," until the investment of the fort was at last complete. Attack and counterattack are described, and a change of weather, with the ground freezing hard at night, yet the Union forces move steadily closer. There are reports of skirmishing, all-out assault, artillery duels, and the deaths of brave men shot by single snipers or killed when charging into massed volleys. The troops are cold, lacking blankets and overcoats, sleeping on the ground, unable to light fires at night lest their glow in the darkness attract enemy guns.

It is no better for the defenders under the Union bombardment, however, and there seems to be a glimmering hope for victory. The crowd feels that hope, although a couple of cynical passersby speak up and break the spell. One of them is described as a "Copperhead," as those who were against the war were sometimes termed.

"Ugh! Ugh!
'Twill drag along—drag along,"
Growled a cross patriot in the throng,
His battered umbrella like an ambulance-cover
Riddled with bullet-holes, spattered all over.
"Hurrah for Grant!" cried a stripling shrill;
Three urchins joined him with a will,
And some of taller stature cheered.
Meantime a Copperhead passed; he sneered.
    "Win or lose," he pausing said,
"Caps fly all the same; all boys, mere boys;
Anything to make a noise.
    Like to see the list of the dead;
These 'craven Southerners' hold out;
Ay, ay, they'll give you many a bout."
    "We'll beat in the end, sir,"
Firmly said one in staid rebuke,
A solid merchant, square and stout.
                    * * *
His yellow death's head the croaker shook:
"The country's ruined, that I know."
A shower of broken ice and snow,
    In lieu of words, confuted him;
They saw him hustled round the corner go,
    And each by-stander said—Well suited him.

The siege of Donelson continues, and day after day the latest news is posted on the bulletin board to be read aloud to the anxious listeners. Union gunboats arrive to bombard the fort, but they fail and are driven off. Snow is falling in Tennessee, and it is freezing, with great suffering among the troops. Wounded men die of cold, some alone in underbrush where they fell, unnoticed, and others in icy camps, where there are no fires. Yet much-needed reinforcements arrive to join Grant's army.

Then a counterattack in force from Donelson bursts against the Union right wing, an attack which "Rolled down the slope like rivers of hell," and the two armies clash and mingle and break up into thousands of single-handed duels "on cliff-side, and down in ravine / Duels everywhere flitting and half unseen. . . ."

The Union men hold and drive the rebels back again.

The reader ceased; the storm beat hard;
   'Twas day, but the office gas was lit;
   Nature retained her sulking fit. . . .

             * * *

That night the board stood barren there,
   Oft eyed by wistful people passing
   Who nothing saw but the rain-beads chasing
Each other down the wafered square,
As down some storm-beat graveyard stone.
But next day showed—

Fresh Union troops move in to take the place of those who had met and
repelled the rebel attack. Confederate positions are methodically stormed by
the Federals and captured, one by one. A day later, "VICTORY!" Donelson
has surrendered:

Grant strikes the war's first sounding stroke
At Donelson.

For lists of killed and wounded, see
The morrow's dispatch: today 'tis victory.

The man who read this to the crowd
   Shouted as the end he gained;
   And though the unflagging tempest rained,
      They answered him aloud.
And hand grasped hand, and glances met
In happy triumph; eyes grew wet.
O, to the punches brewed that night
Went little water. Windows bright
Beamed rosy on the sleet without,
And from the deep street came the frequent shout;
While some in prayer, as these in glee,
Blessed heaven for the winter-victory.
But others who were wakeful laid
   In midnight beds, and early rose,
   And feverish in the foggy snows,
Snatched the damp paper—wife and maid.
   The death-list like a river flows
And there the whelming waters meet.

The majority of Berkshire troops were with Burnside's expedition to the North Carolina coast, and it was those death lists that were most closely scanned by friends and family, from large villages like Pittsfield to the quietest farming communities of Alford, Sandisfield, and Cheshire. Yet Grant's victory at Donelson was everywhere greeted joyfully as a promise of more battlefield success to come. Spirits were restored, and the coming spring campaign was anticipated with more confidence and with the hope that the secessionists would come to their senses and see they must give up their traitorous adventure or be crushed.

For Northerners, there now was a real war hero in Ulysses S. Grant.

While the siege of Donelson was grinding on, Sarah Morewood presented the Pittsfield company of the Thirty-first Massachusetts, the Western Bay State Regiment, with its national color. It was made of silk and bore the motto, "By Courage not by Craft."

Soon afterwards, the regiment would go off to war and join another Benjamin Butler expedition, this one against New Orleans. The men of the Thirty-first adored Mrs. Morewood, who had done so much for so many Berkshire soldiers. When the regiment established its encampment on an island off the Louisiana coast, they would name it "Camp Morewood" in her honor. That she was surely dying of consumption was still kept a secret.

Chapter Eleven

WAR NEWS AND
'LOCAL INTELLIGENCE'

A number of former Allen Guards had enlisted in the new Thirty-first Regiment, including First Sergeant Abraham J. Nichols and Private Daniel Hughes, who joined the company raised and commanded by Captain William W. Rockwell, also of the Guards. All were from Pittsfield.

As was customary, the regiment's newly commissioned officers were given swords and side arms by their friends in emotional private ceremonies that sometimes were reported in the paper, such as the following in the *Pittsfield Sun* on February 13, 1862, describing the presentation to Captain Rockwell, the son of U.S. Senator Julius Rockwell, one of the leading figures in the state:

> On Saturday evening, a few of the many friends of Capt. William Walker Rockwell, of the Western Bay State Regiment, met at the residence of the Hon. Thomas F. Plunkett, on East Street, and presented to the Captain an elegant sword, sash, and belt. The occasion was a very pleasant one, and the youthful officer received the warm congratulations of his friends upon his success in recruiting so soon a full Company for the Regiment, with the true grace and modesty of a soldier.

The presentation speech praised Rockwell, remarking on "the enthusiastic patriotism with which you—true to the spirit of your illustrious grandfather, whose name you bear—volunteered in the ranks of the Allen Guards. . . ." His friends were sure Rockwell would always prove worthy of carrying the sword:

> Let it rust in its scabbard rather than to draw it except in defense of the right, but for that strike manfully, earnestly, heroically; and may you and your brave companions in arms restore the great temple of our liberty—"the beautiful house of our fathers"—our glorious Union of independent States, to its former magnificence and glory.

In reply, the dashing young captain modestly quoted the "old maxim, 'actions speak louder than words,' and I propose to let my actions speak for me."

Another captain of the Thirty-first who had been an Allen Guard was Edward F. Hollister, also of Pittsfield, and two lieutenants were from Berkshire: Benjamin F. Morey of Lee and David Perry of Richmond. The new colonel of the Thirty-first was regular army officer Oliver P. Gooding, a recent West Point graduate and a native of Indiana. For all that Gooding was a professional soldier, the men of the Thirty-first were disappointed to have lost the devoted Charles Whelden because of the political vindictiveness of Governor Andrew and his Statehouse staff. The commissions of most other field officers who had originally been appointed by General Butler to the Thirty-first were approved by the governor. Whelden was also given a new sword, presented by his brother Masons of the local Mystic Lodge.

Berkshire men on the Thirty-first regiment's staff were Robert Bache, major; Elbert H. Fordham, adjutant; Francis E. R. Chubbuck, chaplain (and a professor at the Maplewood Young Ladies' Institute); Charles S. Rust, quartermaster sergeant; and George W. Scary, hospital steward. They all were from Pittsfield.

In Company F of the Thirty-first were five brothers of the Frink family from the town of Washington, the oldest of whom was twenty-seven. A sixth brother wanted to enlist but was turned down because he was only sixteen.

General Butler himself had visited Pittsfield early this year, staying at the Berkshire Hotel. As a companion color to Sarah Morewood's flag, a standard that bore the words "Western Bay State" had been presented by Butler himself.

Berkshire papers followed the movements of the soldiers with reports, long and short, that were mixed in with a wide variety of local and national news, all of it set in small type and crammed into narrow columns.

Articles ranged from accounts of distant war incidents to reports of military promotions for Berkshire men and of plans to raise new companies. War news was alongside reports of local fires—the Lee Episcopal Church burned to the ground just before Christmas—and the regular news of petty crimes and court sentencings. The papers carried announcements of butchers slaughtering prime hogs and a beef farmer's success at bringing a mighty bull to maturity, and told of a young man from Lee shooting a two-foot, ten-pound wildcat out of a tree. There were brief articles on the latest women's fashions, and one or two long articles of advice for homemakers and farmers. A favorite of readers were the short stories—one by Englishman Charles Dickens in 1862—usually with an underlying moral message, and humorous anecdotes were scattered throughout the paper.

In the depths of that Berkshire winter of 1861-62, readers scoured the brief reports of community interest listed under a regular column in the *Pittsfield Sun* headed "Local Intelligence." These days there was heartening news of factories and mills receiving new orders to meet the needs of the war effort. The Berkshire Woollen Company mill at Great Barrington, for example, sent off an order worth $4,000 in "army cloth" and had two more such government contracts in hand, "which will keep them busy for nearly a year longer," wrote the editor.

Another report would be typical of what was to come for Berkshire industry in the next three and a half years:

> Crandall, Bennett & Co., tanners of So. Adams, have furnished $6000 worth of leather for the manufacture of army knapsacks, cartridge boxes, &c., the past few months.

In a day when a decent week's wage for a skilled laborer was thirteen dollars, these were substantial contracts that brought work to Berkshire and promised to make business owners wealthy. The Pontoosuc Woolen Company alone was running sixty looms, power and hand-operated, and more would be needed. Even the looms were made locally, further adding to Berkshire prosperity. At the same time, with more money in circulation, criminals took the opportunity to print counterfeit ten-dollar notes with the name of the Mahaiwe Bank in Great Barrington, and they were passed in Troy, New York.

Along with mounting war news and accounts of Berkshire men in uniform, there were reprints of timely tidbits from other newspapers, such as this from the *Providence (Rhode Island) Journal*, intended for women writing to their men away in the service:

> Ladies will please notice what the Postmaster General says in his report about their omitting to sign their whole names to their letters. When these letters become "dead," he tells us—the impertinent man, to suppose that such letters can ever die—it is impossible to return them to the writers. Mr. [Montgomery] Blair is a gallant man, and we

suppose that he has stated this fact as a curiosity; for he could not be so unsophisticated as to expect that he could frighten ladies into subscribing their names solemnly and formally in full, as if they were signing a will. Think of a love letter signed "Catharine Ann Johnson," instead of "Katie." . . . Or imagine a schoolgirl writing to her friend, and closing with "Jane Euphemia Smith," in full, instead of "Jennie." Oh, Mr. Blair! You may perhaps establish postal regulations in the disloyal States, but you surely cannot think that you are going to have your barbarous suggestion adopted in place of the charming style now in vogue.

Another subject of interest to folk of northern Berkshire, and an indication of how life went on even in wartime, was news that Professor Albert Hopkins of Williams College was "making great improvements on his mountain farm in Williamstown, known as the 'Woodland,' by changing the course of the 'Broad Brook' so as to form a lake over a mile in diameter and by forming a park from a portion of his finest woodland for the elk owned by the College. . . ."

And, as ever, there were robbers at work in Berkshire, including chicken thieves. Two North Adams men said to "have been carrying on extensively for some time" with "hen-stealing" were arrested after one of them was spotted in the act of selling stolen hens. The person who saw them was the farmer from whom the hens had been snatched.

On a sad note, there was notice of the funeral of Michael Mullany, an Irishman who had been living in Pittsfield at the start of the war and had enlisted in the Second Massachusetts at Stockbridge. Private Mullany, twenty-seven, and a stonecutter by trade, died in camp of consumption. Just as poignant was the death by drowning of Mary Lima, wife of Richard Lima, a volunteer away in the Twenty-seventh Massachusetts. Apparently, Mrs. Lima had received her soldier's monthly pay of eleven dollars and had gone celebrating with friends on "Snob Hill." She went missing and was found two weeks later, drowned, in the Green River at Williamstown, presumed to have fallen in while intoxicated.

Soldiers, too, drowned that winter. Four men of the Twenty-seventh Regiment were lost when their rowboat capsized in the waters off Annapolis; two were from Berkshire: Charles Hamlin of Great Barrington and James Bently of Pittsfield.

Intemperance was the bane of nineteenth-century society, and next to the abolition of slavery, the campaign against drinking was the most important of all for those who strove to improve the lives of average people. The Puritan upbringing of the "better class" of Berkshire folk often forbade any spirits in the home, except for medicinal purposes. Others, however, enjoyed imbibing, and for their amusement the *Sun* quoted the following *Courier* report—or at least claimed it was a bona fide *Courier* report:

BAD LIQUOR.—The Gt. Barrington Courier says if Government would purchase a few barrels of the liquor sold in that village, and discharge it at the rebels through a force pump, it would cause a scattering of the army at Manassas; for those who have bought of it declare that "It will kill at forty rods!"

We understand they have a new article for sale at North Adams, known as "razor blade," which is said to be a little ahead of "Manassas."

The more proper women of Berkshire continued to participate in the Ladies' Soldiers' Aid societies, making clothing and other items for the troops. Many attended the regular sessions from 2 to 6 p.m. in Martin's Block, Pittsfield, to make up material, prepare boxes, and accept contributions. By now, with more than a thousand Berkshire men away in various regiments—not to mention the trainloads passing through the county with sick and wounded or carrying Vermont and New York troops on their way to the front—the work of offering them care, comfort, and hospitality was ever more demanding.

On Tuesday week Mrs. C. T. Fenn dispatched to the Pollock Guard at Camp Brightwood another box of valuable articles for their comfort: Among the contributions were fifty pair of "red, white and blue" socks, knit expressly for this Company by the young ladies of the Maplewood Institute. The value of the articles already sent to the soldiers by Mrs. F. and her associates amounts to $497.50.

When possible, friends from Berkshire would make the long journey to visit the soldiers, which was much appreciated, especially when the friend brought tidings from home and much-needed items from the aid societies. Early in 1862, Sylvander Johnson of North Adams visited the Tenth at Washington to see the Johnson Greys, named in his honor. According to the *Sun*, Johnson was "elegantly entertained by the Captain of the Company [Elisha Smart of Adams], who gave a magnificent supper, at which the Colonel and staff and other friends, were also present."

The same edition of the *Sun* reported that the men of the Johnson Greys had sent home to families $1,000 from their pay and also had contributed $150 toward their winter quarters at Camp Brightwood. Another report said that Captain Smart and the Tenth's quartermaster, J. W. Howland of Pittsfield, had come to Berkshire for a brief visit. The officers were likely on company business, perhaps on a buying trip for the men, looking for such things that were neither army issue nor Ladies' Soldiers' Aid society gifts.

Embarking from Annapolis early in January 1862, the First Massachusetts Cavalry regiment and the Twenty-first and Twenty-seventh Massachusetts infantry, all with large contingents of Berkshire men, joined General Burnside's seaborne expedition against the Carolina and Virginia coasts.

Unlike the infantry, which generally campaigned as full regiments, the cavalry would be divided up into small units and assigned to duty, as needed, throughout the theater of war.

One of the captains in the Twenty-first Massachusetts infantry was Henry H. Richardson, who had taken command of the Allen Guards after Henry Briggs had been promoted to colonel of the Tenth regiment. Organized in Worcester, the Twenty-first had a regular officer as its colonel, but when it shipped with Burnside's expedition he chose to remain behind as commander of Annapolis. The reluctance of a colonel to join his men in the field was an inauspicious start for the Twenty-first, yet the regiment was already well regarded. When brigades were being made up for the campaign—several regiments to each brigade—the Twenty-first was the first regiment selected.

Burnside's expedition had opened with an amphibious assault on Confederate coastal fortifications, capturing strategic Roanoke Island. In the assault

After an amphibious landing on Roanoke Island, Union troops struggle through dense underbrush to assault and capture the main enemy fort.

upon the enemy works on Roanoke, the Twenty-first drove the defenders from the fort, and its colors were the first Union flags planted on the works. This assault also captured a Confederate artillery battery's flag, which was sent back to the Massachusetts Statehouse to be placed on exhibit.

The Twenty-seventh Massachusetts—raised in Springfield with men from the western counties—had a Berkshire father and son among its officers: the Reverend Miles Sanford, forty-five, was regimental chaplain, and his twenty-one-year-old son, Charles D. Sanford, was captain of a company that counted fifty North Adams men and many others from Berkshire.

The Reverend Sanford, who had been given a leave of absence from the First Baptist Church of North Adams, was well liked by the officers and men. Still, he was no longer a vigorous young man able to endure the hardships of a campaign, and by now he suffered from chronic illness, as did many soldiers in the expedition. The winter had been unusually cold at their Annapolis encampment, and scores of men had been laid low by fever, thirteen of the Twenty-seventh dying of disease.

From Roanoke, Burnside's invasion pressed on, fighting its way toward the town of New Berne, attacking enemy positions large and small, most of them stoutly defended. In one crucial assault, the Twenty-seventh regiment found itself without ammunition but with orders to join in the charge. It did so, having only the bayonet to fight with, and the enemy was driven from the defenses. By mid-March, New Berne was taken, but now the Reverend Sanford was compelled to resign because of poor health. On Sunday, March 16, the Twenty-seventh regiment, in full battle gear, occupied a church to hear Sanford give his farewell sermon.

Soon after the capture of New Berne, the Union troops were ravaged by disease far more deadly than the fighting, which had been fierce enough. Disease even reached the medical staff aboard the support ships, where a much-revered nurse, Carrie E. Cutter of Warren, Massachusetts—the daughter of the Twenty-first's regimental surgeon—herself fell ill and died. The loss of this beloved "Florence Nightingale of the regiment" brought profound grief to the men despite all their military success.

On March 9, 1862, a momentous naval battle took place in the eastern waters of Virginia between two ironclads: the Union *Monitor* and Confederate *Virginia*, a battle that almost overnight changed the course of naval warfare.

Soon after *Virginia* had ravaged the helpless Union blockading fleet of wooden-hulled ships in Hampton Roads, *Monitor* had appeared and fought her to a draw. Armed with guns mounted by Herman Melville's cousin Guert Gansevoort, *Monitor* kept *Virginia* from again getting in among the blockaders. *Virginia* had the disadvantage of a Union army taking control of the region's shoreline and harbors, and she was forced to retreat upriver lest she be boarded and captured. With the withdrawal of Confederate forces from the advance of General George B. McClellan's invading army, *Virginia* soon found herself cut off from escape and had to be scuttled. The South tried to arrange to buy more ironclads, to be built by the British. Meanwhile, every modern navy in the world was looking to America for the latest development in ironclad technology as it evolved in the heat of actual battle.

Though Melville continued to be ill that spring and stayed in New York, he closely followed naval developments, especially the action between *Monitor* and *Virginia*, about which he would one day write a poem, describing the Northern commander in the turret of *Monitor*. Lieutenant John L. Worden was a friend of the family, and Melville's verse praised him: "First duty, duty next, and duty last; / Ay, Turret, rivet me here to duty fast!"

As did everyone else, Melville anxiously read accounts of joint army-navy expeditions moving against the Southern coast. Not only was one Melville cousin chief of the Brooklyn Navy Yard and mastermind of *Monitor*'s armaments, but another was a gunboat commander operating off the coast of Louisiana, where a major Union attack was expected against New Orleans. Melville also had acquaintances in the Twenty-sixth Massachusetts and the Fourteenth Maine, both regiments stationed on Ship Island off the Gulf Coast and ready for a major move against the Confederacy. Those two New England regiments would be joined by others from Massachusetts that spring, including the Thirty-first from Pittsfield, and Melville personally knew many of the men from Berkshire who would be involved in the campaign for New Orleans.

Melville watched it all from his sickbed, which he was unable to leave even when his favorite uncle, a Gansevoort, died at home near Albany. Melville and his family did not return to Pittsfield until late April, the height of hay fever season and its misery for Lizzie. She would also suffer through another bout of trying to find a housekeeper. The Melvilles always seemed to have difficulty hiring a woman to help around the house, partly because Herman was an extremely fussy and demanding employer. Lacking help made Lizzie's burdens all the more stressful, for she was the one who had to discipline the increasingly rowdy children. Their father was too often lost in thought or in his writing and, even when present, was too indulgent to curb their natural tendency to mischief. The two Melville boys in particular—who attended Miss Drew's school, an hour's walk from home—were often wild when their mother was not on hand to control them, and that made it harder to find and keep a maid.

This spring of 1862, Berkshire folk read detailed newspaper articles about the Thirty-first regiment shipping aboard the steamer *Mississippi* to participate in the coming expedition against New Orleans.

The Thirty-first endured a miserable, seasick journey down the Atlantic coast on *Mississippi*, which also carried General Butler's staff and several companies of the Thirteenth Maine—more than fifteen hundred men crowded onto the vessel. En route from Boston to the Gulf of Mexico, *Mississippi* was first battered by a storm, then ran aground off the Carolina coast. The grounding was perilous, for in trying to get free, the ship was accidentally holed by its own anchor and began to take on water.

As soldiers manned the pumps, hours passed with no help in sight. Everyone knew that if the vessel were unable to get off the sandbar, an enemy warship might appear and have them at its mercy. If *Mississippi* began to sink, then the only escape would be on small boats to the mainland, where the troops would be taken prisoner by the Confederates. Yet another storm was brewing on the darkening horizon when the fortunate arrival of a Federal gunboat from the blockading fleet lifted the spirits of the men, who cheered at the sight of the Stars and Stripes on the vessel. According to a report from a soldier who wrote to the *Sun*,

> [The troops gave] such a shout as might have been raised when the walls of Jericho fell. . . . "Oh how glorious!" and the tear-brightened eye saw such beauties in the Stars and Stripes as had never before been supposed to exist in a piece of American bunting.

The gunboat took many of the soldiers off *Mississippi* in order to lighten her, and much of the transport's cargo was thrown overboard in the hope of lifting the vessel off the sandbar. The wife of General Butler also was taken to the safety of the gunboat. While Colonel Whelden was helping her into a small boat, he lost his new sword, which fell into the sea. (The next day, General Butler gave him another, at least as magnificent.) At last, with the aid of a rising wind, *Mississippi* floated free of the bar. Leaking badly, and with two hundred men at the pumps to keep her from sinking, she had to put in to the next Union-held base for repairs. There, the troops disembarked, and it was more than a week before they reboarded for the rest of the voyage.

More than once, the vessel ran aground again in these unfamiliar waters, and the tedious journey continued until late in March, when the troops gratefully landed on Ship Island, off the Louisiana coast. There, the regiments were assembling for the operation against New Orleans. As planned, the Thirty-first named its camp in honor of Sarah Morewood.

The invasion force included regiments from Indiana, Michigan, and Wisconsin, all of them utterly unprepared for the steamy, malarial climate they encountered while waiting for the naval attack on the lower Mississippi forts. On April 18, floating mortar batteries attacked those forts as the Federal fleet of warships under Flag Officer David G. Farragut fought its way past them and on to New Orleans. The forts were blasted into submission, and the exposed city immediately surrendered without need for a land battle. The outnumbered Confederate forces withdrew rather than bring on a fight that surely would result in the city's being destroyed by Farragut's naval guns.

It was an astonishing victory for the Union, and a devastating defeat for the Confederacy in this hour, for the great Mississippi waterway was closed. The South was in danger of being split in two if Federal forces at both ends of the river managed to unite. Farragut's audacious dash past the forts had been costly in men and vessels, but Melville's cousin, the gunboat commander, survived the battle, as did his craft.

In the wake of the Navy's triumph, the Thirty-first was transported up the river and became the first Union regiment to take possession of the city. The nervous population of New Orleans—and in many cases a dangerously hostile population—mobbed the wharves and streets and had to be pushed back from the waterfront by threat of force. The men of the Thirty-first were to be dispersed in detachments as garrisons for the captured forts and to serve as provost troops—military police—in New Orleans.

With the largest and most important Confederate city and the lower Mississippi in Union hands, campaigns would soon follow to clear the entire river of Confederate strongholds. These included Baton Rouge, about seventy-five miles upriver; Port Hudson, twenty-five miles farther; and Vicksburg, another one hundred and ten miles to the north. For the time being, however, there were too few Union troops in the region to mount an expedition up the Mississippi, and other than occasional guerrilla attacks and the hatred of pro-secessionists in the city, disease was the Northern soldier's worst enemy. Men died steadily from fevers and dysentery, and helpless medical officers could do little more than hope their patients would recover.

As yet, military doctors lacked understanding of how to treat fevers and disease, and the situation would remain that way until Sanitary Commission nurses and workers arrived.

Early in 1862, Sarah Sanders of Savoy received letters from her son, Riley Norcott, saying his regiment, the Thirty-fourth Illinois, was still in Tennessee.

> Cloudy today. It rains a good deal of the time so the mud is very nasty. It will fill a fella's boots to go through it. The bridge across the river is very high and long. It is a sight to look at. We have not had orders to march as yet. We have plenty to eat.

Surely Norcott knew how glad his mother would be to hear that last remark. He soon would be campaigning hard, however, and things would change, as he wrote home a few weeks later.

We have been on a march for the last three weeks. We march from twenty to twenty-five miles a day through mud. Some of the time without anything but bread and meat and some of the time not much of that. I expect we'll stay here long enough to get rested and wash and mend our clothes. . . . I can't keep my mind on anything so you must excuse this short letter.

Not long afterwards, Berkshire heard of the bloody battle of Shiloh on April 6 and 7, at Pittsburgh Landing in western Tennessee, and Norcott's family must have feared for his safety. This was the worst battle of the war so far, with Ulysses S. Grant's army repelling a surprise Confederate attack and once again winning honors, as the Southern troops withdrew, leaving the field to him. The casualties made Bull Run seem insignificant by comparison: more than 13,000 Union soldiers were killed, wounded, or missing; almost 10,700 Confederates. The Battle of Shiloh was yet another blow for the Confederacy, and Grant seemed to be the Union commander of the hour.

To the relief of Mrs. Sanders, her son's next letter arrived, postmarked from Pittsburgh Landing, a few days after the battle. His attitude toward soldiering had sobered.

It is awful to see the dead and wounded laying on the ground. If I am killed or wounded my tent mates will write and let you know it and send my money and pictures to you, for the boys are very nice fine boys and we think a great deal of one another. But I think that I shall come out all right.

For that, his mother could only pray. Another letter in the spring was no more assuring, as Norcott wrote from camp near Corinth, Tennessee, after an engagement. He was becoming a veteran soldier.

One killed, six wounded. The balls flew like hailstones around my head, but I stood up and loaded "old Betsy" and fired as fast as I could. Of the rebels, we found some fifteen and one colonel killed. Raspberries are ripe here and peaches, soon.

Chapter Twelve

ECLIPSE

That spring of 1862, which was especially dry in the East, the Second Massachusetts found itself occupying Harpers Ferry and nearby Charlestown in northern Virginia. Many of the men took the opportunity to visit the site of John Brown's aborted 1859 raid, seeing the arsenal building he had briefly captured, the jail where he had been imprisoned, and the place where he had been hanged. Union officers, such as Captain Robert Shaw, were free to rummage through the abandoned homes and personal papers of high-ranking state officials who had been secessionist sympathizers.

Emotions among the Union soldiers were so high in this time that the very sight of the American flag flying over Harpers Ferry brought tears to the eyes of some. The most moving moment came when the regiment held a religious service in the courthouse where John Brown had been tried and condemned. The regimental chaplain sat in the judge's chair as he led the service. With the regiment was Lee's Adam Miller, who by now had risen from private to sergeant.

In March, the nationally famous author Nathaniel Hawthorne visited Harpers Ferry and was a curiosity to the troops stationed there. Before long, the Ferry and the Shenandoah Valley that it looked toward would not be safe for celebrated New England authors, nor for its soldiers, as the campaign of 1862 began with the coming of a fast-moving Confederate army under General Thomas "Stonewall" Jackson.

In late March, the Union commander, General McClellan, invaded coastal Virginia by landing an army on the peninsula formed by the rivers York and James.

McClellan had worked wonders with the reorganization and training of the Federal army before Washington, but he was under intense pressure from the government to hurry up and strike a decisive blow by capturing Richmond, the Confederate capital. The strategy of using the two rivers as supply routes and advancing relentlessly on Richmond was endorsed by the Union high command, but at the same time, the government required that a large portion of McClellan's army be kept in a defensive position between Washington and Richmond. This force would not be allowed by the politicians to march in support of McClellan's invasion up the peninsula.

McClellan's army was initially blocked by Confederate defenses at Yorktown, the scene of the final decisive battle of the American Revolution in 1781. Yorktown was stubbornly held, and the Federals proceeded to lay siege to it, with General John Barnard of Sheffield in charge of operations, which occupied most of the month of April. A key Union commander was General John Sedgwick, in charge of an army division that included approximately a dozen regiments, among which were the Twentieth Massachusetts and George Massey's Seventy-first Pennsylvania, the Californians. Major Will Sedgwick was a close aide to the general, riding day after day with messages to and from headquarters, always a target of some enemy sharpshooter in this forested country, where an entire regiment could be concealed just a few yards from a road or an open field.

As the siege intensified and the two armies gathered for a major conflict somewhere between Yorktown and Richmond, Sedgwick wrote home to Lenox and his mother, Elizabeth.

> Camp near Yorktown, Virginia, April 13, 1862.
> For myself, I have no presentiment that I shall fall; and I should not consider that I had made any too great sacrifice to the country's cause; and I hardly feel as if I should regret it. . . . I am delighted, dear mother, that you do not allow yourself to feel unnecessarily anxious about me. I shall do my duty, but I shall not commit any folly of bravado, and shall survive this war unless Heaven wills otherwise; in which case we shall all be ready cheerfully to submit ourselves. . . .

Although her son was heroic, Elizabeth Sedgwick could not have been much comforted by his readiness to sacrifice his life "cheerfully." This war was, however, the unfortunate culmination of all she and her fellow abolitionists had striven for these past decades, and there was no denying that it would cost the blood of many fine young men, just like her son, to defeat the Confederacy.

By the end of April, with General Barnard coordinating the construction of Union siege lines and the emplacement of enormous, heavy guns to bombard the Confederate defenders at Yorktown, an enemy withdrawal was expected at any time. The question was whether the main Confederate army under General Joseph Johnston had yet arrived at Richmond to meet the invasion of McClellan's force.

The Twentieth Massachusetts regiment had moved into the front line, taking its turn at picket duty. Captain Frank Bartlett was in command of his company, which frequently exchanged fire with the Yorktown defenders and occasionally clashed with small skirmishing parties. Conditions were miserable, with the encampment under water much of the time, for the region was swampy and the weather damp. Many soldiers were ill, plagued by mosquitoes and wood ticks, with chronic diarrhea being the most severe complaint—a condition that too often could not be cured and resulted in weakened men dying slow and painful deaths.

Bartlett wrote home to his parents in Haverhill that he expected the final "grand attack" to begin within a week, and he would be glad when this "very unpleasant duty" of laying siege was over with.

No glory in being shot by a picket behind a tree. It is regular Indian fighting. I have not been exposed much.

On the morning of April 24, the Twentieth was detailed for routine picket duty in front of the the Union siege lines. Captain Bartlett led his men out to the forward positions, where they scattered thinly across the front, on the alert for enemy movements and keeping Confederate scouts from coming too close to the main Federal army. Bartlett studied the defenses through his spyglass, aware that if the enemy did not withdraw, then an assault against Yorktown would be launched any day.

Though just twenty-one, Bartlett had been required to assume considerable responsibility in overall regimental command during the weeks after Ball's Bluff, when his colonel and major had been prisoners. He took to soldiering naturally, his tall frame filling out so that he was lithe and strong, carrying himself with a bearing that gave him a dignified and soldierly appearance. A fine horseman, Bartlett was especially impressive in the saddle. He was always an excellent example to his company, and his men liked and respected him, as did his fellow officers. Bartlett's future in the army appeared promising if the war should continue for more than another year, as appeared certain, even if Richmond fell to McClellan this summer.

Just before noon, Bartlett took a position behind a tree and knelt to gaze through the spyglass across no-man's-land. After about ten minutes, his left leg was whacked out from under him, and he tumbled, an enemy sharpshooter's bullet having destroyed the knee joint and shattered the shin bone. A litter was sent for, and Bartlett was carried to the rear, wracked with terrible spasms of pain.

By the next morning, the leg had been amputated just above the knee, and Bartlett's military career appeared to be finished. His superior officer and close personal friend, Lieutenant Colonel Francis W. Palfrey of the Twentieth, wrote to Bartlett's family in Haverhill, saying, "Your son was the most brilliant soldier I have known in the Volunteer Army, and I anticipated for him the highest distinction. . . ."

Back in Pittsfield, Mary Agnes Pomeroy would have heard of her friend's tragedy, and that he was going to Baltimore to recuperate in the care of his mother. If, during his recuperation, the letters he had written to his comrades in the field had been written to her with the same sentiments and wording, she surely would have been thrilled.

> I fear daily lest your kind disposition shall cause you to take too much trouble in my behalf. I know that it cannot be convenient for you to write me every day so faithfully; and much as I delight in your letters, I am distressed by the thought that you are putting yourself to too much trouble sometimes. . . . I wish I were with you this pleasant Sunday morning, or at least knew exactly where you were.

Then, again, since it was his mother doing the writing as he dictated the letters from bed, Bartlett would not have been so openly sentimental with Agnes Pomeroy, whom he really hardly knew, and now might never get to know better.

In the great army McClellan had brought onto the Virginia peninsula that spring of 1862 was the Tenth Massachusetts, still awaiting its baptism of fire after almost ten months in the service.

Another regiment also on the peninsula and expecting its own first action was the Confederate army's Second Florida, with Captain Edward A. Perry of Richmond, Massachusetts, developing into one of its best officers, and highly regarded by the men. As was the custom with Southern regiments at this time, there soon would be an annual election of officers, and many thought Captain Perry would make a fine colonel. Also stationed on the peninsula with the Confederate forces was the Seventeenth Mississippi and Captain Claudius Sears of Peru, Massachusetts. After Manassas and Ball's Bluff and more than a year campaigning in the field, Sears was a battle-hardened soldier by now.

An 1841 graduate of West Point, Sears was as yet a lowly regimental line officer, compared with two other military academy graduates in the Confederate service who had been a year behind him—generals James Longstreet and Lafayette McLaws. Yet whatever this Yankee Confederate had learned at the academy—and then had imparted to his students in that Mississippi military school, most of whom likely were now also in the war—he was putting it to good use for the sake of his adopted state. Sears and the Seventeenth Mississippi were held in high repute in the Southern army.

That spring, while the main Union and Confederate forces in the East prepared for full-scale battle on the Virginia peninsula, other fighting was breaking out to the west, in the Shenandoah Valley of Virginia, where the Second Massachusetts was in the corps commanded by General Nathaniel P. Banks. In a series of marches, countermarches, false alarms, and skirmishes, the Second moved back and forth in the valley, trying in concert with other troops to trap Stonewall Jackson's army. Sometimes the Second found itself marching almost to Washington, D.C. Late in May, Jackson surprised the troops under Banks, attacking them in overwhelming numbers and forcing their flight down the valley toward Winchester to avoid being cut off and captured.

The Second fought hour after hour as the rear guard of the retreat, permitting the main body of Union troops to escape. When the town of Winchester could not be held, the Second kept on retreating, covering thirty-two miles and fighting all the way, without a halt. Then another thirteen miles were marched until the Federals crossed the Potomac River at Williamsport and reached safety.

The Second's loss was heavy, with forty-seven killed or wounded and another ninety-four taken prisoner. Among the captured was Major Wilder Dwight of Springfield, a cousin of Will Sedgwick. Dwight had stopped to help a wounded man, and thus falling behind had been captured. Captain Robert Shaw's gold pocket watch had been shattered by a bullet, saving his life.

The Second was commended for valor, its colonel promoted to brigadier general in recognition. From then on, the Second Massachusetts would be known as one of the finest regiments in the Union army.

After defeat in the Shenandoah Valley, the Federal government was afraid of a direct attack on the capital, and at the end of May President Lincoln once more called out state militias.

The Allen Guards responded again, with some new recruits and a number of paid substitutes hired to replace members who could not go. Mustering on short notice and marching through town to the "pealing notes of martial music and deafening cheers of the enthusiastic crowd," as reporter Charles Moulton wrote in the *Berkshire Courier*, they caught the eleven o'clock train to Boston.

Several *Berkshire Eagle* employees went off with the Guards, and Moulton, who also worked for that paper, found himself laboring in an office that "had the appearance of a deserted abode." Formerly only a part-time employee of the *Eagle*, he now had plenty of work to do and was also pretty much in charge of the typesetting department, which he liked. The Guards' service lasted only a few days, however, and once the emergency had passed at Washington, the militia and the *Eagle* typesetters came back to Pittsfield again. Moulton had proved himself able, though, and was given more regular work. He continued to write for the *Berkshire Courier*, signing himself "Chas."— perhaps so the *Eagle*'s publisher would not know he was a correspondent for a competing paper.

Though they had done little more than answer the call, the Allen Guards received a warm reception back in Pittsfield, with a fireworks display, a parade through North Street from the depot to the armory, the inevitable speeches by dignitaries, and a delicious "collation, provided by the liberality of a few gentlemen . . . which was partaken with relish," wrote Moulton.

The unusually dry spring weather finally broke at this time, and on June 5 the *Sun* expressed everyone's relief that "the rain of the present week, which has been copious and was much needed, has been most grateful to the Farmers and everybody else, and entirely changed the appearance of vegetation. The prospect for a good crop of grass and other crops is now most favorable."

Relief did not last long in Berkshire, for word came of heavy fighting on the Virginia peninsula, with clashes that resulted in casualties far worse than those in the Shenandoah Valley.

By late May, McClellan's army had driven the Confederates from Yorktown and was slowly advancing on Richmond. In the reluctantly withdrawing Confederate force were Berkshire natives Sears and Perry, the latter having been elected to replace his regiment's colonel, who had been killed in battle at Williamsburg. On the last day of May, when McClellan's advance troops were within ten miles of Richmond, the main Confederate army under General Johnston counterattacked. Soon, the *Berkshire Courier* and other newspapers published the dreadful news of the two-day Battle of Fair Oaks, numerically listing the dead, wounded, and missing from each company of the Tenth, which was in the thickest of the fighting.

At first, all a reader could do was scan the tally of casualties, which was given without names, and hope and pray for the best. Since everyone knew which company family members or other loved ones were in, the numbers of casualties could only provoke cold fear.

An anonymous article that appeared in the *Courier* seems to have been written by a witness to the engagement.

Unsurpassed Gallantry of the Massachusetts Tenth
Further and fuller accounts of the great battle of Saturday and Sunday, in front of Richmond, show that our victory was most dearly won, and that the battle was prevented from becoming a terrible defeat only by the most persistent and plucky fighting ever witnessed. And we are proud to say that no regiment did braver work, or stood up more unflinchingly in the most difficult and dangerous position than the Massachusetts Tenth.

Colonel Briggs was informed of the approach of a body of rebels; but as he knew the position that [other Union] regiments had held he deemed the report incredible, and went into the woods to see. He had not far to go. There they were, not only in the woods, but through it, and ere an order could be given they delivered their fire full in the rear of the Tenth.

Utter confusion was the result. The regiment broke but it proved to possess that power which has been denied to volunteers, and claimed as the special attribute of old and so-called "regular" soldiers, namely, the power of regeneration. It was rallied, and became once more a complete regiment, with only those out whose bodies lay upon the field. Nay, they did it repeatedly. Four different times they were broken on that day, and four different times the gallant Tenth was rallied and went back into the fight. Let some regular regiment beat that. . . .

The Tenth Massachusetts were hotly engaged. Three batteries also played on the advancing [enemy] line, and still it came on. It seemed as if nothing could stop it. The scene at this time was awfully magnificent. The faint smoke of the musketry arose lightly all along the line just so that the heads of the men could be seen through it; sudden gusts of intense white smoke burst up from the mouth of the cannon all around; bullets shredded the air, and whistled swiftly by, or struck into trees, fences, boxes, or with their particular "chuck" into men; and far up into the air shells burst into sudden flame like shattered stars, and passed away in little clouds of white vapor, while others filled the air with a shrill scream, and hurried on to burst far in the rear.

Every second of time had its especial tone, and every inch of space was packed with death. . . .

The Battle of Fair Oaks, known as Seven Pines to Southerners, cost the Tenth heavily, and Berkshire soon learned just how much it had lost. At the forefront of the fight on that fateful May 31 was the rough-and-ready Captain Elisha Smart of Adams, who recently had bought himself a modern carbine, a breech-loading rifle that could fire six times for every one shot of the conventional rifled musket, which had to be loaded down the muzzle. Smart used this weapon courageously as he covered the withdrawal of his men, stopping to help wounded soldiers get up and escape the oncoming enemy. Then he was hit in the leg and went down, unnoticed, to lie helplessly with a number of others, dead and wounded, who were left behind in the heat of battle.

Confederates appeared, and a Union witness lying nearby said Captain Smart "had words" with one of them. Others say Smart asked for a drink of water. Whatever was said, the Confederate snatched up Smart's carbine and shot him dead, saying, "Take that, you damned Yankee!"

With the Tenth under devastating fire, and after it had broken and been rallied for the second time, Colonel Briggs bent down to kiss the face of one of his dead friends, praying "that God will keep my men is all I care for." At that instant, Briggs was struck by a bullet that went through one leg just above the knee and lodged in the opposite thigh. Suddenly, the outnumbered regiment was being driven back again, and Briggs might have been left on the field if not for the heroism of North Adams's Napoleon "Boney" Blaise, Captain Smart's fellow Johnson Grey, who picked the colonel up and carried him to the rear.

With bullets flying all around, Briggs told the soldier to put him down and save himself. Blaise replied, "I'll never lay my colonel down in a mud hole!" The soldier's hat blew off, but he did not stop to fetch it, so Briggs removed his own hat and jammed it on the man's head. The colonel was carried half a mile to the hospital and was saved, but he would be out of action for months to come. Boney Blaise was promoted to second lieutenant.

A *Courier* letter at this time was datelined "Field Of Battle, June 1st, 1862."

> Yesterday was a hard day for eight companies of the 10th regiment. . . .
> This morning the show opened again, and we regained nearly all we lost yesterday. This morning's engagement was short but sharp . . . and the Bloody Tenth (as it is called) was the first to open fire on the enemy, and held on till orders came to fall back which they did very slowly. Col. Briggs was wounded by a musket ball in both legs, between the knees and the hips, in the fourth charge that was made. This morning he was feeling lively.

A report on the Battle of Fair Oaks published in the *New York Herald* on June 5 quotes Union general Erasmus D. Keyes, himself a Massachusetts man, under whose command the Tenth served during the campaign.

> General Keyes, in a subsequent private conversation with a gentleman from Western Massachusetts, in regard to the fighting at Seven

Pines, and the character of the Tenth, said, "Tell them, when you go back, that I have led a hundred regiments into battle, and never did I see such bravery. I looked back at them as they advanced, while the shot fell like hail, and there never was such a dauntless corps. When the fight was over, I spoke to them of their courage, and they said they had only done their duty, but I have never heard them mentioned in the journals. Their conduct was, and is, unparalleled in the whole war."

At the other end of the Tenth's muskets were Captain Sears and the Seventeenth Mississippi, which was on the edge of the fighting, and the Second Florida, led by Colonel Perry, which lost a total of one hundred and seventy-eight men. The Confederacy also lost General Johnston, wounded at Fair Oaks, and replaced by a fellow Virginian, General Robert E. Lee.

Other Union regiments engaged at Fair Oaks were the Twentieth Massachusetts and the Seventy-first Pennsylvania, the Californians, both in General Sedgwick's division. After Fair Oaks, Will Sedgwick wrote home to Lenox to assure his family he was well. Recently, his mother had met with businessman George H. Laflin of Pittsfield, who had made a visit to the Berkshire troops some time before the fighting began.

Head-Quarters, &c., Fair Oaks, June 11, 1862.
Dearest Mother, I had your sweet letter, written after you had seen Mr. Laflin, day before yesterday. It gave me a lively impression of the far greater anxiety, and consequent suffering, entailed by [the] war upon those at home than upon those who go out to fight.

We, as soldiers are, or ought to be, proof against all uneasiness, except in certain trying moments, which come comparatively rarely, and when the occasion passes, the feeling of care passes also; but you at home, expecting constantly news of a battle fought, and having to wait long for certain intelligence of the result, after it has been fought, are worse off. I feel as if my sympathy were due to you more than yours to me. But I trust you will not fail in adhering to your habitual serene faith. Think of me, always, until you know to the contrary, as destined to be restored to you, safe and sound. It will be quite time enough to grieve when the occasion calls for it.

War, with its deadly instruments and missiles, is far less dangerous than it seems. If one of our 4th of July cannon were accidentally loaded with shell, and the shell should happen to burst near a group of persons, without injuring any, the newspapers and the town-talk would call it miraculous or providential. A hundred similar miracles at least have happened to us within the last 3 days; a hundred shell have exploded, or have passed screeching by without exploding, over ground covered with troops, wagons, and horses; result, one or two horses wounded, and a few darkies and camp-followers (perhaps a few soldiers) badly scared.

Plans were in the works for another regiment to be formed, this one wholly composed of Berkshire men. Major Sedgwick was the most likely candidate to become its colonel, so perhaps the visit of Laflin with Elizabeth Sedgwick was to broach that subject with her.

On June 11, an eclipse of the moon was visible in the East, and that night rockets were fired from Mount Greylock by campers from Pittsfield and Williamstown, who had gone out to see the event. Herman Melville, from his porch at Arrowhead, could have seen both the eclipse and the rockets.

The circus soon came to town, and the Melvilles took the children to it. These days, Lizzie rode their horse Charlie five miles each way to Pittsfield, three times a week, to help with the work of the Ladies' Soldiers' Aid society. Herman continued writing verse, but it brought him little satisfaction, for he considered most of it "doggerel." He even sold a pile of manuscript to a trunk-maker "at a great bargain . . . for ten cents the pound," as he wryly told his brother, Tom, saying the sheets of paper would be used to line the inside of the fellow's new trunks. Before long, Herman would sort through all his writings, keeping a small part of them, and burning the rest.

This was not a happy time for the Melvilles, not only because of Herman's frustrations as a writer and their failure to sell Arrowhead. The war seemed as if it would never end. Never again would there come a time like his first exciting years in Berkshire, before the failure of *Moby Dick*, when the world was brighter and happier, and Melville and Hawthorne went on outings together, visiting the Hancock Shakers, and gleefully running footraces inside the Shakers' round stone barn.

Into early summer of 1862, Will Sedgwick, the Tenth and Twentieth Massachusetts, and George Massey's Californians fought in McClellan's army as it was forced by Lee to withdraw from the outskirts of Richmond.

The worst series of battles was called the Seven Days' Campaign, as a major engagement occurred daily from June 25 through July 1. The battle of June 30 was at Frayser's Farm, where new-made Confederate colonel Edward Perry was badly wounded while leading his men. Like Colonel Henry Briggs of the Tenth Massachusetts, Perry would have to leave the battlefield and be out of action for months to come.

The Union army soon would be compelled to abandon the campaign against Richmond along the Virginia peninsula. Despite the gallantry of the

The dead are collected for burial in the aftermath of the second day of the ferocious
Seven Days' Campaign; the fires are from the burning of dead horses.

Northern soldiers, thousands of whom had died fighting for the Union that spring and summer, the Confederacy had won yet another victory, though also at great cost in the lives of its young men.

One member of the Tenth Massachusetts who could count his lucky stars just then was Charles N. Pike of North Adams, formerly a professional hostler, whose ability with horses brought him to the attention of General McClellan's staff.

Pike was detailed to drive the general's private carriage, and he would retain this position of driver for the commanding general of the Union Army of the Potomac throughout the rest of his enlistment. In addition to McClellan, Pike would drive for generals Burnside, Hooker, Meade, and Grant before mustering out in July 1864 to be an engineer at a train yard in occupied northern Virginia. It would not be long, though, before he was asked by General Grant to come back and serve as his private carriage driver through the end of the war.

Early in July 1862, Will Sedgwick's "Aunt Kitty," Catharine Sedgwick, wrote to his sister, Kate Minot, in Boston, saying Kate soon would see her brother's latest letter and expressing relief that he and General Sedgwick, Catharine's cousin, had been unhurt in the Seven Days' fighting.

I have written to you (ideally) twenty letters since the mail came yesterday, and brought to your mother the first dispatch from Will since the *week of battles*. . . . You will be proud of your brother, Kate, and thankful, most thankful are we all that he and dear Cousin John have passed through such dangers in safety. . . . Your mother is calm, active as ever, and apparently cheerful, but I can see that there is an under swell of anxiety that I much feel will tell on her health. She is fit to be the mother of heroes, and she has certainly transmitted to her son her vigorous, hopeful spirit.

The Sedgwicks were fortunate, but there was much sorrow and weeping in Berkshire this summer of 1862.

Because of "the unhappy state of the country," reported the *Sun*, the Fourth of July came and went without a public celebration in Pittsfield. The Ladies' Soldiers' Aid society in North Adams put on a fund-raising festival, and a similar dinner and ball were held in Great Barrington. On the Fourth, a baseball game was played in Berkshire between the Valley Baseball Club of South Adams and the Taconic Mill Club of Pittsfield. Valley won in a game said to have been the most exciting in recent memory.

On July 5, a bolt of lighting hit a "liberty pole" that had been erected in Pittsfield's park, and the impact surely carried over to the ancient elm nearby. From time to time, the elm's rotting branches crashed to the ground, a danger to passersby. This happened often enough to be a public nuisance, and it would be no surprise to see the beloved old tree topple over one of these days.

Chapter Thirteen

LIVING ON A VOLCANO

The Union cause would enlist another Berkshire man that summer of 1862, as *Courier* reporter and sometime *Eagle* typesetter Charles Moulton of Great Barrington planned to join the new Thirty-fourth Massachusetts then being formed. Moulton had been working part time for the *Eagle*, but also sometimes had to "clerk it" in a grocery and confectionery store to make ends meet. He had to ask his parents to lend him money and complained that *Courier* publisher Marcus Rogers owed him long-overdue back pay.

Two more companies of three-year volunteers had been raised at Pittsfield and were training in the Allen Guards' "armory" in West's Block. One of the captains was Pittsfield attorney Andrew Potter, a North Adams man who also had plied his trade in Barrington. Potter was another Williams College graduate and a graduate of the law school in Albany. The companies soon would join the rest of the Thirty-fourth at Camp Wool in Worcester, and before they left, Sarah Morewood once again rose to the occasion, presenting them a silk American flag with a gilt eagle on the staff.

The Morewoods were enduring some recent troubles of their own, for their little daughter, Annie, had been hit by a falling hay bale that had broken her arm.

In July, Charles Moulton followed the Thirty-fourth to Worcester as a civilian correspondent for both the *Eagle* and the *Courier*. Soon after he got

Early in the regiment's career, the Thirty-fourth Massachusetts drills at Fort Lyon, part of Washington's defensive system.

there, he wrote his mother that he had enlisted, having had a "good position offered me, and I made up my mind that I might as well secure it." Captain Potter had promised Moulton that he would become a clerk of some sort.

"You may think me very foolish at the step I have so suddenly taken," Moulton told his mother, "but I am of a vastly different opinion."

Mrs. Moulton was understandably unhappy at the news and scolded her son for allegedly having tended bar in Pittsfield, a charge he denied, saying he had worked in "a refreshment and vegetable store on Fenn Street and just as respectable a place as there is in Pittsfield, as . . . [the] large numbers of lady customers will testify. It is not a perfect rum hole as you evidently think it is."

In fact, Charles Moulton had made a good decision in joining the Thirty-fourth, and compared to the lot of a soldier in the front line, things would go very well for him.

All over the North, sentiments for fighting to maintain the Union often mingled with the emotions stirred up by calls for the abolition of slavery. The *Pittsfield Sun* was unswervingly conservative, speaking out in virtually every edition against what it considered the fanaticism of abolitionists. On a front page that June, the paper reprinted verse entitled "Abo Bo Lition," which originally had run in the periodical *Vanity Fair*.

"Abo Bo Lition" parodied "Abou Ben Adhem," a popular poem by James H. L. Hunt, which tells of a modest, faithful Muslim soul who prays that the heavenly *Book of Life* will record him as "one that loves his fellow men." The *Sun's* poem, on the other hand, scorned abolitionists such as the Sedgwicks, who would risk destroying the Union by fighting for slave emancipation. According to the poem, Abo Bo Lition is a servant of the secessionist cause and its leader, Confederate president Jefferson Davis.

> Abo Bo Lition (may his tribe decrease!)
> Awoke one night not very well at ease,
> And saw within the shadow of his room,
> Making it mean, and like a stink-weed in bloom,
> A devil writing in a book of brass:
> Exceeding cant had made Bo Lition an ass—
> And to the shadow he said, a little pale,
> "What scribblest thou?" The phantom raised its tail,
> And answered with a leer of sour discord,
> "The names of those who own Jeff Davis lord."
> "And is mine one?" said Abo. "Not quite so,"
> Replied the devil. Abo spoke more low,
> But cheerily still, aching to grasp his pen,
> "Write me as one who hates the Union, then."

> The devil wrote and vamoosed. The next night
> He came again—this time a little tight—
> And showed the names who served Jeff Davis best,
> And lo! Bo Lition's name led all the rest!

That summer, Company H of the Twenty-seventh Massachusetts, stationed on the Carolina coast, sent the Reverend Miles Sanford more than $1,200 for distribution among their families in Adams and Williamstown. Including earlier sums, the company had sent home approximately $1,600.

With increased import duties on goods such as tea, coffee, sugar, and molasses, life in Berkshire and the United States was becoming steadily more expensive, and many families at home without their men were finding it difficult to meet expenses. Often the soldiers' pay was late, or when it was mailed home it could be stolen.

By now, fewer men were interested in joining the military, especially because there was a great need for employees, both on the farm and in the booming workshops, which had more business than ever because of the war. With the shortage of workers, wages went up, and with the rise in wages, price inflation began to develop.

Throughout the summer of 1862, in the face of diminishing enlistments, an advertisement in the *Sun* displayed the American eagle and the national flag under the headline, "RALLY, Irish Citizens of Berkshire!" The ad called upon Irishmen to "Awake! Arise! Defend the Flag!" Indeed, Irish-born men had joined up and would continue to do so in large numbers on both sides of the conflict. They eventually would number 150,000 in the Union army, and virtually all Massachusetts regiments would have Irish-born soldiers in their ranks. German-born soldiers were even more numerous, with some 175,000 in the Union army. (The total number of soldiers who enlisted in the Union army would reach approximately 2.1 million.)

Irish jokes and stories were plentiful these days, and one was told about a "Son of the Emerald Isle" supposedly appearing at the North Adams post office and handing over a letter to his son, who was serving with the occupying Union force in North Carolina. The letter bore a Confederate States five-cent postage stamp with a picture of President Jefferson Davis.

Postmaster Edwin Rogers shook his head: "I don't work for Jeff Davis, and your letter won't be carried a rod with that stamp on it. I don't care if your boy did send you that stamp from North Carolina, and besides, my boss, whose name is Uncle Sam, don't charge but three cents for doing such a job."

At that moment, a young fellow entered the post office and offered to buy the Southern stamp for three cents. The sale was made, and the Irishman bought an Uncle Sam stamp to post his letter.

"Just think of that," he exclaimed with a wink, "Uncle Sam will carry a letter farther for three cents than Jeff Davis for five cents. Be jabbers! I'm a man as will stick to old Uncle Sam, or me name isn't Patrick O'Regan and haven't already got a big state named after me—O-regon!"

The war had turned grimly serious in mid-1862, as indicated by the Union army's mustering out all its regimental bands, which little more than a year earlier had so flamboyantly and cheerfully led their confident comrades marching off to war.

Hodge's Band of North Adams, which had served with the Tenth regiment, was discharged, some of the musicians going home, others remaining with the regiment as soldiers. The bandsmen had been under hot fire, too, risking their lives carrying wounded from the battlefield, and having no weapons to defend themselves. Hodge's Band eventually would reorganize, buy itself new instruments, and begin performing again back home.

Massachusetts' Governor Andrew called for more volunteers, and in response, town "war meetings" were held all over Berkshire. These public gatherings elected boards, made decisions about helping soldiers' families, voted to raise money, and passed resolutions. Since fewer men wanted to join up, towns would have to pay bounties to enlistees in order to meet the quotas established by the Federal government. If a town did not reach its quota of voluntary enlistments, there would be a forced draft of eligible men until the quota was met. Often, volunteers came from other towns, where the enlistment bounty was smaller or where the quota already had been reached. No Berkshire town fell short of providing its quota, and in most cases towns had a surplus of enlistees to their credit.

Many volunteers were found in Boston, where agents of western Massachusetts towns would enlist men to fill quotas. Berkshire towns paid bounties ranging from $100 to $150 per man, this last figure offered by the town of Washington. It was said the bounty was intended as repayment to the enlistee of lost wages, but everyone knew it for what it was: an attractive cash incentive for those who needed it and were willing to risk their lives to get it. At a war meeting in Great Barrington, prominent gentlemen offered the extra incentive of gold and silver watches to volunteers, and one farmer promised a milch cow to the next man who enlisted. Attending Barrington's war meeting was a recovering sergeant, Mark Cottrell, who had been wounded in the Virginia Peninsular Campaign. The audience gave Cottrell three resounding cheers. In ten days, forty men enlisted at Barrington, and other Berkshire towns met comparable success.

Some men, of course, took the money and absconded.

Second Lieutenant "Boney" Blaise of North Adams, who at Fair Oaks had rescued Colonel Briggs of the Tenth Regiment, subsequently fell seriously ill with fever. On July 30, Blaise died in camp.

That August, the *Sun* reported that Susan B. Anthony of Adams, "a noted strong minded Abolition female," lectured at the Baptist Church in North Adams. The *Sun* sneeringly reported that the editor of the north county newspaper, the *Transcript,* had said Miss Anthony's remarks had "for their basis the sound doctrine."

That same month, parts of Berkshire County suffered a terrific windstorm that knocked down trees in Pittsfield and overturned tables set up outdoors for the soldiers training at Camp Briggs, as the Elm Street fairgrounds area designated for the troops had been renamed. (Henry Briggs, now a brigadier general, was at home recuperating from his wounds of the Peninsular Campaign, although he often addressed war meetings and spoke to prospective volunteers.) The windstorm hit Great Barrington especially hard, and in Lenox, carriages were upset by the fierce gusts, their passengers thrown to the ground.

Sometime Berkshire resident Fanny Kemble likely missed the storm, for at this time she was departing from America and from her Lenox home known as The Perch, which she had bought more than ten years earlier. During those years, Miss Kemble had suffered her own personal agony of matrimonial strife and, as a result of her divorce, had been separated from her two beloved daughters—the law usually gave custody to the father. Although they visited their mother occasionally, the girls had spent considerable time at their father's plantation on the Georgia coast.

By 1862, Kemble was in her early fifties, and her daughters were young women, sensitive to the woes of the world and their nation—woes that these

Frances Anne "Fanny" Kemble, pictured in an engraving from a painting by Sir Thomas Lawrence.

days could be overwhelming. Sarah, the elder daughter, had recently married an antislavery Republican from Pennsylvania, and they lived in Germantown, near Philadelphia. Frances Butler, the younger daughter, who was known as "Fan," was close to her secessionist father, Pierce Butler, and attached to the Southern cause. With a famous mother who was known as an abolitionist, Fan Butler was torn between her parents, for she loved them both. A year earlier, Pierce Butler had been arrested for treason and imprisoned in New

York, but after a month was released for lack of evidence. Fan feared that her father, who remained in the North, would be arrested again but not released.

Fan was angry with her mother for being so publicly critical of slaveholders like her father, who by the day's standards was a somewhat benevolent master. As did many of her class, Fan considered Negroes to be a lower race, divinely intended to be cared for by conscientious whites. In her own conduct while helping her father run the plantation, Fan had tried to live up to being a good "Missy," and she was determined to return to Georgia and rebuild after the war, whoever won. Fan knew that Yankee troops had invaded the Sea Islands on the Georgia coast, where the Butler plantation stood. Though the prospects for a final Union victory were as yet faint, the occupation of the Butler plantation by Federal soldiers surely would encourage the slaves to depart, and the rice and cotton fields would be left uncultivated. That meant the Butlers faced financial ruin.

With such painful differences between mother and daughter, it had done Fanny Kemble's heart good when Fan had come to stay at The Perch during the first part of 1862. By summertime, in large part to escape the deepening misery of the war, Fanny had decided to return to England for a while, and she asked Fan to come along and tour Europe with her. Though worried for her secessionist father, the young woman was persuaded to go.

In Fanny Kemble's traveling bags was a yellowing manuscript based on a journal she had kept from late 1838 to the spring of 1839, when she had lived with her husband at the Butler plantation. The journal told of her heartwrenching experiences there, where day in and day out she had been overwhelmed by the sadness of slave life. Letters to friends and entries in the journal had become the raw material for the manuscript, which was presented as being "letters to Elizabeth"—who was, in fact, Elizabeth Sedgwick of Lenox, recipient of many of Kemble's letters from the plantation. Reworking the letters and diary entries and adding essays, Kemble had produced *Plantation Journal,* which unmasked the false notion of happy, carefree Southern slaves that so many Americans and Europeans believed was the reality of plantation life. For more than twenty years, Kemble had resisted submitting the work for publication, although abolitionists had heard about it and some publishers were eager to make her an offer. She had kept it back lest she be accused of unscrupulously attacking her former husband, who could have cut off all contact with the girls when they were younger. Now, however, the daughters were grown.

Kemble's name alone made *Plantation Journal* desirable to many a publisher, for she was not only a star of the stage, but a recognized literary talent as well. She had published plays, letters of travel, and articles for prestigious magazines. Some of her writing had criticized Southern slavery, but most of it was insightful commentary on other aspects of her life and times. With the charm and eloquence that had won the hearts of audiences when she had been a young actress, Kemble's writing had won her an even wider following.

When Kemble left Lenox for England that summer of 1862—for how long, no one knew—she was resolved to publish her memoir of life on the plantation. She must have known that much of British high society would scorn such a journal as a sensationalist tract. Britain had long ago abolished the slave trade, but the country had profited handsomely from commerce with the slaveholding South. Even William Gladstone, the Liberal Party leader who was soon to become prime minister, came from a family that had made its fortune from slave labor in the West Indies. Pierce Butler and the South— indeed many in the North, too—would call her an exaggerator, an opportunist, and even a liar; and certainly young Fan would hate anything that criticized the family plantation and her beloved South.

Fanny Kemble would face all that when the time came. She believed that the truth about slavery must be told, especially because the British government was leaning toward supporting the Confederacy; the public must know what she had seen with her own eyes when she had been the "lily Missus" of the all-powerful "Massa," who ruled absolutely over a thousand black slaves.

So Fanny Kemble bade farewell to Catharine and Elizabeth Sedgwick and war-beleaguered Berkshire, where together they had enjoyed so many contented days in that "happy valley" of the Housatonic—a river she would fondly think of, remembering how it "wanders singing from side to side in this secluded Paradise . . . [and] looks only fit for people to be baptized in. . . ."

At the battle of Malvern Hill, the last fight of the Seven Days' Campaign, the Tenth regiment's George G. Strickland, the twenty-year-old bookkeeper from Springfield and a Stockbridge native, had been wounded in the side by a musket ball.

Strickland had been carried to a barn, where he had remained for four days until taken prisoner and carted in a baggage wagon to Libby prison in Richmond. There he had remained until July 18, when he was exchanged and sent North on a five-day journey to New York. He went to Bellevue hospital, dying there on August 8. His funeral was from the Olivet Church in Springfield, on Sunday afternoon, August 10. The church was crowded with family and friends who paid their last respects before his coffin, which was draped with the national flag and strewn with flowers. A few days later, a poem in Strickland's memory was published in a Westfield newspaper with the heading, "Death of a Soldier. In Memory of G. G. S. of Springfield, who died fighting with the 'Tenth' at Malvern."

Datelined Boston, August 16, and signed "Alvanius," a pseudonym, as was customary, the poem tells of the great Confederate attack at Malvern Hill being repelled, of the "long blue lines" of Union soldiers cheering in victory, and of one fallen man "to whom that sound / Had been the gladdest on the earth below."

. . . for this went thou.
But why should I sit mourning? He and I
Were mates together in a pleasant school.
We toiled and won together. We were friends.
But when the news of the rebellion came,
He went to fight, while I remained at home,
For which I blame myself. My countrymen,
Let us go forth, we who are stout and young,
For from the hills and lakes of Northern Maine,
Down to the borders where the war goes on,
Echoes a universal cry, To Arms!

In Washington, Lincoln and the politicians despaired over General McClellan's failure to capture Richmond. When McClellan was given direct orders to evacuate the Virginia peninsula, he vehemently objected but was overruled and told to return to Washington to bolster the city's defenses. By the time the general had extricated his army from the peninsula that summer, the president had found a more aggressive commander to take charge of a new northern Virginia campaign.

The soldiers in the field, however, loved "Little Mac," as they called McClellan, for he had turned them into a fighting force, and they were furious to hear he was being pushed aside. The men believed that once again their general in the field had been foiled by the misguided machinations of the government, which constantly interfered in military plans. Among those who believed this was Captain Robert Shaw of the Second Massachusetts, son of leading abolitionists, and so did most of the Democrats in the North.

McClellan continued serving the Union as a high-ranking general with his own command, but he was clearly superseded by General John Pope, a Kentuckian, who took charge of Union forces operating against Lee in northern Virginia. Shaw considered the boastful Pope a blowhard. That August, President Lincoln called for another three hundred thousand volunteers, these to serve only for nine months rather than the usual tour of three years.

Early in August, fearing that a full-scale Confederate invasion force would defeat army after army of Federal troops, Catharine Sedgwick wrote to her niece Kate Minot:

> It is strange how cheerily the world goes on, living as we do at this moment on a volcano. But, as I look out of the window on a lawn of the richest clover my eye ever fell on, and on one of the loveliest of sylvan scenes, with the mowers turning up the heavy, new-cut hay to the hot sun, it is difficult to realize that there is any worse evil afloat than the daily showers that discourage the husband-man, and yet a

general dread pervades us all, not without terror, when the cheerful light of day is gone.

The Reverend Henry T. Johns of Hinsdale also felt the weight of the moment, when the next news might tell of Lee's seemingly invincible Army of Northern Virginia again defeating the Union's Army of the Potomac.

If that happened, then little would stand between the battle-hardened rebels and the North. The idea of "Fortress Berkshire" seemed not so far-fetched at this time. The thoughts in the mind of the Methodist Reverend Johns, who was in his mid-thirties, were similar to those of many others watching Berkshire companies muster, regiments assemble, and young men march away. For more than a year Johns had struggled with whether or not to enlist. Now it seemed the fate of the Union was soon to be determined. Years later, Johns wrote a memoir of the war, published as imaginary letters to home, and one dated August 10, 1862, expressed the inner conflict he felt:

> Like many others, I am almost decided to enlist. . . . When victories, "like angel visits, few and far between," illumined the horizon, I have had no special promptings to join the army; but there has never been a signal defeat, that I have not felt the old half yearning, half conviction, that so nearly led me to enlist in the spring of 1861.
>
> As we recede from the seven days' fight before Richmond, we get a clearer view thereof, and are compelled to call it a fearful reverse. True, there were splendid exhibitions of Northern valor, and that is all we have gained. . . . Wisely has the President called for three hundred thousand more men, and now his call for three hundred thousand *more* looks so much like being in earnest, that it calls out the hopeful earnestness of the nation. The country needs the men, and I, for one, feel that no longer can I say "Go!" but "Come!"

Johns would go, and as a soldier, not as a chaplain.

At the time of yet another humiliating Union defeat in the Second Bull Run campaign of August 26-31, Johns enlisted in the Berkshire Guards, Company C of the new Forty-ninth Massachusetts regiment being raised in Berkshire County. This regiment was enlisted for nine months and would be the only one to be made up solely of men representing Berkshire towns. Although some of the Forty-ninth's volunteers would come from outside the county—even from foreign countries—by enlisting at a Berkshire town they would be counted in the quota of men which that community was required to provide. The prime candidate for colonel of the new regiment was thought to be Major Will Sedgwick, serving in northern Virginia on General John Sedgwick's staff.

A few days before Henry Johns enlisted in the Forty-ninth, Pittsfield resident Thomas Reed, thirty-nine years old and with a wife and two children, enlisted for different reasons. Reed saw Pittsfield's $100 bounty as an opportunity to buy a house for his family after his time was up. He was a skilled cabinetmaker, well-educated and worldly. If lucky, he would serve out a two-year enlistment in Company I of the Twenty-first Massachusetts—which was scheduled to be demobilized in 1864—then come home and have a nest egg with which to acquire a house. Both Reed and his wife, Cynthia, were originally from New York City, and he had a brother in Pittsfield who owned a cabinet shop. Company I was known as the Pittsfield Tigers.

Another older Berkshire man who enlisted this summer was Calvin C. Hosford, thirty-one, of Williamstown, who joined Company A of the Twenty-seventh regiment. A painter and mechanic and sometime tailor, Hosford had lived in Wisconsin for most of the past ten years with his wife, Harriet, and three children. He had moved his family back to Massachusetts just at the outbreak of war, and a fourth child had been born in Cummington, where Harriet would live while her husband was away in the army. Signing up in Springfield, Hosford, too, would pocket an enlistment bounty. He joined the Twenty-seventh regiment at its station in the Carolinas, but almost immediately after getting there he came down with fever.

Both families would also qualify for a stipend from state and Federal aid given to soldiers' dependents. In addition to the cash bounty and the thirteen dollars a month a soldier was paid, this bit of extra income offered the hope of financial security and the possibility of saving for the future. With rapidly rising costs, however, and the irregularity of actually receiving the men's pay, life for the family struggling at home generally turned out to be almost as uncertain as that of the soldier.

After reflection upon what he considered enlightening biblical examples, Henry Johns found he could justify the act of killing another man. He also became convinced that war in itself was not wrong; he said Jesus "and His disciples fellowshipped with soldiers and acknowledged them as Christians." And, "Nothing can be more certain than that God is a God of *government*." So, for Henry Johns, it would be a crusade, just as it was a crusade for so many soldiers, North and South.

In August 1862, that crusade in the name of the God-given government of the United States was faltering. With General McClellan forced out of the campaign by Lincoln, the Union army under the incompetent General Pope was completely outmaneuvered, both in the Shenandoah Valley and in northern Virginia. On August 9, a Confederate force under Stonewall Jackson defeated poorly managed Federals at Cedar Mountain in Virginia, where the Second Massachusetts was cut to pieces, with six line officers and forty-nine men killed or mortally wounded, another ninety-nine wounded or captured. Among the wounded was Lee's Adam Miller, now a lieutenant. Shot in the face and having lost an eye, Miller had been taken prisoner. Among those killed was twenty-six-year-old Henry C. Hoxey, a Williamstown farmer. Miraculously, Captain Robert Shaw came out of the battle unhurt, to the relief of his sweetheart, Annie Haggerty, a young New York woman whose wealthy family had a country home in Lenox.

Shaw wrote to Annie, who was in Boston, and reported on the deaths or wounding of their friends in the regiment. He also told her that some men said to have been killed were actually just fine: "How terrible the news has been for you all in Boston this week."

It would get worse. Late in August, Lee and Jackson combined to defeat Pope at the battle in northern Virginia known as Second Bull Run. Thanks to the courage of the troops and officers, the Federals were not routed. The Twenty-first Massachusetts was in the vicinity of the battle, but not in the worst of the conflict. The green Thirty-fourth Massachusetts soon proved its mettle by fighting its way across the Potomac River during the campaign. Among the Union dead at Second Bull Run was the Twentieth New York Infantry's Captain Peletiah Ward, who in 1848-50 had been pastor of the Methodist Church in Lee, and until just before the war had been a minister in Ellenville, New York. Ward had been fatally shot while attempting to raise the fallen regimental colors, even though he was already wounded.

The Tenth regiment, under a temporary commander now that Henry Briggs had been appointed brigadier general with responsibilities for a larger body of troops, found itself on forced marches throughout that campaign and summer. Again and again it was sent to a point of impending crisis, only to be countermarched to another. This was in response to the rapid maneuvering of Lee's army, expected at any moment to strike northward or turn on Washington. The anxiety felt by the North was redoubled after Second Bull Run.

Realizing Pope was a failure, the desperate Lincoln again called on McClellan, whose task it was to find Lee's main army and take it on with every Federal soldier who could be mustered. It soon became clear that part of Lee's force was advancing on Harpers Ferry, and the Tenth was ordered in that direction along with other elements of McClellan's main army, which was cautiously moving northwestward in search of the Confederates.

A few weeks after the Second Bull Run campaign, the Twenty-first Massachusetts suffered heavy losses in a battle at Chantilly, Virginia. The regiment had been surprised by the enemy while advancing through dense woods, mauled by a storm of short-range musketry, and had to fight hand to hand for survival. Fortunately for the newly enlisted Thomas Reed of Pittsfield, he had not yet joined the Twenty-first. And fortunately for the cause of the Union, McClellan was again in command for the coming battle with Lee.

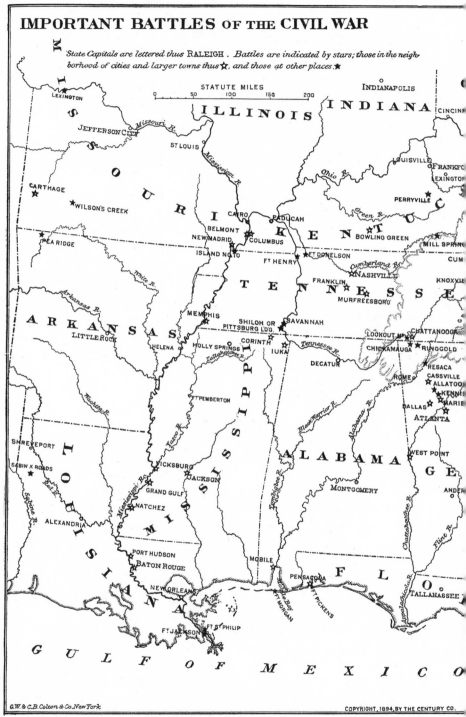

IMPORTANT BATTLES OF THE CIVIL WAR

State Capitals are lettered thus RALEIGH . *Battles are indicated by stars; those in the neighborhood of cities and larger towns thus* ☆, *and those at other places.* ★

STATUTE MILES

0   50   100   150   200

INDIANAPOLIS

LEXINGTON

ILLINOIS   INDIANA   CINCIN

JEFFERSON CITY   *Missouri R.*

ST LOUIS

LOUISVILLE

Ohio R.   FRANKF
LEXINGTON

CARTHAGE   PERRYVILLE

★WILSON'S CREEK   CAIRO   PADUCAH   KENTUC   ☆BOWLING GREEN   MILL SPRIN

★PEA RIDGE   BELMONT   COLUMBUS   CUM
NEW MADRID
ISLAND NO 10   ★FT DONELSON
FT HENRY   *Cumberland R.*   ☆NASHVILLE   KNOXVI

FRANKLIN
MURFREESBORO

MEMPHIS   SHILOH OR   ★SAVANNAH   LOOKOUT MT   CHATTANOOG
PITTSBURG LDG.   CHICKAMAUGA ★★RINGGOLD

HELENA   HOLLY SPRINGS   CORINTH   IUKA   *Tennessee R.*   DECATUR   RESACA
LITTLE ROCK   ★   ROME ☆   CASSVILLE
★ALLATOO
ARKANSAS   KENNE
FT PEMBERTON   DALLAS☆   ★MARIE
ATLANTA

SHREVEPORT   WEST POINT

SABIN X ROADS   VICKSBURG   ★JACKSON   GE

GRAND GULF   MONTGOMERY   ANDER

NATCHEZ   MISSISSIPPI
ALEXANDRIA   ALABAMA

PORT HUDSON   MOBILE
BATON ROUGE   FLO
PENSACOLA
NEW ORLEANS   FT PICKENS   TALLAHASSEE
FT MORGAN
FT ST PHILIP
FT JACKSON

G U L F   O F   M E X I C O

G.W. & C.B. Colton & Co. New York

A few years after the conflict, Century Magazine published this map of key Civil War campaigns as part of its illustrated history, entitled "Battles and Leaders of the Civil War."

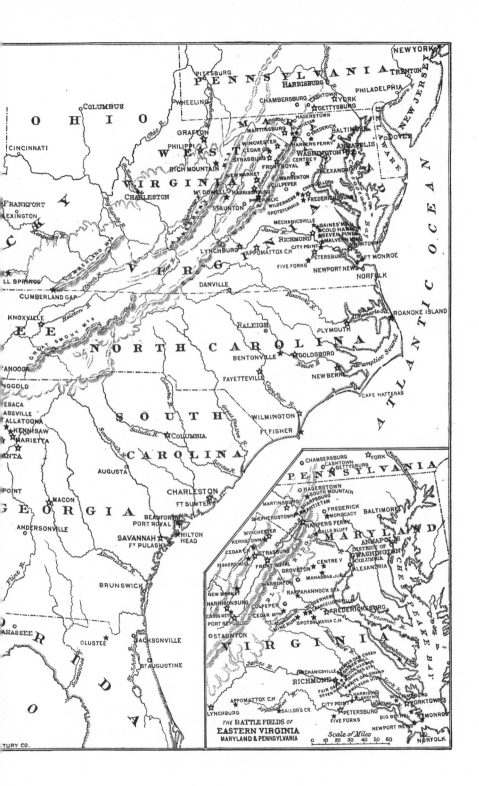

THE BATTLE FIELDS OF
EASTERN VIRGINIA
MARYLAND & PENNSYLVANIA

Scale of Miles
0 10 20 30 40 50 60

Chapter Fourteen

ANTIETAM

In 1862, one more Massachusetts regiment, the Thirty-seventh, was formed with men from the four western counties and based at Camp Briggs in Pittsfield. While he was on sick leave, Colonel William R. Lee of the Twentieth Massachusetts was assigned to command the camp as the new regiment assembled. It was eventually to be led by Colonel Oliver Edwards of Springfield.

The Thirty-seventh had several Pittsfield men on its staff: Alonzo E. Goodrich, lieutenant colonel, Thomas G. Colt, adjutant, and, as quartermaster, Daniel J. Dodge, savior of the old elm years earlier and a veteran of the Allen Guards. Berkshire men captained four of the eleven companies: Franklin W. Pease of Lee, Edwin Hurlburt of Great Barrington, Archibald Hopkins of Williamstown, and Peter Dooley of Cheshire. Six other Berkshire men served as lieutenants, and approximately half the enlisted men were from the county.

The regiment's national color was presented by Sarah Morewood, who was described by the *Sun* as "a lady whose contributions for the soldiers seem to have no limit."

Until the Thirty-seventh regiment left Camp Briggs early in September, the first volunteers who turned out for the new Forty-ninth Massachusetts were quartered in Pittsfield's Burbank Hall. The first company, which would be designated Company A, was made of members of Pittsfield's Allen Guards.

In his memoirs, the Forty-ninth's Henry Johns described the Thirty-seventh's departure, as the soldiers were addressed in the park by Pittsfield Congregational minister John Todd. These days, the goings and comings of soldiers were all too familiar to be much noticed.

> Yesterday, the Thirty-seventh left for Dixie. Under the old elm, Dr. Todd made a farewell prayer. Though it was heard by few, it was a solemn scene. We knew they were bound for the Potomac, and that the exigencies of the times were such that they might be rushed into battle before another Sabbath day.

The Thirty-seventh was being hurried away to bolster the defense of Washington after the Second Bull Run defeat. It took a train to Hudson, New York, then a steamboat down the Hudson River to New Jersey, and another train southward.

Early in September, with Lee's army threatening an invasion of the North, the *Sun* reported that a "monster meeting" was held under the elm in Pittsfield. This huge outdoor gathering, with a number of impassioned speakers, was in response to "the exciting and startling intelligence from the seat of war." The object of the meeting was to whip up enthusiasm for volunteers to complete the town's quota of enlistees. In addition to counting on the patriotism of prospective soldiers, the town offered its bounty of $100 for signing up. That sum would eventually have to be increased, however, for other communities had begun to offer more, workers' wages had gone up, and the war's bloodshed had worsened. Usually, the bounty was given in two parts, half on enlisting and the rest upon leaving the service honorably—alive or not.

In this time, Parthenia Fenn journeyed to New York City to visit wounded Berkshire soldiers in hospitals there. The indefatigable Mrs. Fenn took along boxes of linen and bandages as well as homemade delicacies such as preserves, brandies, and cordials. At 194 Broadway were chambers known as "New England rooms," or the New England Hospital, specifically for casualties from the region.

Also in New York at this time, working as a medical doctor at Bellevue Hospital, was Titus M. Coan, the Williams man who had visited Melville a couple of years previous and had listened to him spout Homer when Coan wanted to hear *Typee*.

On September 15, as the Union army maneuvered to meet the hard-marching Confederates somewhere in Maryland, Major Will Sedgwick wrote a letter, saying, "O, how I long for a few hours' assured rest!" He had been laboring around the clock to perform the duties of a staff officer for General Sedgwick, who was now in command of a larger body of troops, a division of approximately five thousand men. Sedgwick's cousin, Major Wilder Dwight, had by now been exchanged and had returned to the Second Massachusetts Regiment, much to everyone's delight. When he had first appeared, the men had hoisted Dwight on their shoulders and carried him through camp. Like Sedgwick, Dwight immediately went to work, hurrying his regiment forward with McClellan's army. After the humiliation of Second Bull Run, no Union soldier could have been confident of victory. Elements of the two armies clashed around South Mountain, north of Harpers Ferry, in inconclusive engagements. Then one of Lee's wings captured the strategically important Ferry, along with more than twelve thousand Federal troops.

Union troops, including men of the Twenty-first Massachusetts, charge across "Burnside's Bridge" at the Battle of Antietam.

Taking part in that victory was Claudius Sears and the Seventeenth Mississippi, found once again at the most important point in the battle. The Seventeenth was instrumental in driving Union defenders from Maryland Heights, the high ground that commanded Harpers Ferry. Without a rest, Sears and the Mississippians immediately resumed their grueling march toward the Maryland hamlet of Sharpsburg, near Antietam Creek, where Lee desperately needed them in the coming climactic battle with McClellan.

With the site of the final showdown in the developing campaign as yet unclear, and with the North dreading that their own towns would be ravaged, another horror shook all of Berkshire County this September, as a mother and her two little children were brutally murdered in the town of Otis.

The father, George A. Jones, had been away at church on Sunday morning when his wife, Emily, and their children, a boy of four and a girl of two, had gone out picking blackberries. He returned but they did not. Later, a party went to look for them and, after searching for two days, found the bodies concealed in underbrush.

The residents of this hilly eastern section of Berkshire, living in their isolated farms and hamlets, were in a more immediate state of fear as news of the Civil War's latest slaughter reached them.

The main Federal and Confederate armies converged at Antietam Creek, with more than one hundred thousand Americans ranging themselves for a battle to the death. The determined Confederates were flushed with their recent victories, and although the Union army had been demoralized, it was uplifted by the return of McClellan to command. The men trusted him far more than they trusted the politicians who had been pulling the strings of military control and had helped cause the recent disasters—meddling politicians who many thought included President Lincoln.

On the eve of battle, September 16, Major Will Sedgwick rode into the bivouac of his own regiment, the Second Massachusetts, and was cheerfully received by the officers and enlisted men with whom he had journeyed from Berkshire more than a year earlier. There, too, was his cousin Major Dwight, along with his friend Captain Robert Shaw, both of whom he had known since they were children; Shaw's family and the Sedgwicks had of-

COURTESY BERKSHIRE EAGLE

Major William D. Sedgwick, son of Berkshire's leading abolitionist family.

ten visited each other. It was a brief but warm reunion, and soon Sedgwick rode back to resume his endless staff duties. Tomorrow would be a battle like none other, greater even than the bloody Seven Days on the peninsula.

The fate of the Union hung on repelling Lee decisively—if not crushing his army, then at least driving it back to Virginia and preventing the impending invasion.

Major Sedgwick had been glad to see the Second regiment again, but just now he must have been thinking more about his wife and three children, shortly to return from their visit to Germany. The youngest of the girls was a baby he had not yet seen.

The next day, September 17, Catharine Sedgwick wrote to her niece Kate Minot, saying she had "plunged into the melee" of *Les Misérables*, the new French novel by Victor Hugo, a heart-rending tale about revolutionary times and dying for an ideal.

> It is a book that must be read. . . . It deals with the greatest topics of humanity, and in such a mode as is possible only to a mind of the first order. . . . It is solemn, magnificent, and beautiful; full of thoughts that solve the mysteries of history. But you must read the whole book, and no better time than this, when we need to be *diverted* by other miseries than our own.

On that same day, with the thunder of cannon, deafening explosions, and the rippling crashes of musketry all around him, Will Sedgwick wrote a letter of his own to his mother, Elizabeth. He wrote it on a page of his diary as he lay on the field, unable to rise, a bullet in his back. The Battle of Antietam was raging on all sides, and Sedgwick had not yet been found by his comrades or litter bearers.

> While trying to rally our men, a musket-ball struck me in the small of my back, and I fell from my horse. As I write this, I have been lying here more than an hour, powerless to move my right leg. I think the wound must be mortal. I have been praying to God to forgive my sins, to bless and comfort my darling wife and children, my dearest mother and sisters. As I have been lying here in very great pain, shells have been bursting close to me almost constantly. I wish my friends to know that I have fallen while doing my duty as well as was possible, which I can truly assert, and that I have not uttered a groan as yet, lying alone on the hard ground, in the sun, with no friends near.

Not far away, his cousin, Wilder Dwight, also lay alone between the two armies. Dwight, too, wrote to his mother, adding to a letter he had begun that morning and had tucked into a pocket. He told her, "I think I die in victory," and expired where he lay.

Indeed, Lee was repulsed at Antietam, the bloodiest single day of the entire Civil War, and arguably a victory for the North. The Union lost 12,400 killed, wounded, or missing, the Confederates more than 13,700. Lee was compelled to withdraw, his invasion decisively turned back. The Union cause was yet strong, and European nations would have to recognize that the Confederacy was not certain of final victory. Desperately needed British loans were not to be forthcoming as yet.

Will Sedgwick lay there for eight hours, until friends found him and carried him to a farmhouse. Word was sent to Lenox and Boston, and Sedgwick's mother and sister rushed to his side at the military hospital, arriving just before he, too, died.

Lee had been fought to a standstill, and McClellan had proved himself a worthy field general to everyone but Lincoln and the Republicans.

Berkshire men with the Second Massachusetts and those with the Twentieth under division commander General John Sedgwick—himself wounded, but he would recover—fought face to face with the Seventeenth Mississippi and Claudius Sears, battling back and forth over the blood-soaked West Woods and the adjacent cornfields. At one point in the battle, the timely arrival of Sedgwick's troops narrowly rescued the artillery battery of Henry Gansevoort, Melville's cousin, whose isolated guns had been holding back a Confederate attack. The Second Massachusetts suffered about eighty killed, wounded, or missing; the Twentieth had one hundred and thirty-seven casualties. Wendell Holmes, a captain in the Twentieth, was hit in the neck, his second wound, but he would be able to return to action.

Elements of the First Massachusetts Cavalry, with its large number of Berkshire men, were also in the Antietam campaign, although they and their horses were in a weakened condition from prolonged operations on the Carolina coast. In the thick of the battle was the Twenty-first Massachusetts infantry, which participated in the bitter fight over a bridge across Antietam Creek. This bridge was to become known as "Burnside's Bridge" because Union general Ambrose Burnside directed costly frontal attacks to finally capture it. The Twenty-first lost forty-five men at Antietam.

Soon after the battle was over, the Thirty-seventh Massachusetts arrived from the reserves that had been defending Washington, then joined in the cautious pursuit of Lee, as did the Tenth regiment, which had not fought at Antietam.

All the veteran regiments had dwindled from their original thousand-strong establishment to a mere three or four hundred effectives, at most. In the Twenty-first, for example, so many officers had been lost in the course of the last few months that Captain Henry Richardson of Pittsfield had risen to second-in-command. In the Antietam campaign, Richardson had led the men into action. He soon would be promoted to major.

Before long, trains of hospital wagons brought hundreds of medical workers to the field to treat the wounded. Among the workers was Great Barrington nurse Caroline Burghardt, who had made the long, tedious journey from Columbia Hospital in Washington. Part of that journey was by ambulance wagon, passing through crowds of walking wounded, having to move aside for columns of marching infantry and hurrying cavalry, the ambulance jostling slowly along rutted roads jammed with unrelenting traffic. Miss Burghardt and her compatriots labored day after day to save lives and offer what comfort they could to the suffering. Through it all they also had to endure gloomy autumn rains that fell, cold and windblown and merciless.

Lee's invading army withdrew from Antietam, and the North was saved for now from invasion. McClellan was a hero to the Democrats and the soldiers, but a threat to the Republicans, who saw him as a future Democratic presidential candidate. Accusing McClellan of pursuing Lee too slowly, Lincoln and the War Department fired him a second time as the army's commander and replaced him with General Burnside.

Like most of his family, Herman Melville was a moderate Democrat, and he was disturbed and disappointed by McClellan's dismissal. The following is excerpted from Melville's "The Victor of Antietam."

> When tempest winnowed grain from bran,
> And men were looking for a man,
> Authority called you to the van,
>   McClellan:
> Along the line the plaudit ran,
> As later when Antietam's cheers began.
>   * * *
> You, the Discarded, she recalled
> Recalled you, nor endured delay;
> And forth you rode upon a blasted way,
> Arrayed Pope's rout, and routed Lee's array,
>   McClellan:
> Your tent was choked with captured flags that day,
>   McClellan.
> Antietam was your telling fray.

In a letter to a sister not long afterwards, Catharine Sedgwick expressed her deepest agonies of loss and resolve, telling how Will had written, "I have tried to do my duty." Though heartbroken, Miss Sedgwick believed this dying assertion by her nephew was "the simple great truth . . . that takes the sting from death—the victory from the grave. So I am content that my beloved brother's son should die."

With the Forty-ninth at Camp Briggs, Henry Johns walked sentry duty at night.

> After all the bustle of the day, there was something very soothing in the quietness. To be in the midst of a thousand sleeping men, hearing nothing save the measured tread of your fellow-sentries, is like the solemnity of a large city in the small wee hours of the night, or that silence which at times falls on a crowd. It is a capital place for reflecting on what we are leaving, what we are leaving for, and what future we are marching into. . . . Accepting a subordinate's life, that equality may be the birthright of all!

Johns became a commissary sergeant in the Forty-ninth, saying lightly, "there was no military aptitude in me." In his memoirs, he described the companies of the regiment as they assembled at Camp Briggs. For example, he said Company A was "well officered," with twenty-two-year-old Israel Weller as captain; formerly a sergeant with the Allen Guards, Weller was

> well posted in military matters, and having a fondness therefore, will make a superior officer. To his own men he will always be, in thought if not in words, *Is*. Weller. I shall watch Captain Weller's course with some curiosity. He has before him a much harder task than if his men were all strangers to him. They like him, and while he is free with them, they obey him very readily. I fancy he will continue the same cheery, lively spirit, but I mistake the man if he will ever allow a familiarity to degenerate into insolence or disobedience.

Late in September, Captain Frank Bartlett of the Twentieth Massachusetts arrived to take command of Camp Briggs, replacing Colonel William Lee, who had returned to his regiment and led it at Antietam. The wound of Bartlett's amputated leg had healed by now, four months after he had been shot at Yorktown, and he got around well on crutches. His duty was to train the Forty-ninth, although this was not the assignment he wanted. Instead, he longed to return to his beloved Twentieth regiment and take charge of a company again, but Colonel Lee had persuaded him to come to Pittsfield. After all, it could not be denied that an infantry officer on crutches would have great difficulty leading troops into battle.

From the start, the Berkshire volunteers were impressed by Bartlett. Johns wrote: "His appearance denotes much of intelligent energy, and his gentlemanly manner, his soldierly bearing (for he looks the soldier, even on crutches), and our sympathy with him in his great loss have made him at once a universal favorite."

The men had no regulation muskets and still had not been issued uniforms, so they felt somewhat shabby as they paraded in civilian clothing of all colors and shapes. Still, with Bartlett's instruction they were learning to march and maneuver, and though they wore no smart military garb, they felt like soldiers as they answered the drumbeat that called them out for "dress parade" each night.

> Dress parade is followed by supper, and after that we fill up these lovely September twilights and evenings as we see fit, with singing circles, Negro melodies, dances, and occasionally a prayer-meeting, till the drums beat for evening roll-call, which is soon followed by "taps," when lights disappear from all save officers' tents, and quiet rules over the camp.

The men of the Forty-ninth, known as the Berkshire Regiment, were beginning to consider who should be elected as their officers. Johns said the leading candidate for colonel was Great Barrington's Samuel B. Sumner, thirty-two years of age, and "one of our rapidly rising young lawyers, a graduate of Williams College, an ex-State Senator, and a poet and orator of no mean pretensions,"

> and from all I hear, he can have his choice, but he thinks the prosperity of the regiment will be better promoted by choosing a commander from outside.
> He is more than half right there. . . . [Yet] the material for a colonel may be found in our own camp. Two legs are very valuable, but great battles have been won by those who could boast of but one.

The selectmen of Otis offered a reward of $500 for evidence leading to the discovery of the killer of Mrs. Jones and her children. This depressing incident continued to trouble many hearts that autumn, and to it was added a serious outbreak of diphtheria in the southern part of the county.

For the first three days of October, thousands of civilians and soldiers alike tried to put away their troubles for the simple pleasures of the Berkshire Agricultural Fair at the grounds northeast of Pittsfield village.

Harness racing, agricultural and horticultural exhibits, competitions for prize stock and other animals all mingled with a "grand cavalcade of horses" as well as footracing events that were followed by a "spading match" and a plowing match. There were public reports from various societies, and "exercises in the hall" that included music, prayer, and an address by a minister. Outside, the leaves had begun to turn, and hundreds of off-duty soldiers went strolling through the fairgrounds with comrades, ladies, and families. It was during this crisp Berkshire weekend that Frank Bartlett and Agnes Pomeroy fell in love for good. It was a time that the couple would fondly remember.

The Melvilles, too, were on hand to enjoy the fair, for they planned to stay in Berkshire this winter. Their neighbors, the Morewoods, were soon to return to New York City, with doctors insisting that Mrs. Morewood spend some time in a warmer climate to help her lungs recover. She objected, saying there was nothing wrong with her, and went on working for the soldiers as hard as ever, sometimes personally bringing gifts to the men in camp.

Soon after the fair, the war again intruded on Berkshire. The funeral of Will Sedgwick was held from his family home in Lenox. Men from the local Irish community, which held the Sedgwicks in high esteem, carried his coffin the five miles to the Stockbridge burial ground, as once they had carried the coffin of his father, Charles. Men of the Forty-ninth were pallbearers for part of the funeral, which was with full military honors. The long funeral cortege included fifty-four carriages and a company of the Forty-ninth, moving slowly along to the beat of a muffled drum.

Henry Johns wrote:

Yesterday the gifted Major W. D. Sedgwick, of Lenox, was buried. He fell in the ruinous victory of Antietam. Amid the surges of battle, with his dying strength, he wrote in his memorandum book, "I have tried to do my duty." The army has lost a brave and skillful soldier, the nation an *earnest* patriot, and the Forty-ninth an excellent colonel; for, had he lived, there is no doubt he would have been chosen to fill that position. Co. A acted as the guard of honor at the burial, while Captains Sumner, Weller, Garlick, Plunkett, and Lieutenants Francis, Kniffin, Wells, Tucker, Smith, officiated as pall-bearers. They buried him at close of day. The sun was setting and the moon just rising. It was a solemn scene, one long to be remembered. There was the dead hero, and there the Forty-ninth going forth as he had gone, *some* of them perhaps to be brought back like him.

The weekly war news in the papers included stories of men killed and wounded in action, and of anticipated visits by recuperating wounded or by officers who were able to get leave.

There was plenty of other news, of course. In mid-October, a *Pittsfield Sun* editor wrote in the "Local Intelligence" column: "A splendid American Eagle lighted on the old Elm. A friend says this is looked upon by those who believe in mysterious intimations as an evidence of the fact that this town has more than filled its quota."

Apparently, the sighting of a deer in southern Berkshire these days was almost as newsworthy as sighting an eagle, for that autumn the *Sun* reprinted a report published in the *Times* of Hartford, which said a deer had been seen in Monterey. With the county mostly open farmland, much of it grazed by sheep and cattle, and since the old forests had been clear-cut decades ago for lumber and charcoal, deer were quite scarce in Berkshire County.

A news report in 1862 told how Great Barrington had improved communication with the outside world as a telegraph line was finished from the village to Bridgeport, Connecticut. Built by the American Company, the line was completed largely as a result of the efforts of Barrington native Frank Pope, an expert telegraph operator.

As if the South were thumbing its nose at the North, a news item was released stating that a Negro bricklayer had been sold in Charleston for $1,500 in cash, and another seven Negroes, ranging in age from six to thirty-five, had fetched $7,235, "the highest price ever obtained in Charleston."

Also in the Berkshire news was a report that Aaron Holley, originally of Sandisfield, had arrived from his home in Ohio, driving his own team all the way. Holley was accompanied by his third wife, and after a visit with his relations in Berkshire, they intended to return home, driving his team all the way. Holley was ninety-three years of age. He appeared "active, vigorous, and happy," said the *Sun*.

On October 16, the *Sun* reported that "a man named Twining" was suspected of the Otis murders, saying he "had an ungovernable temper, and had had some difficulty with the husband of the murdered woman." Two days before the murder, Twining had enlisted in the Forty-ninth regiment, received his bounty pay, then deserted. His whereabouts were unknown.

Henry Johns wrote that every man of the Forty-ninth respectfully saluted Captain Bartlett, who always returned the salute, even on his crutches, in perfect military style: the back of the right hand to the visor of the cap, then the arm fully extended and brought down to the side.

> You see it is no easy thing to be done *walking* on two crutches, but the Colonel does it, not halting to do it, but while walking on and in the most approved military manner.

Even Bartlett's voice was noble, full of command, and he never cursed, said Johns.

The men were happy when they received uniforms at last—army blues and a broad-brimmed hat. The Berkshire Bible Society did its part by presenting every man with a pocket edition of the New Testament.

> Fully clothed, the regiment has several times marched into town,

creating quite a sensation. Now that they are uniformed, their remarkable *physique* attracts much attention. They are certainly a noble looking body of men.

When not on duty, the enlistees were allowed to go to town to attend church, lectures, and concerts, which they did as squads in the charge of an officer or sergeant. Many heard Massachusetts abolitionist Senator Charles Sumner give an address in Pittsfield, his lecture accompanied by the Hutchinson Family Singers of New Hampshire, who sang antislavery songs that appealed to Johns, an abolitionist like them. Lincoln himself had given the stamp of approval for the Hutchinsons to entertain the troops. General McClellan, on the other hand, had forbidden them from performing in military camps because they enraged so many of those soldiers who did not approve of abolition. This proved to be a small but telling point of friction between "Little Mac," favorite of the Democrats, and "Old Abe" of the Republicans.

An informal election of the Forty-ninth's officers was held, the men choosing their captains and lieutenants, who in turn chose the colonel, lieutenant colonel, and major. Frank Bartlett was unanimously named colonel, Samuel B. Sumner of Great Barrington, lieutenant colonel, and Charles T. Plunkett of Pittsfield, major.

Those results would be confirmed later in official elections, and Johns was pleased.

Not only are the men drilled daily, and are improving rapidly, but the officers also show the benefits of *their* daily drilling by Captain Bartlett. It is a treat to see that man go through the manual of arms. He puts such a finish, such a *vim* to every motion. For two hours at a time he will stand on that remaining leg, till half of us believe he never had any need of the one buried at Yorktown, but it was only a superfluous member or mere ornament. Sometimes we try to see how long *we* can stand on one leg; a few short minutes, and we require the use of both, or find ourselves reeling about like decapitated hens. If the Colonel (I will call him such) needs rest, he takes it as a part of the exercise, so we can not tell which is manual of arms and which rest. The cords of that right leg must stand out like great whip lashes. There is *will* about all this. It is this quiet, intense determination, this fixedness of will, that makes us desire Colonel Bartlett, with but one leg, for our commander, over any other man with the full complement of limbs.

Chapter Fifteen

'FORLORN HOPE'

One enlistee of the Forty-ninth likely had little use for the New Testament presented by the Bible Society: John Mason, reportedly from the Albany, New York, area, was riding in a carriage with a couple of women when he picked a fight with Dalton farmer Henry Harmon on the road. Mason jumped out of the wagon and stabbed Harmon in the belly, ripping it open, then calmly returned to the women and proceeded with them to Munson's hotel in Lanesboro.

There, Mason was soon arrested and charged with murder, a number of witnesses testifying against him. It was subsequently learned that Mason was not the only name he used, and that he had committed a similar crime near Albany, escaping to Pittsfield, where he had enlisted in the Forty-ninth. Mason would be found guilty and sentenced to twenty years in prison.

In early November, the Berkshire Regiment, almost a thousand strong, bade an emotional farewell to friends and family and set off by train for Camp Wool in Worcester, their baggage and supplies having been sent on ahead. Some of the soldiers' families moved in together to be of mutual support while their men were away for the next nine months. Thirty-eight-year-old Corporal John M. Gamwell, born in Tyringham but living in West Stockbridge, was among the oldest volunteers, and as a schoolteacher was well-regarded by his comrades in Company B. One of the regiment's captains was Augustus V. Shannon of Lee, the former singing master who had fled from Texas at the outbreak of the rebellion. More than four hundred and seventy of the troops were farmers.

The weather was bitterly cold, with a snowstorm threatening, and when the regiment arrived at camp well after dark the men were dismayed to find that nothing was ready for them, not even barracks. The storm struck, and Henry Johns thought it the coldest, fiercest of his life. The soldiers had to find what shelter they could, and they tore down fences and sheds to get firewood. There were no blankets and not even coffee, and the Berkshire Regiment suffered miserably through its first night away from home.

In a day or so they were settled, and the entire thousand men squared off for a huge snowball fight. By the end of the month, they would be on their way to Long Island, where they would go into training camp for the winter.

That November, state and national elections gave Democrats notable gains throughout the North, and in the twenty-nine towns of Berkshire, Republican Governor Andrew lost, receiving 3,370 votes to 3,376 for General Charles Devens, the Democratic candidate. Devens had fought at the Ball's Bluff defeat and for a time had commanded the brigade that included the Tenth Massachusetts regiment on the Virginia peninsula. Andrew held on to the governorship, however.

The Melville family prepared to spend the winter in Pittsfield, having rented a house on South Street. They meant to avoid the inconvenience and isolation of Arrowhead in the snowbound months, and this would be easier on everyone, parents and children alike. As they made the move, the Melvilles carried loads of household goods in buggy or wagon trips into town. Melville liked to drive, and he was known for being reckless and going too fast. On November 7, he and his friend, *Eagle* editor Joseph Smith, were passing along Williams Street with a load from Arrowhead when part of the wagon broke down and the horse bolted in fright.

Both men were thrown out, Smith landing on his head, stunned, and Melville seriously injuring his left shoulder, which was broken or dislocated. They were conveyed home by neighbors, and Melville lay abed in extreme pain for days; it would be more than a month before he could get around easily. Melville's already gloomy outlook was even darker now, and he remained dejected much of that winter, brooding and self-absorbed.

Lizzie Melville not only had the war work with Parthenia Fenn as part of her regular duties, but she had a miserably unhappy, invalid husband to care for as well. At least the children were delighted to be living in the village, where they had lots of friends to play with every day.

Trouble erupted among discontented officers of the Tenth Massachusetts, for they did not like their new commander, Colonel Henry L. Eustis of Cambridge, a Harvard engineering instructor and a graduate of West Point. Certainly it would have been difficult for any colonel to replace Henry Briggs, now a brigadier general, but Eustis got off on the wrong foot as soon as he took command late in the summer, after the heavy fighting and serious losses the regiment had suffered.

For one thing, Eustis appeared to lack feeling for the troops, in direct contrast to Briggs, who had actually dug trenches along with them when first they came to Washington. The day he took command, Eustis ordered a dress parade and was unreasonably harsh regarding the appearance of the men, who had been poorly supplied of late, with twenty of them barefoot and others even without trousers. Later, a lieutenant excused some of the men from a drill because they had no shoes, which enraged Eustis, who ordered the lieutenant to have those men carry firewood until told to stop. The lieutenant flatly refused to give the men that order, and he was arrested. His court-martial exonerated him, but he resigned and joined another regiment, where he served honorably until killed in action.

Then Eustis brought in an outside officer to be major—with Governor Andrew's concurrence—which infuriated most of the line officers, who objected to a stranger's being given so important a rank. They waited until the Antietam campaign was over and the fighting done before they resigned, eleven of them together, including Pollock Guard captain Thomas W. Clapp, Captain Samuel C. Traver of the Johnson Greys, and Lieutenant Charles Wheeler of the Pollock Guard. Eustis had them arrested and charged with mutiny, and the news shocked Berkshire, for these were honorable, brave men.

The officers hoped to have their cases heard objectively, but at a time when iron discipline in all ranks was needed to keep the Union army in the field, there was little chance they would have a fair trial. They were discharged from the service. The chaplain of the Tenth regiment wrote a letter to a friend in Pittsfield, and part of what he said was printed in the *Eagle*.

> We are grieved to-day with the result of the trial of our resigning officers, the captains being cashiered and the lieutenants dismissed. I cannot but feel the punishment is out of proportion to the offense. Capt. Clapp has won my admiration for his dignified and gentlemanly bearing. In him we have lost a noble, high-minded officer, and have no idea that his place will be filled by an approximation to his equal. I hope that the ban under which he returns home will not detract from the confidence which he deserves from the public, and that the long and faithful services he rendered his country before this unfortunate affair took place will be duly appreciated.

The *Eagle* editors hoped the case would be laid before President Lincoln with "a good prospect that he will do justice to the discharged officers." That did not happen, and the sentences stood. With the dismissal of Clapp—and since Captain Elisha Smart of the Johnson Greys had been killed—only one of the three captains who had led the high-spirited Berkshire companies away to join the Tenth regiment in the summer of 1861 yet remained in the service: Ralph O. Ives of the Great Barrington Company.

Before long, the Tenth's rigid Colonel Eustis manifested undeniable evidence of alcoholism and even an opium habit, but he remained in command. It was unusual that a West Point graduate of his maturity would still be a lowly colonel, which no doubt gave room for speculation that his superior officers did not have confidence in him. Yet, that spring of 1863, Eustis would be commended for gallantry in action during the Chancellorsville campaign.

Another officer of the Tenth had little excuse, however, for how he brought his own career to an end, and this was a great embarrassment for Berkshire and the Johnson Greys. John W. Howland of North Adams had been regimental quartermaster at the establishment of the Tenth, and in time he rose to be chief quartermaster for the Fifth Corps of the Army of the Potomac, buying supplies and equipment for some ten thousand men, and handling large sums of cash on a regular basis.

By late 1862, Howland had absconded to Canada, having stolen more than $16,500 from the army. He was arrested there in the spring of 1863 by a detective of the War Department and brought back to the United States, where he confessed to having been unable to resist the temptation. Howland had used some of the embezzled money to pay personal debts in Berkshire and elsewhere, and to the chagrin of his debtors, the army demanded the cash be returned. All but $1,200 of the total was eventually recovered.

In the autumn of 1862, Parthenia Fenn of the Ladies' Soldiers' Aid society made another journey to New York City, this time with holiday treats as well as medical supplies for the soldiers in the New England Hospital. She went off just as a howling snowstorm hit the Northeast, one of the few snowfalls to occur in the first half of this unusually dry winter.

The Berkshire Regiment celebrated Thanksgiving of 1862 at Camp Wool, where it was issued new Enfield muskets; finally the men could begin to drill with the real thing. The ladies of Worcester did their part for the Forty-ninth by sewing pockets into their army-issue light-blue trousers.

During the past few weeks, Colonel Bartlett had been away from camp, and he returned wearing an artificial leg and riding a spirited new horse. Bartlett no longer needed crutches, although he kept one slung over his back when he was riding, in case some mishap should damage his wooden leg. The men were delighted to see him, and proud.

Around this time, sheriff's deputies went to Otis Mountain and there arrested Thomas Callendar and his son, James, for the murder of Emily Jones and her children, who had been neighbors. The lawmen took their prisoners, free black men, to jail in Lenox, the Berkshire County seat.

There, James confessed to the murders, saying he and his father had gone out to steal a sheep for food that day and had drunk whiskey that had intoxicated them. Maddened by drink, he said, they had raped the mother, then killed her and the children so there would be no witnesses. The father denied being part of it.

They would be brought before a grand jury at Lenox.

The Twenty-first regiment finally was paid at its encampment on the north side of the Rappahannock River, across from the small Virginia city of Fredericksburg, which was occupied by the Confederates. Like most of the men, Thomas Reed expected an imminent Union advance across the river, and camp gossip suggested that the soldiers did not at all like it. They had seen Confederate earthworks being thrown up on high ground beyond the town, and it was clear that the enemy was ready for General Burnside's attack once he got his army over the river.

On December 2, Reed wrote a letter to his wife, Cynthia, saying he would send her his pay by giving it to the regimental chaplain, who was returning to Massachusetts in a few days and would forward it to her from Worcester. The following day, Reed wrote again:

> Camp in Field near Fredericksburg, Va.
> Dec. 3rd., 1862
> Dear Wife:
> This morning I sent a letter written yesterday in which I intended to have sent the money I got Monday night but the Chaplain preferred carrying the money separate from the letter as he could then carry it about his person, but if in letters, he would be obliged to carry it in a carpet bag, which he considered unsafe. My pay amounted to $30.30 up to Nov. 1st. '62 to which time the men were all paid and I gave the Chaplain $30.00 which he will send you from Worcester by Express. He will leave here tomorrow or next day. . . . [He] told me you would get the money in 10 or 12 days. As soon as you get it write me. You may rest assured that I will spend no money foolishly. I mean to have the benefit of it when I get home, if I live. If not, you and the children will, but I feel assured that an all wise Providence will carry

me safe through and once more I'll enjoy the blessings of a happy home.

Talk about home, let it be ever so homely, it would be a desirable change. I would be satisfied to lie on the bare floor with one of those little stools (I made many years gone by) for a pillow and my blanket to cover me and not say one complaining word. . . .

Reed thought the war would end that winter, but he was troubled by the large number of sickly soldiers he saw every day.

In all my life I never witnessed so many sorrowful looking beings. In fact, despair seemed marked on almost every countenance, and why should it be otherwise, for it is impossible for them to receive that care and treatment they would receive at home, and if they die as many do they are verry quietly laid down to rest and thus their career ends; but I am thankful this war cannot always last, and what a happy time it will be for the boys when they get home.

Less than two weeks later, the people of the North were stunned by news of General Burnside's utterly senseless assault on Lee's strongly entrenched army at Marye Heights, overlooking Fredericksburg.

Burnside sent his troops again and again on direct frontal attacks against a prepared enemy, who mowed them down as fast as they came on. Only the objections of some of his leading generals persuaded the blundering Burnside to call off the slaughter.

One reason for the failure of the attack was that the Union army had been delayed in building pontoon bridges with which to cross the Rappahannock. The Union engineers had come under murderous fire from the Seventeenth Mississippi and Claudius Sears, whose fierce resistance gained Lee at least a day to strengthen his defenses.

Among the courageous Union engineers was Great Barrington's Oliver Harmon, who was serving with a New York unit. Harmon came away unhurt from the exploits of the engineers, who had volunteered to undertake the mission—which someone had aptly called a "forlorn hope."

Federal cannon had bombarded the town of Fredericksburg, where the Mississippians were hiding as they picked off the Union engineers, but Sears's men had held their ground until the Yankees finally got across the river in strength. One of the first three Union regiments to come over the Rappahannock and take on the Mississippians in the street fighting was the Twentieth Massachusetts. The Tenth had crossed downstream, a few miles south of the town.

The First Massachusetts Cavalry was also in the Fredericksburg campaign.

While Mississippi sharpshooters fire from houses in Fredericksburg, Federal soldiers cross the Rappahannock in pontoons; the dead soldier in the foreground lies on a partially completed bridge that was built despite deadly enemy fire from the town.

The tenth regiment, which was kept in reserve, narrowly avoided being among the next troops Burnside wanted to hurl against the enemy. The inexperienced Thirty-seventh Massachusetts, which had been serving in the brigade commanded by General Briggs and then was transferred to one led by General Devens—the recent unsuccessful candidate for Massachusetts governor—experienced its first action at Fredericksburg. The regiment came under direct artillery fire and suffered some casualties, but it did not join the assault. Thomas Reed and the Twenty-first Massachusetts were not so fortunate. Corporal Reed and his company found themselves in line of battle, ordered to charge up a slope littered with the blue of Union dead. At one point, both color bearers of the Twenty-first were shot down as the regiment rushed into withering fire and blinding gunsmoke. The flags were instantly lifted up again, and the regiment charged on, but it soon lost more than a third of its men. Unable to reach the enemy defenses, the Twenty-first had to take cover behind rising ground and from there exchanged unequal fire until after dark, when it was ordered to withdraw. After two more days, the entire Union army retreated back across the Rappahannock, defeated. The Tenth, covering the retreat, was the last regiment to recross.

Burnside was removed from command a few months later.

On December 14, the battle-shocked Corporal Reed wrote home to Cynthia and their children, Emma, sixteen, and "Eddie" (Thomas, Jr.), twelve. Reed considered himself "among the favored ones. Is there not an over-ruling Providence who protects us?"

> Cynth, it is a gay old noise the balls and shell make when bursting and whizzing around your ears but not so much when you have to load and fire and at every step walk over the dead and dying. It's rather sad to see men with their heads blown to pieces who only a moment before were marching by your side.

In a week or two, Reed wrote further about the battle, not sparing his wife the horrible details:

> In the fight of 13th December our colors went down 3 times. One of the color bearers had both arms blown off close to his body by the bursting of a shell and his life was only saved by a book in his breast pocket, which was torn to atoms. The fate of one of the others was not quite so bad. He was shot through the head, while the third one was slightly wounded. . . . Rags we call [the colors], for they are nothing else, they being completely torn in shreds by bullets and covered with blood and brains.

Reed asked whether Cynthia had received the thirty dollars he had sent with the chaplain and said he had sent another letter to their daughter, Emma, enclosing ten dollars. He was impatient to hear the money was safe, especially because he was enduring this soldier's life in order to earn enough to make his civilian life a better one. With the mails often delayed, Reed was anxious for another three weeks about the money sent home, until Cynthia's "verry welcome letter . . . came to hand. . . ."

After the defeat at Fredericksburg, it seemed the North's attempt to save the Union by force of arms might be another "forlorn hope" undertaken with selfless courage and attended by great sacrifice, with little chance of winning final victory.

Claudius Sears was promoted to colonel and transferred westward to take command of a new Mississippi regiment, the Forty-sixth, the last one that

Claudius W. Sears was a native of Peru, Berkshire County, and a graduate of West Point, but long before the war he moved to the South to teach, later enlisting in the Confederate army and rising to become a

state would be able to muster. Brigadier General Edward Perry of the Second Florida regiment and Richmond, Massachusetts, had come back from convalescence in time to lead his brigade, helping to beat back part of the Federal assault at Fredericksburg.

When not serving as provost guard arresting deserters, watching prisoners, or breaking up brawls, the men of the Forty-ninth, still in training on Long Island, could get passes to go into New York City, and in mid-December some of them heard the Reverend Henry Ward Beecher give a lecture. Henry Johns thought him a "provoking character," but said Beecher was unable to touch the "deeper emotion" of the listener's soul. Corporal John Gamwell thought Beecher the "most powerful man I have ever heard."

On December 22, Gamwell went with a friend visiting from Berkshire to look at the Brooklyn Navy Yard, where he saw *Monitor*, which he described in his diary as "unassuming, but nothing dare meet it." Just before Christmas, he enjoyed the city, "decked with evergreens, and all are gay and happy." He attended a concert at Cooper Union that was free to Massachusetts soldiers. Called "Father Kemp's Old Folks Concert," it was "the best thing I ever attended—better than all theaters," he told his diary. Gamwell missed his family, but not just because of the holiday, for his wife was about to give birth.

Gamwell's Christmas Day diary entry read in part:

> How many little hearts at home are made glad by full stockings this morn! How many tears are dropped for the absent one in field or Camp. Goodbye, Noble Fellow—you have done your duty. Your reward will follow in the name you leave to your posterity.

Gamwell celebrated his thirty-seventh birthday on December 29, thankful to be in good health while so many men were "languishing on miserable beds far away from friends and home without hope of ever seeing them in this life."

Two days later, *Monitor* foundered and sank in a storm off the Virginia coast, another unhappy loss to the Union at the end of 1862.

Although overshadowed by the gloom of the Fredericksburg debacle, the fighting on the Mississippi River above Vicksburg put intense pressure on Confederate defenders, although they held out against resolute attacks at places such as Chickasaw Bayou and Arkansas Post.

The 127th Illinois, with South Williamstown's Hamilton Eldridge now its colonel, took part in these engagements, capturing enemy defensive works. Eldridge had his charger shot from under him, and although he suffered severely from fever at times, he was respected as an excellent leader of the regiment, always found at the forefront of the attack. Still, the best of the Union troops could not successfully storm the enemy defenses at Chickasaw Bayou, in Mississippi, and the frontal assaults were reminiscent of Fredericksburg. The Federals, commanded by General William T. Sherman, wanted to renew the attacks and get at the key city of Vicksburg itself. They would soon have to withdraw for the winter, however, and that great bastion of the Mississippi—along with Port Hudson farther downriver—prevented the Union forces from dividing the South in two along the river valley.

At the close of 1862, it appeared that the Confederacy was making good its secession, its armies successful on almost every front. When, in bitter fighting at the turn of the new year and for a few more days into January, a major Union offensive was blunted and stopped at Murfreesboro, Tennessee, the South seemed stronger than ever.

The Thirty-fourth Illinois, with Savoy's Riley Norcott in its ranks, was in some of the heaviest Tennessee fighting. Early in December, before the Battle of Murfreesboro, Norcott wrote two letters home to his mother, Sarah Sanders:

> December 1, 1862. It was very cold this morning, but we set in our tents with a good little fire in the middle so it is very comfortable. One in our company got his leg shot off below his knee. He was a good soldier.

> December 8. Don't expect to stay here much longer for we have orders to have three days rations in our knapsacks and ready to march at a moments warning. There are scouting parties going out every day and have skirmishes with the rebels. All for this time. You need not write again, not until you hear from me. I don't know where we are going to from here. I shant write again until I get to camp.

Mrs. Sanders put the letters away with the rest, not knowing they would be the last from her son. Early in February, a letter from a fellow soldier told that Riley had been killed at Murfreesboro and had been buried in a mass grave.

Since the firing on Fort Sumter less than two years earlier, there had been more than two thousand engagements between North and South. To many in the field, it seemed neither side could defeat the other, and most men were heartily sick of soldiering. Then came what the *Berkshire County Eagle* called "The Great Event of the Age."

President Lincoln chose January 1, 1863, as the decisive moment to issue the Emancipation Proclamation, declaring slaves in secessionist states to be free. Now was the moment to take the ultimate stand against Southern slavery. The war would be to the bitter end, Lincoln was saying, and any foreign power who backed the Confederacy would be condoning the institution of slavery. Not only were the slaves to be free, but Lincoln was more than ever prepared to raise fighting regiments of Negro soldiers. Now they would be enlisted not only from liberated former slaves in captured Southern territory, but free blacks would make up regiments armed to fight for their own cause. Even the most bigoted whites—especially the soldiers—could not deny that thousands of black soldiers joining the Union army would lend much help to defeat the Confederacy.

Few whites, however, expected that blacks would really fight. Instead, they would be laborers, teamsters, guards, thus freeing white men serving in the army to go to the battle front. Blacks would be kept out of the actual fighting, the reasoning went, for it was unimaginable that they would have the grit or courage required to take part in the horrendous, terrifying battles. Yet already there were thousands of black soldiers in new units being formed in the occupied regions of Louisiana and South Carolina, and also in Kansas—usually with the description "native guards." While many were liberated slaves, others were freemen who had never been slaves. How, or whether, they would fight remained to be seen.

Upon hearing of the Emancipation Proclamation, Henry Johns, at the Forty-ninth's camp on Long Island, was proud and relieved and inspired.

> The cause *is* sacred, indeed. . . . We hoped so always; we *know* it now. The Proclamation of Emancipation, dated January 1st, 1863, sweeps from our minds all doubts. The country claims our all. . . . The words have gone forth to be sounded in every slave cabin through the South. "I, Abraham Lincoln, solemnly declare near three millions of slaves free, and will maintain that freedom with all the power of the Government." Grand! never to be forgotten words! words that will grow grander through all the ages; words that will lift up the name of Abraham Lincoln above common names; aye, above the name *Washington*.

Although many in the North refused to say they were laying down their lives for the sake of slave emancipation, men like Johns were thrilled that their cause was now of an even higher order. He looked forward to the raising of black regiments for the final great struggle against the Confederacy.

In one single hour, in some forlorn hope, a man may throw his life against a giant wrong, and in that hour win for truth high vantage ground, and do more for the best interests of the race than by a whole century of peaceful existence.

The words have gone forth. To *all* our flag now means *Freedom*. Those words can never be recalled. The die is cast. We recognize that our nation's life is to be saved by justice and righteousness. . . .

Ere long, men made free by this Proclamation will have the privilege of *fighting* to sustain it. Six months will not roll away before we have many a *corps de Afrique*. Let them come; with their own red right hands let them carve out for themselves honor, freedom, and nationality.

That January of 1863, the Forty-ninth's Corporal John Gamwell had personal reason to celebrate, as his wife gave birth to their second child, another son.

The weather at home was mild, and it was noted that robins and even bluebirds could be heard that winter in Berkshire. Someone wrote a poem for the *Eagle*, praising the beauties of winter and the joys of outings with horse and sleigh. The verses included the line, "Hurrah! then, hurrah for the drifting snow!" A few days later, on February 12, there finally was a real snowfall, good enough for sleighing. A month later came the biggest snowstorm of the season, stopping the trains and closing up the streets of towns, which had to be arduously shoveled clean by volunteers.

One of the features in the *Eagle* that month was an article about Eskimo life, excerpted from a book written by an English explorer.

Chapter Sixteen

NEW SOLDIERS, NEW MONEY

Early in 1863, when the Northern state governments and Washington undertook to raise regiments of free "colored" men, eleven thousand Negro troops were already serving in the Union force occupying parts of the South-eastern coastline, and three thousand more were with Banks on the lower Mississippi. Most had been enlisted—by authority of the War Department—from the local population. There were also five thousand blacks in the United States Navy, a number that would rise to thirty thousand, and soon there would be another sixteen thousand black recruits with the armies operating in the Tennessee-Mississippi theaters. By summertime, there would be ap-proximately thirty thousand Negro troops in the Union army, many of them employed as laborers, but most also drilling as line soldiers, although few as yet had seen action.

Massachusetts ultimately would enlist twelve hundred men for its first Negro regiment and have to start another to accommodate the surplus vol-unteers. In February, Governor Andrew offered Captain Robert Shaw of the Second Massachusetts the colonelcy of the new regiment, which would be designated the Fifty-fourth Massachusetts, the first Negro regiment to be raised in the North. None other than Shaw's father, Francis, came to the Second's encampment at the front to present the governor's offer. Shaw's mother,

Sarah, was an even more radical abolitionist than her husband. For Governor Andrew, there could be no better commander for a black regiment than the veteran soldier son of a leading abolitionist family.

Yet Shaw turned the offer down, for he wanted to remain with the Second Massachusetts, one of the top regiments in the Union army. He wrote about it to his sweetheart, Annie Haggerty, to whom he was soon to propose:

> If I had taken it, it would only have been from a sense of duty; for it would have been anything but an agreeable task. Please tell me, without reserve, what you think about it; for I am very anxious to know. . . . I am afraid Mother will think I am shirking my duty. . . .

Shaw was twenty-five years old and a proven officer who would have been in line for appointment to higher rank in his own regiment. Further, his enlistment would be prolonged if he took command of the Fifty-fourth. He had just another year to go. As he said to Annie, who was in New York then, he wanted "to be at liberty to decide what to do when my three years have expired." Raising a new regiment, training and disciplining the men, was a long-term commitment and sure to be difficult and unrelenting labor. And the mortality rate of infantry colonels was high. Shaw ended the letter by musing that "the hills of Lenox would be a very welcome sight to me, whether they were covered with snow, with grass, or with nothing at all; though just now, I had rather be in New York. I want to see you *horribly* (that is the only word I can think of for it). . . ."

Four days later, Shaw wrote to Annie that he had changed his mind and accepted command of the Fifty-fourth. "Mother had telegraphed me that you would not disapprove of it, and that makes me feel much more easy about having taken it." He said there was no need for him to make his case to Annie for the need for a black regiment, because his mother was with her just then, and Mrs. Shaw was "the warmest advocate the cause can have." What he had to do as colonel was "prove that the Negro can be made a good soldier."

Proving that would not be easy for Robert Shaw or any member of his all-white officer corps, nor for the soldiers of the Fifty-fourth, but it was soon undeniable to Shaw that the men who enlisted were physically and mentally outstanding. Two soldiers in the new regiment were the sons of the famous former slave and prominent antislavery leader Frederick Douglass.

As proud as Massachusetts was to be raising the first black regiment from the North, the Louisiana Native Guards sprang from a militia establishment that had been wearing Louisiana's state uniform even before New Orleans was captured by the Union. Louisiana had permitted Negro militia regiments to exist, and soon after the fall of New Orleans, those units were continued by General Benjamin Butler, who took command of the city. New black regiments were formed, and by early 1863 there were three regiments of Louisiana Native Guards serving in the Union army.

The first Negro regiment officially mustered into the army was the First Louisiana Native Guards, which had a white commander and an all-black corps of officers. That commander was Colonel Chauncey Bassett, a native of Lee who at the start of the war had joined the Eighth Michigan with his late brother Charles.

Immediately after Lincoln's Emancipation Proclamation, members of Berkshire's black community became actively involved in publicly discussing the significance and future prospects of the proclamation, holding lectures, sermons, and discussions. The Reverend Samuel Harrison, pastor of Pittsfield's Second Congregational Church, invited a speaker from nearby Ghent, New York, to give an address on "The President's Proclamation of Emancipation, and the New Responsibilities of the Colored People."

Pittsfield's Reverend Samuel Harrison, instrumental in recruiting men for the Fifty-fourth Massachusetts and later serving as its chaplain, was a key figure in the successful effort to win equal pay for black troops in the Union army.

The Reverend Harrison was also visiting Troy to give his own lectures and to actively encourage men in the audience at "colored men's war meetings" to join the new Fifty-fourth regiment, which began to recruit in February, opening an office in Pittsfield. The *Eagle* said service in the Fifty-fourth was "an excellent opportunity . . . for our colored citizens to refute the slanderers who say that they have not the pluck to become soldiers."

The recruiting effort was immediately an "unexpected success," said an *Eagle* reporter who visited the enlistment office and saw volunteers signing up. He said, "They do not look like men who would be easily frightened." One of the most successful recruiters in western Massachusetts was Sergeant Watson W. Bridge, first sergeant in the Thirty-seventh Massachusetts, who singlehandedly signed up more than seventy men.

Soon, three black recruiters for the Fifty-fourth left Berkshire to find more men willing to enlist. Volunteers Henry Jackson of Pittsfield, H. M. Brewster of Lee, and Phillips A. Backus of Lenox went to Ellsworth, Connecticut, to meet a number of black men who had been drilling under the auspices of that state but as yet had no unit to join. Recruiting for the Fifty-fourth was going well, with Jackson reportedly having enlisted fifty-three men and holding out hope for a full company of approximately one hundred from Berkshire and the surrounding region. The strict physical examination and high health standards would eliminate many—as these did with the white regiments.

The *Eagle* told about Jackson in an article entitled, "Story of a Contraband." The term "contraband" appeared early in the war, when the Federal government declared fugitive slaves from the seceding states "contraband of war," or spoils of war, meaning they no longer belonged to their former masters and were now the responsibility of the government.

Henry Jackson was born in 1827 in Washington, D.C., the son of a slave father and a freeborn mother, and he should have been legally free but had been snatched from his mother's breast and sold at the age of three months. When he was eighteen, and having no formal education, Jackson escaped with the help of a white man from Albany, New York. He later went to Chatham, southeast of Albany and across the state line from Berkshire. First employed on a farm, Jackson later learned the blacksmith's trade, working in the shop nights and mornings to earn his keep, and going to school the rest of the day.

In 1859, Jackson moved to Stearnsville, part of Pittsfield, and married. There he became close friends with the Hancock Shakers, his neighbors, and found employment as a blacksmith with them, earning their respect, a feeling that was mutual. The Shakers were grouped in "families," each with its own workshops, farming operations, and living facilities, though the order was celibate, men and women living separately. The society had large farms and thriving manufacturing shops that usually were in need of extra help, so they often took in outside workers. Jackson worked in the blacksmith shop of the group known as the Church family, according to the *Eagle,* which said "Joseph Patten, the first Trustee of the Church family, rendered him especial assistance in establishing himself in business in the shop where he has since won a high character as a workman, and also the esteem of all who come in contact with him." Then there was the Civil War. According to the *Eagle*:

When the Governor called upon the colored men of the State to rally to the support of the Government, Jackson was one of the first to respond, and being entrusted with a commission to recruit for the 54th Regiment, has been indefatigable and very successful ever since.

With regard to the "capacity of the colored man for taking care of himself in ordinary life," said the newspaper, Henry Jackson's story was "by no means an exceptional one." Although an excellent recruiter, Jackson himself never enlisted.

The Negro community of Berkshire was justly proud of its young men in the Fifty-fourth Massachusetts, but those soldiers were not the first notable blacks to make a mark in the county.

Ever since the 1600s, blacks had been present in Berkshire, some of them freemen, but at first most were servants of Dutch traders from New Netherland, as the colony west of Berkshire was at first known. These traders, with their assistants and slaves, passed through the region while doing business with local Indians and with New Englanders, who had not yet settled the region that became Berkshire. When New Netherland was taken over by the British in 1664 and renamed New York, Dutch influence remained strong in the Hudson Valley, one of the best routes from Berkshire to the outer world, so there was much commerce between the two regions.

Though virtually invisible to historians, blacks in colonial America were part of everyday life, whether as free men, servants, or slaves. In the Northeast, slavery was prohibited early in the 1800s—Massachusetts in 1781 and New York in 1827— but the traditional relationship of wealthy white folk and lifelong black servants continued for decades. Also in Berkshire by mid-century were scores of fugitive slaves who had escaped from the South and been taken into the community rather than journeying on north to Canada. In the 1850s, the "Underground Railroad" had come into being as a secret organization that spirited fugitive slaves to safety. Such practice was illegal and could be severely punished by law, so there was always the danger that authorities, soldiers, or even the slave owner under arms would come in pursuit of escaping slaves.

A few Berkshire people were secret "conductors" or members of the Underground Railroad, among the most prominent being Dr. Henry P. Phillips of North Adams, a much-loved physician and a graduate of the Berkshire Medical College in Pittsfield. Born in Savoy in 1807 into a leading Berkshire family, Dr. Phillips had been an abolitionist since 1840.

There were three "main lines" of the Underground Railroad through Berkshire, which passed the escapees on from hand to hand, hiding them in homes, leading them a little farther on their way to freedom, guiding them, usually at night, over lonely roads, across rivers, and through mountains. One main line came from the west, over the Berlin, New York, mountains to Williamstown and then on to North Adams. From there, the fugitives would cross Hoosac Mountain and the hill towns to Greenfield on the Connecticut River and beyond. Another main line passed through Sheffield and Great Barrington, also aiming eastward to the Connecticut River, and then turning northeast. The third main line was also from the west, over Lebanon Mountain, skirting Pittsfield, where there would have been a federal marshal, and then on to Dalton and eastward.

Fugitives might be led on horseback or hidden under blankets in carts or wagons. The boys of their conductors kept a sharp-eyed lookout ahead and behind for pursuers or for waiting roadblocks set by the authorities. After reaching the next "station stop" with its own conductors, they would leave their charges and return home, exhausted. A Berkshire writer who knew these conductors and their scouts said years later, "[T]hey so skillfully covered their tracks that there was never anything to give them away but some very tired horses in some home barns in the early mornings."

In Berkshire, as in many other Northern communities—especially in the cosmopolitan cities of Philadelphia and New York—some blacks had long ago achieved considerable success. One of the best-known black men in Berkshire was Festus Campbell, born in Louisiana and formerly the slave of a physician, from whom he escaped about ten years before the Civil War.

Campbell came to Pittsfield and was befriended by Dr. Robert Campbell, whose surname he took. From time to time, Festus Campbell was employed as the body servant to several leading gentlemen of the region. One of these was George P. Briggs—eldest son of Governor George N. Briggs—who took Campbell along on overseas journeys. Campbell was brilliant at learning languages, and he amazed and delighted his employers by his ready familiarity with several languages and cultures from Europe to Africa and Asia. He was considered an invaluable companion for Berkshire gentlemen going to foreign countries, and in time became a successful businessman, with a greenhouse in Pittsfield and a popular lunchtime restaurant at the railroad depot.

Tall and straight, always impeccably dressed, and with elegant manners, Campbell was also full of fun, a skilled ventriloquist who could delight companions with his ready good humor. He was a highly regarded member of the Pittsfield Baptist Church, where he taught the Bible school for boys. He sometimes also attended the Second Congregational Church and assisted the Reverend Harrison in conducting services, for Campbell was a fine speaker.

Among the leading black families of Berkshire were the descendants of pioneers named Potter and Jones. Patriarch William Potter, part Mohawk, was a successful farmer in the western part of Pittsfield. Two of his many sons, Morris and Josiah, were outstanding field workers who hired out for wages when they were young and were reputedly unmatched in ability. Morris eventually went West to seek his fortune, and Josiah became a teamster. Another of the patriarch's sons, William, worked for the Julius Rockwell family in Pittsfield until moving to Lanesboro to cultivate a small farm and teach music. Another son, Charles, served with the Fifty-fourth.

Chauncey Jones came to Pittsfield in 1820 at the age of six and had locally well-known sons who were remarkably talented. Among them were Chauncey, a left-handed violinist, and Dennis, a professional angler, expert at fishing for trout. Other well-known blacks in early and mid-nineteenth-century Berkshire included Jack Lloyd, a former New York slave who became a

Lanesboro hostler, and his son Augustus, a wealthy Cheshire lumber dealer. A pioneer barber in North Adams was Ben Williams, who was very successful.

Perhaps the most famous black person of early Berkshire was Elizabeth Freeman, who in 1781 became the first American slave to be legally set free. Known as "Mum" Bett—it was common for elderly black women to be called "Mum," or "Aunt," and for elderly men to be called "Uncle"—she had been abused while the slave of a prominent Ashley Falls resident and had run away, refusing to return. Judge Theodore Sedgwick of Stockbridge, father of Catharine, took up Bett's cause in what became a landmark legal case.

Arguing that slavery had never been sanctioned in Massachusetts and that the state constitution of 1781 outlawed it, Sedgwick won Bett's freedom, and she came to live the rest of her years with his family, taking the name Elizabeth Freeman. Miss Sedgwick remembered "Mumbet," as she fondly called her, from her childhood, describing the dignified Freeman as "queen of the domain." In time, Freeman became a landowner, and after her death at the age of eighty-five was interred in the Sedgwick family plot.

In Williamstown at mid-century lived a well-known, eccentric woman named Dinah, who had a great love for Williams College. Dinah was sure to attend every commencement and knew the professors and scholars by name, reputedly being more familiar with the students than were the college officials. She treated collegians as her equals, and delighted in debating with them, matching quotations, and exchanging repartee. It was said that, as a child, Dinah had been inadvertently left behind in a Williamstown inn by a group of fleeing fugitive slaves. By the 1860s, she lived near the railroad depot with a brother who had returned to the town from the north.

A nineteenth-century Berkshire writer described Dinah's presence at the college's annual graduation:

> It was a day she never missed, be the skies humid or torrid, for handshake, welcoming of former student friends, and farewells to the newly fledged bachelors of art, while none of her acquaintance in the cloud of witnesses gathered there missed her joyous, mirthful, and pleasing greeting. All through those memorable old-time graduation exercises, with her glowing face, beautiful teeth and smiling sprightly chat, she would gracefully glide about the body of the old church on the hill, and from thence to the porch and galleries in quest of literary friends and acquaintance. Clad in her brightest dress and gaily beribboned bonnet, setting off her charcoal blackness, she was a prominent feature of these old-time gatherings and will be remembered by most of the older graduates of this institution. . . .

Two former slaves who had escaped from the South to Berkshire claimed to be members of an African royal family, stolen from their homes as children. One was Prince John Gabriel and the other Prince Williams, both residents of Pittsfield.

One of the most dignified black gentlemen of early Berkshire was Agrippa Hall, a Stockbridge pioneer and Revolutionary War veteran who had been the body servant of the Polish engineer officer Thaddeus Kosciusko, one of Washington's officers. In the 1800s, Hall was a servant of the Sedgwick family in Stockbridge, and Miss Sedgwick predicted that Hall was "one of the few who will be immortalized in our village annals." Indeed, Hall's portrait was painted, and when the new Stockbridge library was finished late in 1864 his picture was hung there. Hall's widow, in her eighties, still lived in Stockbridge at the time.

Another leading Negro family of Berkshire were the Burghardts of the Great Barrington area, one of whom, Henry F. Burghardt of Lee, was in the Fifty-fourth. In 1868, a daughter of this family would become the mother of William Edward Burghardt Du Bois, who was destined to be one of the great educators, philosophers, and social activists of his day. W. E. B. Du Bois would spend his "early days of rollicking boyhood," as he put it, "away up in the hills of New England, where the dark Housatonic winds between Hoosac and Taconic to the sea."

At the start of 1863, a letter to the *Eagle* said the soldiers of the Thirty-fourth Massachusetts had organized another regimental band, though it was unofficial. The new band had sixteen pieces and was directed by Timothy Griffin of Company E, who formerly had led the Great Barrington Cornet Band.

Among the Berkshire men to be found in regiments from other states was Pittsfield's Frederick Taylor of the Seventh Connecticut. In January, the *Eagle* reported that Taylor was sick and in the hospital in occupied Port Royal, South Carolina, but was expected to be discharged soon and "sent North, if able to be removed." Newspapers regularly printed lists of sick and wounded local men in the military hospitals—lists laboriously prepared and updated by Sanitary Commission workers.

Two Florida, Massachusetts, men served in the Twentieth Iowa regiment: Lovell D. Nelson and William Brady. A number of Berkshire men rose to high rank in other states, including Byron Laflin of Pittsfield, who early in 1863 was promoted to colonel of the Thirty-fourth New York regiment, with a Lieutenant Doty of Hancock as his adjutant. In March, North Adams friends of newly promoted Lieutenant Patrick Riordan of the "Irish Brigade" presented him with a sword, sash, and revolver worth seventy-five dollars. When Pittsfield was paid a visit by Lieutenant Chester W. Swain of the famous Berdan's Sharpshooters—a crack outfit—the *Eagle* proudly announced it, which was understandable, because Swain was the former foreman of the newspaper's print shop.

"Lieutenant S. has seen some pretty rough service," wrote the editor, saying Swain was home on furlough after service of eighteen months, "but we are glad to say he looks even better than when he left."

Loyalty to the government was an increasingly important and contentious question in this time, and "Union League" chapters were being formed to promise "unconditional" devotion to the cause of maintaining the Union. By early 1863, one of the first such chapters had been established in Dalton. In some cases, patriotic employers demanded that their workers swear their loyalty. For example, the principals of the Goodrich Company woolen mill of Glendale, in Stockbridge, warned employees that the mill was "loyal territory" and that "disloyal talk" would result in dismissal.

On its front page late this winter, the *Eagle* ran a minister's lengthy sermon on the subject of "unconditional loyalty" and its importance to the Unionist cause. The *Eagle* also pointedly defined the term "Copperhead," which was given to Northerners sympathetic with the cause of the South: Unlike a rattlesnake, said the newspaper, a copperhead gives no warning before it strikes.

The lengthening war was turning out to be a boon for business. Signs of prosperity resulting from supplying the Union war machine could be seen all over Berkshire this spring of 1863, as mills expanded and others operated around the clock.

The paper collar mill of Thomas Colt in Pittsfield was running nonstop to keep up with demand; in North Adams, the O. Arnold & Co. printing works invested $100,000 in new buildings and modern equipment; and in Lee an extensive foundry was added to the McLaughlin Machine Shop. Pittsfield partners C. L. and S. N. Russell were soon to build a new woolen mill on Otaneaque Street; shoe manufacturers in North Adams were prospering; and in the countryside newly planted fields of flax were being grown as a substitute for the Southern cotton that was no longer available to the county's mills.

The *Eagle* applauded the return of flax, saying it was "just like old times," when this crop had been grown locally and spun into thread for weaving linen cloth—that was in the days before cotton had become king for textile manufacturers in the North as well as for the plantations of the South. Nowadays, Egyptian cotton growers were benefiting from the Northern blockade of Southern seaports, and Egyptian cotton was finding its way to Berkshire County. There, mills also turned out vast quantities of woolen cloth for military uniforms. The *Eagle* reported that an Adams manufacturer had placed an order for $50,000 worth of Egyptian cotton, and that in the past year Egyptian production had leaped from 105,000 bales to 180,000 bales.

Some Southern cotton was again reaching New York City from the port of New Orleans, which was occupied by Union troops—including the Thirty-first Massachusetts, now garrisoning the city and its environs. By February, the Forty-ninth Massachusetts would also be in Louisiana, preparing for a campaign to capture Port Hudson and thus take control of the lower reaches of the Mississippi.

For the most part, wool was the only available fiber for Northern cloth these days, and this was a boon to Berkshire, where sheep-raising predominated and many rolling pastures were dotted with thousands of sheep. Because of the increased demand for wool coupled with the forces of inflation, the price of wool was rising, and so was the value of good sheep, as indicated by an *Eagle* report that said a leading Vermont sheep keeper had declined an astounding offer of $50,000 for fifty of his best sheep. "The prices of sheep never ranged so high as at present," said the newspaper, adding that Williamstown's Calvin R. Taft had recently paid $175 for thirty-five sheep, a more normal transaction.

> The high price of wool is turning the attention of western agriculturists also to keeping of sheep, and extraordinary prices are asked and realized. Six dollars a head have been obtained for large flocks in Michigan, and even this is refused now by farmers generally.

It seemed every industry in Berkshire was booming, including fine-quality paper manufacturing, which three years earlier had been in a severe depression. The *Adams News,* reported that countywide more than $923,000 had been invested in writing-paper mills and machinery, an industry with annual revenues of $2 million and employing almost twelve hundred persons. As an indication of the boom at Pittsfield, the newly established Federal income tax listed Taconic Woollen Mills, which paid $1,326 in taxes for November, as consistently paying the highest monthly tax, with a total of $19,527 paid by all Pittsfield businesses from September to November of 1862. By comparison, Richmond businesses paid less than $160 in that period. The lowest Pittsfield taxpayer paid twenty-four cents.

The income tax was crucial to financing the war effort, and taxation was so successful that it gave the industrialized North an insurmountable advantage over the relatively impoverished South, which desperately lacked cash, foreign credit, and manufacturing output. If the North could sustain the will to fight despite the terrible losses in the field, then time would be on its side rather than in favor of the South. With tremendous profits to be made from the war, many on the Northern home front were quite willing to let the conflict continue no matter how many lives were lost or who suffered.

Not all Berkshire prosperity was channeled into private pockets and bank accounts, of course, and this May of 1863, in the very depth of the war, work commenced on a new Stockbridge library that would cost $3,000. Donations from the community came in swiftly, with a surplus of $1,500 raised, and even the building lot was donated. The library was to be finished by the fall.

The arts, too, benefited from the new prosperity, as first-rate performers came through Berkshire this spring, including pianist Louis Moreau Gottschalk, who gave a concert at the Maplewood Institute in Pittsfield. The Louisiana-born Gottschalk was perhaps the most famous American pianist of the day, and had toured all over the country, playing even for President Lincoln and members of Congress.

By 1863, new United States paper money, popularly known as "greenbacks," was in circulation, and it began to replace privately issued paper currency. At the outbreak of war, private currency had been necessary for doing business, buying and selling, because so little government money was in circulation at the time. Local businesses often issued their own notes— usually for amounts under a dollar and nicknamed "shinplasters" because of their doubtful worth—and promised to redeem them, payable in goods or services. Naturally, there were disadvantages, for a shinplaster issued by a business in Tyringham might not be accepted as currency in Williamstown, because it was too time-consuming to make the journey for redemption.

Early in 1863, the newspapers of Berkshire announced that local banks were about to stop accepting shinplasters as currency because greenbacks were so readily available. Yet, even though the banks would no longer accept this private money, said the *Eagle*, "No alarm need be felt by the holders of these necessary evils issued by parties in [Pittsfield] as they are all honest men who will redeem their promises to pay at their own counters."

Postage stamps were also viable currency and regularly used as such, exchanging hands again and again until the stamps were soiled, worn, and virtually useless for posting a letter.

Northern Berkshire was pleased to hear in this time that Governor Andrew now looked favorably upon the continuation of work in the Hoosac Tunnel project.

For all the thousands of men entering the army, there were still enough able-bodied criminals in Berkshire to keep the sheriff busy, including one Gunn, the alleged leader of a gang of chicken thieves, who was locked up in the Pittsfield jail late in the winter. The *Eagle* reported that the sheriff put the troublesome Gunn into a set of handcuffs attached to a chain fixed to a staple driven into a beam, and then "left him to sleep in safety."

> Gunn didn't do any such thing, but by some means drew the staple in the night and skedaddled. The last seen of him was at the Hancock

Shakers, where he tried to induce one of the brethren to relieve him of his uncomfortable ornaments, giving that he had been convicted of liquor selling and escaped. "Go thy way," was the reply, "I think they be rightly on thee." And he went his way "accoutered as he was." We pity the hen-fanciers of Columbia County.

Just over the mountain from Hancock, Columbia County, New York, had another large Shaker community, in New Lebanon. It was unlikely, however, that Gunn found anyone there willing to break his shackles. Although the Shakers were a utopian, communistic sect that willingly took in strangers—"the world's people," as non-Shakers were termed—offering food and lodging in return for honest work, the believers were no starry-eyed idealists who could not recognize a confirmed chicken thief. Especially when he was wearing handcuffs.

Not all the Berkshire news was about criminals or military defeats and casualties or the fortunes of local business. Early in 1863, the *Eagle* announced the marriage of Miss Nellie Stearns of Windsor to Edson L. Harrison, a soldier with the Thirty-fourth regiment, stationed near Alexandria, Virginia. A week later, however, the newspaper ran a retraction, saying the announcement of the marriage was incorrect, and

> Miss Stearns informs us that she is not married to Mr. Harrison, and does not intend to be, and that she has not been to Alexandria, or near it, and of course the whole story was a fabrication of some scoundrel, whose name we have taken means to discover, and shall make known if we succeed. We received the marriage notice from a correspondent who was, probably, himself deceived.

Another week later, the paper said the person who gave the false information about Miss Stearns and Mr. Harrison was none other than Harrison himself, and this was the third time he had lied about a young woman accepting his marriage proposal.

In addition to the dynamic temperance movement active in the county, an unmistakable religious revival had manifested itself all over Berkshire by 1863. Perhaps this revival sprang from reaction to the grinding, daily uncertainties of the war and the heartache of loss and separation. Perhaps it was because religious groups were prospering from the war economy and therefore able to stimulate growth in their congregations and construct new houses of worship. Likely it was a combination of reasons, as the year started off with a national day of fasting and prayer—"to seek aid in the manner of our fathers," announced Governor Andrew. Then followed observances of "The World Week of Prayer," and religious enthusiasm remained strong throughout the spring of 1863. The *Eagle* regularly reported on the religious fervor, with the following being typical:

> The religious denominations of South Williamstown are enjoying a season of religious interest by which all the several churches are benefited. The meetings are held in concert, and work in harmonious action with almost unparalleled success. Already, more than a hundred have become the hopeful subjects of converting grace. Dr. Ransom of Cheshire, who is an evangelist of the primitive stamp, has been preaching to the people with much success.

Likewise, the papers reported unusual expressions of fervor in religious revivals among the Baptists in Florida and at houses of worship in Sheffield, as well as at a series of public lectures at the First Congregational Church in Pittsfield. Lenox, Richmond, and Savoy revivals were noted, in both the Congregational and Baptist churches. In one meeting, the Richmond Methodist Episcopal Church accepted forty people on probation.

In North Adams, the Roman Catholic community was prepared to build a church for $25,000, and the Congregationalists in that town were raising funds for a new house of worship of their own. One S. Whitten of Colrain, a community across the Franklin County line, announced he would double his promised thousand-dollar donation if all previously committed donors also doubled theirs.

As the northern Virginia weather turned milder at the end of winter, Pittsfield's Corporal Thomas Reed and his Twenty-first Massachusetts were loaded aboard transports and sent down the coast to Newport News, Virginia, a posting that suited him just fine. There was little sign of serious action in the offing, and the troops had plenty to eat, including an abundance of the finest oysters Reed had ever tasted. He insisted that Cynthia not try to send him things that would cost her money, adding that he was as comfortable as he could make himself, though homesick and longing for her.

Reed also shared with her some soldier slang, the sort of vernacular that had developed among the troops.

> Cynth, I never get the blues and am quite contented. You see I make necessity a virtue. What I can't help I endure, but home to me has lost none of its pleasures. . . . Now to tell the truth I can think of no one I would like to see more than *my old gal Cynth.* I candidly believe I should *boo-hoo right e-out*, as the Yankees say.

Reed said he was sending presents of things that had been taken from some of the destroyed homes at Fredericksburg—"Contraband of War," as he described it. These included rings, two buttons "that are pure Secesh and were never soiled by Northern hands until they came into my possession," a brass ring from a hotel chandelier, and some tobacco. He told Cynthia not to expect him to get leave any time soon.

> You allude in your letter to persons getting furloughs; it is *a big thing in Canterbury*. If a person has money enough to pay his expenses home and back again, then there is not much difficulty in getting away, on the contrary if he has not got the rocks it's useless for him to think of seeing home.

Soon afterwards, Cynthia mailed him cash, and Reed sent it right back, admitting, "I am sadly in need of money but not bad enough to take money that you need more than me." He was extremely troubled that Cynthia and the children were suffering because he had not been paid in months. His family had found another place to live, and he was concerned that Cynthia would overexert herself in the move. He told her to hire what help she needed and to pay them when he sent her the money.

> [W]hat worries me now is how you are to get along. As yet I cannot say definitely when I shall be paid off. When I get it I will send immediately.

On March 20, Reed had to report that in usually balmy coastal Virginia he was writing with benumbed fingers, and that the army was experiencing "one of the severest snow storms that I have witnessed since the cold weather set in last Fall." He said the regiment was expected to move off on transports soon, but he did not know where. He also asked Cynthia to send him a stamp with each letter she wrote so he could use it to write back, for he had no money to buy his own stamps, which cost three cents.

By mid-April, the Twenty-first had been transported back north by steamer and then cross-country by cattle car, arriving in hilly Kentucky. The regiment was not paid until then, when Reed received fifty-two dollars, representing four months of service. He was seeing little action other than occasional forays in futile pursuit of rebel raiders, who attacked supply wagons and trains and stole everything they could carry off, including the mail. Reed was sorry not to be able to send all the money home, especially because Cynthia needed it during the move.

> Enclosed I send you ten dollars. I am afraid to send more at a time as the mail is likely to be attacked. . . . Cynth, I would willingly forgive

all Uncle Sam owes me if I could have been there to help you as I once was, but I live in hopes that the time is not far distant when we shall again enjoy each others society.

Soon, Reed and the regiment were comfortably situated at Mount Sterling, Kentucky, carrying out provost duty and winning the respect of the locals, who were glad for the stability and peace after war had swept back and forth over them. Here, there was little hard work to be done and even less soldiering in the field, and Reed's health was good. The occupying Massachusetts soldiers were well-liked by the civilians, and Reed told of men becoming involved with local women. He, of course, was not.

The boys are most of them having a gay time with the gals; they are with few exceptions engaged to be married, no time fixed upon and if I'm not much mistaken never will be.

Chapter Seventeen

1863: A SPRINGTIME OF DEFEAT

At the sprawling military camp on Long Island, Henry Johns was the Forty-ninth's quartermaster, responsible for issuing supplies, which meant he was likely to be behind the lines when the others went into action. Yet Johns was determined never willingly to be confined to a safe place when the call to arms came.

Although the regiment had been busy with duty as provost guards—arresting more than twelve hundred men absent without leave in New York City—some of the men were falling ill and dying, even here in training camp. Green troops had to learn soldiering the hard way, not only by repetitious marching, drilling, and handling of firearms, but also learning how to stay dry and warm, to eat properly and avoid contracting the fevers that were so common among unseasoned troops. Men who did not take care of themselves would become ill, and recovery was never certain in an army camp.

Johns thought it best that the weak and sickly be weeded out now and go home to recover, before they had to be sent back from the front, doomed to die:

> [W]e are going to the most unhealthy part of the South, . . . where many of us will find graves even if we never see an armed rebel. . . .
>
> Four months have passed away and no pay. This delay works out

real suffering to soldiers' families, especially in those States that do not provide State aid to the families of volunteers. Bless Old Massachusetts! Her provident legislation assures us that *our* families are not entirely destitute. [Soldiers also] need money, if for nothing else, to buy tobacco. You may preach anti-tobacco with some hope of gaining a few converts anywhere save in camps. Give a man very many unemployed hours, and tobacco, if not a necessity, is a wonderful solace. The pipe, the fine-cut, makes up the deficiency in quantity or quality of food, and is a positive, indescribable luxury. The sutler trusts each soldier to goods amounting to two dollars per month, but as most of them have exhausted the credit, the prospect of going South without money is anything but pleasant.

By late January, the Forty-ninth had been loaded aboard the steamer *Illinois* and sent down the coast toward the Gulf of Mexico and eventually New Orleans. It was a miserable, stormy journey, and the men were almost all seasick. One suffering fellow at the ship's rail accidentally let his false teeth fall into the ocean. As the regiment proceeded southward, the weather grew warmer and more humid, a drastic contrast to the winter temperatures of New England. The climate would soon become even more steamy, with mosquitoes rampant, and men would fall feverish and die. Colonel Bartlett worried about how hot Louisiana would be in July.

"We are likely to find out, I guess," he wrote in his journal, feeling sickly himself, although his men did not know it. "Three hours of a cool northern breeze, and a good dinner at home . . . would make me all right."

By February, the regiment was in Louisiana. Despite the burden and pain of his artificial limb—a "ball and chain of a leg," he called it—Bartlett sternly drilled his men, inspected their camps, and supervised the digging of earthworks. He even grabbed a shovel himself to show how it was to be done. Henry Johns said, "The soldierly neatness of our Colonel is apparent in the superiority of our rifle-pits over those thrown up by other regiments. . . ."

The Forty-ninth might be sneered at by older regiments as just a nine-month outfit that would be here and gone before anyone noticed, but Bartlett treated them like three-year men. They took pride in how they performed as well as in their daily dress parade, when he required them to turn out wearing white gloves with spic-and-span uniforms and firearms. Bartlett curbed the Berkshire-born tendency to hold public gatherings, as they did at home to democratically discuss problems or questions. This was a "task of peculiar delicacy," wrote his biographer. But he did it, and at the same time pushed them to be good volunteer soldiers. As a result, the Forty-ninth gradually earned the respect of the older, three-year regiments, although it had yet to prove itself in battle.

As quoted by his biographer, Bartlett told the men he was pleased with how they were drilling, loading, and firing, and he said "if they would only do as well, keep as steady, and fire as coolly in a real action as they did then, not fire until they got the word from me, no matter how near the enemy might approach them,—when they did fire, aim low, at the enemy's knees (if near),—they need not be afraid of anything under heaven in the shape of an enemy."

The Forty-ninth believed in Bartlett, and when the spring found them marching back and forth on inconclusive maneuvers in the lower Mississippi valley, they had willingly put their lives in his hands. Bartlett harbored one private dread, which he expressed in his journal: "I only hope I shall not get shot until after I have had the regiment in one good fight, for really they seem to be so entirely dependent on me, that if I should get knocked over at first, I don't like to think what would become of them."

The Forty-ninth was nothing like the veteran Twentieth Massachusetts regiment, which Bartlett had longed to rejoin, and in which he once had preferred to be a captain rather than be "colonel of any regiment that might be raised." The Twentieth was recognized as one of the best regiments in the Union army, and Bartlett's experience with it set high standards for the Forty-ninth.

Herman Melville had seen the shining qualities of Frank Bartlett during the time the new regiment was being raised in Berkshire. Melville and Bartlett had attended social events together, including at the Morewoods, where the colonel was a favored guest. Struck by how young Bartlett was to be bearing such great responsibility, Melville later wrote verse entitled "The College Colonel."

> He rides at their head;
> A crutch by his saddle just slants in view. . . .
>
> A still rigidity and pale—
> An Indian aloofness lones his brow; . . .

In northern Virginia, the Thirty-seventh Massachusetts regiment was—like the Forty-ninth—also suffering from lack of pay, and at one point was six months in arrears. A soldier wrote back to the *Eagle* that "the richest man in the regiment was an officer who had $4.50 in hand."

Not only were active soldiers not being paid their salaries by the government, but the families of soldiers who had died were also suffering from the War Department's many shortcomings. By March 1863, the widow of Pittsfield's John Merchant—Merchant had been killed at Ball's Bluff serving with the Twentieth regiment—still had not received a penny from his pension. The *Sun* reported the comforting news that Mrs. Merchant had a surprise visit at her home on East Housatonic Street from a group of friends who gave her sixty dollars in cash and more than forty dollars' worth of household goods and other valuable items.

In mid-March, Captain Robert Shaw (not yet officially a colonel) took leave from the Fifty-fourth's training camp near Boston and traveled to Berkshire to visit Annie Haggerty and her family at their country home in Lenox.

Shaw and his fiancee called on the Sedgwicks, and he related to them his last meeting with Will Sedgwick on the evening before Antietam. Having spent time as a student in Germany, Shaw would have been able to converse freely with Will's widow, Louisa, in her own language. He wrote to his mother about the visit to his late friend's family:

> I had a great deal to tell about him. His little girl wanted to hear all about her father. His mother is one of the most patriotic women I have seen, and seemed to feel proud that her son had died for his country.

Shaw got back to Boston just before a blizzard hit western Massachusetts after a relatively snowless winter. In a subsequent letter to Annie, he told about his regiment's volunteers from Berkshire: "To-night we received quite a large squad of men from Pittsfield. They seem to be very patriotic up there."

Although the Fifty-fourth was successfully recruiting, the regiment was not having such an easy time when it came to the promised financial support of the national government: the bounty of one hundred dollars was not to be paid until the termination of the enlistment, unlike the bounty for whites, which was paid half on entering the army and half on discharge. The black soldiers reluctantly accepted that, as long as they were paid the thirteen dollars a month that was paid to whites. Governor Andrew had promised just that, as did the regiment's official recruiting posters, but the reality would be seen on payday.

Rumor was that the Fifty-fourth would be sent to the Carolina coast, near New Berne, and there brigaded with other black regiments that had been raised locally from liberated slaves. Before the regiment departed, Shaw and Annie Haggerty were to be married in New York City and would honeymoon in Lenox.

In early April, George Massey of Richmond, Massachusetts, was mustered out of the Seventy-first Pennsylvania—the California Regiment—for medical reasons. Massey, the former schoolteacher, had seen considerable action from the very first, and after four months in Libby Prison had suffered much in his health and could not have kept up with the hard marching his regiment was about to do in the coming spring campaign. He was leaving a year before his enlistment was up, but since it was not easy to receive a medical discharge, he must have been seriously ill or disabled.

That spring, Berkshire families connected with the Thirty-seventh were stunned and heartsick to hear that one of the regiment's favorite young officers was absent without leave.

Lieutenant Thomas F. Plunkett, Jr., had been a promising staff officer serving with General Devens, when he took a five-week furlough and never returned. The *Eagle* editor expressed dismay, beginning a short report by saying, "It is with the utmost pain and reluctance, . . ." Certainly whatever Plunkett had witnessed and endured in his half year at war must have been horrible, but other good men were enduring it, many even thriving as soldiers on a crusade for the Union. The folk at home seemed unable to understand why such a "brave and able officer" who had been "highly esteemed" by all, should have deserted.

Whatever Plunkett's reasons and wherever he was—it was said he had gone to Europe—there was not much room in Berkshire for forgiveness.

Late in April, Plunkett's Thirty-seventh regiment moved out to take part in another storming of Marye Heights above Fredericksburg in northern Virginia. The regiment was in the Sixth Corps, commanded by Major General John Sedgwick, part of the Army of the Potomac that now was led by Major General Joseph Hooker, a Massachusetts man.

Hooker, who had replaced the incompetent Burnside, hoped that Lee would mistake the Fredericksburg assault for the primary Union offensive. While the Confederates were distracted, Hooker's main army would march around to attack Lee's left flank. If Lee held Marye Heights in strength, then the diversionary Union attack surely would end in another bloody repulse, but Lee cunningly withdrew most of his army and went to meet Hooker's main force at the crossroads called Chancellorsville.

The Tenth and Twentieth Massachusetts regiments also took part in the Marye Heights assault, although the Twentieth was not in the heaviest fighting. The battle was described in a letter from a soldier of the Tenth that was published by the *Berkshire Courier*.

Letter from the Tenth
Banks's Ford, Va., May 5, 1863

Mr. Editor;—As I have but little time to write, I can only give you a short account of the battle here.

The 6th Corps occupied Fredericksburg . . . and immediately prepared to storm the enemy's works. While the infantry were getting ready the artillery engaged and succeeded in silencing the enemy's battery. Everything ready, the order came to "charge," and immediately the column commenced to advance. The enemy poured a sharp fire from their rifle pits on the advancing column, and our men fell thick and fast, but on we pressed; and on reaching the foot of the hill, sent up a defiant shout and rushed upon them, capturing a large number of prisoners and two pieces of artillery. . . .

The enemy fell back about three miles and took a position in a dense wood, and prepared to give us battle. At 5 p.m. the light brigade forming the front line charged into the woods, and were repulsed with heavy loss, the 93d Pa., losing their colors. The second line advanced and were met by a division of the enemy, and also forced to fall back. The third line (our brigade) . . . then advanced and poured a galling fire on the advancing foe, which checked them, and on our column pressed and drove them into the woods, and ending the fight for this day. . . .

The assault on Marye Heights succeeded. For the Thirty-seventh, Tenth, and Twentieth Massachusetts regiments, the victory was bittersweet revenge. Unfortunately, the gallantry of the attacking force was wasted, for Hooker's Army of the Potomac was soundly defeated by Lee at Chancellorsville. In the main army was the Second Massachusetts, fighting hard and with success, but at last being forced to withdraw with the army.

While the rest of Hooker's army was retreating across the Rappahannock, the Tenth regiment came under heavy fire at Salem Heights, losing sixty-six men killed or wounded. The Thirty-seventh, too, was heavily engaged, holding an exposed position in John Sedgwick's line, repelling several attempted enemy advances, and helping prevent yet another Confederate victory. So, too, was the Twentieth in this engagement at Salem Heights. At dusk, the Thirty-seventh covered the unhappy withdrawal of Sedgwick's force back across the Rappahannock, leaving Fredericksburg and Marye Heights again in enemy hands.

The First Massachusetts Cavalry regiment also was in the Chancellorsville campaign, and for the first time had been gathered in strength as many of its various detachments were collected—although not its four companies serving in Florida campaigns. Further, almost three hundred new recruits from Massachusetts were added to the regiment. Whether or not the main armies were fighting pitched battles, cavalrymen were constantly on the move, skirmishing, taking prisoners, and being taken prisoner. Cavalrymen died in ones and twos, for the most part, but they died day after day, and their casualties were comparable to those of the infantry.

About the only solace the North could take from the disaster at

Chancellorsville was that Stonewall Jackson, one of Lee's key generals, had been killed. Jackson's remarkable battlefield successes were so well known in Berkshire that the *Eagle* printed a front-page article about his military career and death, which was accidental, caused by Confederate pickets firing upon his staff as it rode down a darkened road.

At Chancellorsville, Confederate Brigadier General Edward Perry of Richmond, Massachusetts, fell ill with typhoid fever. Still, Perry remained in command, determined to march with his brigade wherever Lee might direct them—and that likely would be in a full-scale invasion of the North.

As the Battle of Chancellorsville raged, Robert and Annie Shaw spent their brief honeymoon at Lenox. Shaw wrote happily to his sister that the weather was beautiful, and "I have been in quite an angelic mood ever since we got here . . . and I haven't felt envious of anyone. Excuse this short note, for I am *dreadfully* busy." He said they had "only been off the place once." The newlyweds were reading George Eliot's 1860 novel *Mill on the Floss*, which they had read together when he had visited her at Lenox three years earlier.

Then Shaw heard that his regiment was to be sent to the front on May 20, in less than two weeks. He cut his honeymoon short by three days, and the couple headed back to Boston.

That spring of 1863 brought Berkshire the sad news that the much-admired Major General Edwin V. Sumner, another high-ranking Massachusetts officer, had died of illness after a stellar career through the first years of the war.

Sumner, who had been in his early sixties, had a personal connection to Berkshire, having been employed as a stage driver there as a young man. It was said he had been encouraged to join the army by an officer (and future general) who had been a passenger when the stagecoach had flipped onto its side while negotiating one of the treacherous Berkshire hill trails. The frightened team had been dragging the toppled stagecoach along, veering close to the precipice, and the officer clambered out a window and demanded the reins. Young Sumner ordered him back inside, then proceeded to stop the horses safely.

The officer was so impressed that he persuaded Sumner to enlist, then saw to it that the promising fellow had every opportunity to advance in keeping with his abilities. Sumner had a long and much-decorated military career. He was promoted for courage and outstanding generalship at the Battle of Fair Oaks and distinguished himself at Fredericksburg and Antietam, rising to command a full corps before falling ill in the winter of 1862-3 and resigning from active service. He would be sorely missed in the desperate Union effort to turn back Lee's greatest invasion of all.

On May 14, the Forty-ninth Massachusetts marched toward its first real engagement after more than three months of tedious soldiering in the hot Louisiana sun—"Lousyana," the men called the place, because of the infestations of lice that plagued them.

Many of the regiment's men had already died of fever and exposure in camp. Henry Johns said, "Death has been busy among us. The soul-eating monotony has often been broken by the funeral procession." He wrote brief obituaries of the recent dead, placing their company's letter-designation in parentheses:

> Morton Olds (F) died here March 21st. Fever was his foe. He was a steady, even-tempered farmer boy, of eighteen years of age, from Sandisfield.
>
> Fever also struck low in death, March 22nd., Eugene W. Pierce, Sergeant (B), of Windsor. He died, I believe, as he was returning to this place, but was buried at New Orleans. His father came on to visit him, but death had finished its work ere his arrival. He was one of our reliable farmer boys, aged twenty-one years, with bright eye, denoting no ordinary intelligence. . . .
>
> Nelson B. Stetson, Corporal (K), died at the General Hospital . . . of fever. He leaves a wife and a child. He was one of Windsor's best soldiers, a farmer, aged twenty-eight years. . . . I attended his funeral. We went to the hospital, where hundreds far away from home are learning the hardest lesson a soldier or any one can learn, "to suffer and be strong." Roses in full bloom perfumed the fresh air blowing from the river, but very many were wrapped up in the insensibility or delirium of fever, inhaling, perchance, the fragrance of flowers that grow around the old homestead and cooling their fevered brows with breezes from their native hills. We went into the "dead room." There were several corpses there, each one marked with the name, company, and regiment of the deceased. Discarding the coarse coffins furnished by the government, we tenderly placed all that remained of our comrade in a neat coffin . . . and bore him [to] . . . the foot of a tree just bursting into bloom, on the shores of the Mississippi, [where] we buried him. . . .
>
> Near this grave Charles Bartholomew of the same company is buried. He was a boy of eighteen, from Sheffield. Fever closed his career yesterday. In the army, burial follows death speedily. Neat headboards are placed at each grave, on which names and regiments are painted. For a few years those boards will tell who for their country did die; then they will disappear, and nothing but the heaped mounds will eloquently speak of that class, who, martyrs at a bleeding nation's

call, were yet denied the proud privilege of dying on a field of strife. The authorities are preparing a cemetery to receive our dead, but these scattered graves seem more eloquent to me than any well-ordered grave yard.

In that second week of May, the Forty-ninth advanced into enemy-held territory in an expeditionary force under the overall command of General Nathaniel Banks. It moved up the east side of the Mississippi toward the stronghold of Port Hudson, where several thousand Confederates were stubbornly hanging on, even though they knew they soon would be surrounded and besieged.

The Forty-Ninth had previously taken part in exhausting forced marches that had pretended to threaten Port Hudson, but actually had been only feints, intended to hold the enemy troops in position and allow other Union regiments and naval gunboats to operate more freely. Johns lamented the great suffering his regiment had endured while waiting to go into action. There were fewer than four hundred and fifty effectives, in part because some companies were on detached service, but mainly because of losses to death and illness.

Alas! how changed we are from the men who marched in that celebrated "feint" on Port Hudson. Then, we were worthy of any foeman's steel. Now, we are but spectres. Our sick list stands seven officers and two hundred and ninety-five "enlisted men." We do full duty as long as possible. Many of the "well" properly belong to the sick list. . . .

COURTESY IMAGES FROM THE PAST

A Harper's Weekly *depiction of the doomed attack at Port Hudson in May of 1863, where the Forty-ninth Massachusetts charged through an almost-impassable tangle of fallen trees and branches directly under the fire of the enemy's fort.*

On the decisive advance against Port Hudson, the Forty-ninth marched sixteen brutal miles in one day while guarding a supply train. Colonel Bartlett, too, was seriously ill, and at times had to accompany his men in a wagon or carriage. Often, headquarters countermanded marching orders, and the regiment was forced to wearily retrace its steps and return to camp.

Also in the Union forces operating in the lower Mississippi valley were two Williams College men: General Charles C. Dwight and Colonel Jasper Hutchins.

On the morning of May 21, near the hamlet of Plains Store, Louisiana, the Forty-ninth was ordered into column for an advance. Henry Johns knew a fight was in the offing, so he borrowed a gun, left the quartermaster's department, and hurried to join the troops.

The regiment was soon deployed into line of battle—companies formed up shoulder to shoulder, in two ranks, fully extended to the right and left, with battle flags at the center. Although no enemy could be seen, cannon fire opened up on the Union troops, including the Forty-ninth. Fighting seemed to be raging all around, but the Berkshire Regiment moved forward with no sign of enemy troops. The Forty-ninth was under Lieutenant Colonel Samuel Sumner, because Colonel Bartlett was too feverish.

Henry Johns advanced in the line of battle, "determined I would walk in the path of duty, though it led to the jaws of death."

> Slowly we pressed our way. Soon, wounded men and bleeding horses were brought to the rear. Shells shrieked and bursted. Our first battle had begun. A strange sickness came over me. I doubted if it were right for *me* to fight, and was tempted to retreat to the safety of the quartermaster's department.

Johns stayed.

In the minor engagement known as Plains Store, the untested Forty-ninth maneuvered coolly, some of the companies firing volleys at enemy artillery batteries concealed by trees, but for the most part never seeing the Confederates, who were beyond tree lines and dense groves. With cannonballs and musket bullets flying all around, the Berkshire regiment behaved like well-disciplined soldiers, wheeling and marching upon command, advancing resolutely into open fields lashed by gunfire, and standing their ground. Johns felt "wild blood leap" when volleys were fired by his regiment. "I had heard the 'joy of battle.' I understood it then." Captain Israel Weller advanced into a dark wood to scout, and a cannonball whizzed narrowly past him, but he kept on going before finally turning back to report what he had seen.

When there was a lull in the firing, Johns said that Sumner "Right there put us through some tactics," calling for the manual of arms drill with their muskets, "so as to increase our self-possession."

And self-possessed the Berkshire men were on their first day under fire, though Plains Store is little remembered as a Civil War engagement. On that day a broken Union regiment came pell-mell out of the trees and rushed toward the waiting ranks of the Berkshire Regiment. The Forty-ninth might easily have caught the panic and run away, too, but it stood there as hundreds of hastily retreating men shouldered through its ranks and fled to the rear. There was no enemy pursuit, but the Berkshire men were ready if it had come. At Plains Store, the Forty-ninth proved its steadiness under fire, and the Union force camped that night on the battlefield, a token of victory.

Nineteen Union soldiers died in this minor battle, with eighty wounded and a few missing. The Berkshire men suffered four wounded, including Lieutenant Joseph Tucker of Barrington, who lost a leg to an exploding shell. Johns wrote that Colonel Bartlett sent word to the surgeons "to be sure and have his leg cut high enough," for "[h]is own cut was too low down and often he suffers much."

If the Battle of Plains Store and the next few days of action seasoned the Forty-ninth, the all-out assault against Port Hudson a few days later, on May 27, nearly destroyed the regiment. The inept General Banks hurled his army in a frontal attack against an enemy completely concealed by fortifications that were protected by a deep ditch. Union soldiers had to cross rough ground thickly strewn with fallen tree limbs so entangled that it was almost impossible even to walk, and at the end of the rush there was the ditch. Banks planned for a vanguard of soldiers to carry heavy "fascines"— bundles of branches—and throw them into the ditch to make a bridge. He asked for volunteers for the vanguard, five unmarried men from each company of each regiment.

Henry Johns volunteered, but his company's quota was filled by drawing lots from the thirteen who offered to go. In the attack, he would carry a gun instead of a fascine. Major Charles T. Plunkett, six feet six in his stockings, offered to lead the volunteers, but that honor went to the lieutenant colonel of another Massachusetts regiment. One of the officers who would go with the advance troops was Lieutenant Thomas Siggins of Company D, the Barrington company, and another was Lieutenant Robert T. Sherman of Egremont, Company E—even though Sherman was sick. Of the entire Berkshire Regiment, only two hundred and thirty-three were still available for duty.

Also taking part in the main assault were the three hundred remaining effectives of the Thirty-first Massachusetts regiment, which had been operating that spring up and down the Mississippi, from Baton Rouge to the environs of Port Hudson. Some troops of this regiment were stationed in New

Orleans, as were men of the Forty-ninth, most of them on the sick list and doing light duty.

Another of the volunteers for the vanguard was Frederick Deland from Great Barrington, at eighteen years of age finally old enough to go to war. Deland later wrote about the assault on Port Hudson, telling of the wait before the attack was launched.

> I shall never forget that night. We were encamped in a beautiful grove of oaks. The full moon arose, and shed its silvery light through the branches, and glistened on the long line of shining bayonets. The men had lain down to get what sleep they could. As I looked at my comrades I knew that ere the morrow's sun should set some would be numbered among the dead.

General Banks had devised a bad plan of attack, and Bartlett was against it, but the colonel was resolved to obey orders and be at the head of his regiment, even though he could not lead it on foot. Bartlett mounted his spirited horse and went to the front of the regimental battle line. The attack began, and as Bartlett urged his men forward, his mount leaped high over the obstacles, astonishing everyone who saw it. Friend and foe alike marveled at Bartlett's horsemanship and gallant courage. He was the only man on horseback.

"I knew my chances for life were very small," Bartlett wrote. "But I had to go on horseback or not at all. So [I] prayed that life and limb might be spared, and went in."

So did the Union force, storming the enemy's works, rushing through terrible gunfire, obstructed and slowed by the tangle of brush and tree limbs that made them easy targets. Bartlett immediately caught the attention of the Confederates. In the assault alongside the Berkshire Regiment were the black troops of the Louisiana Native Guards under Lee's Chauncey Bassett. Their reckless bravery impressed and inspired Henry Johns.

Firing from behind earthworks, the Confederates massacred the heavy-laden men carrying the bundles of branches. Lieutenant Sherman fell, shot in the head and breast, and Lieutenant Siggins went down, shot in the throat. Then the enemy turned their guns on those following close behind. John Gamwell was struck by a cannonball that took off a leg, but when a friend, William Kniffen, also of West Stockbridge, stopped to help him, Gamwell urged Kniffen to fight on and not try to save him.

Colonel Bartlett, too, was shot and fell from his horse, severely wounded in the right wrist and slightly in the foot. When Bartlett was carried away, Lieutenant Colonel Sumner took command, only to be wounded in the shoulder. Henry Johns did not write about his own deeds that day, but he and three other men of the Forty-ninth, including young Deland, would be awarded the Congressional Medal of Honor for what they did in that doomed assault on Port Hudson. The others were Second Lieutenant James Strong of Pittsfield and Corporal Francis E. Warren, like Johns, of Hinsdale.

For all their courage, the Union soldiers had little chance of success. Assault after assault was driven back. The Louisiana Native Guards charged six times, getting farther than any other Union regiment, as indicated by the positions of their dead. Johns said hundreds of black troops fell "to lift up their race from the degradation of centuries, . . . and the survivors, heroes all, sadly but triumphantly returned." Some Union soldiers, including the Forty-ninth and the Second Louisiana, got into the outer defenses, but not enough made it, and the attack at last was decisively repelled.

In the space of less than three-quarters of an hour, eighty of the Forty-ninth became casualties, sixteen killed outright, and many others fated to die of their wounds. Among the dead on the field was John Gamwell. Thomas Siggins would survive, but Robert Sherman was mortally wounded. Of the eighteen officers of the regiment who went into action, eleven were hit, one of the few uninjured being the tall Major Plunkett, though he had been a prominent target. Plunkett was the ranking officer to next take command, for Bartlett was on his way to New Orleans and home, and Sumner would need weeks to recuperate. The Forty-ninth's losses were comparable to those of the rest of the attacking force, which suffered one-third casualties in the futile assault. The Thirty-first had approximately thirty casualties.

Later in the war, it was learned that Confederate commanders had told their men not to shoot at Bartlett, because he was so courageous. Poems were written about that day, one by the wounded Lieutenant Colonel Samuel Sumner, entitled "The Charge of the Forty-ninth."

> "Forward, now, the Forty-ninth!" the General's mandate came;
> "Attention, Third Battalion!" was the Colonel's prompt exclaim;
> Now, you sons of Berkshire, your crowning hour has come,
> Prove your fond fidelity to ancestry and home!
>
> * * *
> "On the right, by file in line!" rapidly we form;
> "Forward march! Guide center!" Now the fiery storm,
> With redoubled fury, vexes earth and sky,
> As our glorious banner greets the foeman's eye.
>
> * * *
> Ah, what rebel cunning had prepared the way!
> Felled trees, logs, and branches in our pathway lay;
> Still our flag moves forward! aye, and not alone,
> For our line of battle bravely holds its own.

Bartlett falls, and Sumner cries "Onward! Onward!" and then he is shot. "Yet our boys undaunted . . . strive to gain the ramparts . . ." But they cannot, and the survivors at last must take cover in the tangled limbs and branches strewn in their path, and there await the coming of darkness, when they can retreat, lifting up wounded friends and carrying them back to safety or to die.

Friends at home, and kindred, ah! what would you say,
Could you see your petted Forty-ninth today!

This, at least, in future say, with honest pride,
"Berkshire boys right nobly fought, and bled, and died,"
Ever let their actions be rehearsed in story,
And their names encircled with a wreath of glory.

Chapter Eighteen

THE DREADED INVASION

On May 28, the day after the hopeless attack on Port Hudson, the streets of Boston were filled with the largest crowd ever to see a regiment depart, perhaps the largest crowd in the city's history. More than one hundred policemen led the parade, clearing the regiment's line of march to the Statehouse for the presentation of its colors by Governor Andrew.

The troops were preceded by the famous Gilmore's Band, playing the stirring "Battle Hymn of the Republic," with the verses about John Brown's body. More than a thousand strong, the new regiment awed spectators by its perfect discipline and fine appearance. The parade was described in the memoirs of a company commander:

> All along the route the sidewalks, windows, and balconies were thronged with spectators, and the appearance of the regiment caused repeated cheers and waving of flags and handkerchiefs. The national colors were displayed everywhere.

A newspaper of the day reported:

> Vast crowds lined the streets where the regiment was to pass, and the Common was crowded with an immense number of people such as

only the Fourth of July or some rare event causes to assemble. . . . No white regiment from Massachusetts has surpassed the Fifty-fourth in excellence of drill, while in general discipline, dignity, and military bearing the regiment is acknowledged by every candid mind to be all that can be desired.

With Colonel Robert Shaw at its head, the Fifty-fourth Massachusetts Volunteer Infantry marched to the waterfront and boarded the steamer *De Molay*, "en route for rebellious soil." Thus wrote the memoirist, Captain Louis F. Emilio, a Salem man who had served with the Twenty-third Massachusetts and now commanded the Fifty-fourth's Company E. Approximately one hundred and twenty men enlisted in Berkshire. Great Barrington's Orrin G. Smith, formerly of the Second Massachusetts, was first lieutenant of Company G. Watson Bridge of the Thirty-seventh, instrumental in recruiting men from western Massachusetts, was the captain in command of Company F.

The Fifty-fourth stood for the highest ideals of the black population of the North, most of whom had been born free, and its men were determined to prove themselves the equal of any soldiers, though it cost them their lives. Yet even as the regiment filed onto the steamer to stand at the rails and wave farewell to family and friends, the question of equal pay had not been resolved. There were rumors that the Federal government would offer them only seven dollars a month, half what the white soldier was paid. As far as the Fifty-fourth was concerned, they would not accept anything less than equal pay.

This spring, the *Eagle* reported that Stephen J. Field, a Stockbridge native, had become an associate justice of the Supreme Court of the United States. A son of the Reverend David Dudley Field, Justice Field previously had been chief justice of California.

"The Minister's Boys" was the headline for an article in a New York newspaper about the Reverend Field's remarkable sons, as the *Eagle* related in its own article:

> David Dudley Field, lawyer in New York; Rev. Henry M. Field, D.D., our neighborly editor of the *Evangelist* [a weekly religious publication]; Cyrus W. Field, who hopes to lay a second sub-Atlantic telegraph; Hon. J.E. Field, present President of the Senate of Massachusetts; and Judge S.J. Field of California. Who says that ministers' sons do not turn out well?

This May, Berkshire read in the newspapers' "Regimental Reports," as casualty lists were euphemistically termed, that Frederick H. Smith of the Thirty-seventh Massachusetts regiment had died in northern Virginia the previous month. Smith had been the soldier correspondent who had written to Berkshire about the Allen Guards' adventures.

Colonel Bartlett of the Forty-ninth was taken to Baton Rouge, where the ball was removed from his shattered wrist, buckshot from his foot. He was in great pain and remembered too well being carried on a similar journey after his wound at Yorktown a year earlier.

The wound in the wrist suppurated, and the hot weather put the doctors in fear of an infection that could kill him. They worried that the wrist would become inflamed and the arm have to be amputated. "We must pray not," Bartlett wrote home.

Male nurses sat by his bedside for hours, day and night, dripping melting ice onto the wrist to keep down the inflammation. It appeared to be no use; there was no improvement. One evening the surgeons examined the wound and decided it was too risky to try to save the hand. They went to fetch their instruments for amputation, and when they returned to operate it was getting dark, which required another delay while candles were brought. According to his biographer, Bartlett "had a feeling, nothing more, that if he was to lose another limb, he would like better to have it done by daylight, and he asked them if it would make any real difference if they should wait till morning." The doctors consented and left for the night.

By morning, when the surgeons prepared to operate, they thought the wrist looked a little better, though they dared not hope for recovery. They postponed the operation until the afternoon. Another examination indicated slight, but noticeable, improvement, and the operation was put off again. As the days passed, the wound began to heal, and the hand was saved, although Bartlett would not have full use of all the fingers.

Berkshire mourned the loss of so many in the Forty-ninth at Port Hudson, among them Albert Allen of Sandisfield, twenty-two years of age, whose brother had died in the fighting at Vicksburg. Mount Washington lost eighteen-year-old Luther Funk, who "fought and fell at his father's side," wrote Henry Johns. Both son and father, David Funk, had enlisted together.

> Parental love could not save him, but by his grave has placed a good headboard to note the place of his burial. This done, and the lonely father turns again to meet the foe.

Upon hearing that the son of her friend the Reverend Orville Dewey had come out of the Port Hudson assault unscathed, Catharine Sedgwick wrote to the minister to say she shared his joy, which

must have risen in an anthem of . . . praise, almost lifting the roof
from the dear old ancestral home, when you heard that your son had,
with so good a will—a will so strong and victorious—paid his debt
for his country, and that he was *safe*—

The Reverend Dewey, originally of Sheffield, was one of the country's
leading Unitarian ministers. He headed a church in Boston that was attended
by Lizzie Melville's family, the Shaws, and had officiated at the funeral of
Lizzie's father.

This spring, the Twenty-seventh Massachusetts, with Captain Charles
Sanford of Adams and a large contingent of northern Berkshire men, was
campaigning in the forested swamps and creeks of coastal North Carolina.
Some of the best Confederate troops and officers of high rank—including
generals D. H. Hill and P. T. Beauregard—had been sent to eliminate the Union
presence along the coast.

There were frequent skirmishes and always a threat of ambush, as well as
the ever-present sickness that laid men low. At this time, the Twenty-seventh was operating in such difficult circumstances that it daily averaged two
hundred and thirty men undergoing medical treatment for wounds or ail-
ments.

In one action, Captain Sanford led troops of his and a Pennsylvania regiment in a charge against enemy works, capturing the Confederate camp and
one hundred and seventy prisoners. These engagements were relatively small,
but they were deadly. Just as it was for cavalry on the move, infantrymen
serving in the Carolina coastal region were frequently exposed to danger and
death. The Twenty-seventh suffered slow but steady attrition, and as was common in all the theaters of war, many more men died of disease than from
wounds.

Berkshire's losses in the Twenty-seventh, though not suffered in famous
battles, were noted, one by one, in the local press.

On June 11, along with the news of the Forty-ninth's repulse at Port Hudson,
and with the dreaded Southern invasion of the North expected to break out
of Maryland at any moment, the papers of Berkshire reported that James
Callendar had been tried in a special term of the state Supreme Judicial Court
for the Otis murders the previous year. His father, Thomas, had not been
charged.

Defense attorney Norman W. Shores of Lee contended that the confes-
sion had been forced from Callendar and therefore should be inadmissible as
evidence. After deliberating only twenty minutes, the jury found the defen-
dant guilty, and he was sentenced to be hanged.

Also on June 11, the Eagle reported that Robert E. Lee had already marched northward into Maryland with 90,000 men. The advance of the Confederates was announced in an unusually large headline: "Invasion of the Loyal States by the Rebel Forces."

Although the Eagle writers did not know it, Lee was maneuvering toward Harrisburg, Pennsylvania, where he could establish himself in a defensible stronghold, be resupplied by foraging from the land, and get reinforcements from Richmond. Lee would then consider whether to attack Baltimore or Philadelphia. Washington was too strongly protected by defensive works engineered by Major General Barnard of Sheffield. Further, General Hooker's still-powerful Army of the Potomac was between the invaders and the capital. If all went well for the Confederates, Lee would select the field of battle most favorable to him, take a strong defensive position, then wait for the Union army to attack.

As the Union's top military engineer, General John Barnard of Sheffield designed Washington's miles of defensive works, such as this heavy Parrot gun emplacement at Fort Stevens.

In reaction to Lee's invasion, militiamen all over the North were being called out, including in Berkshire, and the sounds of drums and marching feet could be heard everywhere.

Stationed on the Georgia coast that June, the Fifty-fourth Massachusetts got off to a troubling start as some of its soldiers were ordered to join in the pillaging and destruction of evacuated Darien, a pretty little town on the Altamaha River, near Pierce Butler's plantation. Shaw was furious, considering such raids to be "barbarous warfare" that hurt innocent civilians and gave the black troops a bad reputation.

This operation was under the command of Colonel James Montgomery, known for leading bloody guerrilla raids during the civil strife in Kansas before the war. After he had raised some blacks to help resist secessionists in the Kansas-Missouri region, Colonel Montgomery had been reputed to be one of the white officers most fitted to lead Negro troops. Now he commanded liberated slaves who had been formed into South Carolina native guards. Embittered by the brutality of "Bleeding Kansas," Montgomery took satisfaction in ruthlessly destroying secessionist plantations and towns and freeing slaves who sometimes enlisted in his regiment. In fact, he had little regard for his Negro troops, whom he ruled with an iron hand.

Shaw did not like Montgomery, calling him a "bushwhacker" who "burns and destroys wherever he goes with great gusto and looks as if he had quite a taste of hanging people and throat-cutting whenever a suitable subject offers." Shaw noted, however, that Montgomery allowed no swearing, drinking, or tobacco in his camp. On one occasion, a deserter from a native guard unit was brought before Montgomery, who had him summarily shot. Shaw objected, and in a letter home to his family wondered why Montgomery was never investigated for this illegal act. Shaw was glad when the Fifty-fourth was to be transferred to Hilton Head, near Savannah, farther up the coast, where it would not be involved in Montgomery's raids. Unfortunately, Montgomery's regiment was also ordered to the same vicinity.

Before leaving for Hilton Head, Shaw visited the Butler plantation on St. Simons. It was "an immense place and parts of it very beautiful," he wrote home, though he noted the house was dilapidated. He thought of his family's dear friend, Fanny Kemble, now in England, and wondered what it must have been like for her more than twenty years ago, as the wife of the "Massa." Only ten slaves remained at the plantation, all of them aged. Though Pierce Butler had sold off three hundred of their family and friends before the war, they still considered him a good master.

When Shaw told them he knew "Miss Fanny, they looked very much pleased, and one named John wanted me to tell her I had seen him."

On June 13, Thomas Reed wrote home from Mount Sterling, Kentucky, to say he and the Twenty-first regiment had been paid off and that twenty dollars was on its way by express to Pittsfield. Reed said he was glad to receive newspapers from home—the *Eagle* and a Boston paper—which told of the battle at Port Hudson, where so many Berkshire men of the Forty-ninth had fallen. He remarked that those with minor wounds were likely out of danger for the remainder of their nine-month enlistment.

I noticed the names of the Pittsfield boys who were wounded at Port Hudson. I think the boys were very fortunate in getting off being so slightly wounded, for I expected to hear of the death of some of my acquaintances. . . . [W]e had been again ordered to the front, and the orders countermanded much to the satisfaction of the boys. We're so much pleased with the place that we would dislike to leave, still when the occasion requires our presence elsewhere we are ready at a moment's warning.

Reed did not finish this letter until the next day, for the Twenty-first was suddenly called away to oppose a raid by enemy cavalry. Reed and his comrades marched out of town, then back again, and had to remain awake and on duty all night before the alarm was over.

Soon, Reed found himself in an even better situation, as he became a regimental clerk: "It is not quite as laborious as carrying a gun, but there is heaps of business of a perplexing nature which taxes my energies exceedingly." Indeed, clerking was extremely demanding work, with long hours and great responsibility for a fortune in supplies. Reed proved to be excellent in his new position. He eventually became part of the quartermaster's staff, responsible for shipments of supplies and equipment to the troops on the front line—at times while they were in the heat of battle and desperately needed the food and ammunition that Reed managed. He expected to be paid more than the common soldier's thirteen dollars a month and held out hopes for this to Cynthia.

On June 14, General Banks ordered yet another frontal attack on Port Hudson.

The weather was brutally hot, the road a "furnace of fire," said Henry Johns. "An hour after sunrise or an hour before sunset and it is seemingly as hot as at noon." In the past two weeks, the Union siege had been gaining ground steadily, driving the enemy from forward earthworks and digging new advanced trenches at night. Attacks with limited objectives were launched from the advanced trenches, or troops fired from them to force the Confederates to retreat to other defensive works. Those abandoned positions, in turn, would be occupied by the Union men, and the process repeated. The noose on Port Hudson steadily tightened.

Artillery fired back and forth, but even more effective were the snipers, who wreaked havoc in both armies. Men were shot dead just when they thought they were safely behind cover and had lifted a canteen to take a drink. Soldiers stopped wearing the cooler straw hats they could buy from locals, because the hats made them conspicuous targets for sharpshooters. The Union soldiers were constantly in danger, and they died daily, many prostrated by disease and sunstroke, with at least fifty a day lost to the besieging army of about thirty thousand men. Conditions were far worse for Port

Hudson's starving defenders—as was the case with the large Confederate army besieged by Grant up at Vicksburg. Still, there was no sign of surrender at either place, and the assault on June 14 was intended to coordinate with a similar push against Vicksburg.

There were worries that new Confederate forces were gathering in the rear of the two besieging armies, so Port Hudson and Vicksburg must be forced to surrender soon. No one knew what would come of Lee's invasion of the North, but something decisive had to be done here in the Mississippi valley in case Lee triumphed. So the next attack at Port Hudson went forward, another "day of fearful slaughter . . . relieved only by the grand heroism of the sons of New York and New England," wrote Johns.

The Forty-ninth lost eighteen killed or wounded, including David Funk, who was wounded in the head and shoulder but would survive. The Thirty-first Massachusetts was also in this useless assault and lost another thirty men. At one point, the Thirty-first came under such heavy fire that it had to lie down in line of battle, unable to advance and unwilling to retreat, but remaining that way through the entire sweltering day with bullets zipping past, kicking up the dirt, all too often finding a target.

After the failed assault, the desultory siege resumed.

On June 19, the enlistment time of the Forty-ninth was officially up, but the army showed no sign of letting them go. Other nine-month regiments with Banks had publicly complained that they wanted to go home, as was their right, yet they had been threatened with punishment as mutineers. Only when the War Department allowed the men to leave was their time considered up. The Forty-ninth wanted to be there when Port Hudson surrendered, but they were heartily sick and tired of the siege and slaughter. And they continued to die, one by one. At times, less than one-tenth of the original regiment was fit for duty and present in the trenches before Port Hudson.

Joseph Wolcott, a young Sandisfield farmer, was killed by a sharpshooter on June 23. When the regiment had departed Berkshire, Wolcott's wife and family had moved in with the family of Lieutenant Barton D. Deming, of the same town. Lieutenant Deming had been killed in the May 27 assault. Wolcott was buried near his friend.

Johns wrote of the wives: "A mutual agony now seals their solemn sisterhood."

Around this time, a soldier-correspondent in the Tenth Regiment with the Army of the Potomac in northern Virginia sent a report to the *Berkshire Courier*, addressed to "Friend Rogers," meaning part-owner and manager Marcus Rogers, who had purchased an interest in the paper early in 1862.

A native of Mill River in New Marlboro, Rogers had lived for a time in Pittsburgh, learning the newspaper trade, so that when he took over the *Courier* he was thoroughly experienced in the business. In his late twenties, the remark-ably dynamic Rogers had already designed and built a newspaper folding machine, an invention that eventually earned him a small fortune. He was known as an erudite mathematician, astronomer, talented poet, and world traveler, but as a publisher he took close interest in the mundane affairs of his readers. His attention to the daily comings and goings of the community won readers to the *Courier*, and the weekly's circulation expanded rapidly during the war years. Rogers's innovations earned the respect of other newspaper men, and he was asked to explain his methods in an address to an association of editors and publishers. That address was widely reprinted across the United States and even in Great Britain.

With the North hanging on every bit of news from the front, the letter from the Tenth would have been devoured by Rogers's anxious readers. As was common with soldier-correspondents, the letter is signed only with the writer's initials. It was surely Pittsfield native Charles A. Gilmore, who had been employed as a printer in Great Barrington and was a correspondent to the *Courier*.

Fairfax Court House
June 21, 1863
Friend Rogers:—I have been obliged to delay writing you, as our con-stant moving hither and thither has prevented me doing so at an earlier date.

Friday, 12th—We crossed the river last evening at 6 and relieved the 98 N.Y. as skirmishers. The enemy's sharp-shooters commenced firing on our regiment as we were deploying, and kept it up until we reached the skirmish line. Only one man was hit, (A.B. Parker of Co. G) through both legs, severe. This morning at 5 o'clock, we were relieved and marched back to the rifle-pits as reserves. [General Hiram] Berdan's sharp-shooters have completely silenced the rebs, and not one dare show his head above the pits. At 7 p.m. the enemy threw a few shells at our ammunition train across the river but did no damage, except killing one horse.

Saturday—Expected an attack on our left flank this morning, and everything was ready to meet it, with orders to hold our position at all hazards; but, as our movements were made in sight of the enemy, they probably had the desired effect as no attack was made. At 9 a.m. a thick cloud of dust was seen rising along the line of the Bowling Green road, which proved to arise from a heavy column of Lee's troops moving to our right. Up to 7 p.m. nothing has been heard from it.

Sunday—Last evening at eight o'clock a heavy thunder shower burst upon us, which lasted about two hours, and leaving the night very dark, and the order came to be ready to move at a moment's notice. At midnight the whole corps had recrossed the river without firing a gun. The troops bivouacked for the night back of Falmouth, and at daylight this morning the column was in motion, with orders to report at Stafford Court House, which place we reached at 5 p.m., a distance of about 16 miles. Bivouacked for the night, and received orders to march at 10 o'clock.

Monday—Started on the march last night according to orders, to report to Dumfree's, a distance of about 18 miles, which place we reached at 12 p.m., to-day. Bivouacked here for the night and drew three days rations.

Tuesday—Started on the march this morning at 2 o'clock, with orders to report at Fairfax Station, which place we reached at about 5 p.m. after a march of about 20 miles. The sun shone very warm all day, and the column was enveloped in a thick cloud of dust, and but very little air stirring, on the whole march.

Nearly 60 men have fallen from sun-stroke to-day out of the 3rd (our) division. Heavy firing was heard to-day . . . towards the Potomac.

Wednesday—Started this morning for Fairfax Court House, where we are at present waiting orders, or for Lee to make his appearance. The cause of the heavy firing yesterday was a collision between a body of Stuart's cavalry, and a body of cavalry under Kilpatrick, which resulted in a complete victory for the latter, who drove the enemy from the field and captured nearly one hundred prisoners.

Nothing of importance has transpired up to to-day. Yesterday (20th) a heavy thunder shower came upon us, and lasted all day and night leaving the roads in a very bad condition for travel.

A large number of prisoners have passed here en route for Washington. In one squad there was 80 of Stuart's cavalry; in another squad about one hundred men belonging to Jackson's Corps. A long train of ambulances have passed this morning filled with wounded rebels.

The men in the Tenth are in very good spirits, but many are rather foot-sore. The men that have been off on detail from the regiment have all been ordered back. This increases the size of the regiment greatly, and decreases the duty for each man. Co A is all right. . . . As I close a heavy cannonading is heard to-wards the Potomac above Washington. With high hopes of some excitement soon, I remain,

Yours &c.,

C. A. G.

One of those who collapsed with sunstroke on that forced march toward Gettysburg, Pennsylvania, was John Atwood of North Adams, a Johnson Grey.

Atwood was taken to the division field hospital, delirious and dehydrated. One of the nurses caring for the many men who had been prostrated in that hot weather was another soldier of the Tenth, William Mason, of Company K, an Englishman who served as a nurse throughout the war.

The cavalry action mentioned was likely the battle at Aldie Court House, one of several major cavalry engagements in this campaign. The First Massachusetts cavalry regiment, with its large contingent of Berkshire men, was in Brigadier General Hugh Kilpatrick's command, as was the "Barrington delegation" in the Second New York cavalry. At Aldie, the Union troopers, so often scorned by the Confederate cavalry, launched a number of sharp attacks, with the First cavalry regiment opening the battle by leading Kilpatrick's column through the town. For some time, the regiment bore the full brunt of the battle as it held the ground until reinforcements came up. The First lost heavily, with twenty-four killed and one hundred and thirty wounded or missing. Berkshire soon learned that two of its men, troopers C.T. Chapman and Joseph Blake, had been taken prisoner at Aldie, and Blake was wounded.

On a scout, Federal cavalry watch for the advance of Lee's army during the Gettysburg campaign.

Although virtually all the officers of the First cavalry regiment were from eastern Massachusetts, the assistant surgeon was Dr. Oscar C. DeWolf, a graduate of Berkshire Medical Institute in Pittsfield. Before the 1863 campaign, DeWolf had paid a visit to Berkshire that was mentioned in the *Eagle*.

The Aldie battle and other related cavalry engagements were crucial for the reconnaissance efforts of Union commander Joseph Hooker, who needed his troopers to break through the enemy cavalry screen and locate Lee's army. By now, Lee was threatening Harrisburg, Pennsylvania, the state capital, where civilians were panic-stricken, the trains full of people loaded down with baggage, and the statehouse almost evacuated, its papers, books, and paintings being frantically packed.

On June 30, the Fifty-fourth regiment was mustered to be paid in its camp on St. Helena Island, near Hilton Head. When the army paymaster offered them only ten dollars a month, the same pay given to the contraband regiments, Colonel Shaw bristled. He wrote to Governor Andrew that he refused to have the regiment paid unless they received the same thirteen dollars as white soldiers, as they had been promised.

The men concurred with the colonel, even though their families at home—and they themselves—badly needed the money.

In the last days of June 1863, while Federal forces rushed through the heat of summer to head off Lee's invasion of the North, President Lincoln abruptly removed General Joseph Hooker as commander of the Army of the Potomac. In Hooker's place came dependable, professional Major General George Gordon Meade, who drove his troops toward Lee's army for the decisive battle.

The Federal army was strung out for fifty miles, desperately hurrying to confront the enemy from a strong position that he would be obliged to attack. Lee was doing the same, and both armies were driven to the brink of endurance, even before the fighting began. The nation held its collective breath to see what would happen.

Chapter Nineteen

THE NORTH RISES AGAIN

W hile in the East the Union and Confederate armies converged on Gettysburg, on the Mississippi River Grant was slowly strangling Vicksburg and Banks held on tenaciously to the siege of Port Hudson. In Lee's Army of Northern Virginia was the sickly Brigadier General Edward Perry and his battle-hardened Florida brigade, part of the Third Corps commanded by the brilliant Lieutenant General A.P. Hill; trapped in Vicksburg with his newly raised Forty-sixth Mississippi was Colonel Claudius Sears.

South Williamstown's Hamilton Eldridge, who had been promoted that spring to be colonel of his 127th Illinois, was with the Federal forces before Vicksburg. In May, during an all-out assault at Vicksburg, Eldridge had seized his regiment's colors and carried them into the enemy's defensive works. The Union attack had been repelled, but Eldridge was brevetted—nominally promoted for his outstanding effort—to the rank of brigadier general. As the siege continued, Eldridge proved himself one of the top Union commanders, although he was suffering from the debilitating "break-bone fever" caused by the malarial climate.

Eldridge's duties were made somewhat easier by an intelligent mare he had captured to replace his original horse, which had been shot from under him. At one point, Eldridge and some picked men were ambushed while out on special duty, and he narrowly escaped on horseback into the thickets and swamps. As darkness fell, he had become lost. With enemy patrols seemingly on every side, Eldridge could only give his mare her head, and she miraculously brought him safely back to camp.

A few days later, Eldridge retraced his trail and found that the horse had picked its way, in the darkness, along the trunk of a large, fallen cottonwood tree that spanned a deep chasm.

As the vanguards of Meade and Lee clashed at Gettysburg, Berkshire read of a new enlistment bounty being offered—the astounding sum of $402. Some men already in the service felt cheated by the smaller size of their own bounties, and in the case of those first regiments to enlist, such as the Tenth Massachusetts, there had been no bounty paid at all.

The Battle of Gettysburg opened in full force on July 1, and the Tenth and Thirty-seventh were coming on as fast as they could. They arrived on the battlefield on the second day, after rapid marching for more than a week. The Thirty-seventh and the Tenth were serving together in the Sixth Corps under General John Sedgwick.

Along with the Sixth Corps went the First Massachusetts cavalry. Riding a day and a night with scarcely any rest, the regiment soon became engaged at Gettysburg, although it would spend much of the battle guarding a couple of thousand prisoners, who were herded away from the field.

The Tenth and the Thirty-seventh went into a supporting position at the left of the Union line and slept that first night "on their arms," with weapons close at hand and prepared to go into action. As the battle raged the next day, the regiments were marched back and forth, often at the double-quick in spite of the smothering heat, and positioned to support the front line, ready to dash in. On July 3, a Saturday and the third day of battle, Lee opened a mighty artillery barrage on the Union positions just as the Thirty-seventh was marching behind the lines. The regiment came under devastating fire that instantly caused more than thirty casualties. "Not a man shrank," wrote a regimental historian, and the regiment moved into a sheltered position near the high ground known as the Round Tops.

The Second Massachusetts, which also had endured the forced march to Gettysburg, fought on the right of the Union line throughout the battle. Although the main Confederate assault on the third day was at the center of the Union line, the Second was fiercely engaged with enemy attempts to turn the Union right flank. The Second attacked and captured Confederate positions, but abruptly found itself cut off by the charge of another enemy force. The Second had to turn and fight its way back across the same field to regain its original position. Losses were heavy, more than one hundred and twenty dead, wounded, or captured out of approximately three hundred engaged,

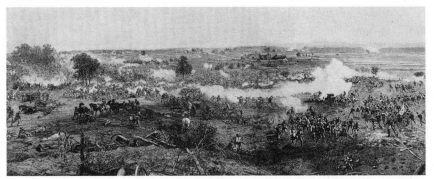

The high tide of the great Confederate assault at Gettysburg was met by Federal troops near the clump of trees to the left; the arrival of the Twentieth Massachusetts was crucial to stopping the enemy breakthrough

including the Second's lieutenant colonel, who was killed.

The Twentieth Massachusetts—minus Captain Wendell Holmes, who was recuperating from a leg wound suffered a few weeks earlier at Chancellorsville—was at first held in reserve. On that third day of battle came the great Confederate assault, led by Major General George E. Pickett, as fifteen thousand howling soldiers charged the center of the Union line. In that do-or-die charge was Perry's Florida Brigade, though its commander was too sick with typhoid to take part. Under a torrent of gunfire, the Confederates rushed the Union line, and despite terrible losses, seemed about to burst through. At that key moment, Union troops rushed up to repel the point of the Confederate attack, and leading that crucial countercharge was the Twentieth Massachusetts. In this, perhaps its most important single exploit of the war, the "Harvard Regiment" suffered one hundred and twenty-seven casualties out of the two hundred and thirty officers and men who went into action at Gettysburg—the greatest loss in battle of any Massachusetts regiment. Its colonel, lieutenant colonel, two majors, an adjutant, and a surgeon were killed.

Pickett's charge was thrown back, and with its bloody ebb went the Confederate States' last hope to force the Union and the world to recognize its secession as irreversible. Southern casualties included eighty-one killed or wounded in Perry's Florida regiment, and his brigade claimed to have suffered the highest percent of casualties of all the Confederate brigades in the assault. Worse was to come for the South: as Pickett's charge was being defeated, the defenders of Vicksburg were preparing to surrender to Ulysses S. Grant.

Colonel Claudius Sears was captured at the fall of Vicksburg, and would remain a prisoner for six months before being exchanged. In this time, he was quite ill, but his reputation had been made in various actions during the prolonged Vicksburg siege, and he was in line to become a brigadier general.

Robert E. Lee retreated slowly from Pennsylvania, ever prepared to turn and fight, and the Tenth and Thirty-seventh Massachusetts regiments were in the cautious pursuit, which meant more hard marching and always the risk of another battle. The men were bone-weary, and the Thirty-seventh had more than one hundred and eighty soldiers without shoes. The First cavalry was also in the pursuit of Lee, but the Union army never moved quickly enough or in enough strength to bring on another battle.

At the end of July, the Thirty-seventh was refitted and sent to New York City, where its duty was to help prevent violence in the streets; earlier in the month, riots had broken out in protest of new Federal draft laws. The regiment remained for several weeks encamped at Fort Hamilton, and while there it won praise for its discipline and excellence in drill. The Second regiment, too, was chosen for this service, remaining camped at New York's City Hall Park until early September, when it returned to Virginia. The Second soon would be heading westward by rail, in the command of General Hooker, to support Federal operations in Tennessee.

News of the Gettysburg and Vicksburg triumphs had not yet reached Berkshire on July 4. Much of that day it rained hard in Berkshire County, where for the second year the celebration had not been observed with the traditional large-scale public display. That spring and early summer had been dry until now, and the rain was welcome, especially because there were no parades or outdoor festivities to be spoiled. In rain-drenched Pittsfield, "Not a bell was rung or a cannon fired," wrote the *Eagle*. "There was neither orator, toast, or jubilant music, procession or public fireworks."

People otherwise made the most of the holiday, however. When the rain relented, the young women and teachers of the Maplewood Institute took carriage excursions and had a picnic, small American flags flying on their carriages. Later in the day, people went into the streets, even before the news of the great victories had come in, and spontaneous fireworks "enlivened the evening," said the *Eagle*.

National flags were displayed everywhere, including one that had "passed through the fire" of Second Bull Run, and another—little more than tatters—that had been brought back by Colonel Whelden from Louisiana, where secessionists had taken it down from a captured Federal fort. Whelden had discovered the flag in storage and had lent it to a Union gunboat that flew it in battle on the Mississippi. The flag had been torn by shot and shell before it was returned to Whelden, who hung it on this Fourth over the door of his Pittsfield pharmacy. Above the West Street residence of the Briggs family floated the Stars and Stripes that had been flown by the Tenth regiment at Camp Brightwood.

When word of Gettysburg and Vicksburg flashed to Berkshire, the *Eagle* headlines expressed everyone's joy: "Glorious News! Week of Victory! Triumph in Pennsylvania—Total Rout of the Invading Army! Vicksburg Fallen! Hurrah! Hurrah! Hurrah!" The *Eagle* called its reports "[T]he most glorious record which has illustrated any week of the War."

At Pittsfield on the night of July 6 there was a "fine display of fireworks," and a huge bonfire lit up North Street. The next day bells rang, more fireworks went off, and cannon boomed all over the county to celebrate Gettysburg and Vicksburg. The *Eagle* editorial was under the title "Victory":

> One word, one thought, one feeling, has filled all hearts, has been first upon all tongues, has thrilled every hearer. Victory continued, glorious, almost unqualified, has been ours—has been our country's. It has swept out of sight all political differences between loyal men, has sunk all petty and selfish considerations and made the success of the country the first consideration with all. We rejoice that it is so— but let us not imagine that the struggle is over, and that no more remains for us to do. Now is the time for the most strenuous effort. Whoever has held back before, no man must now withhold his effort. Victory is won, its fruits must be secured.

That "most strenuous effort" was to require two more years of war and suffering, as the proud and stubborn South fought for every foot of ground, costing America hundreds of thousands more dead and wounded before the war ended.

Brigadier General Henry S. Briggs, former commander of the Tenth Massachusetts and the Allen Guards, could take profound pride in what his regiment had achieved. Briggs's war wounds kept him from further active service, but he was a valuable member of various military boards at Washington, and he would remain in the service until the end of the war.

Herman Melville's verse about this momentous time in the country's history was entitled "Gettysburg: The Check." It likens the Confederates to Philistines, worshipers of the idol god Dagon, whose "foredoomed" fall comes as "God walled his power, / And there the last invader charged."

> He charged, and in that charge condensed
> His all of hate and all of fire;
> He sought to blast us in his scorn
> And wither us in his ire.

The invader was "repelled by sterner pride," and in the end thousands of Confederate dead lay upon the field after Pickett's Charge like the wreckage of ships that a storm had swept in from the sea:

> Before our lines it seemed a beach
> Which wild September gales have strown
> With havoc on wreck, and dashed therewith
> Pale crews unknown—

The Melvilles were finally preparing to leave Arrowhead, to which they had returned that spring from their rented house on South Street. As much as the Melvilles loved Berkshire, they were excited to be returning to New York to take ownership of a home on Twenty-sixth Street that had belonged to Allan Melville, Herman's wealthy brother. In May, Allan had sold them the house as part of a trade, along with cash, in return for Arrowhead.

On July 3, Allan had come up with his family to visit and to look over Arrowhead. Lizzie Melville disliked Allan's wife, Jenny, considering her haughty, with a patronizing attitude toward country folk and Berkshire, and even toward "poor, simple Arrowhead," as Jenny described the farm. Jenny intended to modernize Arrowhead in keeping with her elevated social status, and she would bring along efficient maids to manage the place.

With the great Union achievements on the battlefield, it seemed only a matter of time before the war would finally be over, so Herman and Lizzie intended to enjoy their last summer in Berkshire. Still, they worried about the health of Sarah Morewood. These days, Lizzie regularly went to see Mrs. Morewood over at Broadhall, as her home was called, for she was weak and seldom went out anymore. She suffered from intense headaches and had been compelled to all but stop her efforts for the soldiers.

With two of the four Melville children away in upstate New York visiting relatives, and Jenny Melville agreeing to watch the other two, Herman and Lizzie took the opportunity for a farewell carriage trip around Berkshire. Traveling as a happy, unencumbered couple, they would see again many of those places that had meant so much to them in thirteen years of living here.

"Glory! Hallelujah! Amen! Port Hudson is ours, and the Mississippi is open." Thus did Henry Johns begin his July 13 letter from Baton Rouge, announcing that "the Confederacy is split in two; the backbone of the rebellion is broken."

With the fall of Vicksburg to Grant, the Confederates at Port Hudson knew their cause was lost and that there was no point in further bloodshed. They had barely a week's food left, and the determined Yankees had proven too stubborn to give up the siege. The Union troops entered battered Port Hudson on July 8, and even before the surrender ceremonies took place the defenders left their works by the hundreds and made their way toward the Union men, who were allowed to converse with them. They spoke of the siege and shook hands with specific men they had been trying to shoot down for weeks. A number of men on both sides, particularly the West Point officers, had known each other before the war. The Union soldiers shared their food and tobacco; the garrison had but one delicacy to offer: homemade light beer, which they had in large quantities.

For Johns and the Berkshire men, their victory was a mighty achievement, especially in the wake of the simultaneous Union successes at Vicksburg and Gettysburg.

> We put God and humanity on our side and have gone from triumph to triumph. The 4th of July has been resurrected. Again its inspired truths, all undiluted, fall from the lips of America on the ears of an expectant world. . . . 1863 is proving its kindredship to 1776. The child is nobler than the parent. The glory of the latter day is above that of the former.

There would be more marching and more action for the men of the Forty-ninth, though their enlistment time had been up weeks ago. These would be minor brushes and skirmishes, but more Berkshire boys would fall and others would die of fever, lingering in camp or hospital when they should have been sent home. A Lanesboro lad, David Winchell, was bathing in the Mississippi when he got in too deep and drowned, for he could not swim.

Colonel Bartlett spent a few days in New Orleans in mid-July, suffering from the heat and from the agony of bone splinters that were working their way out of his wounded wrist. He then sailed for New York and journeyed on to his family in Massachusetts, where he took a month to recuperate and prepare to meet the Forty-ninth back in Pittsfield for its final mustering out. Already, Bartlett was planning to accept the colonelcy of another Massachusetts regiment, and he hoped some of his Forty-ninth would re-enlist to serve with him again. He was only twenty-three years of age.

In mid-July, the Fifty-fourth Massachusetts went into action on James Island, South Carolina, taking part in a movement by several Union regiments against the southerly defenses of Charleston. The enemy was ready and reinforced, however, and the Federal troops were separated by waterways that made it difficult for them to support one another in battle.

Early on the morning of July 16, the Confederates launched a full-scale counterattack, the main assault aimed at the Fifty-fourth and at the Tenth Connecticut, which was posted across a river to the Fifty-fourth's left. The enemy was intent on isolating the Connecticut regiment, and if the Fifty-fourth were driven back, the Connecticut men would be cut off from retreat. The outnumbered Fifty-fourth gave ground slowly, its skirmishers becoming trapped in small groups that resisted fiercely in deadly encounters with enemy cavalrymen. Some of the

Fifty-fourth were killed, others taken prisoner, but the regiment held on long enough for the Connecticut troops to escape from their exposed position.

The Fifty-fourth also gained time for the main body of Union troops to form up and prepare for battle, and as a result, the Confederate attack was not resumed. The Connecticut troops immediately conveyed their gratitude to the Fifty-fourth, and an army newspaper described their feelings.

> The boys of the Tenth Connecticut could not help loving the men who saved them from destruction. . . . [P]robably a thousand homes from Windham to Fairfield have in letters been told the story how the dark-skinned heroes fought the good fight and covered with their own brave hearts the retreat of brothers, sons, and fathers of Connecticut.

This sharp engagement, the regiment's baptism of fire, cost the Fifty-fourth fourteen dead, eighteen wounded, and thirteen missing. Some of the missing no doubt were prisoners who might be executed because they were black men under arms against the Confederacy. The secessionist government had declared that captured former slaves who enlisted in the Union army were liable to a death sentence, and their white officers could face the same fate, as accused inciters of slave rebellion. Though the Fifty-fourth had few former slaves in its ranks, the men still were in danger of execution if captured.

In the next two days, the Fifty-fourth had to withdraw under cover of darkness and, along with the rest of the Union force, leave its forward positions. This rapid move involved difficult marches through swamps and across watercourses, without rest even to stop and eat. There was little food available anyway, so the regiment pushed on through blistering heat that burned a man's skin through his clothes. They were ordered to Morris Island, where the Confederates had an artillery battery, called Fort Wagner, commanding the entrance to Charleston Bay.

On the night of July 17, these hungry and bone-weary men were carried, thirty at a time in one longboat, to an old steamer waiting to transport them. Suddenly, they were swept by a fierce thunderstorm that inundated them. They kept on loading the steamer, soaked through as well as exhausted and very hungry. Colonel Shaw personally supervised that night-long embarkation, and was the last man into the longboat as it pulled for the steamer at dawn on July 18. The officers had a meal aboard the steamer, but there was nothing for the enlisted men. Later that morning, the regiment landed and marched along a sandy island, passing camps of Union soldiers who cheered them for their exploits a few days earlier. That did the Fifty-fourth good, but their bellies still were empty. All they had to eat was a box of water-soaked hard tack they found by chance on the beach. It was devoured, and on they went for another six miles in the Southern sun.

As they marched, they sang out the popular song "When This Cruel War Is Over." That evening, they boarded another steamer and were transported across to Morris Island, where they waited on shore for further orders, still without food.

The commanding Union general thought Fort Wagner had been bombarded into rubble and would offer little resistance to a determined attack. He believed that no more than three hundred demoralized, shell-shocked defenders were still in the fort. In fact, Wagner had been reinforced with fresh troops numbering seventeen hundred men and had plenty of artillery. Moreover, the garrison expected the Union attack. The Fifty-fourth was offered the honor of leading the assault, and even though his men were starving and had scarcely slept for days, Shaw could not resist accepting. He and his regiment had something to prove.

In the early twilight, the six hundred available troops of the Fifty-fourth moved along the beach in a column several men wide, with the sea lapping at their right. The rest of the army was to follow on close behind. Fort Wagner was more than sixteen hundred yards away. Shaw had given orders not to fire, but to rush over the parapets and use the bayonet. The regiment advanced steadily, muskets sloped over their shoulders. Now Wagner was a thousand yards away. It remained silent. Darkness was falling. The order came to advance at quick time. The beach narrowed as the regiment approached the fort. The men on the right were trotting in the water.

At the front and center of the attacking column was the Stars and Stripes, and beside it Colonel Shaw. Three hundred yards. All was still. The final assault was about to begin, but no man was to fire until the fort was reached. Captain Emilio described that rush through gathering darkness, "with eyes strained upon the colonel and the flag, [the regiment] pressed on toward the work, now only two hundred yards away. . . ."

> At that moment Wagner became a mound of fire, from which poured a stream of shot and shell . . . mingled with the crash and rattle of musketry. A sheet of flame, followed by a running fire, like electric sparks, swept along the parapet. . . .

The Fifty-fourth did not flinch, but "changed step to the double-quick, the sooner to close with the foe," charging through the storm of lead, men dropping on every side. Shaw led them right to the top of the parapet, the Fifty-fourth's flag-bearer beside him. Fallen officers and men littered the approach to the fort, among them Lieutenant Orrin Smith and Ralph B. Gardner of Great Barrington, Henry Burghardt of Lee, and George Waterman of Lenox—all wounded. Scores had been hit. At the top of the parapet, Colonel Shaw waved his sword for the men to come on, and then he fell, shot dead.

Under destructive musket and artillery fire, the Fifty-fourth Massachusetts fights its way to the enemy-held ramparts of Fort Wagner, losing Colonel Robert Shaw, near top right with sword, and soon being forced to withdraw.

The color sergeant, too, went down, but the Stars and Stripes were lifted up by Sergeant William H. Carney of Company C, a New Bedford man. Carney planted the flag on top of the parapet, and men of the Fifty-fourth clambered up to join him. Brutal fighting began with musket butt and bayonet. Carney was severely wounded twice. The struggle was fierce, but short-lived.

The Union men were driven back. Though wounded, Carney somehow managed to save the colors, taking them with him in the withdrawal. For some time, the shattered Fifty-fourth lay down a short distance from the fort, exchanging fire as the main Union force attacked another part of Wagner and was likewise repulsed. Captain Emilio found himself in command of the regiment, for all the superior officers were dead or wounded. He received the national flag, but knew it was impossible to rally the troops in the darkness. Emilio withdrew his men farther back, and the regiment's survivors regrouped. He positioned them in line of battle to meet any counterattack, but none came. By midnight, the firing ceased. The Tenth Connecticut eventually arrived to relieve the Fifty-fourth, which marched away to the rear.

The Union losses in the assault on Fort Wagner were devastating, more than fifteen hundred, with some regiments losing all their officers. Seven of the ten regimental commanders were casualities, two of them killed. In addition to Colonel Shaw, the Fifty-fourth had lost more than two hundred and fifty killed, wounded, or missing of the six hundred who went into battle.

For his gallantry under fire, Sergeant Carney would be the first black soldier awarded the Congressional Medal of Honor. Carney would recover from his wounds and continue to serve in the Fifty-fourth. He and three other soldiers were singled out in the official report of the battle, and would be given special medals by the commander of the army's Southern Department; among those honored was Private George A. Wilson of Pittsfield.

On July 27, the leading Confederate States senator William Loundes Yancey, fire-eater secessionist and former Lenox Academy and Williams College student, died in Montgomery, Alabama, at the age of forty-eight.

Governor Andrew came out to Berkshire from Boston in mid-July, and while there he met with the Reverend Samuel Harrison of the Second Congregational Church to ask the minister to visit the Fifty-fourth, which as yet had no chaplain. The Reverend Harrison, who was forty-five and not in condition for a prolonged tour of the front lines, agreed to go because many of the enlisted men needed to have religious services led by a clergyman of their own color and to find solace in talking with him.

Harrison arrived on the South Carolina coast on September 1 and found the regiment encamped on sandy, sun-scorched Morris Island. The men were laboring nightly, digging trenches that crept ever closer to the defensive perimeter of Fort Wagner. A full-scale siege was being conducted against Charleston, including punishing bombardments of Fort Sumter, now little more than a ruin in the center of the harbor. During the day, the heat was ferocious, and flies and sand fleas tormented everyone. The Fifty-fourth's camp was not within musket range of the enemy defenses, but from time to time an unexpected round or shell crashed in from Confederate artillery in the various works protecting Charleston harbor. There had been no rain for almost a month, and the only relief was bathing in the sea. Six hundred men were still with the regiment, including many who were sick. It was much the same with the white regiments, but at least they could count on receiving their promised pay.

The officers of the regiment elected the Reverend Harrison chaplain, meaning he was the Fifty-fourth's first black officer. The government had no intention of commissioning blacks, however, and there would be prolonged controversy over his rank, as well as the amount of his rightful pay. Harrison made a brief trip back to Berkshire on personal business, then returned to serve with the regiment, even though his health was not good. He would be compelled to resign that fall and return home to recuperate, continuing to petition vigorously for full pay to the black soldiers.

Chapter Twenty

THE BERKSHIRE REGIMENT'S HOMECOMING

Early in August, the Forty-ninth prepared to head home after a few days in New Orleans, where it was to board a steamboat for the slow journey up the winding Mississippi to Cairo, Illinois, and then by train homeward.

The regiment served as provost guard in the city, where it was reunited with Berkshire friends from the Thirty-first, including Captain Willie Rockwell. The captain had been kind to some Forty-ninth men who had been captured the previous month and then paroled and left to find their way to safety. The parolees had reached New Orleans, and Rockwell got them food and clothing, giving his own money to help them get back to their regiment.

Before the Forty-ninth boarded the steamboat, more men died of illness, including two Clarksburg farmers, both family men, and in the same company: G. Benedict Niles, twenty-nine, died of heart disease, and Augustine Aldrich, twenty-three, of an abscess in his side. Savoy farmer A.H. Maranville of Company B, aged thirty-eight and married, also died in this time. Of Maranville and the others, Johns expressed how many of the men felt about dying for the sacred cause of the Union: "There is life in *his* death."

Several officers of the Forty-ninth Massachusetts, after returning from the war
l-r: seated, Colonel W. Francis Bartlett—his arm in a sling—and
Major Charles T. Plunkett; rear, Lieutenant Colonel Samuel B. Sumner,
Adjutant Frederick A. Francis, and Surgeon Frederick Winsor.

On a hot Monday, August 10, Herman and Lizzie Melville drove their buggy
away from Arrowhead and headed south to Great Barrington. August 1 had
been Herman's forty-fourth birthday, and though he was no longer the phe-
nomenal young author electrifying America, he felt more content these days.
This journey would be a sentimental farewell to Berkshire, but mingled with
the welcome relief of the Union victories.

At Barrington, the Melvilles stopped for lunch, and from there they drove
to Mount Everett, a favorite spot for sightseeing in the Taconic Mountains.
They spent the night at an inn and the next day went to the romantic and

beautiful Bash Bish Falls on the state line with New York, where they again spent the night. Then they drove into Copake, New York, and followed the highway northward a few miles before turning east through the Taconics to stop again at Barrington for a meal. From there they went further east to Monterey and lodged for the night beside Lake Garfield.

On Thursday, the Melvilles drove through North Becket and into the Berkshire hill towns. That night was spent at Peru Hill, and the next day they continued north and east to Cummington, where William Cullen Bryant had been born. They went to Savoy Hollow and stayed the night, and on the following day, Saturday, returned to Pittsfield. They were just in time for the return of the Berkshire Regiment, and everywhere were signs of making ready, as banners and garlands festooned the village streets, almost everyone excited and happy.

Lizzie soon was doing her part, working with Parthenia Fenn to prepare a hospital in a building on the south side of the village park. Colonel Frank Bartlett arrived on August 19 and stayed at Broadhall with the Morewoods. Herman Melville had plenty of opportunity to appraise, up close, this zealous and honorable young hero—seeing the wounded arm in a box sling and observing how Bartlett got along so well with the artificial leg. Melville admired the colonel. One evening, before the regiment returned, the Liederkranz Singing Society of Pittsfield appeared at Broadhall to serenade Bartlett and the Morewoods. The colonel thanked them with an appropriate and modest speech. Sarah Morewood somehow found the strength to serve refreshments to everyone.

Sarah Morewood of Pittsfield and New York was one of the many self-effacing women who worked unceasingly for the welfare of the soldiers.

It soon was reported that Bartlett had been offered command of a new three-year regiment, the Fifty-seventh Massachusetts, to be enlisted from the western part of the state. He would accept.

The Forty-ninth's train journey home was met at virtually every town and station with welcoming crowds and delicious food the likes of which the men had not envisioned for more than half a year. Henry Johns wrote:

> We had been worrying ourselves about the emptiness of our purses;
> we knew not that the great heart of the North was alive to our coming.

. . . [S]ome kind souls would throw apples into the passing cars; then, at small stations, we would see miniatures of the "dear old flag" flying, and whole baskets of fruit would be handed in. . . . Our trip was one continued ovation.

From southern Illinois, Indiana, through Ohio and Pennsylvania, and into western New York, the train rattled on, stopping often, and local folk would bring tobacco, eggs, milk, even blackberry brandy at times. The soldiers traveled in cattle cars while the officers were in carriages, but the enlisted men were more comfortable than their superiors because they had more room to lie down. Some could only lie down, they were so weak. At every stop, there was generous care for these wounded and sick: "[W]oman's kindness came to us with an unexpected and touching power," said Johns. Women came into the cars to "bathe their brows and wash hands and feet that long had been guiltless of water."

Like angels they hovered over these wrecks of human strength, and, like angels, wept not, lest the tears welling up from overcharged hearts should hinder them in the discharge of their loving but hurried duties.

Johns wrote that through all of this, and while Berkshire families at home were preparing for the happy reception in Pittsfield, one soldier was uneasy and said so to his friends. Sergeant Myron Nichols, a twenty-six-year-old farmer from Otis, with a wife and child awaiting him, had "a presentiment that he would never live to see Berkshire," Johns said. On August 21 as the regiment's train passed through Little Falls, New York, just a few hours from home, Nichols fell from the cars and was killed. No one saw him fall, and the regiment only heard about it by telegraph when they reached Albany, too late to send word to Pittsfield, less than an hour away.

Other men were dying, expected soon to pass away at home, but Nichols had come through all of it, a steady and reliable soldier.

"Has death no relenting?" Johns groaned.

In Albany at 1:30 a.m. on August 22, the regiment was served sandwiches and coffee. The men washed up and put on their "best toggery, so as to look as well as possible under the gaze of Berkshire. To have marched into Pittsfield in all our dirt and rags would only have been an affectation of heroism," said Johns. There were fewer than six hundred and seventy men left of the more than one thousand who had set out last year. Leaving Albany at seven on a clear summer's morning, they were carried by passenger cars the rest of the way, through Columbia County, New York—"never did any country look so beautiful"—crossing the state line, "and with a joy too deep for cheers, felt we were again in the dear old Commonwealth whose principles we had gone forth to uphold and extend. The booming cannon and . . . cheers at last told us we were at home."

In Pittsfield, the soldiers stepped down from the carriages onto the depot platform and into adoring throngs estimated at more than ten thousand people, most of whom had traveled to the station in early-morning darkness and had been waiting impatiently since then. The men embraced their loved ones, and only after an hour or so did the regiment at last form up in the parade column. By then, the fifty sick and wounded had been carried to the hospital readied by Parthenia Fenn, who was helped by many other women, including Lizzie Melville and Lucy Rockwell, the mother of Captain William Rockwell in New Orleans. The Forty-ninth then marched off to the blaring of brass bands from North Adams, Albany, and Lee.

The parade was led by a brass band followed by a large cavalcade of citizens carrying red, white, and blue pennants, then companies of firemen and another band, a couple of social groups carrying their own banners, and yet another band, then the Forty-ninth. The *Sun* wrote:

> At the front of the regiment rode its heroic commander, Colonel Bartlett, mounted upon a splendid horse, which he took with him to Port Hudson, having but one arm at liberty, the other one not yet being recovered from the wound. . . . His soldier-like bearing, and the enthusiasm of the regiment at meeting him again . . . prove him to be one of the few of our many officers who honor their positions more than their positions honor them.

The happy parade wound its way up Depot Street, down North Street and South Street, to East Housatonic Street and Maple Street (now Appleton Avenue), up East Street, and finished at the north side of the park by the Old Elm. The South Street house the Melvilles still rented was decorated with flags and festoons; Herman described those haggard soldiers in his poem "The College Colonel" as a "remnant half-tattered, and battered, and worn, / like castaway sailors . . . stunned / By the surf's loud roar. . . ."

"The College Colonel" describes the monklike Bartlett, which description would fit many a devoted Civil War leader, of both North and South:

> He rides at their head;
>   A crutch by his saddle just slants in view,
> One slung arm is in splints, you see,
>   Yet he guides his strong steed—how coldly too.
>   * * *
> A still rigidity and pale—
>   An Indian aloofness lones his brow;

He has lived a thousand years
Compressed in battle's pains and prayers
Marches and watches slow.

* * *

It is not that a leg is lost,
    It is not that an arm is maimed,
It is not that the fever has racked—
    Self he has long disclaimed.

Lieutenant Colonel Samuel Sumner followed Bartlett on horseback, and after him came the tall Major Charles Plunkett.

The streets were decorated with flags, banners, flowers, and bunting of red, white, and blue over a triumphal arch at the corner of East Street. A banner near the depot read, "How are you, Forty-ninth?" Others had sayings such as, "Welcome Home," "Constitution and Union," and "Aren't you glad you've come?" Some had the names and dates of the regiment's engagements, and St. Louis businessman Thomas Allen, still summering in Pittsfield, had a personal sentiment on his banner: "The Free Navigation of the Mississippi." Suspended from the Pittsfield Bank and the Backus Block were flags and a large banner trimmed with black, inscribed with: "In Memoriam—the Fallen Brave." As the regiment passed beneath this one, every cap was raised, wrote Johns.

It was a beautiful and affecting sight—those hardened, sun-burned men, happy at regaining once again their native hills, turning from the cheers and congratulations of the crowd to heave a sigh or drop a silent tear to the memory of "the fallen brave." . . .

On the Old Elm and over the banquet tables hung the slogan, "Only the brave deserve the FAIR." After the welcome ceremonies, the men were reunited with relatives and friends for the feasting, more music of brass bands, and songs from the Pittsfield Liederkranz. Their loved ones were the only faces the men were more pleased to see than that of Colonel Bartlett, said Johns, who recalled what the colonel had said as they had prepared for the rush against Port Hudson on May 27: "Boys, do nothing that you will be ashamed of when you meet your friends in Berkshire."

The Berkshire Regiment had done all their colonel asked of them, and more.

It would not be long before Melville's family departed from Arrowhead. First, though, they would enjoy the annual Agricultural Fair in October, for the children did not want to miss that. Also, there was the failing Sarah Morewood to comfort.

Frank Bartlett went to the mineral springs at Saratoga to recuperate, and while in Pittsfield he stayed with his relations as well as with the family of his sweetheart, Agnes Pomeroy.

In this time, Lizzie Melville presented the Berkshire bar association with a bust of her famous father, Judge Lemuel Shaw, which was to be placed in the county courthouse at Lenox. Also, the Reverend Orville Dewey came out from Boston to baptize the three of the four Melville children who had not yet been christened.

There were many people for the Melvilles to visit and bid farewell, both in Berkshire and in upstate New York, but on their week-long drive around the county in August, Lizzie and Herman Melville already had taken leave of the beautiful Berkshire countryside.

That summer of 1863, Thomas Reed of the Twenty-first Massachusetts was in Lexington, Kentucky, serving with the regimental headquarters and supply staff. In the army less than a year, Reed still had more than a year to go in his enlistment, and he was weary of the service.

> Cynth, I often wonder if the time since I left home appears as long to you as it does to me; it really seems as though I had been away from home full five years, yet I cheerfully bide the time when you and I will sit side by side as in days of yore, and merrily pass the time away. I should like to engage in two or three more battles before war ends so that I can have a good account to render of myself. As yet I have no scars rec'd in defense of my country but for all that there is many a poor Reb were he alive to speak could testify to my effort in suppressing the Rebellion.

Alarms came and went for the Union troops occupying Lexington as Confederate forces sought to get a foothold in Kentucky. A highly placed quartermaster was court-martialed for embezzlement of regimental funds and diverting supplies to his own use, but Reed retained his position as a clerk on the staff. He even was given the luxury of boarding at the Broadway Hotel; but after a year of sleeping on the ground in a tent, he was "so unused to the accommodations [that I] cannot sleep on a bed when night overtakes me. Think, *If my dear Cynth were with me* [I] would enjoy myself much better but where is the use of speculating in fancied imaginations. . . ."

In August, contemplating reports of the glorious welcome home for the Forty-ninth in Pittsfield, Reed sighed about having one more year to serve. He felt sorry for the suffering the Forty-ninth had to go through in Louisiana and was glad they had received so much "praise for their bravery and soldierly conduct in the service." He was told that daughter Emma was soon to be married, although he would not be there to see it. He thought her too young at seventeen, and wrote, "had she waited a year or two longer she would have acted and thought differently in the matter." He did not doubt that her future husband, John Scace, was a fine man, but he wished Emma to marry someone more prosperous. They would wed that September, and from Kentucky, there was nothing Reed could do about it.

There were plenty of war troubles to worry about, as in mid-September a Confederate army mauled a Union force at Chickamauga Creek, a few miles south of Chattanooga, Tennessee. The defeated Union general, William S. Rosencrans, whose army managed to retreat toward Chattanooga, had a Williams man, James A. Garfield, as chief of staff. Garfield was a close friend of his Williams classmate Brigadier General Hamilton Eldridge, who had served with distinction while leading the 127th Illinois with Grant's army at Vicksburg. Eldridge recently had resigned his commission because of persistent illness and returned to his law practice in Chicago.

Despite the defeat of Rosencrans, Garfield was promoted to major general after the Battle of Chickamauga. He soon would resign and be elected as a congressman from Ohio.

At dawn on September 7, as the men of the Fifty-fourth regiment were preparing to join in another assault on Fort Wagner, a rumor came that the fort had been evacuated the previous night by the Confederates.

It was no rumor. When it was confirmed that the enemy had indeed slipped away from Wagner, the Union soldiers cheered, throwing up hats, dancing and shouting for joy. Other enemy strongpoints also had been abandoned, and the entrance to Charleston harbor was forced that much more open. All the Union troops had fought and worked for during this siege of fifty-eight days, all they had sweated and bled and died for, seemed worthwhile on that day, as regimental flags and the Stars and Stripes went up over Fort Wagner, a ruined hulk that would be rebuilt with one of its batteries renamed Fort Shaw.

The Confederates were not giving up easily, however, and Fort Sumter, huddled and crumbling, was still occupied. Yet, there was a pervading sense in the Union army that the war was being won, and it was worth all the effort. The commander of the Union Department of the South wrote to the troops:

> The scene where our country's flag suffered its first dishonor you have made the theater of one of its proudest triumphs.

The Fifty-fourth had shared a full measure of the struggle, and of the victory. Yet the men still had not been paid, more than three months after departing Massachusetts.

The regiment's work here was far from over, for Charleston still held out. The next months witnessed major artillery battles and fights between ironclads in the harbor, and Sumter resisted a couple of poorly organized Union assaults. The Fifty-fourth continued to dig and construct fortifications. Some men from the regiment were given thirty-day furloughs, allowed leave by shifts. Later that September the rainy season set in. On September 27, the paymaster arrived in camp, but once again the men refused to accept the offer of ten dollars. The paymaster returned three days later, but with the same results.

On this day, Colonel James Montgomery, the former "Bleeding Kansas" guerrilla leader and reputedly effective commander of black troops, came into camp to address the regiment. The Fifty-fourth's present colonel, Edward N. Hallowell, was on leave recuperating from wounds. As Captain Emilio put it, "Montgomery . . . made the men a remarkable and characteristic address." That address was paraphrased as follows:

Men: the paymaster is here to pay you. You must remember you have not proved yourself soldiers. You must take notice that the Government has virtually paid you a thousand dollars apiece for setting you free. Nor should you expect to be placed on the same footing with white men. Anyone listening to your shouting and singing can see how grotesquely ignorant you are. I am your friend and the friend of the Negro. I was the first person in the country to employ nigger soldiers in the United States Army. I was out in Kansas. I was short of men. I had a lot of niggers and a lot of mules; and you know a nigger and a mule go very well together. I therefore enlisted the niggers, and made teamsters of them. In refusing to take the money offered you, and what you are only legally entitled to, you are guilty of insubordination and mutiny, and can be tried and shot by court-martial.

Actually, Montgomery went even further in his insults, but Emilio thought what he said was "improper to repeat. The colonel seemed to be unaware that his remarks were insulting, and most of the men he addressed [had been] born free."

Despite this blunt attempt at intimidation, the Fifty-fourth staunchly continued to refuse unequal pay.

Thanks to the efforts of the Sanitary Commission, supplies of ice, raspberry vinegar, pickles, and other relative luxuries were provided to the Fifty-fourth, which had little cash of its own with which to purchase the necessities that made a soldier's life more comfortable. Donated funds were available to purchase certain items, including tobacco, dried apples, lime juice, and

writing paper. Also, "contraband" friends from nearby towns regularly provided the regiment with a welcome supply of fresh vegetables.

For some weeks, Thomas Reed was stationed with the quartermaster's staff
of the Forty-eighth Pennsylvania regiment while his Twenty-first Massachusetts was at the front. In that time, he ate extremely well, for the Pennsylva-
nians were generous with food for their troops. Then the Forty-eighth went
to the front, and the Seventh Rhode Island took its place in Lexington. Reed,
a native New Yorker, did not like the change, for the Rhode Islanders skimped
on supplies, reducing the required portions of food in order to save money.

> [The Rhode Islanders,] after the true Yankee style have already com-
> menced shaving on the rations and this much I will assure you, a
> person must be very hungry indeed to eat the rations they cook. . . .

Reed made up for this by purchasing his food from civilians. At the time,
the headquarters staff of General Ambrose Burnside, the new regional commander, wanted Reed to join them—quite an honor, which indicated how
accomplished he was. He hoped he would be paid more if that transfer were
made, for his pay had still not been increased for assuming the regimental
quartermaster clerk's position. That pay, as ever, was seldom on time, nor did
it come when Cynthia needed it most.

> Cynth, you don't know how much it worries me to think that you are
> without money and yet have it not in my power to help you. Well,
> the only consolation I can offer is this. I will use every endeavor to
> get it and will send to you as soon as possible on receipt of it. 10
> months from today the time of our Regiment is up and then let any
> man talk to me about re-enlisting and I won't be responsible for the
> consequences.

That fall, Reed was detached from the Twenty-first to be a clerk on
Burnside's inspector-general's staff for the Department of the Ohio, as the
military theater was designated. The force Reed was with was the Army of
the Ohio, and he had a "soft thing," as his friends in the service termed it.
Yet, he worried about rumors that Burnside might be replaced by General
Joseph Hooker, which could mean a wholesale change in staff, and he would
be back toting a musket at the front.

Early that October of 1863, while Herman Melville was in New York working with contractors readying his house on Twenty-sixth Street, Lizzie took
the children to the agricultural fair in Pittsfield. Sarah Morewood appeared

at the fair on the sixth, looking as well as could be expected, but at least she was out.

A few days later, on October 15, Lizzie paused in her labors preparing for the move from Arrowhead—where carpets were rolled up, most things in boxes—and strolled over to Broadhall for a visit. She was startled to find the doctor there and was told Sarah was dying. Lizzie hurried up to her friend's room, arriving just in time, for Sarah soon died. She was thirty-nine.

Lizzie had never experienced someone's death before, let alone that of such a dear friend. She was steady enough, however, to help dress Sarah for burial. Herman was not able to get back in time for the funeral, though he was invited to be a pallbearer. He would later write "The Mound by the Lake," which reflects upon women like Sarah Morewood and Parthenia Fenn, who had given so much to the volunteers.

> The grass shall never forget this grave.
> When homeward footing it in the sun
>   After the weary ride by rail,
> The stripling soldiers passed her door,
>   Wounded perchance, or wan and pale.
> She left her household work undone—
> Duly the wayside table spread,
>   With evergreens shaded, to regale
> Each travel-spent and grateful one.
> So warm her heart—childless—unwed,
> Who like a mother comforted.

On October 15, the Thirty-fourth Massachusetts saw its first action. Operating in the western Potomac region, the regiment had been marching and countermarching for months, responding to enemy threats and imagined threats without coming under fire. Near Berryville on this day, enemy cavalry struck in force and captured a Maryland regiment, and the Thirty-fourth was ordered out in pursuit. It carried on a running battle for miles as the Confederates slowly withdrew, often turning to fight. At times, the Thirty-fourth was almost on its own and came under severe fire again and again.

Once the Confederates had been decisively driven off, the pursuit ended, with the Thirty-fourth losing two of its color guard killed and eight men wounded. By the time the regiment returned to camp, it had marched thirty-six miles, fighting constantly for at least six of those miles. The engagement was known as the Battle of Berryville.

Shortly after Sarah Morewood's funeral, Herman Melville returned to Pittsfield and gathered up his family and their possessions for the final move to

New York City. The Melvilles left Berkshire for good in the second week of November 1863.

From Knoxville, early in November, Thomas Reed told Cynthia he was "enjoying myself first rate," having "easy times" and a "soft living," and expected to draw an additional $12 a month for working on the army headquarters staff.

Reed's superior officer even presented him with a "splendid" new uniform, "which I think will last a year if I am not too hard on [it]." He was on horseback almost every day and, after serving in the field so long, was used to sleeping in his pants: "[S]uch are our habits that I should feel unlike myself were I to undress and go to bed. However when I get home you can give me a few lessons and as I learn easily it will not take long before I am a civilian and retire as you do."

It troubled Reed, however, to see many Union soldiers going barefoot and in rags in the city because their shoes and uniforms had worn out campaigning. What was worse, these men were owed back pay and were destitute, unable to buy new gear. He believed that problems transporting supplies and equipment were to blame for the poor condition of the men, not neglect on the part of the Federal government. Reed's work was hectic and demanding, and he suffered worsening eyestrain, but he was otherwise healthy.

By late that autumn, a Confederate advance had hemmed in the Union forces at Knoxville, and a mighty battle was brewing at Chattanooga, Tennessee, where General Grant was in command of Federal forces. The enemy was making a decisive push with all available resources to drive the Union troops out of eastern Tennessee and Kentucky. At Burnside's headquarters, Reed was in the midst of intense organizational and logistical work, upon which the soldiers in the field depended for their very survival as a fighting force. Supplies were running low, and for a while even the headquarters staff was reduced to only one-quarter of its daily rations.

Grant soon would be victorious in the Chattanooga campaign, and his reputation as the most effective commander in the Union army would lead him eastward to Washington to take overall command of the Union forces in the field. The siege of Knoxville was lifted as the enemy withdrew, but Burnside resigned, and Reed again thought a whole new staff would take over, and he would be ordered to rejoin his regiment in the field.

Late in November, the Massachusetts state legislature resolved to make up the deficiency in the pay that had been offered to the Fifty-fourth regiment. Henceforth, announced Governor Andrew, this regiment and the Fifty-fifth, also recruited from blacks, would be paid from the state treasury, and also would receive everything due them from the day they were first mustered into service.

On behalf of the regiment, and with all due respect to the governor,

Colonel Hallowell replied that the men of the Fifty-fourth had enlisted just like all other soldiers from Massachusetts and, as Captain Emilio put it, "would serve without pay until mustered out, rather than accept from the United States less than the amount paid other soldiers." They again turned down their unequal pay.

Their reasons were articulated in a letter from an enlisted man to a "friend of the regiment," Theodore Tilton, who passed the letter on to a Boston newspaper. The letter reminded the state of its promises to treat the Fifty-fourth equally. The men had "swallowed the insult offered us by the United States paymaster, contenting ourselves with a simple refusal to acknowledge ourselves different from other Massachusetts soldiers." Without mentioning Colonel Montgomery's name, the letter also commented on "insult and intimidation," which "we quietly refused and continued to do our duty."

> Imagine our surprise and disappointment . . . to find [the Governor proposing] to pay this regiment the difference between what the United States Government offers us and what they are legally bound to pay us, which, in effect, advertises us to the world as holding out for *money* and not from *principle*,—that we sink our manhood in consideration of a few more dollars. . . .

The letter continued, "[T]he regiment whose bayonets pricked the name of Colonel Shaw into the roll of immortal honor can afford to be cheated out of their money, but not out of their manhood."

The siege of Charleston continued and, month after month, the Fifty-fourth did its duty without accepting a penny of unequal pay.

John Atwood of the Tenth Massachusetts recovered from his heat prostration that fall of 1863, and one day was surprised to be asked to represent his state by carrying the Massachusetts colors in a parade through Gettysburg. Also asked to carry colors was fellow Tenth member William Mason, the English-born nurse from Springfield.

That parade took place on November 19, and in it was none other than President Lincoln, riding on horseback, and apparently not feeling very well. With the flags of every state borne aloft, the procession went through Gettysburg on a chilly late-autumn day, the streets lined with thousands of people as the procession made its way to the new military cemetery. Atwood, flanked by a soldier on each side, found himself marching up to Cemetery Hill, where an immense platform had been erected, large enough to hold several hundred people, including speakers Lincoln and former presidential candidate Edward Everett of Massachusetts.

Atwood sat just twenty feet away from the speaker's podium.

The principal address was delivered by Everett, who had given a speech at Pittsfield early in 1861. A noted and colorful orator, he talked for two hours, going into great detail about the war. At last, the president rose to offer some "appropriate remarks" he had composed on the train from Washington. John Atwood of North Adams was there when President Abraham Lincoln delivered the Gettysburg Address. Atwood later said he heard every word distinctly.

Chapter Twenty-one

THE DEPTHS OF WAR

The men of the pacifist communal sect known as Shakers—whom Melville liked to visit—were able to avoid being drafted thanks largely to the direct influence of their leaders, called elders, two of whom went to Washington and met with the president. After hearing their case, Lincoln agreed they should be exempted from service on the basis of their nonviolent beliefs.

The Shaker communal villages in Berkshire County at Hancock and Tyringham and just over the New York line in New Lebanon were part of a larger network of seventeen such communities scattered from Maine to Kentucky, with a total membership of just under thirty-five hundred. The Shakers, formally known as the United Society of Believers in Christ's Second Appearing, considered work as an expression of faith and inner purity, their motto being "Hands to work, hearts to God." Founded in the Berkshire-Albany area in the late eighteenth century, Shaker communities had thriven for the first half of the 1800s, their members mostly employed in agriculture and small-scale manufacturing. The Shaker-made reputation for high quality had established the order as an important producer of common household goods and agricultural equipment, from brooms to furniture, packaged seeds to pharmaceuticals, which were sold all over the country.

The Shakers had reached their zenith by the Civil War period, with new converts becoming scarce in these years. A celibate order dependent on con-verts for membership, the "Believers," as they called themselves, expected that an imminent return of Christ would bring the wholesale conversion of many thousands. With the Civil War came unheard-of technological progress in America, mass production, swift travel and shipment by railroad and steam-boat, improved communication and roads, and the rise of cities. The rural life and industry of the Shakers were overtaken by mass manufacturing, and the lure of ready cash to be had in booming population centers attracted those who might otherwise have sought a more spiritual existence. Fewer young people were interested in joining the order, and by the middle of the 1860s, the sect had lost much of its dynamic.

During this time, the Shakers suffered greatly in places such as war-scorched Kentucky, where their villages endured the thievery of soldiers from both armies, which swept back and forth across the state. Yet even in the North, war taxes were heavy, placing a financial burden on the villages, and from time to time Believers would be drafted by their local communities and had difficulty certifying their status as pacifists. Sometimes, Shaker men were imprisoned for refusing to serve in the military, requiring legal wrangles be-fore release was gained.

Still, the Shakers of Berkshire wholeheartedly supported the Union cause and donated considerably to the soldiers' aid groups. The Mount Lebanon Shaker leaders communicated regularly with Lincoln—the elders who had visited the president in 1862 had been from this village, which was the spiri-tual and administrative headquarters for the Shaker order. In 1864 they sent him the gift of a Shaker-made chair, for which he personally wrote to thank them. They genuinely worried about the welfare of the president, whom they considered a friend.

In the fall of 1863, Captain Ralph Ives of the Tenth regiment and Great Barrington had gone to visit a Virginia family living a distance from the camp and had been captured by enemy raiders.

Taken to Libby Prison in Richmond, Captain Ives soon found himself embroiled in a momentous controversy between the warring governments. The Confederacy wanted to make an example of two Federal officers, in ret-ribution for two of its own captains having been sentenced to death after being captured while recruiting behind Union lines in Kentucky. That death sentence had been commuted to hard labor, and the two Confederate officers were forced to wear a ball and chain, punishment that contravened under-standings regarding the treatment of captives. In order to force the Federal government to desist, the Confederacy had lots drawn by the Union captains imprisoned at Libby to see who would be put under the same circumstances as its two men. Ives was one of the two Union unfortunates, and he was put to hard labor, wearing a ball and chain until February 1864, when both governments finally relented.

Since her health was failing, the elderly Catharine Sedgwick lived these days with the family of her niece Kate Minot in West Roxbury, near Boston, seldom visiting Berkshire. She was in her mid-seventies.

Late in the summer of 1863, Miss Sedgwick went to stay for the last time at the original Sedgwick family home in Stockbridge, a place that meant so much to her. Since she suffered from severe and unpredictable attacks of epilepsy, she was forced to give up visits to Lenox to stay with her sister-in-law, Elizabeth Sedgwick, who lived with the widow and children of her late son, Will, and was also unwell. In one seizure, Catharine Sedgwick was unconscious for so long that it was thought she would die. She recovered and later wrote an acquaintance, "I receive gratefully my life from day to day. . . ."

Miss Sedgwick was very weak, and when she departed Stockbridge that fall, it was her farewell to Berkshire.

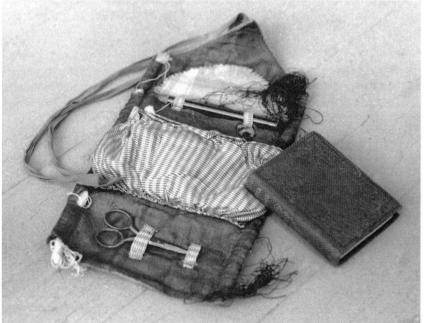

COURTESY JAMES N. PARRISH

Many Civil War volunteers received a "Soldier's Housewife" sewing kit such as this one, which was presented to the Forty-ninth's Private W.J. Karner of South Egremont by the local Ladies' Soldiers' Aid society, along with the pocket New Testament.

At the end of 1863, more than one hundred members of the Tenth Massachusetts re-enlisted for another three years, each man collecting a bounty of approximately $700 and earning a thirty-day furlough. Those who did not re-enlist would be mustered out this coming July and would get no furlough. Among the men not re-enlisting was Charlie Gates of Lee, who had decided to return to the farm. Before Gates's time was up, however, there would be plenty of soldiering and some of the very worst fighting of the war.

In the seven or eight months after Gettysburg, the Tenth had been stationed in northern Virginia, where the Union and Confederate armies sparred, probed, and threatened, but generally avoided full-scale battle. Each had sent strong reinforcements to the Kentucky-Tennessee theater, and among these was the Second Massachusetts, which had gone by rail that fall to Chattanooga.

Late in 1863, the Twentieth Massachusetts regiment had been heavily engaged at Mine Run and Bristoe Station in northeastern Virginia, counter-ing probes by Lee and turning them back. Also campaigning in Virginia was the Thirty-seventh Massachusetts, which went on hard marches at the end of this year but was not involved in major action. The Twenty-seventh Massachusetts regiment, collected from its various stations along the Caro-lina and Virginia coast, was sent to Norfolk and Portsmouth, Virginia, as the provost guard for those towns. The armies went into winter quarters, a welcome respite from the most difficult campaign season thus far.

At New Orleans, the Thirty-first Massachusetts found itself changed from infantry into cavalry. Although they enjoyed comfortable quarters in a former factory, the soldiers had to learn how to ride, to care for their mounts, and to handle the cavalryman's carbine, a short-barreled rifle. Equipped with sabers and revolvers, the Thirty-first would be called the Sixth Massachusetts cav-alry, although officially it would keep the designation as the Thirty-first, of which the men were understandably proud.

In December, Pittsfield's Willie Rockwell, a captain of the Thirty-first, died of illness in New Orleans. He was twenty-four.

From Knoxville, Tennessee, just before that Christmas of 1863, Thomas Reed sent his family in Pittsfield the respectable sum of seventy dollars. Reed wrote, "I think you must have been sadly in want, wasn't you? Well, you know that good things come slow." His fortunes continued to rise as he became a clerk in the commissary department, responsible for trainloads of supplies.

In January 1864, Reed's Twenty-first Massachusetts was asked to re-enlist for the duration of the war. The regiment's time would run out in late summer. Men who re-enlisted would be paid the bounty and given a month of furlough, during which they could go home. Reed was torn by the choice. As much as he wanted to leave the army that summer, he was tempted by the re-enlistment bonus. Further, he had a very good situation in the commissary department, where he likely could wait out the rest of the war and survive to go home again. Still, civilians with his clerking experience were earning high wages these days, as much as one hundred dollars a month, and he might find himself with a good job if he left the army that summer. Back in Berkshire, the cost of living had gone up so fast that even the normally conservative clergymen were uniting to ask that their salaries be increased by thirty-three percent. At the same time, new mansions were being built by local business-men who were prospering from the war, and appearing in Berkshire lately were newly rich—phenomenally rich—tycoons from New York and Boston on the hunt for places to build estates.

Lincoln was calling for another two hundred thousand soldiers, and Berk-shire was faced with the possibility of the draft forcibly taking men away. Again the drumbeat of enlistment went around the county, and many young men joined, but not enough to fill the quota of 1,693 for this latest call-up. The largest town quota was Pittsfield's, with 312 men required, followed by Adams at 238; the smallest was that of New Ashford, obligated for six enlist-ees. Peru, with eleven men called for, already had provided thirteen, and Sandisfield had exactly met its quota of forty-one.

To make up the shortfall of a given town, the army threatened to draft from it the number of men needed. Only volunteers received bounty money, and draftees received just the soldier's monthly pay of thirteen dollars.

Some towns falling short on the quotas renewed efforts to recruit willing fellows from other towns, sometimes as far away as Boston. There were more instances of men signing up, receiving their bounty money, and skipping out. An extreme example of such fraudulence occurred early in 1864, when ten men purportedly from Greenfield offered to sign up as part of Hinsdale's quota, each to be paid $150 bounty from the town.

The ten volunteers, who were put forward by a middleman acting as agent, collected $1,500, were brought to camp for muster, and vanished the next day, without a trace of either them or the town's money.

In January of 1864, Stewart's Cornet Band of North Adams enlisted to serve as the band of the brigade that included the Tenth Massachusetts. Though the army no longer permitted regimental bands, brigades and larger units could have them. Brass bands provided the most popular musical entertainment of the day, and Stewart's, led by Edward Stewart, would do much for soldier morale.

That February, a comet was visible to the naked eye in the constellation Cassiopeia, which by nine o'clock at night was nearly in the zenith of the heavens.

In mid-February of 1864, the steam-powered sloop of war U.S.S. *Housatonic* was anchored at its station as a blockader just outside the bar to besieged

Charleston Harbor. Launched at Boston in 1861, the vessel was named after the Housatonic River, which rises in Berkshire and wends its way southward through Massachusetts and Connecticut to Long Island Sound. Since September 1862, *Housatonic* had served in the blockade of Charleston, preventing the Confederacy from easily receiving supplies into, or shipping goods from, this important harbor.

On the night of February 17, an officer on watch saw what appeared to be a plank moving through the water toward the ship. Looking more closely, he realized it was some hostile device, being propelled right at the side of *Housatonic*. Alarm bells rang, and guns were manned, but they were too late to be depressed far enough to shoot at whatever was approaching. There came a dull explosion underwater, and the *Housatonic* shuddered. She had been fatally holed in history's first successful submarine attack.

The submarine was H.L. *Hunley*, built in Mobile, Alabama, and fitted with a long pole on the end of which was a torpedo with ninety pounds of explosive. The torpedo was pushed against the target vessel and secured by a barbed spike, then the charge was fired by a crewman of *Hunley* pulling a lanyard. *Housatonic* went to the bottom, losing five men, the rest of its crew scampering to safety up the rigging, which remained above the surface in those shallow waters.

Hunley, the first submarine ever to sink a warship in combat, also went down, with the loss of her entire crew of nine.

In major cities throughout the North, plans were underway for holding enormous Sanitary Fairs this summer, at which funds would be raised to finance the effort to care for the troops. New York, Chicago, and Philadelphia would have the largest fairs and would manage to raise millions of dollars in a wide range of ways, from auctioning fine artwork, rugs, and furniture to selling homemade baked goods, handmade quilts, artful or amateur photographs, and offering exhibits of all kinds—whatever would bring in a dollar.

The town of Adams caught the spirit early in 1864 and planned for its own Sanitary Fair in March. Folk in other Berkshire towns decided it would be best for all if the county supported Adams rather than dilute the effort by holding several fairs in different communities. One of the attractions at the Adams fair, which was held in North Adams, were two British brass cannons captured from a Confederate vessel that had tried unsuccessfully to run the Federal blockade. Daniel Dodge of Pittsfield arranged to have the cannons brought to the fair, and also to exhibit a "John Brown pike," one of the spears that Brown planned to issue rebelling slaves had he succeeded in sparking an uprising in the South back in 1859.

The Adams Sanitary Fair raised $3,300 to aid the soldiers.

Early in 1864, reinforced by one hundred and twenty new recruits, the Fifty-fourth Massachusetts embarked on a steamer for a campaign in Florida. The men were eager for a change from the hot and sandy Carolina coast, but it was unfortunate that the unlikable Colonel James Montgomery would be one of the expedition's leaders.

That February, the Fifty-fourth took part in the capture of Jacksonville, Florida, which was only weakly defended. The Union expeditionary force moved inland, and with it went some companies of the First Massachusetts cavalry that were operating as an independent battalion. This battalion soon would be enlarged by added companies and then designated the Fourth Massachusetts cavalry.

At first, Confederate resistance in Florida was light, but reinforcements were gathering to contest any Union advance. The general commanding the Federal expeditionary force was explicitly ordered not to go too far from the main base at Jacksonville, but the leadership of the campaign was the same group of officers that had misjudged the defenses of Fort Wagner last summer and had ordered the failed assault. Once again, they made the wrong decision—flouting direct orders from the high command—and advanced their force into the jaws of an ambush in country thick with tall pine forests ideal for a surprise.

The subsequent Battle of Oulstee was essentially a fighting retreat for the outmaneuvered Union soldiers. At a crucial moment in the fight, the "colored brigade," composed of the Fifty-fourth Massachusetts and the First North Carolina Native Guards, made a stand to give the main body of the expeditionary force a chance to withdraw. As the men of the Fifty-fourth marched to the battle front, passing retreating Union regiments, they heard many warnings to turn around before they were wiped out.

The brigade went into line of battle, and as it prepared for the enemy assault, the Fifty-fourth shouted a bitterly ironic war cry: "Three cheers for Massachusetts—and seven dollars a month!"

The Union men fought off repeated enemy attacks, and then came a moment when the Fifty-fourth found itself alone, having been unaware of the withdrawal of the Native Guard regiment. No orders came to retire, so the Fifty-fourth stayed in position, holding the main body of Confederates at bay. Captain Emilio wrote:

> It would seem either that the position of the regiment was forgotten, or its sacrifice considered necessary.

As daylight began to fail, the Fifty-fourth was almost out of ammunition, its dead and wounded lying all around. Still no orders had come to withdraw, but the enemy was closing in on the flanks and firing from cover. When a fresh supply of ammunition was brought up, spirits rose until it was seen that the cartridges were of the wrong caliber, useless. By now, Colonel Hallowell had become separated from the regiment, which was being led by Lieutenant Colonel Henry N. Hooper. The sound of gunfire passing along the right and left flanks told that the enemy was about to cut off all retreat. Then Colonel Montgomery appeared and, as Captain Emilio recalled, "seemed determined to retire [the regiment] in his bushwhacking way. . . ." Emilio recounted what Montgomery said: "Now, men, you have done well. I love you all. Each man take care of himself." The men looked at one another, uncertain, wondering whether they were supposed to break and make a run for it, to scatter like guerrillas, not stand and fight like the trained infantrymen of a proud regiment.

> [T]his plan did not please Lieutenant-colonel Hooper, [who] . . . shouted "Rally!" and a line was again formed. . . . Lieutenant-colonel Hooper . . . briefly addressed the men, ordered bayonets fixed, and exercised the regiment in the manual of arms to bring it completely under control. . . . The regiment was then directed to give nine loud cheers to make it appear we were receiving reinforcements. In line of battle faced to the rear the Fifty-fourth then marched off the field. . . .

The wrong-caliber ammunition was thrown into mud holes, the wounded hoisted onto shoulders or carried in blankets slung between men, and the regiment gradually withdrew, prepared at any moment to give battle. There were several brushes with enemy troops, but the Fifty-fourth reached the expeditionary force safely. This was a shining moment for the regiment, for it had withdrawn in the face of the enemy, in perfect order and with firm discipline, even though it had been told by a ranking officer to break and run.

Of the almost two thousand Union casualties suffered at the Battle of Oulstee, the Fifty-fourth lost eighty-seven men.

Soon afterward, the regiment was brigaded with the Fifty-fifth Massachusetts, another black regiment. There was little action during the rest of that balmy Florida springtime, however, and with the monotony of camp life came more rumors about the regiment's equal pay being approved by the Federal government. They were just rumors, however. At home, their families were suffering, some even forced to enter county poorhouses.

The officers of the Fifty-fourth wrote to the government, and Massachusetts representatives tried, unsuccessfully, to have Congress pass bills for equal pay. Nothing had been achieved, and friends of the regiment as well as the soldiers' home towns helped their families by contributing money and clothing. Through it all, the soldiers unswervingly stuck to their principles, continuing to demand equal pay.

In April the Fifty-fourth embarked from Florida and returned to Morris Island, that dismal place with its hordes of flies, where the Confederates were still holding on to Charleston and fighting for every inch of ground.

That same month, Henry T. Johns sent the manuscript of his book, *Life with the Forty-ninth*, to a printer in New York.

Since the time of the Battle of Berryville in mid-October 1863, Great Barrington's Corporal Charles Moulton of the Thirty-fourth Massachusetts had been on detached duty as clerk in the provost marshal's office at Harpers Ferry. His regiment's next action was in a daring midwinter expedition of seventeen hundred men up the Shenandoah Valley in support of a cavalry raid on enemy salt works, but Corporal Moulton did not have to go with the regiment into the cold and danger. Like Thomas Reed, he was more valuable to the army as a clerk with a pen than as an infantryman with a musket.

When the Confederate commander, Lieutenant General Jubal A. Early, led a powerful force in pursuit, the Union expedition narrowly escaped, with the Thirty-fourth herding along more than one hundred prisoners.

During the winter of 1863-64, Pittsfield's Thomas Reed was injured by a crate falling on his foot. Reed dared not ask for time off to recuperate, for he might lose his "soft" position with the commissary department in Knoxville. He labored on, keeping his pain to himself, except when writing home.

Reed told Cynthia of his work, which included supervising the unloading of a steamboat carrying seventy thousand pounds of bacon and fifty thousand of "hard bread." He had to account for all the crates as a work gang of thirty men carried the freight from steamboat to wharf: "[Y]ou might as well believe it's as much as the Boy cares to attend to and have the figures come out all right."

Reed was good at his work, and when he told the other clerks he was planning to go home when his time was up, they "unanimously declared I should not, because each one of us has a separate department to manage . . . and it would be a shame to create a vacancy by my leaving." Reed was tempted by the bounty money to stay in the service. He even had an offer to work for the army as a civilian clerk, with high wages, but

> I would be a heap glad to go home and see my Gal Cynth. I some-
> times think money enough never was made to induce me to remain
> here after I get my discharge and yet I know full well that the inter-
> ests of my dear ones at home require all the efforts I can exert to
> make them comfortable and if I can do so by any sacrifice of my own
> I will most cheerfully do it. But when I do get home, I'm just going to

have an easy time for at least a month or two and shall want some of your assistance, too.

Reed hotly objected when Cynthia told him their fourteen-year-old son, Eddie, wanted to enlist as a drummer boy. Reed said Eddie was too young, and that most of the drummer boys who had so eagerly joined up early in the war had quickly gone to their graves.

In the spring of 1864, Colonel Frank Bartlett was presented with a sword by the people of the town of Winthrop, where his father's family resided. Bartlett had just taken command of another regiment, the Fifty-seventh Massachusetts, which he had raised that spring. Known as the colonel who rode into battle with a crutch slung over his back, he was quite famous, and the presentation ceremony was reported by the *Boston Herald*.

> Yesterday afternoon the citizens of Winthrop assembled at their Town Hall for the purpose of presenting a sword to their fellow citizen, Col. Wm. F. Bartlett, of the 57th Mass. regiment. . . . The Colonel made a modest and becoming response, expressing his thanks . . . and his determination to remain in the field until the war was over.

Though he endured excruciating bouts of pain in his amputated leg, Bartlett prepared to lead the new regiment south. In the Fifty-seventh were a number of Berkshire Regiment veterans, who had re-enlisted to serve with him.

Herman Melville and his brother, Allan, journeyed to Washington, D.C., in April, where they acquired a pass—arranged by Massachusetts senator Charles Sumner—to visit troops at the front. Melville passed through Alexandria, where Brigadier General Henry Briggs was in command, and then journeyed to the camp of the Second Massachusetts cavalry, among whom Melville had friends. He rode out on an expedition with them, accompanied by Pittsfield's Dr. Oscar DeWolf, surgeon to the cavalry brigade.

For the first time in ages, Melville thoroughly enjoyed physical activity, and he was even temporarily unburdened from his painful sciatica. He would write "The Scout Toward Aldie."

> The sun is gold, and the world is green,
>   Opal the vapors of morning roll;
> The champing horses lightly prance—
> Full of caprice, and the riders, too . . .

* * *

How strong they feel on their horses free,
  Tingles the tendoned thigh with life;
Their cavalry-jackets make boys of all—
With golden breasts like the oriole;
  The chat, the jest, and laugh are rife . . .

Toward evening, gunfire was heard from up ahead, and word came back that enemy cavalry were in line of battle. The Union troopers formed up in a column of four, drew out their carbines, and charged. Melville charged with them, though no enemy force was met.

Not long after, Melville was introduced to General Ulysses S. Grant, the new general-in-chief of Union forces. Grant had come east from a triumphant career in the western theater, and now he was to lead the final crushing of the stubborn Confederate army of Robert E. Lee. Grant's initials, "U.S.," were said to signify "Unconditional Surrender."

Chapter Twenty-two

THE WILDERNESS
AND A JOURNAL

Colonel Bartlett and his Fifty-seventh regiment departed Massachusetts
on April 18, arriving in northern Virginia within two weeks. Three days after
the regiment reached the front, and before Bartlett even had time to visit his
friends stationed nearby with the Twentieth, the Battle of the Wilderness
erupted, and the new regiment was hurled into savage fighting.

It began with the clash of two army corps—the Federal corps was the
Sixth, under Major General John Sedgwick, and included the Tenth and
Thirty-seventh Massachusetts. Earlier in the war, the first phase of a battle
might have been joined by single regiments or brigades, but now the scope of
the conflict was so immense that a full corps with twenty or more regiments
was the common unit of maneuver. As Sedgwick's force took on the Confederates, more and more corps from each army marched up to join the fray. The
fighting was bloody, desperate, but neither side could get the upper hand.
Upon entering this battle, Bartlett wrote in his diary, "I believe I am prepared
to die."

At eleven that morning, after the Fifty-seventh had been fighting for three
hard hours, there came orders to charge past a Union regiment that was lying
down, frozen in place, unwilling to attack. The Fifty-seventh rushed right over

them, and Bartlett's division commander roared, "Glorious!" Soon after, Bartlett was struck on the head, a glancing blow by a bullet that made him reel in the saddle. Stunned, he lay on his horse's neck and rode to the rear for treatment. He agreed, only reluctantly, to be sent in an ambulance back to Washington.

This was Bartlett's fourth wound.

The Battle of the Wilderness opened a whole new phase of the war—an even more merciless one—as Grant launched enormous assaults straight at the Confederates. He was willing to accept high losses in order to sap and ultimately break the enemy's strength. Coupled with the courage of the veteran soldiers on both sides, Grant's total-war tactics brought on ferocious struggles in the close quarters of Virginia's forests and swamps, where the Confederates were strongly dug in and refused to retreat.

In the Wilderness fighting, the new Fifty-seventh suffered a staggering two hundred and fifty casualties, including Bartlett. The Tenth, Twentieth, Twenty-first, and Thirty-seventh Massachusetts were also in the battle, and the First Massachusetts cavalry was engaging enemy troopers not far away. Serving with the cavalry were two Williamstown brothers, Charles and Walter Jennings. Charles, the older brother, had been wounded at Antietam while serving with the Twenty-first Massachusetts, had recuperated, and then enlisted in the cavalry, joined by his brother. Walter had been only sixteen, too young to join up, but he lied about his age.

Fighting surged back and forth in the Wilderness, with part of the forest bursting into flame, killing many wounded who could not escape. The conflict ended only when both armies were utterly exhausted. The Federals suffered more than 17,600 casualties, the Confederates approximately 7,500, and Lee had held his ground against Grant's frontal attacks. Yet, everyone knew it would soon start again.

It did, as Grant maneuvered to outflank Lee and cut him off from Richmond. The next major action was the Battle of Spotsylvania Court House, which started on May 8 and raged for almost two weeks, the largest, most prolonged engagement to that time. Grant intended to continue his bludgeoning tactics until the foe was drained of manpower, but the Confederates had plenty of fight left and would not surrender until there was absolutely no other choice, and even then they sometimes fought fanatically to the death.

On that first day of Spotsylvania, the Tenth was dismayed to learn that their former commander, Brigadier General Eustis—the man who had cashiered so many fine officers of the regiment—was found to be intoxicated. General Grant himself, along with corps commander Sedgwick, saw that Eustis's brigade was not being maneuvered properly, that his regiments were being given conflicting orders. Sedgwick, mortified with embarrassment, immediately relieved Eustis of command and put Colonel Oliver Edwards of the Thirty-seventh in charge of the brigade (Edwards had originally been adjutant of the Tenth).

On the second day of battle, the much-loved Sedgwick was killed by an enemy sharpshooter. Though his death would be mourned throughout the Union army, there was no time for sorrow while the fighting still raged. On May 10, the third day of Spotsylvania, the Federals launched a general attack against entrenched Confederates, and twice were repulsed with heavy casualties. The day ended with near breakthroughs in the enemy line, but the Confederates held on. While the infantry gathered for yet another clash, cavalry engagements were going on all around, and in one raid against a key railroad junction, the First Massachusetts Cavalry lost twenty-eight men, including Williamstown's Lieutenant Edward P. Hopkins, the son of Albert Hopkins, the much-admired Williams professor.

Without rest, the cavalry regiment joined a forced march to a crossroads

Berkshire men fought in the Civil War's most prolonged close-quarters combat, which raged at the "Bloody Angle" in the Battle of Spotsylvania during the Wilderness campaign in northern Virginia.

known as Yellow Tavern, where it fought in a daylong battle against Confederate troopers under the famous cavalry general J. E. B. Stuart. The Federals won, and Stuart was mortally wounded.

The conflict at Spotsylvania resumed as the two armies, like enormous wild beasts, tore at each other. Before dawn on May 12, the Confederates counterattacked the lines of the Sixth Corps, striking directly at the Tenth and Thirty-seventh Massachusetts regiments, which were holding a position that became famous as "The Bloody Angle of Spotsylvania," arguably the fiercest fighting of all the Civil War. A heavy rainstorm deluged the soldiers, but the struggle went on for twenty-four hours. The Tenth expended three hundred rounds per man, the Thirty-seventh four hundred; sixty rounds were generally carried into battle. When ammunition was low, bayonets and musket butts did their murderous work, and at times the hostile forces occupied opposite sides of the same earthworks or fence line, fighting from just a few feet away. Men died from surprise bayonet thrusts through wooden breastworks that separated the two armies in some places.

After dark on the twelfth, the fighting paused, and front-line Union regiments such as the Tenth and Thirty-seventh were relieved, going to the rear, where they collapsed with exhaustion and immediately fell asleep. In the middle of the night, the Thirty-seventh was jarred awake by warning yells from their relief troops, who were retreating from an enemy attack. Though out of ammunition, the Thirty-seventh hurried back to the front and held the position with only the bayonet until more ammunition was brought up. Then they fired into the darkness all that night. Morning revealed that the Confederates had fallen back.

So went the Spotsylvania conflict, day after terrible day. The Berkshire men of the Tenth, Thirty-seventh, Fifty-seventh, and the First cavalry regiments were in the very worst of it. Grant and Lee threw everything they had at each other until May 19, when Grant made another flanking movement around Lee to force the Confederates to withdraw toward Richmond. In the Wilderness and Spotsylvania battles, the Tenth Massachusetts regiment lost one hundred and eighty-six men, the Thirty-seventh more than two hundred and thirty, the First cavalry eighty-six, and the Fifty-seventh almost three hundred and fifty. In the next few weeks, these regiments would continue to suffer heavily, with the Fifty-seventh losing its next commander and another thirty-six men in one engagement.

The Twenty-first Massachusetts, most of its men not long back from a month's furlough as re-enlistees, lost more than one hundred men in these conflicts. Major Henry Richardson, former commander of the Allen Guards, had rejoined the regiment just before this campaign, having been on detached service for some months. Although at the forefront of the action, Richardson had miraculously never been wounded.

In the Virginia campaign of 1864 were other Union regiments with individual soldiers from Berkshire, among them the Eighty-third New York, with Lieutenant Charles H. Barker of Adams, whose three years had been up just before the Wilderness, but he had re-enlisted. Lieutenant Barker was mortally wounded in the battle, dying in the hospital on May 10.

Confederate Brigadier General Edward Perry, Berkshire native, was severely wounded at the Wilderness while leading his Florida Brigade, and for the rest of the war would be a member of the reserves, stationed in Alabama. His brigade was wiped out.

On May 19, the day the Spotsylvania battles ceased, Nathaniel Hawthorne died in his sleep at Plymouth, New Hampshire, at age sixty. Hawthorne's death was another sign that the prewar era was fading away, never to return.

To the southeast of the Wilderness-Spotsylvania fighting, a comparatively minor but fierce battle took place that May, as Union forces advanced toward the city of Petersburg, the defenses of which were a key to Richmond. The Twenty-seventh Massachusetts was in this offensive, which was stubbornly opposed by Confederate defenders, solidly entrenched. Led by the intrepid General P. T. Beauregard, the Southerners stopped the Union troops, who were commanded by General Benjamin Butler. In the struggle, the Twenty-seventh fought valiantly, as each army launched attack and counterattack. In one disastrous episode, a major portion of the regiment was trapped at Drury's Bluff on May 16, and almost two hundred and fifty taken prisoner, including its colonel. (The next commander of the regiment would be Captain William H. Clark of Pittsfield.)

Sixty-five men of the Twenty-seventh were killed or wounded at Drury's Bluff. Among the dead was Captain Charles Sanford, twenty-four-year-old son of the Reverend Miles Sanford of North Adams, former chaplain of the regiment. The Confederates buried Captain Sanford on the battlefield.

Shortly afterwards, Sanford's mother was in a small room on Bradford Place, North Adams, at work with other members of the Ladies' Soldiers' Aid society, when the message came about her loss. A Berkshire writer later said, "If a rebel shell had burst above these devoted women's heads there could not have been more consternation, or if a rebel sword had pierced that loving mother's heart, it could not have inflicted a more cruel wound."

Most of the captives from the Twenty-seventh were taken to notorious Andersonville Prison, where more than one hundred and twenty eventually would die from neglect. One of the prisoners was Corporal Eldad E. Moore of Lee, who was determined not to die in captivity. Also among the captured was Williamstown's Calvin Hosford, whose health since he joined the service had never been good. Before the prisoners were brought into Andersonville, they had been robbed of everything by the guards—their money, valuables, clothing, even their family photographs, these last often taken with a cruel sneer. All pleading to keep at least the photographs was in vain, and Hosford is quoted as saying, "[O]ur hearts sank, and a new sense of the satanic spirit of our foe overwhelmed us."

The soldier who quoted Hosford was a young captive from Sheffield, already in Andersonville when the Twenty-seventh men arrived: Robert H. Kellogg had been serving with the Sixteenth Connecticut regiment when taken prisoner. He was surprised to see how the newcomers from Massachusetts had been so completely dispossessed of everything, a new intensifying of brutality on the part of the enemy. Kellogg's journal described his own arrival at Andersonville. Before coming there, he had heard rumors of terrible conditions in Confederate prison camps, but had thought them only fabrications intended to frighten Union troops and dissuade them from surrendering. When he walked into the place, however, Kellogg saw what Calvin Hosford later saw:

> Our blood almost froze with horror and made our hearts fail within us, [for] . . . before us were walking skeletons covered with filth and vermin. . . . [C]an this be hell?

It was.

There was little food at Andersonville, no shelter, no water for washing, almost no clothing or blankets, and the guards—who seemed chosen for their cruelty—had a free hand with the helpless prisoners. Yet the defiance of the suffering Union men expressed itself in their will to live, and sometimes in their acts of patriotism. When July Fourth arrived that year, the captives sang Union songs all that day and night, thousands of voices lifted against the oppression that could kill them, but could not break their spirits. For this, they were harshly punished by food being withheld for several days, though there was little enough of it to begin with. Hosford suffered from scurvy, his limbs withering, joints stiff, so that he could scarcely move.

Lee's Eldad Moore was strong enough to escape when he had the chance, and that came not long after arrival in Andersonville, when some prisoners were put on a train for transfer to a camp near Charleston. Moore jumped off and ran into the woods. He fled for seventy-five miles before soldiers with bloodhounds finally caught up with him and brought him to another camp. Moore was determined to try again, though his guards warned they would shoot him if he did.

Catharine and Elizabeth Sedgwick's dear friend Fanny Kemble was again the center of attention in Britain now that her sensational *Journal of a Residence on a Georgian Plantation* had been published. The British release early in 1864 was followed that summer by publication in the United States, with the late Colonel Robert Shaw's father, Francis, arranging for Harper Brothers to publish the American edition.

Many in Britain refused to believe Miss Kemble's graphic description of the slaves' oppressed, dehumanized life on the plantation. In Britain it was generally thought that Southern slaves were fundamentally happy with their lot, enjoying a simple, carefree life that gave them security, a place to live, and food. Other readers thought it indecent that the *Journal* so nakedly depicted the harshness of life for the Butler slaves. Such readers also considered it extremely improper for a divorced woman to reveal such things about her former husband's personal life. Many daughters of respectable British families were warned never to open Miss Kemble's book, but they did, of course, and with all the gossip and publicity, the *Journal* sold well.

It was said that anyone who picked up the book could not put it down, and Fanny Kemble became the controversial subject of many heated discussions.

With regard to its effect upon Britain's attitude to the Civil War, the *Journal* made the government uncomfortable enough with Southern slavery that politicians began to lean more in the direction of neutrality. A sympathetic lord presented a copy of the book to Queen Victoria, who was reportedly moved by it, further strengthening the hand of anti-intervention forces in Britain. Admiration for the "sporting gallantry" of the Confederacy (as one lord had put it) was considerably diminished. Reviews of the *Journal* generally adhered to the political leanings of the publications.

American response to the *Journal* was comparable to that in Britain. Many readers admired the book, and others despised it, according to their political inclinations. *Harper's Weekly* promoted it as "the most powerful anti-slavery book yet written," and a reviewer in the *Atlantic Monthly* said, "A sadder book the human hand never wrote."

Miss Kemble described not just the slaves' dismal living conditions, ruinous physical work, and degradation, but also how the human spirit of slaves was suppressed, even their right to worship. In one of the letters to "Dearest E," Elizabeth Sedgwick, Miss Kemble told that "Pierce Butler's people"

> have petitioned very vehemently that he would build a church for them on the island. I doubt, however, his allowing them such a luxury as a place of worship all to themselves. Such a privilege might not be thought well of by the neighboring planters; indeed, it is almost what one might call a whity-brown idea, dangerous, demoralizing, inflammatory, incendiary. I should not wonder if I should be suspected of being the chief cornerstone of it, and yet I am not: it is an old hope and entreaty of these poor people, which I am afraid they are not destined to see fulfilled.

In some homes in the South, the *Journal* was secretly read in private.

In May of 1864, another Union warship was commissioned with a name that honored Berkshire: U.S.S. *Pontoosuc* commemorated the original Pontoosuc Plantation, the eighteenth-century tract that had been developed into Pittsfield.

Pontoosuc was a side-wheel steamer, approximately two hundred feet in length, armed with a dozen modern naval guns. Built for the navy by a

Portland, Maine, shipbuilder at a cost of $157,000, *Pontoosuc* would remain in service until mid-1865. She would be sold about a year later for less than $7,000.

In May, the large Hudson River steamboat *Berkshire* caught fire and was destroyed, with much loss of life. Several passengers were from the county, but they escaped unhurt.

Railroads were steadily becoming dominant in western Massachusetts, but taking a steamboat between Albany or Hudson, New York, and New York City remained a popular and enjoyable method of travel. Bulk goods such as farm produce, timber, paper, iron, coal, and tanned leather were still more easily and cheaply shipped by water than by rail, so there was lots of business for steamboat companies on the Hudson, which was an important artery for Berkshire. Passengers enjoyed a scenic and restful journey on the river and could even take a cabin and sleep part of the time. The comfortable steamboat was a contrast to the jarring rattle, noise, and smoke of trains, which derailed often enough to be a real hazard to passengers.

In mid-June, after delays caused by printer's problems, the memoir *Life with the Forty-ninth*, by Henry Johns, was published in a first edition of five hundred. The frontispiece was a portrait of Frank Bartlett, arm in a box sling as a result of his wound at Port Hudson.

The book was well reviewed by the *Springfield Republican*, and the *New York Tribune* ran an extensive article with excerpts that covered several newspaper pages. Johns would bring the Forty-ninth so much attention that some Berkshire men whose own regiments had far more glorious and much longer terms of service would resent a nine-month regiment being the sentimental favorite. Still, the Forty-ninth was the only regiment wholly raised in the county, and the only one known as "The Berkshire Regiment."

Among the many nationally prominent "Berkshire-borners" was Sheffield's Frederick A.P. Barnard, the former University of Mississippi president, who had returned north at the start of the war. In 1864, Barnard became the tenth president of Columbia College, a small undergraduate institution for men in Manhattan. He would hold that post for nearly twenty-five years, in which time the college would be transformed into a major university.

Barnard strongly advocated women's education, so much so that when a women's college was founded in New York in 1889 it was named Barnard College in his honor.

Early summer of 1864 brought Frank Bartlett the happy news that he would be promoted to brigadier general. Among the youngest in the army to hold such a high rank—on the sixth of June, Bartlett had turned twenty-four—he still suffered recurring pain in his amputated leg, but the promotion invigorated him, and he wrote in his diary, "Vive la Guerre!" "Hurrah for war!" He was eager to get back to the battlefield.

In mid-1864, signs of increased prosperity were everywhere in Berkshire, though not necessarily for the families of soldiers, whose pay was worth little these days. The Fifty-fourth's families were even worse off, depending on what friends and benefactors of the regiment could do for them, for their men still had not been paid.

Berkshire industry was at full tilt, turning out a wide array of goods, from army blankets and uniform cloth to shoes, buggy whips, pig iron, paper, and building stone—all of it needed to feed the war effort and, lately, to satisfy the appetites of the new rich. There was plenty of work in Berkshire, whether in the mill or quarry or on the farm, and cash flowed freely throughout the county.

A new Roman Catholic church was in the planning stages for Pittsfield, its foundation laid this summer. Named St. Joseph's, and built of stone, it would replace a twenty-five-year-old wooden church. In Lenox, Catholic residents also began to raise money for a new church. In Pittsfield, many people wanted to build a public library, for the splendid new Jackson Library in Stockbridge, completed after two years of work, had made the other towns long for their own. The Pittsfield Library Association currently rented some rooms to house their books, and its members now called for the real thing. Also inspired by the Stockbridge library, residents of Lee began agitating for a new library building.

Another sign of Berkshire's prosperity was seen with the move to incorporate the North Adams Gas Light Company, and street after street in Adams, as well as in other Berkshire towns, was being illuminated by gaslight. There was also a scheme to connect Pittsfield with a railroad line to New Haven, Connecticut. The junction was planned for Lee, and Berkshire towns on the line began to subscribe to stock in the project, with sums of $50,000 to $100,000 contributed per town.

Work on the Hoosac Tunnel in northern Berkshire progressed under the management and funding of the Commonwealth of Massachusetts, but it was difficult to find reliable workers because so many men were away at war. Excavating the shaft, twenty feet wide and twenty-four feet high through the mica slate of Hoosac Mountain, required hundreds of laborers working long hours with hand-drill, pick, and shovel. Black powder blasted the rock apart, but explosions left dangerous cracks and unseen weaknesses that resulted in sudden collapses. Men died regularly in rockfalls.

At one point, crews of hard-case toughs were hired off the streets of New

The Hoosac Tunnel east portal.

York to labor in the tunnel, and they often became involved in petty crime and hell-raising in nearby Adams and in the settlements of workers at the east portal in the town of Florida. One day, a mob of sixty New York men conspired to raid the construction company's store at the west end of the tunnel, but manager J. Henry Orr pulled a gun and threatened to shoot the first man who tried anything. Orr turned them back, protecting $14,000 worth of company goods.

In this same period, paymaster O. P. Rice was driving a buggy with the payroll through the town of Florida when men jumped out and grabbed for the bridle of his horse. The robbers, however, were foiled by the spirited black trotter, which rose up and struck at them with its front hooves. In the next moment, as one writer described it, before the thieves "could recover their surprise, [Rice's buggy] was thundering away at a 2:40 gait."

The tunnel employed more than three hundred and fifty men in 1864, with an annual budget of $300,000, and as much as $5,500 a month paid to the workers, a tremendous benefit for nearby towns.

In Lee, where the paper-making industry in particular was flourishing, a building boom began, as mill owners built new homes. One New York City newspaper used a thousand dollars' worth of Lee paper each day. Further, experimental work was underway at a Lee paper mill to develop a process of making paper from wood pulp instead of rags, which was the usual method. This innovation would come to fruition just after the war, and Berkshire's seemingly inexhaustible forests of spruce, poplar, and hemlock would bring a whole new era of paper production to the county.

The nature of industry and business was changing in the county, but not all for the better. West Stockbridge had been an important marble town since 1824, its high-grade stone used in Boston's Statehouse, New York's City Hall, and in a college at Philadelphia. By 1860, even though the coming of railroads promised easier shipment of stone, the accessible marble veins had been exhausted, and the quarries were soon abandoned.

On the other hand, a small but telling success could be seen in Pittsfield, where the "apothecary" of C. D. Mills installed a modern soda fountain, which *Eagle* editor Joseph Smith enthusiastically described as the "most beautiful and best" he had ever seen. With a newly patented "ice cream" fountain as the centerpiece, it had an Italian marble counter top and silver faucets surmounted with eagles.

One of the many Berkshire folk who had left the county before the Civil War and had done well was Henry Shaw Wheeler of Lanesboro, now a resident of Poughkeepsie, New York. In his mid-forties, Wheeler was a nationally famous humorist writing under the name Josh Billings, whose country wit and wisdom—expressed with disarming phonetic spellings—caught the fancy of newspaper readers.

Among Wheeler's admirers was President Lincoln, who considered Josh Billings the "funniest man in America" and regularly related Billings's anecdotes at cabinet meetings to lighten the mood. In an upcountry New England dialect, Billings parodied his former Berkshire neighbors, folk who appeared outwardly to be governed by strict Puritanical morals. The strait-laced ministers of mostly Congregationalist Berkshire preached that drinking and carousing were sinful, but Josh Billings knew how his folk really lived. Berkshirites were as down-to-earth as anyone, despite the pretensions of self-righteous upper-class squires and the "divines," as ministers were termed. (Coincidentally, in 1818, the year Wheeler was born, the Reverend Dr. Stephen West had been dismissed after fifty-six years as the authoritarian pastor of the Congregational church in Stockbridge; Dr. West had been accused of "intemperate drinking.")

Billings spun rambling narratives about home life in northern Berkshire:

> The village ov New Ashford . . . iz one ov them towns that dont make enny fuss, but for pure water, pure morals, and good rye, and injun bread, it stands on tiptoez.
> It was settled soon after the landing ov the pilgrims, bi sum ov

that party, and like all the Nu England towns, waz, at one time, selebrated for its stern religious creed, and its excellent rum and tanzy.

It may seem a leetle strange, tew these latter day saints, tew hear me mix up rum and religion together, but i had an Unkle, who preached God's word in the next town south ov New Ashford, 80 years ago, who died in due time, and went to heaven.

This genial old saint alwus took, on week daze, three magnificent horns ov rum and tanzy, and Sundaze he took four.

I hav no doubt it lengthened out hiz time, and braced up hiz faith.

But i wouldn't advise enny ov the yung klergy ov to-day tew meddle with rum and tanzy, az a fertilizer.

The tanzy is all rite—it grows az green and az bitter az ever; for man kant adulterate it, but rum haz been bedeviled into rank pizon.

One sich horn az mi old unkle used tew absorbe between hiz sermons on Sunday (5 inches, good and strong) would disfranchise a whole drove ov preachers now. . . .

But times and men hav altered, and so haz rum and tanzy.

I dont want them good old times tew cum back agin, we aint pure enuff now tew stand them, neither are we tuff enuff.

Throughout the war years, Josh Billings reminisced about Berkshire, spouting country philosophy with sophisticated irony and offering humorous insights into human nature. Billings charmed readers whose country had been torn apart by the war, telling them of living in the shadow of Mount Greylock, a "grate giant mountain tew guard you," and of Berkshire streams with their "dancing" trout that jump into your fishing basket, and of "rattlesnaix." He spoke about home and hearth and peacetime, for which many a homesick soldier, North and South, ached: "If yuh luv a mountain, cum up here and see me." Billings said he wished he could stay by that mountain, because there he was "az happy and az lazy az a yearling heifer . . . [without] a kare on mi mind, not an ake in mi boddy," and he meant to remain there "till mi munny gives out, and shall cum bak tew the senseless crash ov the city, with a tear in mi eye, and holes in both ov mi boots."

Billings's native Berkshire wit cheered up thousands of war-weary readers in army posts and naval stations, just as it cheered up the beleaguered President Lincoln and his cabinet. Lincoln surely would have agreed with the Billings observation that "The man who is as kind and courteous to his office boy as he is to a millionaire, is a gentleman."

Independence Day of 1864 turned out to be a bit more exciting than some Pittsfield folk would have liked, as a stray rocket crashed through the front window of a shop on North Street. That window held a display of fireworks that were ignited and went off, reported the *Eagle*, sending "a small battery of infernal machines about the heads of the occupants of the store."

The good news this week was that a prolonged region-wide drought finally broke with drenching summer storms.

Chapter Twenty-three

THE BEGINNING OF THE END

On July 25, 1864, there occurred a symbolic event that spoke of Berkshire's having changed forever: the towering Old Elm in Pittsfield had to be cut down.

For too long the straggling dead branches at the top of the gray-white trunk had been breaking off and crashing to the ground, a threat to passersby as well as to the young elm trees growing nearby. Reluctantly, Pittsfield's selectmen resolved to have the tree felled, and at the park this afternoon there appeared woodsman Sylvanus Grant, the fellow who had volunteered for the army early in the war but had been turned down because he was black. A melancholy crowd gathered to watch this passing of an era in Pittsfield and Berkshire. A historian described the moment:

Sylvanus Grant, who felled the Old Elm.

> [A] heavy rope was tied to its trunk to secure its downfall on the south side, the axe was laid at its base, and at six o'clock in the evening it came crashing to the earth with a great assemblage of people as

witness of its downfall. When it struck the highway there were evi-
dences in its decayed limbs that in its old age it had been smitten
with a third thunderbolt. There was a great scramble by relic hunters
to secure these top branches, and even twigs, bark and leaves were
hastily gathered up by these for preservation.

The selectmen of the town then claimed the remains of this aged
forest monarch which had for so many years towered . . . above its
fellows, and put them up at auction. . . . A portion of the tree was
afterwards carved into cups, crosses, and other articles, a wooden
chair of its wood was given for use in the Town Hall and another to
the First [Congregational] Church. Dr. Robert Campbell and Hon.
Thomas Allen were also the owners of two small tables which were
constructed from its branches, while many smaller relics from trunk
and bough are yet sacredly preserved.

The winning bid for the greater part of the trunk of the Old Elm would be
handed over to Mrs. Fenn for the Ladies' Soldiers' Aid society. The winner
was storekeeper Elijah H. Dodge, a longtime Pittsfield resident who had served
as a state legislator. Dodge, who paid ten dollars for the prize, died suddenly
within two weeks of the event, and before the tree trunk could be sold and
"work[ed] up into keepsakes," the barn in which it was stored burned down,
the precious elm wood consumed with it.

In 1856, Joseph Smith, editor of the *Eagle,* had written "The Gray Old
Elm of Pittsfield Park," evoking the love of Berkshire folk for the tree and all
it represented.

> And dearly the sons of the mountain vale,
> Wherever their exile be,
> Will thrill as they list to the song or tale,
> If it speak of their home and thee.

Many a Berkshire soldier would come home and be dismayed to see the
Pittsfield elm gone. Indeed, much would have changed since he left.

The 1845 local poet who signed with the initials "C. P. R." and wrote "The
Old Elm Tree" closed with:

> The pride of the village it long hath been,
> And the voice of envy hath said,
> That clad in mourning we all shall be seen
> When our idol tree is dead.
> Be it so, methinks it is unkind to mock
> Our worship, if such it be,

For age hath made most venerable
That stately old elm tree.

The annual rings indicated that the Old Elm was at least three hundred and forty years old.

In the mid-nineteenth century, Dalton paper-makers were developing—and much later successfully patented—a method of installing silk fibers in banknote paper to foil counterfeiters. During the war, government currency paper was manufactured in Crane's mills in Dalton and would remain in production there into the twenty-first century. The Cranes coined the term "bond" paper, which originally meant paper suitable for bank notes. By the end of the war, a special mill was in operation at Dalton to produce attractive bond writing paper to appeal to women, and Crane began turning out an average of five thousand pounds of "Ladies' Paper" a year.

Government currency was in wide circulation these days, and the bills known as "postal currency" that had been in use were no longer seen. This was just as well for Adams and Pittsfield manufacturer William Pollock, benefactor of the Pollock Guard. Pollock strongly resembled Salmon P. Chase, secretary of the treasury, whose image was printed on many of those Federal bills. The Pittsfield National Bank had issued its own bills with the portrait of Pollock on them, since he was a leading investor in the bank. Local residents, it was said, were suspicious of using the Federal bills until they saw what appeared to be the respected Pollock's image on them—actually that of Chase. Then they readily accepted the Federal bills, asserting that "Pollock had signed it with his face."

For all that business was booming in Berkshire, and the Pittsfield area was considered a manufacturing center of national significance to the war effort, taxes were burdensome, and "war prices" had increased the cost of goods by more than forty percent.

Also troubling were dreaded "incendiary fires" that were being set in northern and central Berkshire, destroying homes, barns, abandoned mills, and outbuildings. When a Pittsfield boardinghouse caught fire that fall, a young woman was killed jumping from a window while trying to escape.

Frank Bartlett had not been seriously hurt by the glancing gunshot wound to his head at the Battle of the Wilderness, but his stump still caused him severe pain, and for a time it was difficult to wear an artificial leg.

In Washington, the highly regarded Bartlett could have had an "easy berth," as he phrased it, but, he told a friend, "If I am of any value, it is in the field, in the *actual handling* and *government* of *troops*." He visited New York and Pittsfield early that summer of 1864, then went to his family home in eastern

Massachusetts. Back at Washington in mid-July, Bartlett saw Wendell Holmes being mustered out along with other veterans of the Twentieth Massachusetts, although so many of this regiment re-enlisted that it remained a fighting force and took part in the ongoing siege of Petersburg that summer.

Bartlett wanted to get back to the front, and by July he was there, also in the siege of Petersburg, in the steaming heat of Virginia. The fortifications of both armies were labyrinths of trenches, and nowhere was it safe, as musketry and cannon fire were almost constant. Stockade fences were built to protect horses and livestock as well as men, and the walls of Bartlett's log headquarters pattered steadily with the drizzle of lead balls and shrapnel. Going to inspect his men each day was dangerous, and even in the rearward lines men were hit regularly, with four officers from the Fifty-seventh being hit—one killed, three severely hurt—soon after he entered the trenches.

> It is wearing to body and mind, this being under constant fire. People at the North, who are enjoying themselves and thinking of nothing but making money, little appreciate what this brave army is enduring every day and hour for them. . . . I wish some of the patriotic (?) ones at home who are making speeches (and money), would just come out here and spend a week. . . . They would not care to go down to the lines where the men are day and night fighting for their security and safety.

Bartlett's command was a brigade of 1,300 men, made up of six Massachusetts regiments and one from Pennsylvania, regiments that had started out with a thousand men apiece. By now, General Grant had sacrificed in killed, wounded, or missing more than sixty percent of the original army he had taken into the 1864 campaign, but he had received reinforcements by the thousands, another capability the South could never match.

On July 30, in the middle of the night, Bartlett led his brigade through a "covered way," as a protected corridor in the maze of trenches was called, and took a position in the front lines, where they prepared to attack. Just before dawn there was a tremendous explosion, as a Union mine was set off under the enemy fortifications, throwing debris and Confederate bodies high into the air. Federal sappers had dug a tunnel under no-man's-land to the Confederate trenches, so that its detonation blew a hole in the enemy's earthworks. Union troops surged forward after Bartlett, who was on foot, leading his men into the massive crater caused by the explosion. In the same division as Bartlett, but attacking in the third wave, was the Twenty-first Massachusetts, which had no more than one hundred men fit for duty.

Thousands of Northern soldiers crowded into "the Crater," as it became known, there to be confronted by an unexpectedly steep approach to earthworks that the enemy had immediately reoccupied. The top Union commanders failed to coordinate a broader attack against the enemy line, a failure that turned the surprise assault at the crater into a nightmare of hand-to-hand fighting, the attacking troops caught in a devastating enemy crossfire. Bartlett wrote in his diary about the disorganized confusion inside the crater, as more and more Union troops poured in under heavy fire and were unable to get out again:

> I got up to the enemy's works about as soon as anyone. Got into the crater. Took the first and second lines of the enemy. Held them till after one, when we were driven back by repeated charges. I fought them for an hour after they held the whole line, excepting the crater where we were, their flag within seven feet of ours, across the work. They threw bayonets and bottles at us, and we returned, for we got out of ammunition. At last, to save further slaughter, there being no hope of our being rescued, we gave it up. That crater during the day I shall never forget. A shell knocked down a bowlder of clay on to my wooden leg and crushed it to pieces, killing the man next me. I surrendered to General Mahone.

Bartlett wrote this diary entry while on his way to the officer's detention center at Danville, Virginia. He would later be transferred to Libby Prison in Richmond to await exchange. That would take more than two months, and Bartlett would be seriously ill much of the time.

Although Herman Melville got some of Bartlett's history slightly wrong, the closing stanza of "The College Colonel" distills his war experience:

> But all through the Seven Days' Fight,
> And deep in the Wilderness grim,
> And in the field-hospital tent,
> And Petersburg crater, and dim
> Lean brooding in Libby, there came—
> Ah heaven!—what *truth* to him.

The Twenty-first regiment had managed to fall back from the bloody chaos of the crater, but twenty-four of its men were killed, wounded, or captured, one of the mortally wounded being its commander, Captain William Clark of Pittsfield.

During the Petersburg siege, Major Henry Richardson of Pittsfield and the Twenty-first suffered his first wound, a serious one, taking a bullet in the thigh. After recuperation, he rejoined the regiment, but his three-year enlistment would expire along with the majority of the men's that August.

When those who had not re-enlisted left the regiment, there would be only seventy-five men remaining. They would find themselves reorganized into a battalion of three companies.

Thomas Reed of the Twenty-first was eager to leave the army. Stationed at City Point, Virginia, a supply base for the sieges of Petersburg and Richmond, Reed appeared to be safe from the dangers of war, such as the defeat at the Crater, where his Twenty-first regiment had paid such a high price for the ineptitude of the leaders: General Ambrose E. Burnside finally resigned, after yet again having overall responsibility for another Union debacle.

Reed was not completely safe, however, for he narrowly missed being involved in a freak accident behind the lines, as he told Cynthia.

> While sitting at the table writing yesterday morning about eleven o'clock, I heard a heavy report in the direction of City Point which I supposed to be a heavy siege gun on one of the gun boats, but judge of my surprise when I learned about an hour afterward from those who had just come from the landing that an explosion had taken place on board one of the barges lying at the wharf discharging ammunition and had communicated with the warehouse in which the ammunition was stored—blowing the building and all others in the vicinity to atoms. . . . [N]ot less than two hundred and fifty lives must have been lost. . . . I think as I have been in luck thus far I shall be favored 10 or 11 days more and then good bye to the Army.

In July of 1864, Lieutenant General Jubal A. Early led a fast-moving Confederate force of ten thousand men around the main Union army and made directly for Washington. Most of the Federal soldiers were bogged down in the campaign against Richmond and Petersburg, so Washington was only lightly defended. There were fears that Early could actually enter the capital, which would be a disastrous setback for the North.

The Confederates, however, found themselves confronted by the formidable defensive works devised by John Barnard of Sheffield, chief engineer for the Union and brother of Columbia's new president. Though no more than a few thousand soldiers were in the District of Columbia at the time, many of them invalids, there were hundreds of cannon that could be quickly moved from place to place in the fortifications. Barnard had made it possible for a small number of troops to sustain themselves in strong redoubts, forts, and entrenchments and behind palisades until reinforcements arrived.

Throughout the war, Barnard was the engineering expert most essential to the Union cause. He never won the fame or glory of a combat commander in the field, but Barnard labored tirelessly, and with great skill, behind the scenes. Instead of leading some heroic assault, he served the country in other crucial ways: building Washington's defenses, developing field fortifications in northern Virginia, and supervising the making of maps.

From the very start of the war, Barnard's engineering tasks had been complex and difficult, made all the more so because of the lack of good maps. Maps were one of the most critical requirements of the army in the field and the navy operating along the coastline, yet at the beginning of hostilities maps were scarce, and the most basic troop movements were often compromised by not having them. Before maps were available, military units and supply wagon trains had to move almost blindly in battle situations, for the officers had little idea what lay across the next ridge or was hidden beyond a grove of trees.

From the start, Barnard led a prodigious Federal mapmaking effort to gather information about northern Virginia and the Washington area. As described by a field assistant, his plan was to produce a

detailed survey [that] shows all the important topographical features of the country which it embraces; the main roads, by-roads, and bridle-paths; the woods, open grounds, and streams; houses, out-buildings, and fences; with as close a sketch of contour as the hidden character of the country would allow—producing in all a map by which any practicable military movement might be studied and planned with perfect reliability.

The resulting new maps produced by the military's cartographic department were essential to Union armies in the field as well as to naval squadrons blockading Southern bays, river mouths, harbors, and ports. Barnard's first mapmaking efforts were interrupted in July of 1861, when Federal troops were defeated at Bull Run and forced to retreat from Virginia, a defeat that in large part was the result of the Union commanders' lack of accurate maps. Mapmaking immediately resumed under direct orders from General McClellan, and Barnard's remarkably detailed map of the Washington area was issued on January 1, 1862.

At the scale of one inch to a mile, this was the first good map of northern Virginia and the District of Columbia ever published. The information was gathered by every possible means, including daring cavalry patrols as well as the close questioning of travelers, enemy deserters, and fugitive slaves. Also informative were interviews with Southerners sympathetic to the Union cause, as was the extensive use of spies, including private detectives, who risked their lives by entering enemy territory in disguise. Hydrogen-filled balloons tethered close to the front lines and carrying aloft observers who could see for miles were another effective way to locate Confederate positions and watch troop movements.

Thousands of roughly drawn maps of small areas were incorporated into revised maps of the larger region. When a map was ready, it was printed and issued to the military, and as the war went on Federal maps were printed by the thousands, something never before seen in America. Approximately 44,000 printed maps, charts, and sketches were distributed to the military in the second year of the war, more than double the distribution in the year 1861, and upwards of five times the average annual distribution of prewar years. Almost 66,000 maps and charts were printed during 1864, which included more than 22,000 military maps and field sketches.

In addition, maps were compiled and printed by the army's Corps of Engineers, which was under Barnard's direct command. In 1864, he reported that almost 21,000 map sheets were furnished to the armies in the field. In 1865, the final year of the war, this figure was almost 24,600. The Confederates could not compete in mapmaking, and usually were compelled to rely on captured Federal maps.

When General Early dared raid Washington in mid-1864, John Barnard's other achievement—the erection of defensive works—turned the Confederates back. In Barnard's official "Report on the Defenses of Washington," published after the war, he described what Early faced when he appeared before the city:

> From a few isolated works, covering bridges or commanding a few especially important points, was developed a connected system of fortification by which every prominent point, at intervals of 800 to 1,000 yards, was occupied by an inclosed field-fort, every important approach or depression of ground, unseen from the forts, swept by a battery . . . and the whole connected by rifle-trenches which were in fact lines of infantry parapet, furnishing emplacement for two ranks of men and affording covered communication along the line, while roads were opened wherever necessary, so that troops and artillery could be moved rapidly from one point of the immense periphery to another, or under cover, from point to point along the line.

Although Northern newspapers indignantly complained that Early's force could have marched with ease into weakly garrisoned Washington, the Confederate general himself discovered otherwise, as he explained after the war, saying the fortifications "were found to be exceedingly strong," and

> [A]s far as the eye could reach, the works seemed to be of the same impregnable character.

Barnard, who soon would be promoted by Grant to brigadier general, served as chief engineer of the Army of the Potomac from 1861 to 1862, as chief engineer of the Department of Washington from 1861 to 1864, and as chief engineer of all Union armies in the field until the end of the war in 1865.

When General Early fought his way back from the threshold of Washington, the Thirty-seventh Massachusetts was one of the regiments sent in pursuit. The men had just been equipped with new Spencer repeating rifles, which gave them tremendous firepower.

The Thirty-seventh was among the first Union regiments to be so equipped, and when their picket firing, alone, shattered a much larger enemy force late that month, it was clear that repeating rifles could change the face of war. In the Battle of Opequan that September, the regiment would demolish an enemy brigade and silence an artillery battery with its new rifles, "sweeping everything before them," said a historian, and win "high commendation." Repeating rifles in the hands of the Thirty-seventh were not due all the credit, however, for at one point the regiment was out of ammunition, and far in advance of the main army, when it held its ground with only the bayonet until reinforcements came up. Colonel Edwards was brevetted brigadier general for his regiment's services that day.

Also at Opequan was the Thirty-fourth Massachusetts, which had been fighting hard all that spring in northwestern Virginia, with heavy losses, especially at New Market in May. There, it had more than two hundred and twenty killed, wounded, or captured, half its total strength. Many Berkshire men were in Company K, which suffered severely in the fight. The regiment was under the command of Lieutenant Colonel Andrew Potter of Pittsfield because its colonel, Williams graduate George D. Wells of Boston, was in command of the brigade.

At one point, Colonel Wells could not get his vastly outnumbered regiment to withdraw from an unsupported, exposed forward position under heavy enemy fire. The regimental historian said Wells at last "seized the color-bearer by the shoulders, faced him to the rear, and finally led the remnant of his command back to its former position." Wells himself was slightly wounded but did not leave the field.

After New Market, General Franz Sigel, the commander of the force in which the Thirty-fourth served, was awed by its fighting ability, which he had witnessed for the first time. General Sigel said the Thirty-fourth was "the best regiment and has the best commanding officer I have ever seen."

Lieutenant Colonel Potter was seriously wounded in action that June, when more than one hundred and ten men were casualties at the Battle of Piedmont. At the Battle of Opequan, the regiment had another one hundred and ten casualties. It fought through late autumn, almost constantly on the march, and fiercely engaged time and again. Colonel Wells was killed at Cedar Creek in mid-October, when of two hundred and fifty men taken into action, almost one hundred were casualties. The following spring the regiment would resume fighting, joining the siege of Petersburg. Potter would return to the Thirty-fourth and become the brigade commander.

The Tenth regiment's Charlie Gates, the underage boy who had run away from the family farm in Lee to join the Barrington Company, was a model soldier, who did not drink or smoke. In a memoir written after the war, Corporal Mark Nickerson of Gates's company described a harrowing moment in a battle that could have been any one of the Tenth's many fierce engagements.

> My right hand man was Chas. Gates from Lee, Mass. He was one of my chums, was about my age and I thought a great deal of him. As brave a boy as ever shouldered a gun. During the second charge of the enemy he suddenly put his hand to his face, withdrew it, looked at it, and then said to me, "Nick, I guess I am a goner." I saw blood flowing down his face as he fell out of the ranks, and thought to myself "Shall I ever see him alive again?" It unnerved me. He was the best friend I had in the army, and I shouldn't believe he was a goner until I had to.
>
> I wanted to follow him and see how badly he was wounded, but the enemy was coming nearer and I must stay in my place and help to beat them back. As I was thinking of Gates and what a good friend he had been to me, suddenly he stepped back into his place again and said to me, "Nick, it is nothing serious. I'm all right. I'm worth a dozen men yet." I was so glad I didn't know how to express myself. If there had been a lull in the battle I believe I should have dropped my gun and hugged him then and there. (Remember we were scarcely more than boys.) But the enemy was coming nearer all the time and that meant business for the "Blue Coats." I just slapped him on the back and said, "Bully for you, now we will give it to them." And give it to them we did, for we worked like beavers, loading and firing for all we were worth. The blood and sweat rolling off his face made him a ghastly spectacle to behold.

In midsummer of 1864 the men of the Tenth who were not re-enlisting set out for home and for final mustering out. The remainder were consolidated, along with the Seventh Massachusetts, into the Thirty-seventh regiment. At the same time, Brigadier General Eustis, who faced "charges of neglect of duty and general inefficiency," according to a War Department dispatch, resigned from the army.

The veterans of the Tenth arrived by train at Springfield to a rousing welcome and were mustered out the first week of July. Charlie Gates took a train

*"The Berkshire Boy's Return" was a popular post-war lithograph, depicting the homecoming
of Lee's Charles Gates from his service with the Tenth Massachusetts.*

to Becket, then walked along a winding road through the Berkshire hills
toward Lee and home. Contemporary poet Kate Putnam Osgood immortalized the departure and return of Gates in her "Driving Home the Cows,"
published, during the war, in *Harper's Weekly*. Gates had never been seriously
injured, regardless of the "empty sleeve" that can be attributed to Osgood's
poetic license. In these, the final stanzas, Charlie's father is finishing the chores
his absent son normally would have been doing.

> The summer days grew cold and late,
>   He went for the cows when the work was done;
> But down the lane as he opened the gate,
>   He saw them coming, one by one,—
>
> Brindle, Ebony, Speckle and Bess,
>   Shaking their horns in the evening wind,
> Cropping the buttercups out of the grass,
>   But who was it following close behind?
>
> Loosely swung in the idle air
>   The empty sleeve of army blue;
> All worn and pale from the crisping hair
>   Looked out a face that the father knew.
>
> The great tears sprang to their meeting eyes;
>   For the heart must speak when the lips are dumb;
> And under the silent evening skies
>   Together they followed the cattle home.

Chapter Twenty-four

THE END IN SIGHT

One of the saddest and most troubling aspects of the war was how to handle the bodies of dead soldiers. In many cases there was no choice but to bury them, often in mass graves, on the battlefield. In other instances the men died in hospitals or in camps, and the decision had to be made by family or close relations whether to ship the body home in special airtight boxes or bury them in a local military cemetery.

The *Eagle* published a sobering and disturbing article entitled, "Returning Bodies of Deceased Soldiers."

The cost of bringing home from Washington the bodies of deceased soldiers is a subject concerning which there is frequent inquiry. The Winsted (Ct.) Herald says that a gentleman whose son was recently brought through from Washington to Winsted gives us the following estimation:

The ordinary freighting lines decline this class of transportation, and turn it over to the Express companies. The latter, before they will receive a body, require either that it shall be embalmed and boxed, or that it shall be enclosed in a metallic, air-tight coffin. The embalming process (which is effected by ejecting the blood from the veins and arteries by a force-pump, and injecting a preservative liquid) costs invariably $30. The cost of a metallic coffin is $18 to $50. The express charge to Winsted is $22. Hence the cost of bringing a body home after it reaches Washington is $40 at the lowest—$52 if embalmed; and in the latter case a coffin is still necessary before final burial. The incidental expenses are also considerable, and it is doubtful if a less sum than $125 would serve to cover the return of a body from any of the regiments about Washington. It is hardly possible to effect such a return without the personal attendance of some friend, and every step is attended by some incidental expense.

This, in a day when a soldier was paid thirteen dollars a month.

Relatives of Charles Barker of Adams, who had died from wounds suffered in the Wilderness in the spring of 1864, went South to find his grave. Barker had died in the military hospital at Fredericksburg, but even with the help of friends from his company in the Eighty-third New York, the search for where he lay was unsuccessful. No one knew where he had been buried, and now the family at home would never know.

The North Adams family of Charles Sanford, killed at Drury's Bluff while serving with the Twenty-seventh regiment, also sought their son's grave, but with success. The Reverend Miles Sanford went to Virginia immediately after news arrived of his son's death. Though buried on the battlefield by the enemy, Captain Sanford's body was located with the help of regimental surgeon Dr. H.J. Millard of North Adams. That summer of 1864, the Reverend Sanford returned to Berkshire with his son's remains, which were interred in Hillside Cemetery in the new "soldiers' lot."

The Reverend Albert Hopkins of Williams College, whose cavalryman son had been killed that spring, took part in the funeral service, held at the Reverend Sanford's Baptist church and attended by many mourners. Stewart's Cornet Band led the procession, which included thirty men of Sanford's Company H, who fired three volleys of musketry in salute over the grave.

On August 4, the re-enlisting veteran members of the Thirty-first Massachusetts regiment arrived back in their home state for a month-long furlough. They deserved a rest, after spending four hard months campaigning along the Red River under the less-than-competent General Banks. The enemy had routed Banks at every turn, and the entire expeditionary force—infantry, cavalry, supply wagons, and armed gunboats—had been forced to retreat to the Mississippi.

Colonel Chauncey Bassett of Lee led his Louisiana Native Guards Negro regiment throughout the ill-fated Red River campaign. On May 26, the Lee weekly newspaper, *Valley Gleaner*, reported that Bassett's regiment had been "destroyed on a gunboat." The colonel's death was confirmed by a *Gleaner* story on June 23, which reported that, after being wounded, he "fell into the hands of the enemy and was conveyed to a house nearby where he lived but a few days."

One man of the Thirty-first was still in the army but no longer serving with the regiment: a year previous, First Sergeant Abram J. Nichols of Pittsfield, formerly of the Allen Guards, had been appointed captain in a New Orleans Negro regiment, the Second Infantry Corps d'Afrique. That regiment became the Seventy-fourth U.S. Colored Infantry, and Nichols served with it until this month, when poor health forced him to resign and return home. Nichols was one of approximately 7,000 white commissioned officers in black regiments.

While on furlough in Massachusetts, the Thirty-first was officially redesignated infantry once again, but upon returning to New Orleans was remounted as cavalry and served in that capacity, fighting guerrillas, and scouting a wide territory along the eastern shore of the Mississippi. The Thirty-first proved effective, hunting down two notorious guerrilla leaders and killing them, thus earning the commendation of General Sherman himself, something not easily won.

On August 13, Thomas Reed told Cynthia to stop sending him letters, for he was about to head for home, expecting soon to be mustered out at Worcester. All he need do was wait for his final pay, and then he would come directly to Pittsfield.

As it turned out, the military bureaucracy was slow to release Reed and the other men of the Twenty-first Massachusetts who were not re-enlisting. No provision was made even to get them prompt transportation home, let alone to pay them on time. It was not until August 21 that Reed was at last aboard the steamer *Ellen S. Terry* and writing "Homeward Bound!" on the heading of his letter. The returning men of Reed's regiment were delighted to be going home, but they were "with nary a red [cent] in their pockets."

Meanwhile, the Union army under Grant, including the remainder of Reed's Twenty-first regiment, was again moving against Confederate defenses at Petersburg and Richmond. That fall, the remaining seventy or so members of the regiment would be transferred to the Thirty-sixth Massachusetts. Reed wrote about seeing twenty-four steamer transports loaded with troops heading up the James River toward the front.

> Now Cynth keep up your courage for I am more confident now that I shall see you than I have been at any time since I left. There was some heavy fighting about to take place just as I left and our boys have been truly fortunate in getting out of the scrape.

The returnees from the Twenty-first went by steamer to Washington, and then on to New York City, where they boarded a train to Massachusetts. Passing through Connecticut, Reed dozed contentedly in his seat across the aisle from William Phipps, another returning soldier from Berkshire. Suddenly, a mighty crash jarred Reed awake, and he found himself under splintered seats, with "scalding hot water pouring" on him, steam choking him so that he could not breathe. He was trapped, "wedged among the ruins," thinking "how hard it was after having fought on so many battle fields and being out of the way of bullets, then when returning home to meet with a death still more horrible than anything on the field."

Reed yanked his coat over his head and struggled to get clear of the wreckage. His train had collided with another, and four or five carriages had been thrown from the track. The other locomotive had come to rest against the side of his car, and steam spouted from the engine's burst boiler. Reed got out, later to write home: "I don't think I could have lived five minutes longer inhaling the hot steam." The unfortunate William Phipps was so severely injured that he had to be sent to the hospital.

Reed insisted Cynthia not worry about him and said he would be home within a week. The Federal government still did not cooperate, however. In mid-September, Reed wrote from Boston: "We have been promised from day to day that tomorrow we would get our pay, thus time has passed, and still we remain unpaid." He promised that as soon as the money came, he would "return to my Gal, not to leave her again very soon."

Later that autumn, Thomas Reed finally got back to Cynthia in Pittsfield, and with his rightful pay.

At its station before Charleston, much of the duty of the Fifty-fourth Massachusetts regiment involved guarding several hundred captive enemy officers. The prisoners were always looking for a chance to escape, but the Fifty-fourth carried out its duty perfectly, allowing no one to get away, and at the same time winning even the respect of the Southerners.

On September 28 came the electrifying news that the Fifty-fourth was to receive equal pay at last, and would get, retroactively, everything the Federal government owed them. After eighteen long months, stoically refusing seven times to be paid and defying the threats and insults of men like Colonel Montgomery, the regiment was rewarded with an unforgettable moment of triumphant joy. An officer wrote that after the Fifty-fourth was paid, a "carnival prevail[ed]."

> The fiddle and other music long neglected enlivens the tents day and night. Songs burst out everywhere; dancing is incessant; boisterous shouts are heard, mimicry, burlesque, and a carnival; pompous

salutations are heard on all sides. Here a crowd and a preacher; there a crowd and two boxers; yonder feasting and jubilee. In brief, they have awakened the "pert and nimble spirit of mirth, and turned melancholy forth to funerals."

It took two full days to pay the Fifty-fourth, which was again approaching full strength, with nine hundred men. More than $170,000 was paid out, and while plenty was spent lavishly and wastefully by these young soldiers, more than $53,000 was immediately sent home by express, with more following until $100,000 was sent to family and loved ones. The regiment also contributed more than $1,500 to a future monument for Colonel Robert Shaw, to be erected near the spot where he fell. (After the failed assault on Fort Wagner, Shaw had been buried by the Confederates in a mass grave at the base of the ramparts.) Other freedmen serving as soldiers or living as civilians in this military department also contributed to the Shaw monument fund until more than $4,000 was raised.

There was a problem, however, for the action of the waves was eroding Morris Island and made the site unfavorable for a monument. Instead, the Shaw fund was devoted to the establishment of a free school for black children in Charleston when peace came.

With the war decisively going in favor of the Union, some of the worries of Berkshire folk were lifted, but the threat close to home persisted: from Stockbridge northward, arson destroyed additional houses and barns. Week after week, reports came in of new fires.

Harnessing water for firefighting as well as for industrial power was one of the motives behind the ground-breaking for the Waconah Reservoir in Windsor in September. The dam, to be placed above the falls, would be thirty-six feet high and two hundred and forty long, covering one hundred acres with a reservoir twelve feet deep. Most of the manufacturers along the East Branch of the Housatonic, who would benefit from the water power, were contributing to meet its cost.

That fall, the presidential election again revealed the deep political rifts in Berkshire. Pro-Lincoln Republicans were backed by the *Berkshire Eagle* and its publisher, Henry Chickering, and pro-McClellan Democrats were staunchly supported by the *Sun*, whose publisher, Phineas Allen, was a delegate to the Democratic convention in Chicago. The *Eagle* minced no words, calling the Democrats "Copperheads," and accusing them of being willing to concede Southern secession for the sake of peace. In his turn, whenever Allen gave speeches at Democratic political rallies, he often sarcastically referred to the president as "a particularly handsome man named Abraham Lincoln."

A pro-Lincoln gathering in Pittsfield during the 1864 presidential election.

For some weeks during the campaign, war news was almost pushed off the newspaper pages, but the fifty-fourth annual Berkshire Agricultural Fair got its usual front-page treatment when it was held in Pittsfield that October.

The election came in November, and with it Lincoln's victory. Berkshire County overwhelmingly backed the president, giving him more than 3,500 votes to approximately 2,500 for McClellan. Every town but Dalton and Cheshire went for the president. In Adams, the result was 759 for Lincoln to 199 for McClellan; Pittsfield, 683-591; Great Barrington, 429-211; Lee, 352-242, and Williamstown, 266-243.

Massachusetts was strongly for the Republicans, and Governor Andrew was re-elected for another one-year term.

Reported or not, the war was still raging that fall, the South still refusing to yield.

The Second Massachusetts was one of only a handful of eastern regiments serving in General William T. Sherman's lean and tough army of westerners that was driving deep into the heart of the Confederacy. More than five companies strong thanks to reinforcements and to enough of its members re-enlisting, the Second retained its official designation, adding the honorific of "veteran regiment," as did all regiments that re-enlisted in adequate numbers. After a month-long furlough this past winter, enjoying a rousing reception in Boston, the re-enlisted soldiers of the Second had come back in time to join Sherman's march to Atlanta, which had begun late in April.

Fighting, marching, driving the foe steadily back, Sherman's veterans were handpicked, the best troops in the western theater. That May, the Second fought at Resaca, Georgia, then at Cassville and New Hope Church, meeting the enemy head-on or carrying out flanking maneuvers that forced the Confederates to withdraw. By the end of July 1864, the Second had fought under Sherman to the outskirts of Atlanta, taking part in the bloody battle at Peach Tree Creek on the twentieth. Union attackers forced the Confederates into defensive works around Atlanta, and more flanking maneuvers were combined with attack and counterattack until Atlanta was evacuated on September 1.

Sherman's triumphant army marched in, and the Second enjoyed the honor of pitching its tents in the city hall park. During six weeks or so of Union occupation, the regiment served as Atlanta's military police. When Sherman resumed his campaign, he ordered much of the city burned to the ground. The Second was one of the last regiments to leave the place. On went Sherman's ruthless invasion, destroying everything of military value in its path—railroads, bridges, cotton warehouses, telegraph lines—the men foraging off the land so that many plantations were looted and burned. Maneuvering rapidly in the open in direct contrast to Grant's sledgehammer tactics for the trench warfare against Richmond and Petersburg, Sherman made his next objective Savannah and the sea, then on to Charleston.

When he was near Charleston, Sherman was surprised to run across the widow of the late General Thomas Childs, a native of Berkshire, veteran of the War of 1812, and former comrade of Sherman's from their service in Florida before the Civil War. General Childs was the son of the redoubtable Dr. Timothy Childs, a leading Berkshire figure in the decades before the war. Sherman had lost track of General Childs after their time together in Florida, when Childs had been a major in the army, Sherman his subordinate. Childs had served in the Mexican War and risen to the rank of brigadier general, then moved to South Carolina with his family. His only son was in the Confederate army.

When the vanguard of Sherman's invasion finally linked up with Union soldiers serving along the Georgia and Carolina coasts, the first troops they met were men of the Fifty-fourth Massachusetts regiment, which had been campaigning between Savannah and Charleston. The Fifty-fourth made the long-awaited junction with the Westerners in mid-January 1865, and a month later marched into Charleston, evacuated by the enemy after a Union siege of more than three years.

COURTESY BERKSHIRE ATHENAEUM

Sergeant William H. Carney of the Fifty-fourth rescued the national colors at the Fort Wagner repulse, winning him the Medal of Honor; after the war, Carney moved from his residence in eastern Massachusetts and settled down in Berkshire County.

By 1864, the gallantry under fire of black soldiers had awakened new prospects for Negroes in America, and although racial prejudice was rampant in both North and South, it was apparent that, if given a fair chance, the black man could succeed just as well as the white man. With the tumultuous social changes of the Civil War, the possibility of a better life for blacks was within sight.

Perhaps the single most influential black man in Berkshire at the time of the Civil War was the Reverend Harrison of Pittsfield, who for some months had served as chaplain to the Fifty-fourth. Since the rank of chaplain was officially an officer's position, Harrison was due the pay of an officer; but because he was black and not permitted to be an officer, army bureaucrats refused to pay him any more than ten dollars a month. Early in 1864, Governor Andrew vigorously petitioned Lincoln to have Harrison's case addressed, and the president placed the matter before the attorney general. That spring, the judgment was that Harrison deserved full pay, thus paving the way for the official acceptance of Negro officers in their own regiments.

With the economic and social transformation brought on by the Civil War, including the overnight abolition of slavery and the well-publicized heroism of black volunteers, the way of life of the Negro community of Berkshire County was changing. Real opportunity and higher social standing would be slow in coming, however, just as full pay for the Fifty-fourth was so long delayed. Yet, it would come. Mirroring the new attitude of many Americans, contemporary poet and playwright George Henry Boker of Philadelphia wrote about the charge of the Louisiana Native Guards at Port Hudson. Boker's verse, "The Black Regiment," composed in the style of the immensely popular "Charge of the Light Brigade" by Tennyson, was published in the *Eagle*.

> "Freedom!" their battle-cry—
> "Freedom! or leave to die!"
> Ah! and they meant the word,
> Not as with us 'tis heard,
> Not a mere party shout:
> They gave their spirits out;
> Trusted the end to God . . .
>
>   * * *
>
> Glad to strike one free blow,
> Whether for weal or woe;
> Glad to breathe one free breath,
> Though on the lips of death . . .
>
>   * * *
>
> This was what "freedom" lent
> To the black regiment.

Chapter Twenty-five

PEALS FROM EVERY TOWER

L ee's Eldad Moore of the Twenty-seventh regiment escaped again that fall of 1864 and was on the run for eight days, covering two hundred miles through enemy territory.

Moore was wearing an old Confederate jacket that had been forced on him by guards, and one day he decided to casually stroll past the sentry at the gate. He made it to the Union lines at Atlanta on October 19. Soon after, when on a Federal train heading north, Moore found himself captured once again, this time by guerrillas who attacked the train. Wasting no time, he escaped from the guerrillas, getting back to Atlanta and onto another train, which took him safely homeward to Berkshire by November.

Moore later said that each time he was on the run he had been harbored and protected by local blacks, who had never betrayed him, though they would have suffered terrible punishment if they had been caught helping a fugitive Union soldier.

In mid-December 1864, the scurvy-crippled Calvin Hosford of the Twenty-seventh learned that he was to be released from prison, along with other disabled prisoners. His "limbs were drawn double," according to one description, and he could barely stand, but the guards placed a ghastly condition to his being released: Hosford had to be able to go, on his own power, from the stockade to the rail line, a distance of one mile.

He did it. It took an entire day, but he did it.

Calvin Hosford went back to Berkshire and his family, but was so ill that he could only stay a month. He returned to the military hospital at Annapolis, Maryland, to remain there until July of 1865, when he went home for good.

Catharine Sedgwick was too weak to write very much, her eyes failing so that she could not read, which was her special passion. Miss Sedgwick's time as author and correspondent was virtually at a close, though her mind was clear, and she was able to pen a line or two from time to time.

In December, she sent a dictated note to her dear friend the Reverend Orville Dewey, to tell about the death of her sister-in-law, Elizabeth Sedgwick, who had been ill for a long time: "Since I wrote you, my heroic sister has passed on—a blessed release in all senses—most blessed to her, if we can believe . . . that Death gives more than it takes away."

Miss Sedgwick told the Reverend Dewey about two female cousins who were working in a New Jersey military hospital, saying they were

> good soldiers in a holy warfare. What a different consecration from that of nuns! How blessed are the single women of our country, who have found such new and blessed channels for those affections which crave and will channel! Surely more acceptable to God is the tending and solacing of sick soldiers than protracted prayers kneeling upon stone floors.

At Hancock Shaker Village on the western edge of Pittsfield stood a massive stone barn, round in shape, and so unusual that it was one of the most famous agricultural structures in the country. With its novel layout for milking and haying the dairy cows, the "Round Stone Barn" symbolized Shakerdom's excellent workmanship and innovative genius.

On December 1, at seven in the morning, the barn was discovered to be on fire, and despite every effort by local firemen to save it, it was destroyed, along with $3,000 worth of hay. The barn had cost more than $10,000 to build about twenty years earlier. Its thick foundation and circular stone walls could be salvaged, however, so it would be rebuilt promptly.

No one was ever found guilty of this particular arson, but around this time two Stockbridge residents, brothers James and Jeremiah Tracy, were arrested and charged with fires that had occurred in that town.

Two days before Christmas, a huge brawl broke out in Pittsfield as dozens of returning Adams and Pittsfield men who had been serving short, hundred-day terms in the army clashed at the train depot. The outnumbered police were powerless to stop the fighting, which lasted an hour and resulted in some ugly fractures and stab wounds. Just as things were quieting down and the battlers seemed to have had enough, a gang of Pittsfield roughs appeared and pitched into the Adams men again.

Only the arrival, and prudently quick departure, of the train for Adams brought an end to the fighting. Pittsfield was scandalized by the inability of its lawmen to do anything while the train depot was a battle ground, unsafe for law-abiding citizens.

In the desperate effort by the Confederates to turn aside Sherman's relentless invasion, Southern brigadier general Claudius Sears, who had been taken prisoner at Vicksburg and subsequently been exchanged, had led a division in the unsuccessful Confederate defense of Atlanta in 1864. Sears then took part in a daring Confederate invasion of Tennessee, an attempt to cut Sherman's supply line, but the Confederates were defeated at the Battle of Nashville in December.

In that battle, a shell struck Sears's horse, blowing off one of the general's legs, and a few days later he was captured again.

In February 1865, the *Eagle's* Joseph E. A. Smith announced his resignation after ten years as editor. He would go on to become Pittsfield's chronicler, taking up the task of writing a history that would require another ten years to complete.

One of the last events he reported upon for the *Eagle* was a devastating fire in downtown North Adams, which consumed three blocks. The fire was accidental, reportedly caused by a lamp having been left lit after a late-night dancing party had ended and everyone had gone home.

The Thirty-seventh Massachusetts was one of the best-regarded of any regiment in the Union army, and it was in almost all the major engagements between Grant and Lee late in the war.

Though the fate of the Confederacy was all but decided, the Union army had to fight constantly to find a way to break the enemy defenses. Forts and trenches had to be stormed, attacks had to be supported, and men died of wounds and of cold in that early spring weather, which was freezing and stormy. On the morning of March 25, 1865, the tireless Thirty-seventh prepared to reinforce a counterattack on Fort Stedman in the Richmond-Petersburg defenses. The enemy had just captured the fort in a desperate attempt to break the Union siege. When the Union attack succeeded without need for the Thirty-seventh, it was in part thanks to the gallantry of the Fifty-seventh Massachusetts, the unit raised and first commanded by Frank Bartlett, who was at his family's home in Winthrop, recovering from imprisonment, his health broken.

Bartlett and Agnes Pomeroy of Pittsfield became formally engaged in January 1865, and he looked back on 1864 as "an eventful year for me in more ways than one." He prayed that the end of 1865 would find him "a better man, and more deserving of God's mercy and goodness and the love of my darling Agnes."

In February, Corporal Daniel Hughes of Pittsfield, a former Allen Guard, was mustered out of the Thirty-first regiment at Camp Carrollton, Louisiana. Corporal Hughes went home at last, safe and sound, having served his country since the spring of 1861.

General Sherman drove his men through stormy weather and flooded roads to chase the remnants of Joseph Johnston's ragged but defiant army across the Carolinas. The Second Massachusetts was frequently engaged with an almost fanatical enemy, the fighting as brutal as it was hopeless for the South. Yet the killing continued. On March 16, Sherman and the Second Massachusetts defeated a portion of Johnston's army, and a few days later an audacious counterattack by Johnston at Bentonville was repulsed. Johnston kept his army together and continued to retreat, Sherman at his heels.

Around this time, the First Massachusetts cavalry, reduced to battalion size by now, closed its illustrious career by serving as mounted pickets guarding the rear of the army at Petersburg. Before long, the First would be brought farther back to the defenses of Washington and would serve as provost guard for the Army of the Potomac.

The Twenty-seventh Massachusetts had been transferred back from Virginia to the Carolina coast. Of the original seven hundred and forty-four men who had gone to Virginia in May of 1864, fewer than seventy remained. There had been new recruits to bring the regiment up to an effective strength of about two hundred and sixty. The Twenty-seventh resumed the close-quarters skirmishing in the swamps and forests it had known during its first year of service, and though the war was almost over, the fighting and marching were hard.

In February of 1865, Lee's Charlie Gates had grown weary of farming and joined the army once again, this time in the Twenty-seventh. By the time he got to the front, however, there would be nothing left of the regiment to join, as in March the Twenty-seventh was attacked and surrounded by a vastly superior enemy force. Desperately trying to break out, rallying around its standard bearers, two of whom were shot down, the Twenty-seventh finally had no choice but to surrender. Seven were killed, forty wounded, and one hundred and forty-seven captured. Only a handful of stretcher bearers were able to escape. The prisoners were marched to Libby Prison in Richmond, where they were immediately paroled and sent back to the Union lines. Upon their return, the men were given a month's furlough to Massachusetts; it was the end of their active service.

That month, the Thirty-first Massachusetts joined the campaign against the important port city of Mobile, Alabama, which was captured within a month after hard marching but little fighting on the regiment's part. From then until the end of the war, the Thirty-first "knew only the pleasant side of soldier life" in Mobile, according to its official historian. The regiment would remain in service until September 1865, five months after the surrender of the main Confederate armies.

That March of 1865, Shaker elders wrote to invite President Lincoln to make a secret, incognito, visit to Mount Lebanon, where he could find "a place of rest for body and mind."

> We will meet and receive you as sympathizing friends, brothers and sisters in Christ, who regard you as a servant of God to humanity. . . .
>
> We will ask for no favors, and you shall hear no complaints; nor any petitions, except to God for the restoration of your health and that you may be strengthened to accomplish your allotted task in the order of Divine Providence.

Lincoln did not make that visit to the Shakers.

Through a dense, predawn fog on Sunday morning, April 2, 1865, a Union force that included members of the Thirty-seventh, Thirty-fourth, and Sixty-first Massachusetts regiments attacked and finally broke through Lee's defensive lines at Petersburg.

The Sixty-first was composed largely of veterans who had re-enlisted, with a good number of Berkshire men, among them Henry Johns of Hinsdale, formerly of the Forty-ninth, now a captain, and a participant in the assault.

At one point, the men of the Thirty-fourth found themselves pinned down on a steep slope before an enemy battery known as Fort Gregg. They could keep their positions only by sticking bayonets into the ground to avoid sliding downward. After half an hour spent unable to advance or retreat, they recklessly surged forward and captured the fort. The charge was led by Egremont farmer Robert I. Gardner, a first sergeant in Company K, who swung his musket as a club to clear the way. The attackers then turned captured enemy cannon on other Confederate positions and cleared them.

Among the Thirty-fourth's dead was Christopher Pennell of West Stockbridge, later memorialized by a writer and poet from the regiment, whose brief tribute to Pennell would fit many a comrade:

Brave Christopher Pennell—with noble ambition leaving his many
friends to serve on another field, and falling at last before Petersburg.

After the Union breakthrough, the Confederates had to retreat from
Petersburg and abandon all hope of defending Richmond any longer. On April
3, Lee's army evacuated Richmond, leaving the city's elected representatives
to meet with the Union officer of the day—the duty officer in overall charge
of a specific part of the line—in this case General Oliver Edwards, former
colonel of the Thirty-seventh Massachusetts. Accompanying Edwards at the
dawn meeting was a small body of troops mainly made up of men from the
Thirty-seventh. Later that day, the regiment entered the city to preserve
order until an occupying garrison was in place, but their rest was short-lived,
and on they went with Grant to pursue Lee's army.

For what they did to help breach the enemy lines at Petersburg, the Congressional Medal of Honor would be awarded to three members of the Thirty-
seventh regiment, including Corporal Richard Welch of Williamstown, who
captured a flag. The Thirty-fourth's Sergeant Gardner, of Egremont, also would
be awarded the Medal of Honor for his "gallant conduct in battle."

In New York City on the day Richmond was evacuated, Herman Melville
examined his wartime verse and began to gather and revise it into a collection for
publication under the title *Battle-Pieces*. Philadelphia author George Henry
Boker had already published his *Poems of the War*, and New Yorker Walt Whitman,
who had been a nurse in Union hospitals, had brought out *Drum-Taps*.

Melville's finished work would not be based on the experience of observing battles first-hand, but he would research periodicals and read memoirs to
develop verse that accurately placed historical events in the larger context of
the war's history. Commemorating the capture of the Confederate capital,
Melville's "The Fall of Richmond" was subtitled, "The Tidings Received in
the Northern Metropolis," and it opens:

What mean these peals from every tower,
   And crowds like seas that sway?
The cannon reply; they speak the heart
   Of the People impassioned, and say—
A city in flags for a city in flames,
   Richmond goes Babylon's way—
     Sing and pray . . .
Well that the faith we firmly kept,
   And never our aim forswore
For the Terrors that trooped from each recess
When fainting we fought in the Wilderness,

And Hell made loud hurrah;
But God is in Heaven and Grant in the Town,
And Right through might is Law—
God's way adore.

On April 3, the same day Melville began to look over his verse, Shaker sister Cecilia De Vere at Mount Lebanon dreamed of a "great crime" taking place in a theater.

Union troops harried Lee's retreat from Richmond, fighting his army's rearguard actions all the way.

The Thirty-seventh, armed with those devastating Spencer repeating rifles, took part in important clashes that were obstinately fought on both sides. At the Battle of Sayler's Creek on April 6, the last major engagement between the armies of Lee and Grant, Private Charles A. Taggart of Otis captured an enemy flag and won yet another Medal of Honor for his regiment and Berkshire County. Forty of the two hundred remaining members of the regiment fell as casualties in this campaign.

The Thirty-seventh's Captain Archibald Hopkins of Williamstown officially received a brevet promotion to lieutenant colonel in honor of his conduct at Petersburg.

Also in the pursuit of Lee were the Thirty-fourth and Sixty-first Massachusetts regiments, both skirmishing frequently. (The Fifty-seventh Massachusetts had been sent to garrison duty in Washington.) The Thirty-fourth was part of a force that made a hard two-day march to plant itself squarely on the line of Lee's retreat, and on the night of April 8, the Union men confronted the vanguard of Confederate troops who were intending to clear the way for their army's escape. The vanguard commander had thought the Union force in his path to be only cavalry, but—as the regimental historian wrote—instead he "beheld the firm ranks of the Thirty-fourth and its fellow regiments. The surrender of Lee's army followed. . . ."

General John S. Barnard was one of only a half dozen or so of the highest-ranking Union officers with Grant and Lee in the house at Appomattox for the signing of the final terms.

Melville wrote "The Surrender at Appomattox (April 1865)."

As billows upon billows roll,
    On victory victory breaks . . .

Berkshire was delirious with joy at the news of Richmond's fall and then, a week later, at Lee's surrender. The Eagle reported the celebrations:

The news . . . transformed Williamstown into a Bedlam. The streets glowed with bonfires while horns, drums, fifes, bells, and muskets mingled their jargon. At Williams College speeches were made. . . . President [Mark] Hopkins said his heart was too full for speech, but announced . . . that tomorrow would be a holiday in college.

Final recitations were in progress at Williams when the students heard of Lee's surrender, and they rushed, cheering, to the chapel, without waiting to be formally dismissed. There, they sang "America" and the Doxology, and bells rang everywhere. The college chapel bell was so vigorously rung that it came loose from its fastenings and crashed down to the belfry floor—falling no further, fortunately for the ringers below.

And elsewhere in Berkshire:

Seldom has sleepy old Stockbridge been so aroused from its usual somnolence as when it heard of the capture of Richmond and sur-render of Lee, which events were signalized by a general jubilation, with guns, drums, bells, and bonfires. . . . No sooner had the telegraph ticked off the welcome news, than the bells "tolled" it to the people. In the evening bonfires blazed . . . and gunpowder and bad tobacco smoke made the night as gloriously hideous as the most enthusiastic could desire.

Pittsfield was "a blaze of glory," with the news of Lee's capitulation inspir-ing even more festivities than did the fall of Richmond. On Monday night, April 10, with bells ringing and flags flying everywhere, the business district was illuminated "until a late hour," and many residences lit every lamp and candle and lantern they had.

All the buildings in the business portion of the village were lighted, and all the store windows on North Street were brilliant with lights, flags, colored lanterns, etc. . . . the illumination was thorough and complete, and no doubt the most perfect ever witnessed here.

A cannon, expected to come from Albany, did not arrive, so the fire worshipers had to console themselves with rockets &c., of which the display was good.

The *Berkshire Courier's* headlines read: "THE END! Surrender of Lee! Overthrow of the Rebellion," as the people of the Great Barrington area gathered on April 10 at the town hall, where songs of rejoicing were written and sung on the spot.

In the "Local News" section of the *Eagle* edition that described the celebrations, a brief paragraph reported on a new state militia company being raised in North Adams. Arthur M. Tinker had been chosen captain, because "None of those who had seen service would take the office."

On April 14, the residents of Berkshire County saw the sun turn an ominous, deep red, and everyone wondered fearfully what was happening. At the Richmond home of iron miner Garrett J. Murphy, his wife, Ellen, heard people lamenting that the end of the world was at hand, and others—who had not heard of Appomattox—said it was an omen that the Northern armies had been defeated. Mrs. Murphy could only think of her brother, a soldier away at the war, from whom she had not heard in some months.

The next morning, on April 15, came the dreadful news that President Lincoln had been assassinated the previous day while watching a play at Ford's Theater in Washington.

One week after the rapture of Appomattox, the *Courier* headline was: "The President is Shot! Great National Calamity."

Under the title "A Nation Mourns," the editorial read:

> The sound of rejoicing over the near approach of peace has been hushed by the cries of mourners, whose voices are heard throughout the length and breadth of the land. . . .
>
> After four long years of civil war, while the Angel of Peace was announcing glad tidings to the people, our chosen leader is suddenly called away, as if his task were done. . . .

The *Eagle* editorial commentary was under the headline "President Lincoln Murdered."

> At many times during the war have we witnessed exhibitions of great public grief, but never anything like this upon us now, which has bowed every reasoning head and almost broken every loyal heart.

Lincoln's funeral in Washington was held on April 19, and in Berkshire all places of business were closed between noon to 6 p.m. and draped with black cloth, nearly every store window showing a patriotic exhibit and the Stars and Stripes. Bells tolled from 11 a.m. to noon, followed by church services, the churches draped in black funeral cloth. The First Congregational Church of Pittsfield, like many others in the county, was filled to overflowing, and mourners stood outside to listen to the service.

For Berkshire, it was as Melville wrote in "The Martyr":

There is a sobbing of the strong,
And a pall upon the land; . . .

Johnston and the last Confederate army surrendered to Sherman in North Carolina on April 29, and the war was over.

The Fifty-fourth Massachusetts had been in combat right to the eighteenth of the month, skirmishing in South Carolina against die-hard Confederates at Boykin's Mill. This was one of the last clashes of the Civil War, and it required a charge by the Fifty-fourth, costing the regiment another fifteen men killed or wounded. With the cessation of hostilities, the Fifty-fourth did garrison duty in South Carolina, including in the city of Charleston, until it journeyed to Boston for mustering out on September 1.

Sheffield's Robert Kellogg, former sergeant major of the Sixteenth Connecticut, published his book, *Life and Death in Rebel Prisons*. Sheffield Medal of Honor winner Frederick Deland of the Forty-ninth and Great Barrington would write his own war memoirs, entitled "Forlorn Hope," which he would read to a reunion of the regiment in 1885.

In celebration at the close of the war, two enormous "Grand Reviews" of Union troops paraded through the streets of Washington.

In Washington on May 24, there was a "Grand Review" of mainly Sherman's victorious army. The Second Massachusetts marched in this review, as did the Sixty-first. Led by generals and their staffs on horseback, and with the resounding music of brass bands and drum corps of sixty or eighty instruments, thousands upon thousands of sunburnt, lean soldiers marched behind their tattered regimental colors, proudly parading twenty or more abreast through the city they had fought so long to defend.

The cavalcade went on all day, regiment after regiment. At times there would be solid ranks of only cavalry with sabers drawn and gleaming in the spring sunlight, taking an hour to pass by. Dozens of battalions of black sappers carrying their picks and shovels, and hundreds of polished artillery pieces passed by, the guns ranked four or six wide across the street. This was a mighty display of the military power of the Union, but it was only a portion of the force that had conquered in the East and South.

On June 8 there was a second grand review, just as enormous, just as spectacular and thrilling, this one with Grant's army, and in it was the Thirty-seventh Massachusetts. The Thirty-fourth regiment was in camp four miles north of the city, but did not take part in the review, nor did the First Massachusetts cavalry, which was on escort duty outside Washington.

In Berkshire, the next great celebrations of victory and peace came on Independence Day, and North Adams in particular made the most of it with festivities that one writer considered "probably the most enthusiastic of all the earlier or later events of that anniversary in Berkshire County, and [which] really marked the passing away of good old observances of that character."

The day was "ushered in at sunrise by the ringing of bells, and a National Salute of one hundred guns from Robinson's Hill," said the *Transcript*. At mid-morning, with the arrival of the trains from Pittsfield and Troy, the parade formed up in front of the Berkshire House, with Stewart's Cornet Band at its head. The procession marched through town to the Baptist church, which swung wide its doors—first for the ladies, who had the galleries reserved for them. There, the Reverend Sanford opened the program, which was highlighted by the reading of the Declaration of Independence.

Two large naval flags hung across the summit of Church Hill, suspended from the steeples of the churches. One flag, belonging to John Welch, a resident of North Adams, had flown from the masthead of the warship *Brooklyn*, which had been in many of the major naval engagements of the war. The other flag had been rescued from the bark *Cavallo*, when it was captured by the Confederates. The man who rescued this flag was *Cavallo*'s first mate, Martin Stickney, also a resident of the town.

After the exercises there followed a free dinner, contributed by the Berkshire House, on the grounds of the Methodist church. The meal was accompanied by speeches and proclamations and the reading of letters from Governor Andrew, Senator Sumner, and others, followed by a speech from Mark Hopkins, president of Williams College.

One of the day's features was a street performance by the "Tarnal Critters," young businessmen of the village who "gave all the spectators their fill of laugh and fun." Continuing a twenty-year tradition of such annual performances, the Tarnal Critters, wearing disguises and costumes, put on skits, read humorous poems, and gave speeches. With slapstick and inside jokes, they made good sport of—"put hits on"—everyone from the local fire company to Williams professors, from Pittsfield's prominent men to former Confederate president Jefferson Davis. There was even a mock state legislator, Ethan Spike, who gave a blowhard speech to his "feller Tarnal Critters" that would have appealed to Josh Billings: "As I haul my eyes over your intellectooal and sweaty forms and features, assembled together on this here great and enormous day. . . ."

The celebrations culminated that evening in a fireworks display for four or five thousand spectators seated on "fence boards, blankets and the green turf" on the west side of Sugar Loaf Hill. Many of the fireworks had suffered water damage in transit from the factory in Boston, and "but few pieces were worth seeing," said the *Transcript*, "besides the beautiful bomb shells which exploded high in the air with a galaxy of colored stars." Nevertheless, whenever it was discussed years later, the North Adams Independence Day of 1865 was remembered fondly as the last "good old-fashioned" Fourth.

After all the effort and sacrifice in the name of the Union these past four years, many Berkshire folk would agree with their own Josh Billings that: "2 sta is 2 win."

A group of Civil War veterans, some in their Allen Guards uniforms, gathers with friends for a photograph after performing at Burbank Hall in 1872 in a play entitled "The Drummer Boy of Shiloh"; they include, seated l-r, Brigadier General Henry S. Briggs and Captain Israel C. Weller.

COURTESY BERKSHIRE EAGLE

Chapter Twenty-six

AFTER THE WAR

In mid-1865, the wealthy Thomas Allen of Pittsfield and St. Louis suggested immediately wiping out the immense national debt by selling two hundred thousand shares of $10,000 notes to America's rich—the "capitalists," the *Eagle* called them, using a relatively new expression. No one took Allen up on his plan.

The Civil War had cost the Federal government $6.19 billion, and the national debt stood at $2.85 billion. This did not include the soldier pensions and expenses for the burial of veterans—which costs would, by 1910, reach an estimated $11.5 billion.

To honor of the Fifty-fourth, there was a great parade through the city of Boston on September 2 and a final review by Governor Andrew from the Statehouse steps.

The *Boston Evening Transcript* wrote:

> The Fifty-fourth Massachusetts Regiment . . . now returns crowned with laurels, and . . . have had such a reception to-day as benefited an organization the history of which is admitted to form so conspicuous a part of the annals of the country.

In a ceremony at Boston on December 22, 1865, Massachusetts regiments officially deposited their national and state flags and regimental colors in the Statehouse.

Members of the regiments were invited to follow their colors one last time, marching in a procession through the city, beginning and ending at the Common, and cheered by a huge crowd all along the way. Governor Andrew described it as "a pageant, so full of pathos and of glory."

The Second regiment, with some fifty men present, deposited three flags and two staffs from which the colors had been shot off; the Tenth, thirty men, two flags; the Twentieth, fifty-nine men, two colors; the Twenty-first, twenty-five men, six colors; the Twenty-seventh, fourteen men, three colors; the Thirty-first, eleven men, five colors; the Thirty-fourth, thirty-six men, two colors; the Thirty-seventh, four men, four colors; the Forty-ninth, four men, two colors; the Fifty-fourth, sixty men, two colors; the Fifty-seventh and Fifty-ninth, consolidated, sixty-one men, two colors; the Sixty-first, sixty-one men, two colors.

Herman Melville's *Battle-Pieces*, published by Harper Brothers in August 1866, was unfavorably reviewed for the most part, and went almost unnoticed in his lifetime. The verse was described as too difficult, too deep, too sympathetic to the South, writ-

The tattered colors carried into battle by the Thirty-seventh Massachusetts after being deposited at the Massachusetts Statehouse at the end of the war.

ten too rapidly, too rough, too detached, too lacking in feeling for the actual experiences of those who were at the battle front—and one critic even said it was, for Melville, "a further step toward popular oblivion."

This was yet another disappointment to Melville. As one scholar said more than a century later, perhaps he had overestimated his readers and their ability to comprehend the work. Not until late in the twentieth century would *Battle-Pieces* be rediscovered and re-evaluated. Then, some of the poems would be considered important contributions to Civil War literature and worthy of standing with Melville's finest achievements.

The Melville family at Arrowhead from now on would be that of the wealthy brother, Allan, and the house would know the giddy whirl of the new Berkshire "Gilded Age" society. The county was increasingly becoming fashionable, as the immensely rich, who for the most part had made their fortunes from the Civil War, began to build country homes there.

Several Berkshire communities allotted portions of their burying grounds for military men. The *Eagle* wrote about Pittsfield:

> It is not well that these men should be forgotten, as so many of our soldiers, who fell in former wars, have been. Let us then set apart one of the most beautiful spots in our beautiful cemetery, to receive the remains of those who may be brought home, and erect in it a suitable monument to bear the names, not only of those, but also of their comrades who sleep in nameless graves under the sod which they died to redeem for their country.
>
> A spot like this would add new and holier consecration to the cemetery. Strangers would visit it with the reverence due to the tombs of heroes. The present generation, familiar with the excitements, the anxieties and dangers, under which the sleepers went out from us—would turn to their resting place with a deeper thrill each year, and their descendants would visit it with an ennobling pride forever. Perhaps in some future hour of our country's peril, the youth of Pittsfield may be inspired with equal self-devotion by the thought that she did not forget even the humblest of those who at her call went forth to die.

Near the end of the war, Florida's Brigadier General Edward A. Perry had gone into hiding, unwilling to surrender, but still suffering from his wounds. With his wife and her aunt caring for him, Perry had hidden in a cave, while they had lived in a cabin nearby. The occupation force of Union soldiers would have been pleased to discover and imprison him.

At the end of hostilities, Perry resumed his civilian life in his adopted state of Florida, but there is no record of his ever signing an official surrender document, which Confederate officers were required to do by the peace terms. Perry returned to the practice of law, becoming a champion of Florida's rights during the oppressive period of Reconstruction, when much of the South was looted by unscrupulous "carpetbaggers" from the North.

So prominent was Perry in Florida that he was elected governor and served from 1884-88. He died the following year, at the age of fifty-eight.

After his release in mid-1865, Mississippi's Brigadier General Claudius Sears returned to teach at Mississippi State University in Oxford, where he would be a professor of mathematics until 1889. Sears answered to the university chancellor, Alexander P. Stewart, a former Confederate general who had been his superior before the war at the U.S. Military Academy, and with whom he had served near the end of the Civil War. Sears apparently did not care for Stewart, once telling an associate, "I was under him at West Point; I was under him in the army; I am under him now; and I reckon I will be under him

The dedication of the Soldiers Monument erected at Park Square, Pittsfield, in 1872.

in hell." Sears died in 1891 at the age of seventy-three. Sears and Perry were two of the most notable Berkshire natives to serve in the Confederate forces, but there were others. For example, in 1897, William H. Chamberlain, originally of the Coltsville section of Pittsfield, wrote a letter to the editor of the local *Saturday Blade* to tell that, of fifteen boys he remembered as schoolmates in 1852, ten had been in the Union forces, and five, who had gone South before the war, had fought for the Confederacy.

The remains of Charles Barker of Adams, who died of wounds soon after the Wilderness conflict, were never recovered, but a silver badge he had owned was.

A Binghamton, New York, man moved to Virginia after the war, and one day his wife bought the badge from a local woman who said she had cut it from the uniform of a dead Union soldier. The inscription on the badge was, "Co. B, 9th N.Y.S.M., war 1861." The man subsequently moved back to Binghamton, where he was persuaded by a friend to place a "lost and found" advertisement in the *National Tribune*, a newspaper published for soldiers and former soldiers.

Barker's family had a photograph of him wearing that badge on the uniform coat of his Ninth New York State Militia regiment, which was designated the Eighty-third New York Volunteers. The family remembered how, when home on leave, he had said the badge might be a comfort to them one day. These relatives learned of the advertisement and acquired the badge, which was presented to Barker's mother, then eighty-five years of age. It was, indeed, some comfort to her.

In the family plot of the Adams cemetery stands a plain marble cross in memory of Charles Barker.

In Knoxville, Tennessee, in the spring of 1874, Laura Smith Richardson, a native of New Marlboro, was the head of a ladies' committee that procured flowers for decorating the graves of soldiers, both Northern and Southern. Mrs. Richardson, who was in her late forties—her maiden name was Catlin—was having difficulty finding enough flowers so early in the year. One day, she saw a pile of miniature American flags in a store, and the idea flashed to her of placing a flag on each soldier's and sailor's grave.

The idea was adopted by her committee, and on May 30, 1874, a ceremony was held at the local cemetery, with Andrew Johnson, former president and former governor of Tennessee, as guest of honor. While Johnson spoke, hundreds of miniature flags fluttered over the graves, and in that moment a new national tradition was born.

One of Hinsdale's two Medal of Honor recipients, Francis E. Warren of the Forty-ninth, went out west as soon as the war was over, and by 1868 had established himself as a prominent sheep-rancher in Wyoming Territory. He became governor of the territory, and after Wyoming became a state, served as senator. Warren was the father-in-law of John J. Pershing, commander of the American Expeditionary Force in World War One and later Chief of Staff of the Armies of the United States.

In 1880, Chicago attorney Hamilton Eldridge, originally of South Williamstown and a Williams College graduate, was instrumental in winning the presidency for his former classmate and close friend James A. Garfield of Ohio. When the Republicans could not settle on a candidate at their convention in Chicago that year, Eldridge telegraphed every Williams College alumnus he could locate and called upon them to send their own telegrams to the Republican delegates from their states to demand they vote for Garfield—then the least likely candidate to win the nomination. Eldridge also arranged for Garfield to receive a resounding cheer from the audience as soon as he showed himself on the convention hall floor. The result was that Garfield became the nominee and won the presidency.

*Lee's Memorial Hall was dedicated in 1874 in memory of those from the town
who served in the military during the Civil War.*

In July of the following year, after less than four months in office, President Garfield was at the Washington, D.C., railroad station, on his way to Williams College for the annual commencement, when he was fatally shot by an assassin.

Of the three hundred and seventeen Williams College men who served in the Civil War, one was a major general (James Garfield), fifteen were brigadier generals (three of whom were killed); and two were naval officers, one of whom would become a rear admiral. Thirty-six men from the college volunteered for the Sanitary Commission. Thirty Williams men died in the war.

A few years after the war, Parthenia Fenn once again took the lead in providing what Pittsfield's former soldiers needed: a commemorative statue.

Mrs. Fenn and the women of the town worked hard to raise the first $3,000 for the committee to design and commission the Pittsfield Soldiers Monument, which finally cost $7,000 and was dedicated on September 24, 1872. Cast from condemned cannon donated by Congress, the life-size bronze figure of a color-bearer stands at the west end of the park, on the spot where most of the local soldiers gathered before departing for the war. The sculptor was G. Launt Thompson of New York.

On plaques affixed to the pedestal are the names of Pittsfield men who died while in the service.

General William Francis "Frank" Bartlett, who would never recover from war-related disabilities that constantly plagued him, had the honor of unveiling the statue. Bartlett was now a much-loved adopted son of Pittsfield, manager of the Pomeroy family ironworks in West Stockbridge. Illness followed illness for Bartlett, but he was a shining example of a noble spirit in a fragile body. He was Harvard's commencement speaker in 1874 and an honored guest at patriotic and civic events from his birthplace, Haverhill, to New York City. He firmly opposed taking revenge against the South, called for reconciliation, and was a leading light in the cause of national healing. Bartlett's eloquence "thrilled the hearts of thousands," said a biographer.

One of Bartlett's business enterprises was an ironworks in Richmond, Virginia. There, in the spring of 1875, he was the guest speaker at a convention of former Confederate soldiers, who welcomed him with a great ovation. He told them, "[W]hen the passions of the time pass away, posterity will honor genius, patriotism, and chivalry without regard to the flag under which it was exhibited or the uniform it wore."

That same year, Bartlett declined offers from both Massachusetts Democrats and Republicans to be their candidate for lieutenant governor and governor, respectively. His health was failing again.

Bartlett's business enterprises were not as successful as his public career, for three of the four manufacturing operations he participated in were destroyed by fire, and the fourth failed. As a result, he lost most of his personal fortune, and coupled with his poor health, this stress contributed to his steady decline. He was

This silver cup with gold lining and raised enamel decorations commemorating General Francis Bartlett's various ranks was presented by the officers of the Twentieth Massachusetts to Bartlett's newborn son, Edwin, as the first boy born to any of the regiment's former officers.

COURTESY BERKSHIRE MUSEUM

vulnerable to sudden relapses, such as the illness that seized him in New York City early in 1876, when he told a friend, "[M]y nerve force is exhausted, and I have used my strength faster than I have made it."

In September, a daughter was born to Agnes and Frank Bartlett, their fourth child after three sons. Bartlett was physically enfeebled, but it was a delight to him when baby Edith was christened in his room that November.

Bartlett died a few weeks later, on December 17, 1876, at the age of thirty-six. On a cold, bright winter's day, he was buried in Pittsfield Cemetery, widely eulogized as the single most outstanding soldier Massachusetts had sent to the Civil War. John Greenleaf Whittier wrote a poem commemorating the generous spirit of this young hero's quest to rebuild America:

> His fame who led the stormy van
> Of battle well may cease,
> But never that which crowns the man
> Whose victory was Peace.

COURTESY BERKSHIRE ATHENAEUM

The statue of General Bartlett sculpted by Daniel Chester French; the plaster cast is at Berkshire Community College, Pittsfield.

In 1904, a statue of Bartlett by sculptor Daniel Chester French of Stockbridge was dedicated in Memorial Hall of the Statehouse in Boston. Soon afterward, French presented a plaster cast of the statue to Berkshire County, to be placed in the county courthouse in Pittsfield.

At the time of Bartlett's funeral, one anonymous contemporary, who was reputed to have had "few equals in judging of character," said, "The Massachusetts of this generation has bred no so heroic a character as that of the man whom she will bury, with sadness and with honor, in Berkshire, this week."

In a generation of heroes, there was no higher compliment.

At an annual reunion banquet of the Forty-ninth Massachusetts in Pittsfield on May 21, 1867, former lieutenant colonel Samuel B. Sumner of Great Barrington read a poem he had written for the occasion. General Bartlett was

in the audience as Sumner's verse recapitulated the history of the regiment
with ample humor and filled with appropriate sentiments:

How strange a thing is memory: as I gaze
This night on comrades of those fruitful days,
When arméd cohorts thronged on every hand,
And war's alarms and thunders shook the land;
I am not here,—but backward, far away,
My inmost thoughts and recollections stray,
And bygone scenes are passing in review,
Which, haply, I may reproduce to you.

Sumner told of recruiting the regiment, and of those first days at Camp
Briggs, when "'twas drum-beat morn and night, and tramp, tramp all the day. . ."

The boys complained of homesickness;—the discipline seemed hard;
And ever and anon, at night, the rascals ran the guard.

Of course, "all the belles in town" admired their "stunning dress-parades,"
and the food was "exceeding good," their appetites "glorious," and they drank
coffee so strong "'twould kill at forty rods." Pittsfield hospitality and the late,
dear Sarah Morewood were lauded. Then came orders to leave for Worcester,
where the men were enthralled by the "bewitching" local ladies with their
"charming smiles." None too soon, the regiment departed for camp on Long
Island, otherwise "each bachelor . . . [would] have been decoyed and married." The events in camp and as provost troops for New York City were
recalled, as was the rough, seasick voyage to the South, when

A disposition seized us to keep the vessel's side,
And cease our conversation, and only watch the tide.
We found some strange attraction in the briny surge beneath,
And many a mouth was wide agape,—and Charlie lost his teeth!

Then to Louisiana and New Orleans, where Berkshire friends in the Thirty-
first welcomed them, reminiscing about home, about places where they would
like to "peep in, / Of dinners that we used to eat, and beds we used to sleep in."
Next, they went into camp at Baton Rouge,

And here, until the fourteenth day of March, we lay at ease,
When General Banks conceived a plan, with force and arms to seize
The stronghold of Port Hudson;—but here let the Muses rest,
I'll sing that olden ballad; it will aid our memories best.

Sumner then recited a ballad, "The Passage of Montesino," written by him and several others while on the campaign. It was rich with inside jokes and sarcasm regarding commanders such as Banks. Most of the ballad's more insulting, and likely vulgar, humor was not included in the collection of Sumner's verse published after the war—as he said in a footnote, "the printing of which would be a matter of doubtful propriety." In the poem, Banks praises the disgruntled regiment for making a hard, fruitless march to the Mississippi and back, which the general declared to have been a great military achievement and a "gallant deed."

The men did not think so. Sumner quotes Banks as saying:

"And in the long hereafter,
　　Be this your glorious boast;—
'We went with Banks's army
　　To Port Hudson . . . almost!'"

After the ballad there followed, in Sumner's poem, a serious description of the fighting, of the "fearful struggle" for Port Hudson, and of the "nameless graves afar beneath that Southern sod. . . ."

O, if no other impulse moved our hearts to gather here,
To hold one brief communion, with each recurring year;
Our duty still were plain enough, since, haply, we survive,
Their sacrifice to count, and keep their memories alive.

Nor did the "scarred and shattered" men in that room escape unscathed from the war. Then Sumner changed pace and mood: "I have sung as impulses moved me. . . . Let us banish the sadness. . . . The conflict is over. . . ."

And as time shall roll on, let us happily gather,
　　Now and then one more glance retrospective to cast;
With a fondness and longing, unlessened, but rather
　　More deep, as our years recede into the past.

And now, let the generous cup be o'er flowing
　　With grateful libations, potential to cheer;
The rapture of social enjoyment bestowing,
　　As we strengthen the ties of our fellowship here.

NOTES

PROLOGUE

Famous individuals from nineteenth century Berkshire County included William Miller, originally of Pittsfield, who founded the apocalyptic sect known as Millerites and predicted that the end of the world would occur in 1843 with the advent of Christ in the body. When no such phenomenon occurred, the Millerites dissolved, some forming other religious groups. Miller died in 1849.

Edwin D. Morgan, New York governor from 1858 to 1862, was born in the town of Washington, Berkshire County, and became active as a merchant, broker, and banker; he resigned as governor to enter the U.S. Senate as a Republican, which party he had helped create while serving as its national chairman, achieving the election of Lincoln in 1860.

John Z. Goodrich of Stockbridge, one of the early editors of the *Berkshire County Eagle* when it was based in that town, was also a founder of the Republican party, serving as chairman of its national organizing committee.

John Thompson of Peru was founder and president of the First National Bank in New York, and later founded Chase National Bank.

Thomas C. Durant of Lee was a chief figure in the construction of the Union Pacific Railroad, and would be one of those who had the honor of driving the ceremonial golden spike when the continent was finally spanned by tracks in May 1869.

Theodore Sedgwick 3rd of Stockbridge and Lenox was the leading figure in the organization of the first World's Fair, held at the Crystal Palace in New York City in 1853.

Cyrus Field's transatlantic cable failed a few weeks after being laid in 1858, which was the second attempt at laying it, the first having been unsuccessful in 1857. Field's third attempt, in 1866, was successful.

CHAPTER 1

In 1860, Berkshire County had a population of approximately 55,000; Pittsfield, with around 8,000 inhabitants, was the largest community and the main railroad center, while Adams—which included North Adams at this time—was second with almost 7,000 persons.

Berkshire County could boast of several "firsts" in the nation by 1860, including the first cooperative cheese factory, established in Cheshire (1801), and the first county agricultural fair (1810); the fair was started in Pittsfield by Elkanah Watson, a merchant and former owner of Broadhall, the farm later purchased by the Morewoods.

The first college alumni association was formed at Williams College (1821), and the first village improvement society was established by the Laurel Hill Association in Stockbridge (1853). Williams also held the first intercollegiate baseball game (1859), losing 32-73 to Amherst College.

Cheshire also produced the first plate glass manufactured in the United States (1853).

For advocating peace, former president Franklin Pierce was considered a traitor and turncoat by many, which was not true.

Englishman Long John Howell, who settled in Springfield, was another former member of the Light Brigade in the Crimean War; he eventually served in the Sixth and Twenty-fifth Massachusetts infantry regiments. The Second Massachusetts Infantry had a color bearer who had served as a color bearer in a Russian regiment during the Crimean War.

CHAPTER 2
In 1854, Julius Rockwell of Pittsfield was elected to the U.S. Senate from Massachusetts.

CHAPTER 3
At the start of 1861, John G. Barnard of Sheffield was a major of U.S. engineers and served on a Navy Department "board of conference" for preparing plans to blockade the Southern coast, some of whose fortifications Major Barnard knew first-hand.

The military lineage of Western Massachusetts and specifically the Tenth Massachusetts volunteer infantry regiment traces back to 1639, when the Springfield Train Band was mustered into service to defend the region from attacks by Indians. During eighty-five years of frontier wars, the train band (reorganized in 1662 as the Hampshire Regiment) saw almost constant action. In King William's War (1689-1697), the Hampshire Regiment captured Port Royal in Acadia (Nova Scotia) for the British Crown.

The Hampshire Regiment saw duty in Queen Anne's War (1702-1713), King George's War (1744-1748), and the French and Indian War (1753-1760) during decades of conflict with the French, Canadians, and their Indian allies. The Hampshire Regiment was again reorganized in 1748 into the North and South Hampshire Regiments. In 1763 the Berkshire Regiment was formed.

In 1775, the Berkshire Regiment was reformed into four battalions for service in the Revolution. The battalions were at the siege of Boston, and with General Washington in the Long Island Campaign and at Trenton, Princeton, and Monmouth. Some Berkshire Regiment companies were with General Benedict Arnold at Quebec and Saratoga. The regiment also took part in battles in Rhode Island and New York. Another reorganization took place in 1792, when the regiment became known as the 9th Division (Berkshire County) Volunteer Light Infantry Companies. The 9th Division was mobilized in the War of 1812 to protect Boston, but saw no fighting.

In 1834, the Light Companies reformed into the Regiment of Light Infantry, the first regiment in Massachusetts to be issued rifled muskets. On April 24, 1840, the light regiments of Berkshire and Hampden counties were reorganized into the Tenth Regiment of Light Infantry, the immediate predecessor of the Tenth Massachusetts.

CHAPTER 6

Pittsfield's David Campbell had given the drum to the Cushing girls and so was honored by their company's being named the Campbell Guard.

During the first Battle of Bull Run, after the tide had clearly turned against the Federals, General John G. Barnard was in company with one of General McDowell's staff officers. The staff officer asked Barnard, his superior, whether he agreed with ordering up reinforcements to take positions that would cover the Union retreat, which was becoming a stampede. Barnard agreed, and even though McDowell, the army's commander, was not on hand, these two officers took the initiative and responsibility for ordering troop movements that, in the end, saved the main Union field army from an even worse defeat.

CHAPTER 8

In September 1861, Melville had a portrait taken at Rodney Dewey's photographic studio on North Street in Pittsfield.

CHAPTER 9

Another version of what happened to the Massachusetts officer's commission for Charles Whelden was given in a 1916 *Berkshire Eagle* article, unsigned, which claimed that Whelden told the writer that Colonel Gooding of the Thirty-first had visited him in Pittsfield around 1889, at which time Gooding had "professed to be dissatisfied with the way Whelden handled his regiment, so when Whelden's commission, signed by Governor Andrew, came to New Orleans, Gooding held it." The problem with this scenario is revealed when one considers Andrew's bitter fight with the War Department over the state's prerogative to raise regiments. Would Andrew have permitted a regular officer to so insolently interfere with a state commission at that time—even Whelden's? Certainly Andrew would have known about it if Gooding had "held" Whelden's commission.

CHAPTER 10

For much of the mid-nineteenth century, Berkshire Medical College in Pittsfield was one of the country's leading institutions educating physicians, and for a time annually turned out more doctors than did the medical school at Harvard—a staunch rival then. With Pittsfield being an important railroad center, Civil War wounded were constantly streaming through, sometimes being cared for on the way by staff of the college. In the summer of 1862, Berkshire Medical College became affiliated with the Federal government's overburdened system of military hospitals.

George F. Root's musical abilities apparently hark back to colonial-era antecedents who also had music in their blood, and they sometimes enjoyed secular music more than their Puritanical local laws would permit. In 1761, one landlord Root of Great Barrington "did wittingly and willfully suffer and permit singing, fiddling, and dancing in his dwelling-house, there being there a tavern or public house." Root admitted his crime and was fined ten shillings and court costs.

CHAPTER 11

After the battle at New Berne, North Carolina, a Massachusetts officer found an old flintlock, dated 1825, which had been manufactured at the Pomeroy musket works in Pittsfield. The musket was eventually sent back to the city and donated to the Berkshire Athenaeum, the forerunner to the institutions that divided to become the library of that name and the Berkshire Museum.

In the attack on New Orleans, Melville's cousin, Edward G. Curtis, was commander of the gunboat *Sciota*, which served as the flagship of Farragut's fleet captain, Henry H. Bell; the vessel was fortunate in this action, having only two men wounded.

CHAPTER 13

After the defeat at Second Bull Run, General John Barnard took charge of building even stronger defenses around Washington, which included fortifications on the north side of the city, clearing fields of fire, and opening up campsites by felling whole forests of trees. With Barnard's oversight, "Heavy details of new troops were furnished daily, and the men, carefully selected, easily and cheerfully got through an immense amount of work in an incredibly short time," according to a report by Lieutenant Colonel Richard B. Irwin, then an assistant adjutant general for the U.S. Army.

CHAPTER 14

On October 16, the *Pittsfield Sun* published a letter from Henry W. Bishop, a prominent attorney and judge in Lenox, eulogizing Will Sedgwick; a portion follows:

> On the first day of October last after night fall was brought into this quiet village the dead body of the late William Dwight Sedgwick. Around his paternal home were gathered his former associates, neighbors, and friends, with faces downcast and bedewed with tears, to receive, and look upon the lifeless lineaments of him, who from his childhood they had loved, whose brave and generous spirit they had admired, of whose intellectual powers and attainments they were proud, whose kind and cordial greetings they fondly recollected, and whose bravery, and decision and energetic will, promised to make his birthplace one to be long remembered by the good, the benevolent, and courageous. It was a sadly impressive scene. It will never be effaced from the memory of its witnesses. Solemn silence expressed the profound grief of the bearers. Face spoke to face of sorrow too great for utterance, and the countenance disclosed emotions of the heart too intense for the tongue's expression. The leaden missives of the battle field do not pause to discriminate. Could heroism and love of country have procured exemption from the fatal slug, the manly form of Sedgwick would now be erect. . . .
>
> The ways of Heaven are not our ways, and we bow mournfully but with patient acquiescence to the blow which has bereft us of an associate, the dearest, the most beloved, and most respected of all.

William D. Sedgwick's monument bears the inscription: *Dulce et decorum est pro patria mori*. "It is sweet and honorable to die for one's country."

CHAPTER 16

The Fifty-fourth Massachusetts Infantry was the most famous all-black regiment, but the commonwealth produced two more such regiments, both of which had noteworthy careers: the Fifty-fifth Massachusetts Infantry and the Fifth Massachusetts Cavalry.

CHAPTER 17

Samuel C. Armstrong was one of the former Williams College students who became a prominent Union officer, distinguishing himself at Gettysburg as a captain with the 125th New York Regiment, and later commanding the Eighth and Ninth U.S. Regiments of Colored Troops. At the war's end, at age twenty-six, he was brevetted a brigadier general. Armstrong was a close friend of Williams president Mark Hopkins and married a Stockbridge woman. After the war he founded the Hampton (Virginia) Normal and Industrial Institute for educating blacks, which became one of the earliest black colleges, and survives today as Hampton University.

One young Union general with later Berkshire connections was Francis C. Barlow, who built a home after the war in Lenox near the home of Robert G. Shaw's widow. Barlow was at one time a tutor to the young Shaw, and he married Shaw's sister Ellen in 1867. Gravely wounded at Antietam, but later returning to the service, he was the model for the Union officer in Winslow Homer's well-known painting "Prisoners from the Front."

Another Shaw brother-in-law was George W. Curtis, a leading literary figure of the day. Curtis was married to Shaw's sister Anna, and they had a summer place in Ashfield, just east of Berkshire. He was the main speaker at the dedication of Pittsfield's Civil War statue described in Chapter 26.

Joseph Tucker, who was wounded in the Forty-ninth's Port Hudson campaign and had to have a leg amputated, became a Massachusetts lieutenant governor after the war. His letter describing the amputation is quoted in David Wood's history of Lenox.

CHAPTER 20

As the Forty-ninth made its way home, another tragic death occurred when Ezra Van Deusen fell overboard in the middle of the night. The incident was recorded in a letter by Egremont's Raymond H. Brown, who related what his friend and Forty-ninth member Henry Van Tassell told him:

> Ezra was most uneasy to get home and when the regiment was returning home on a steamer going north up the Mississippi River, a whole bunch of men were sleeping, wrapped in their blankets, on the upper deck, which had no railings. Ezra Van Deusen walked in his sleep and went overboard. Hen. Van Tassell said that he was on the lower deck caring for the horses, saw the blanket go down alongside . . . and heard the yell "MAN OVERBOARD." He said that they stopped the steamer, but no trace of Ezra Van Deusen could be found, and he said he felt quite sure that he was hit by the paddle wheel of the steamer.

In September 1867, Melville presented Bartlett with a copy of *Battle-Pieces*. It is reported that, in the late 1990s, a Berkshire book dealer said this copy of *Battle-Pieces* had been recently sold to someone outside the county.

Melville's address in New York City was 150 East 18th Street.

CHAPTER 23

More than one illustration of "Driving Home the Cows" was made, one of which hangs in the Stockbridge Library and is commonly known as "The Berkshire Boy's Return." Another was published in *Harper's Weekly* along with the poem.

During the Civil War years, there was a racehorse known as "The Berkshire Boy," owned by Henry Smith of South Adams.

CHAPTER 25

The Reverend Orville Dewey (1794-1882) was one of the country's leading Unitarian ministers in the days when Unitarianism was a great force in New England life, and he held important pastorates in Boston and New York. A native of Sheffield, Dewey graduated from Williams College in 1814. Along with William Cullen Bryant and David Dudley Field, he was among the leading members of the Berkshire Jubilee planning committee composed of emigrants. (A similar planning committee was organized locally.)

Before the war, Dewey was severely criticized both by abolitionists and by his Southern friends because, while he was antislavery, he was also antiabolitionist. He feared that insistence on abolition would break up the Union.

For the rest of his life, Pittsfield's Daniel Hughes of the Allen Guards and the Thirty-first Regiment was well-known in the county for taking particular pleasure marching in every parade he could.

Many years after the war, South Egremont's William J. Karner told a story he had kept bottled up since the Lincoln assassination in 1865.

Karner, an enlistee in the Forty-ninth, had avoided active service when influential relations got him a clerking job in Washington. He resided in a third-floor room next to a boardinghouse in which lived Mary Surratt, who later was convicted as a conspirator in the assassination and hanged. In his 1920 memoirs, Karner described how he often saw a group of men meeting at Surratt's, sometimes gathering on the back porch.

"On the supposition it was a boarding house, I paid very little attention to them[, but] from later developments I have no doubt they were the people that were arrested and convicted for complicity in the assassination."

The very day of the assassination, Karner was exercising in a local gym when the well-known actor John Wilkes Booth came in to see the manager, a friend of his.

> The manager introduced me to Booth and we shook hands. Almost immediately, Booth turned, walked across the room, then came back, waved goodbye and left the room. As his manner had been stagy, I remarked, "Mr. Booth must have come from rehearsal," to which the manager replied, he thought "J.B. had been indulging too much." I thought no more of it until the following morning while reading the paper. I recalled the meeting of the previous day, and the thought flashed through my mind: If there was a detective at the gym, could he connect the manager and myself with Booth and the tragedy?

Dreading he might be arrested as a conspirator, Karner said nothing about all this for years to come. Eventually, he became a leading engineer and was employed as the purchasing engineer and personnel agent for the construction company building the Panama Canal. It was not until he was more than seventy years old that he told the full story—one of his listeners was his grand-niece, Lila Parrish of Great Barrington.

CHAPTER 26
In 1881, sculptor Daniel Chester French, who had studios in New York and at Glendale in Stockbridge, carved a marble bust of W. Francis Bartlett, which was placed in Memorial Hall at Harvard University; its plaster cast is on permanent display at Chesterwood, the sculptor's studio and museum in Glendale. The full-length bronze statue, completed in 1903, was placed in the Statehouse's Memorial Hall, and the plaster cast is at Berkshire Community College, Pittsfield.

Following are Berkshire enlistment statistics from *History of Massachusetts in the Civil War*, published in 1868.

According to the returns made by the selectmen in 1866 from all the towns in the county, it appears that the whole number of men furnished by Berkshire for the war was five thousand three hundred and fifty-six. . . . Every town in the county furnished its full quota of men upon every call made by the President, and each had a surplus at the end of the war, with the exception of Mount Washington and Tyringham, and these had the exact number required of them. No town in Berkshire, nor in the State, fell short of its quota.

The aggregate expenditure of all the towns in the county on account of the war, exclusive of the money raised and expended for State aid to the families of volunteers, was five hundred and ninety thousand six hundred and ninety-seven dollars and nineteen cents ($590,697.19). The amount raised and expended by all the towns for State aid to the soldiers' families during the four years of the war, and which was reimbursed by the Commonwealth, was two hundred and sixty-two thousand forty-nine dollars and sixty-one cents ($262,049.61), making a grand total of $852,746.80.

The Adams Free Library was built in 1897, with its second-floor Memorial Hall honoring local Civil War veterans and serving as the meeting place for their organization, known as the Grand Army of the Republic (G.A.R.). The local post was named after Charles D. Sanford.

President William McKinley came to town to lay the library's cornerstone. During the ceremony, McKinley declined to accept a seat in a special elevated chair that had been custom-made for him. He said he never wanted to be set above anyone else.

At the turn of the twenty-first century, the G.A.R. hall in the Adams library remained as one of only two such halls still in existence in the Northeast. While others met their demise after the last G.A.R. members passed away, the Adams hall continued, unaltered, as a storage space until late in the twentieth century when it was reopened for community use—still with the original light fixtures in place.

On Tuesday, May 17, 1904, the North Adams correspondent of the *Springfield Republican* wrote the following article under the headline: "Will Read Lincoln's Address."

An interesting feature of the Memorial Day exercises in this city will be the reading of Lincoln's speech at the dedication of the national cemetery at Gettysburg by a man who heard it as it fell from the lips of the martyr president.

This man is John Atwood of C. D. Sanford Grand Army [of the Republic, Adams] post, who saw three years of hard service in the Civil War. He was a member of Company B, 10th Massachusetts regiment, and it was through a peculiar train of circumstances that he happened to be present as a color bearer on the memorable occasion of the dedication of that great cemetery, where rest the remains of valiant Union soldiers. . . .

Mr. Atwood served on the North Adams police force for five years, retiring when the force was reorganized at the time the town became a city eight years ago. He is a very quiet and modest man, and not given to exploiting his military experiences. For this reason there are comparatively few people of the city who are aware of the part he took at the dedication of the great cemetery at Gettysburg, and undoubtedly the story will come as news to many of his comrades in Sanford post. He is in his 65th year, but is remarkably preserved, and does not look to be over 50.

That speech of Lincoln's will be read in many places on Memorial Day, but in very few by one who was present when it was delivered by its immortal and beloved author. The evening after the [Gettysburg] dedication, a reception was held, at which Mr. Atwood shook hands with Lincoln, and so his memory of the great war president is very vivid.

SELECTED BIBLIOGRAPHY

BOOKS

Armstrong, Margaret. *Fanny Kemble, A Passionate Victorian*. New York: The MacMillan Company, 1938.

Birdsall, Richard D. *Berkshire County, A Cultural History*. New Haven: Yale University Press, 1959.

Blight, David. W., ed. *When This Cruel War Is Over—The Civil War Letters of Charles Harvey Brewster*. Amherst, Massachusetts: University of Massachusetts Press, 1992.

Boatner, Mark Mayo, III. *The Civil War Dictionary*. New York: David McKay Co., 1959.

Bowen, James L. *Massachusetts in the War 1861-1865*. Springfield, Massachusetts: Clark W. Bryan & Co., 1889.

_____. *History of the Thirty-seventh Regiment Massachusetts Volunteers in the Civil War of 1861-1865*. Holyoke, Massachusetts: Clark W. Bryan, 1884.

Brooks, Robert R. R., ed. *Williamstown, The First Two Hundred Years 1753-1953*. Williamstown, Massachusetts: The McClelland Press, 1953.

Bryan, Clark W. *The Book of Berkshire*. Springfield, Massachusetts: Clark W. Bryan & Co., Publishers, 1889.

Coerner, Christopher. *Sheffield 1733-1983*. Sheffield, Massachusetts: Sheffield 250th Anniversary Committee, 1983.

Cohen, Hennig. *The Battle-pieces of Herman Melville*. New York and Windsor, Ontario: Thomas Yoseloff, 1963.

Derby, W. P. *Bearing Arms in the Twenty-seventh Massachusetts Regiment of Volunteer Infantry During the Civil War, 1861-1865*. Boston: Wright & Potter, 1883.

Dewey, Mary E. *Life and Letters of Catharine M. Sedgwick*. New York: Harper & Brothers, Publisher, 1872.

DeWolf, Mark Howe, ed. *Touched with Fire—The Civil War Letters of Oliver Wendell Holmes, Jr.* Cambridge, Massachusetts: Harvard University Press, 1946.

_____. *Justice Oliver Wendell Holmes, The Shaping Years: 1841-1870*. Cambridge, Massachusetts: The Belknap Press of Harvard University Press, 1957.

Dornbusch, Charles E., ed. *Military Biography of the Civil War*. 4 vols. New York: New York Public Library, 1961.

Drew, Bernard A. *Great Barrington*. Great Barrington, Massachusetts: Great Barrington Historical Society, 1999.

Drickamer, Lee. C. and Karen D. Drickamer, eds. *Fort Lyon to Harper's Ferry—The Civil War Letters of Charles H. Moulton*. Shippensburg, Pa.: White Mane Publishing, 1987.

Du Bois, W. E. B. *The Souls of Black Folk*. New York: Gramercy Books, 1994.

Duncan, Russell, ed. *Blue-eyed Child of Fortune—the Civil War Letters of Colonel Robert Shaw*. Athens, Georgia, and London: The University of Georgia Press, 1992.

Dyer, Frederick A. *A Compendium of the War of the Rebellion*. Des Moines: Dyer Publishing Co., 1908.

Editors et al. *Battles and Leaders of the Civil War*. Four vols. New York: Castle Books, 1956.

Editors et al. *Berkshire, The First Three Hundred Years: 1676-1976*. Pittsfield, Massachusetts: The Eagle Publishing Co., 1976.

Editors et al. *The Berkshire Hills*. Compiled and written by members of the Federal Writers Project of the Works Progress Administration of Massachusetts. New York: Funk & Wagnalls Co., 1939.

Editors et al. *The Berkshire Jubilee Celebrated at Pittsfield, Massachusetts*. Albany: E. P. Little, 1845.

Editors. *Centennial Celebration of the Town of Sheffield*. Sheffield, Massachusetts: Centennial Committee, 1876.

Editors. *History of Berkshire County*, Vol. I. New York: J. B. Beers & Co., 1885.

Editors. *Massachusetts Soldiers, Sailors and Marines in the Great Civil War*. 9 vols. Norwood, Massachusetts: Norwood Press, 1931.

Editors. *Picture History of the Civil War*. New York: American Heritage Publishing Co., 1960.

Emilio, Luis F. *History of the Fifty-fourth Regiment of Massachusetts Volunteer Infantry, 1863-1865*. Boston: The Boston Book Co., 1894.

Field, David D. *A History of the County of Berkshire, Massachusetts*. 2 vols. Pittsfield, Massachusetts: S.W. Bush, 1829.

Fox, William F. *Regimental Losses in the American Civil War, 1861-1865*. Albany, New York: 1889.

Garner, Stanton. *The Civil War World of Herman Melville*. Lawrence, Kansas: The University Press of Kansas, 1993.

Headley, Phineas C. *Massachusetts in the Rebellion*. Boston: Walker, Fuller & Co., 1866.

Higginson, Thomas W. *Massachusetts in the Army & Navy 1861-1865*. 2 vols. Boston: Wright & Polten Printing, 1896.

Hyde, C. M. *Lee, The Centennial Celebration and Centennial History*. Springfield, Massachusetts: Clark W. Bryan & Co., Printers, 1878.

Kemble, Frances Anne. *Journal of a Residence on a Georgian Plantation in 1838-1839.* Edited by John A. Scott. New York: Alfred A. Knopf, 1970.

Leyda, Jay, ed. *The Melville Log: A Documentary Life of Herman Melville, 1819-1891,* 2 vols. New York: Gordian Press, 1969.

Lincoln, William S. *Life with the Thirty-fourth Massachusetts Infantry.* Worcester, Massachusetts: Noyes, Snow & Co., 1879.

Long, E. B. *The Civil War Day by Day.* Garden City, New York: Doubleday & Co., 1971.

Newell, Joseph K. *Ours: Annals of the 10th Regiment, Massachusetts Volunteers, in the Rebellion.* Springfield, Massachusetts: C. A. Nichols & Co., 1875.

Palfrey, Francis W. *Memoir of William Francis Bartlett.* Boston: Houghton, Osgood and Co., 1878.

Phinney, Jane B. *Taking the High Road.* Savoy, Massachusetts: Town of Savoy, 1997.

Quint, Alonzo Hall. *The Record of the Second Massachusetts Infantry, 1861-1865.* Boston: James P. Walker, 1867.

Roe, Alfred. *The Tenth Regiment Volunteer Infantry, 1861-1864.* Springfield, Massachusetts: The Tenth Regiment Association, 1909.

Rudolph, Frank, ed. *Perspectives: A Williams Anthology.* Williamstown, Massachusetts: Williams College, 1983.

Schouler, William. *History of Massachusetts in the Civil War.* 2 vols. n.p., 1868.

Sears, Stephen W. *To the Gates of Richmond—The Peninsula Campaign.* New York: Ticknor & Fields, 1992.

Sedgwick, Sarah C. and Christian S. Marquand. *History of Stockbridge, Massachusetts, A Chronicle 1739-1939.* Great Barrington, Massachusetts: 1939.

Smith, J. E. A. *The History of Pittsfield, Massachusetts, from the Year 1800 to the Year 1876.* Springfield, Massachusetts: C.W. Bryan & Co., 1876.

Spear, W. F. *History of North Adams, Mass. 1749-1885.* North Adams, Massachusetts: Hoosac Valley News Print House, 1885.

Spies, Mary-Joy, ed. *Yours Only, Thomas: Letters from a Union Soldier.* Valhalla, New York: MileHigh House Books, 1999.

Spring, Leverett W. *A History of Williams College.* Boston: Houghton Mifflin Co., 1917.

Stackpole, Edward J. *The Fredericksburg Campaign.* New York: Bonanza Books, 1957.

Tague, William, and Robert B. Kimball, eds. Richard V. Happel, text. *Berkshire—Two Hundred Years in Pictures.* Pittsfield, Massachusetts: Berkshire Eagle, 1961.

Taylor, Charles J. *History of Great Barrington 1676-1882.* Great Barrington, Massachusetts: n.p. 1918.

Wood, David H. *Lenox, Massachusetts Shire Town.* Lenox, Massachusetts: Town of Lenox, 1969.

Wright, Constance. *Fanny Kemble and the Lovely Land.* New York: Dodd, Mead & Co., 1972.

MANUSCRIPT SOURCES AND PRIVATELY PUBLISHED

Brown, Raymond H. "Egremont, as Remembered in His Letters." Collected by James N. Parrish.

Deland, Frederick N. "Forlorn Hope." Address to the 1885 reunion of the Forty-ninth Massachusetts Regiment.

Deland, Frederick N. "Some Recollections of the Civil War." Pittsfield: Claxton Printers, 1909.

Gamwell, John M., Doris Gamwell Wendell, ed. "Civil War Diary of Cpl. John M. Gamwell, Co. B 49th MV." Bridgeport, Connecticut: n.p., 1987.

Hosford, Calvin C., Karen W. De Hond, ed. "Andersonville Diary: April 1864-December 1864." n.p., May 1867.

Hughes, Daniel. "Daniel Hughes and the Eighth and Thirty-first Massachusetts Regiments." Atlanta: n.p., 1967.

Johns, Henry T. *Life With the Forty-ninth Massachusetts Volunteers.* Pittsfield: Printed for the author, 1864.

Karner, William J. *Recollections.* Boston: Thomas Todd Co., 1920.

Lewis, Joseph W. *Berkshire Men of Worth.* New York: The Educational Press, 1931-1937.

Nickerson, Mark. "Recollections of the Civil War by a High Private in the Front Ranks." n.p., 1991.

Stone, James H. "Williams College During the Civil War." Williamstown, Massachusetts: n.p., 1848.

Sumner, Samuel B. and Charles A. Sumner. *Poems.* New York: The Authors' Publishing Co., 1877.

Torrey, Rodney W. *War Diary of Rodney W. Torrey 1862-1863.* Windsor, Massachusetts: Printed for the author, n.d.

NEWSPAPERS, PERIODICALS

Adams News and Transcript, Adams, Massachusetts.

Berkshire County Eagle, Pittsfield, Massachusetts.

Berkshire Courier, Great Barrington, Massachusetts.

Berkshire Eagle, Pittsfield, Massachusetts.

Berkshire Hills, Pittsfield, Massachusetts.

Berkshire History, Berkshire County Historical Society, Pittsfield, 1971—.

Harper's Weekly, New York, New York.

Hoosac Valley Transcript and Recorder, North Adams, Massachusetts.

Pittsfield Sun, Pittsfield, Massachusetts.

Springfield Republican, Springfield, Massachusetts.

Valley Gleaner, Lee, Massachusetts.

ARTICLES, ADDRESSES, REPORTS

Barnard, John G. "A Report on the Defenses of Washington to the Chief of Engineers, U.S. Army." Professional Papers of the Corps of Engineers, U.S. Army, No. 20, Washington, 1871.

Bell, William F. "The Civil War Death of Lenox's Willie Sedgwick." *Berkshire Eagle*, Pittsfield, Massachusetts, May 27, 1996.

Bishop, Henry W. "Major William Dwight Sedgwick," Letter In Memoriam to the *Pittsfield Sun*, October 10, 1862.

Brewer, D.C. "Williams in the Late War." *Williams Literary Monthly*, April 1886, 1:405-412.

Carman, Bernard. "Up Pop Two Berkshire Men as Rebel Generals." *Berkshire Eagle*, Pittsfield, Massachusetts, October 24, 1959.

Carman, Linda. "Invisible Community Project Marches On." *The Advocate*, Williamstown, Massachusetts, January 7, 1998.

Carter, Franklin. "The College and the Civil War." *The Gulielmensian*, Vol. 57 (1914) pp. 32-36.

Chapman, Gerard. "Mum Bett's Bold Challenge." *Berkshire Eagle*, August 25, 1981.

Editors. "Idea of Flags for Graves Conceived by New Englander." *The National Tribune*, Washington, D.C., May 21, 1942.

Editors. "Last Allen Guard Member Recalls Day When Snappy Company Marched to War." *Berkshire Eagle*, Pittsfield, Massachusetts, January 18, 1936.

Editors. "Incidents in the Career of Local Regiments." *Berkshire Eagle*, Pittsfield, Massachusetts, n.d., 1916.

Feibelman, Herbert U. "Life of Edward Aylsworth Perry." *The Florida Law Journal*, July 1949.

Latham, Ronald. "Magic of the Berkshires: Pittsfield Commemorative Streets." An address to the Berkshire Institute of Lifelong Learning, February 4, 1998.

Livermore, Mary A. "Massachusetts Women in the Civil War." Report for the U.S. Sanitary Commission in Boston, n.d.

Roan, Bette. "A Civil War General and a Private." *Berkshire History*, Vol. IV, Fall 1983.

Turner, Steve. "Berkshire Blacks: The Struggle for Equality Began Two Centuries Ago." *Berkshire Eagle*, Pittsfield, Massachusetts, August 28, 1976.

Weaver, C.P. "The First Black Soldiers." *The Washington Post*, September 30, 1997.

INDEX

Illustrations and maps are indicated with **bold type.**

ABOUT THE AUTHOR

Stuart Murray is the author of twenty-two books, most related to American history. These include *Rudyard Kipling in Vermont* (a book-of-the-year finalist in biography for *Independent Publisher* in 1997); *Washington's Farewell*; *The Honor of Command: General Burgoyne's Saratoga Campaign*; and *America's Song: The Story of "Yankee Doodle"* (book-of-the-year bronze medalist in history for *Foreword Magazine* and finalist in history for *Booklist*). He is also author of two books about Norman Rockwell: *Norman Rockwell at Home in Vermont* and (with James McCabe) *Norman Rockwell's Four Freedoms: Images that Inspire a Nation*. He has written eleven novels of historical fiction, and he has edited numerous other books. He and his family live in Columbia County, New York.